VIENNA

T0326878

Richard Cockett is a historian and journalist, a
and senior editor at *The Economist*. He is the author of seven books,
and a member of the Institute for Advanced Study in Princeton.

Further praise for *Vienna*:

'In Richard Cockett's compelling and beautifully researched book,
prewar Vienna, like fifth century Athens, enabled the intellectual
and cultural foment that shapes our thinking even now. Cockett's
writing sparkles and his insights startle, forcing us to reconsider not
only an Austrian city, but how genius fed on genius to generate all
we now know as modernity.'
Andrew Solomon, author of *Far From the Tree*

'I consider myself lucky if I read one book a year that really changes
how I think about the world; in that regard, I am very lucky, because
the year is still young and I've already read such a book.'
Stephen Dubner, *Freakonomics Radio* podcast, April 2024

'Cockett makes a convincing case for paying greater attention
to the city and its legacy . . . He weaves together a rich cast of
characters who each played a part in this intellectual culture.'
Emily Schultheis, *Foreign Policy*

'A panoramic portrait of Viennese culture and society . . . Vienna
has shaped the modern world more than any of us care to realise.'
Luka Ivan Jukic, *History Today*

'Explains how the Austrian capital not only produced generations
of brilliant minds but also ruthlessly disposed of them.'
Alexej Koroljow, *Der Standard*

'The cast of characters is glittering . . . Cockett does a fine job of
explaining why Vienna produced so many impressive men and women.'
Bruce Bawer, *American Spectator*

'Fascinating . . . The story of Vienna's role as a radical cultural centre.'
Benedict King, *Oldie*

'Impressive . . . The ideas and images and ideologies that fermented around the Austrian capital in the first third of the twentieth century go on percolating around the globe today.'
Christopher Bray, *Tablet*

'Cockett dramatically expands our understanding of how Viennese intellectual life of this period shaped the modern world . . . It's useful to remember the cities and times that have broken the mould.'
Samuel Gregg, *City Journal*

'An excellent survey and introduction to the miracles of Viennese science, philosophy, and culture, earlier in the 20th century.'
Tyler Cowen, *Marginal Revolution*, Book of the Year

'Glorious . . . There is enrichment on almost every page. And with it, a wealth of fundamental insights into the production and exploitation of useful knowledge.'
Charles Emmerson, *Engelsberg Ideas*

'A rich and fascinating book. Pre-war Vienna was a cauldron of ideas – ideas that were mostly extinguished in Austria, but exported to the Anglo-American world. Richard Cockett makes a compelling case for how they continue to shape our lives.'
David Edmonds, author of *The Murder of Professor Schlick*

'Richard Cockett allows us to savour the heady days of Viennese café culture, which, as he vividly demonstrates, brewed the richness and boldness of the modern era. From art and music to economics and science, he reveals the city's extraordinary and pivotal contributions to contemporary life.'
Paul Halpern, author of *Flashes of Creation*

'A kaleidoscopic journey through the twentieth and twenty-first centuries. In Richard Cockett's hands, Vienna is the origin of the contemporary world.'
Janek Wasserman, author of *The Marginal Revolutionaries*

VIENNA
HOW THE CITY OF IDEAS CREATED THE MODERN WORLD

RICHARD COCKETT

YALE UNIVERSITY PRESS
NEW HAVEN AND LONDON

Copyright © 2023 Richard Cockett

First published in paperback in 2024

For information about this and other Yale University Press publications, please contact:
U.S. Office: sales.press@yale.edu   yalebooks.com
Europe Office: sales@yaleup.co.uk   yalebooks.co.uk

Set in Adobe Caslon Pro by IDSUK (DataConnection) Ltd
Printed in Denmark By Nørhaven A/S, Viborg

Library of Congress Control Number: 2024934840
A catalogue record for this book is available from the British Library.
Authorized Representative in the EU: Easy Access System Europe, Mustamäe tee 50, 10621 Tallinn, Estonia, gpsr.requests@easproject.com

ISBN 978-0-300-26653-5 (hbk)
ISBN 978-0-300-27936-8 (pbk)

10 9 8 7 6 5 4

For brave, beautiful Harriet

Contents

Part III Emigrants and Exiles

Illustrations

Acknowledgements

This book has been long in the making, even if circumstances conspired against my actually starting to write it until 2020. Perhaps a word of explanation is in order. I first encountered the Viennese, specifically the 'Austrian School' economists, during the early 1990s when I was writing a book about the counter-revolution in economic thinking that led to Thatcherism in Britain.[1] I am just old enough to have corresponded briefly with Karl Popper before his death in 1994. However, I let the Viennese be at this point, presuming that their outsize influence had been confined principally to the field of political economy. Over the following decades, however, I gradually discovered how wrong I had been; in any field that I read and wrote about, from business to advertising, from philosophy to shopping malls, from espionage to modern ceramics, there was usually a Viennese at the root of it.

Surely there was a significant story here, a missing piece of twentieth-century history. My instincts were confirmed by the great historian of central Europe, Norman Stone, who first encouraged me on my way. But it was another historian, Jonathan Haslam, then the George F. Kennan Professor in the School of Historical Studies at the Institute for Advanced Study (IAS) in Princeton, who eventually furnished me with the means to write this book. He invited me to apply for a year's research fellowship at the IAS, where I spent 2020–21 as the Elizabeth and J. Richardson Dilworth Fellow in the school of history. It is to the IAS that I owe my primary debt of gratitude; unencumbered by teaching duties, the institution affords a rare opportunity in modern academia to just focus on research and writing.

My other institutional debts are mainly to *The Economist*, which allowed me to take the year off from my day job to go to the IAS in the first place, and to the London Library, a private members' library in St James's Square. As chance would have it, my year at the IAS happened to coincide with pandemic lockdown; not only could I not travel to Princeton for months, but for a while, as all the libraries in London (and elsewhere) shut their doors, so it looked for a few alarming weeks as if I would be unable to do any work on this project at all. But the London Library came to the rescue, without fail sending out boxes of books to my home during the cruellest of the Covid months. I owe a great deal to the dedication and helpfulness of all the staff at the library.

I want to record my heartfelt thanks to one family in particular: Bob Mayo has been a staunch friend throughout and encouraged me to study Michael Polanyi; his younger brother Edward similarly encouraged me to grapple with the younger Polanyi, Karl; Susan regaled me with tales from the Vienna Woods; and Catherine provided me with the perfect place to write, a little cottage in Norfolk adjacent to an old mill once populated by Karl Popper and other scientists and sages referred to in these pages.

Many other people have helped me to shape the ideas in this book, often over the course of many years, in Britain, America and Vienna itself. Sometimes I have benefited from brief, but absorbing, conversations; with others I have taken up far too much of their time, sometimes over decades. I wish to record my debt to the following: Mitchell Ash, Ananyo Bhattacharya, Steven Beller, Gerhard Benetka, Judith Beniston, Doris Berger, Mark Berry, Peter David, Edmund Fawcett, Johannes Feichtinger, Gary Gerstle, Anthony Gottlieb, Malachi Haim Hacohen, Eva Jablonka, Allan

Janick, Stuart Jeffries, Jane Kallir, Eric Kindle, Elisabeth Klaus, Paul Lerner, Cheryl Logan, Christopher Long, Cathy Malchiodi, Marguerite Mendell, Nick Midgley, Gerd Müller, Birgit Nemec, Helena Newman, Andreas Novy, Eva Nowotny, Oliver Rathkolb, Wolfgang L. Reiter, Günther Sandner, Noam Saragosti, Stefan Schwarzkopf, Radmila Schweitzer, Chandak Sengoopta, Karl Sigmund, Quinn Slobodian, Friedrich Stadler, Richard Straub, Klaus Taschwer, Edward Timms, Francesco Torchiani, Peter Wallace, Rob Wallach, Janek Wasserman and Andrea Winklbauer. Often I took their advice and guidance, sometimes I did not; the responsibility for the result is entirely mine.

This is my third outing with Yale University Press, testimony, I hope, to an easy and productive working relationship. Heather McCallum commissioned this book, whilst Julian Loose saw it through the editorial process assisted by Frazer Martin, and Eve Leckey proved to be a first-class copy editor; my deep thanks to all of them. David Camier-Wright is as exacting a fact-checker as one could hope for; my gratitude to him for going over the text with his usual rigour. Lastly, and most importantly, I must thank my son Joe, who provides a lot of the necessary distraction when the going gets tough, and Harriet, my wife. As a professional writer and editor, she read several drafts of the book, improving it every time, and as a wife reminds us all how powerful love can be, even in the face of the utmost adversity. This book is dedicated to her.

Richard Cockett
Hammersmith, February 2023

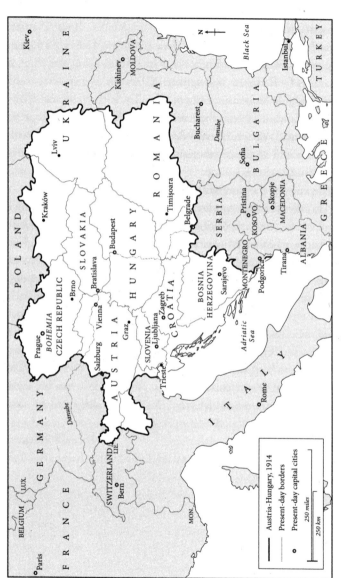

The Austro-Hungarian empire at its zenith.

Introduction

Why Vienna?

To hold that a European capital on the banks of the Danube lit the spark for most of Western intellectual and cultural life in the twentieth century may sound like an absurdly extravagant claim – yet this is the flame that runs through my book.

While students, politicians and thinkers feel they must study the rise to power by America in the twentieth century as a proxy for understanding modern global history, I would contend that they should be reserving some of their energy for Vienna. Or at least the vibrant, radical, extraordinary iteration of the city that was eventually crushed by the rise of fascism in the 1930s.

Post-war Western history is often considered in terms of the 'Americanisation' of European politics and culture, as the principal victor of the Second World War exerted its freshly minted hard and soft powers. But this book argues for a new perspective on the currents of transatlantic influence; often, the Americans were merely recycling ideas that had originated in Europe back to Europeans, and the Viennese were the most striking contributors to this intellectual back and forth. This aspect of the creation of an 'Atlantic community' is only now being explored by writers and scholars.

Certainly, the American Century, as declared by the journalist Henry Luce in 1941, was by no means the one-way street that is often depicted.[1]

In truth, no one who has looked closely can challenge the reality of Viennese influence across an astonishingly wide range of intellectual and cultural production, from nuclear fission to shopping malls, from psychoanalysis to the fitted kitchen. The argument, surely, is only one of degree. Other scholars have explored select elements of this phenomenon, but my book sets out to chronicle the city's impact on the West across the full range of human endeavour for the first time. Furthermore, it is worth remembering that this story is about a *city* shaping the modern world, rather than a country, or an empire. And not even a large city at that: you can still traverse its main cultural quarter (the 1st District) in half an hour at a brisk pace.

Chronicling Vienna's extraordinarily talented men and women also leads us straight to the roots of so many contemporary global issues. For as well as producing some of the era's most enlightened and humane people and ideas, Vienna was unique in also producing some of the most pernicious and destructive pathologies in modern history: Nazism, organised anti-Semitism, and extreme ethno-nationalism. In the end, the city crumbled under the weight of its own contradictions, and I follow both tempers, the constructive and the destructive, in this book. These are the essential contradictions of our own era. To understand the trajectories of contemporary societies and politics, particularly in the West, we first have to understand how and where so many of them started – in Vienna.

The matrix of innovation

The text that first prompted the claims to Viennese exceptionalism in the realm of ideas was *Fin-de-Siècle Vienna: Politics and Culture*, by the Princeton historian Carl Schorske (first published in 1980). Schorske's elegant and persuasive volume is the bedrock for those interested in Vienna and the history of ideas, inspiring writers, artists and scholars to comb over the subject in ever more detail.

My enquiry explores many of those questions that Schorske provoked, but never fully answered, about the sheer breadth of Vienna's influence. As his title suggests, he dwelt entirely on the now very familiar *fin de siècle*, the glittering metropolis of Sigmund Freud, Alfred Adler, Gustav Mahler, Alfred Loos, Arthur Schnitzler, Robert Musil and Gustav Klimt, the setting for so many subsequent plays, memoirs and films (most recently Tom Stoppard's *Leopoldstadt*). Like others before me, however, I have considerably widened the historical focus.[2] I argue that any claims for Vienna's primacy can only be made if this chapter in the city's history is considered along-side the lesser known but transformative interwar period. These were the years of 'Red Vienna', when the city council embarked on a radically ambitious democratic experiment in human evolution – arguably the first of its kind.

By taking this synoptic view, as the historian Edward Timms argued, 'the case for seeing the city as a matrix for innovation becomes much stronger . . . conflating the creative convulsions of the declining Habsburg Empire with the ideological dynamics of the interwar period'. At every level, Timms reminds us, 'there was a dramatic *radicalisation*' after the First World War.[3] This is the real key to Vienna's sway over Western culture and ideas, for better and for worse.

Moreover, I have attempted to cleave Vienna from the suffocating embrace of 'German studies'. Too often, the 'Austrian' contribution to the history of ideas in the twentieth century is subsumed into histories and studies of 'German-speaking' diasporas and émigré communities. This sort of generic classification, however, does Vienna a gross disservice, as the city's mental landscape was decis-ively different from that of Germany in several respects. Indeed, to a large degree Vienna defined itself *against* Germany's intellectual and enlightenment history, and this is one reason why its citizens were so efficacious in the West. Particularly during the Cold War, for example, they were critically important in providing a new political lexicon that allowed the West eventually to triumph over the totalitarianism of both right and left.

Who is Viennese?

The scope of the book rests largely on how I have chosen to define 'Viennese'. Some words of explanation are therefore needed. The city was, of course, in prosaic terms a spatial, geographical entity, enclosed within administrative boundaries that shifted over time. However, as I argue in Chapter 1, Vienna was also a cultural and intellectual creation in and of itself.

The most obvious point of difference with other great capital cities is that Vienna was composed largely of immigrants, often from the farthest ends of the Austro-Hungarian empire. They settled there to contribute to, and benefit from, the world's most dynamic, and perhaps tolerant, intellectual community. This is how the Viennese of these pages always defined themselves, resisting all the other ethno-nationalist, religious or gender-specific labels forced upon them by others, however well-meaning. Austrian 'culture', by contrast, was an entirely different affair, as will become evident.

In today's debased currency of ideas, these Viennese might be derided as 'people from nowhere'. But they saw themselves passionately and unreservedly as 'people from somewhere' – that somewhere being Vienna. That is one reason why *this* Vienna, of Stefan Zweig's *The World of Yesterday*, continues to exert such a hold on the imagination. Indeed, it *should* enthuse those who believe in a European culture stretching from Dublin to Kyiv, regardless of whether or not that culture has to be enshrined in the political institutions of the European Union. To be brought up, to be educated and to work in Vienna was to share in a particular, unique, open and cosmopolitan environment, even if it was anathema to some.

So for my purposes I include as Viennese in this book all those who were educated in the city and contributed to its intellectual achievements, even if they were not born there. For instance, I devote considerable attention to Charlotte Bühler and Ernst Mach, even though the former was born in Berlin and the latter spent a substantial amount of his career in Prague. Yet both clearly had a major impact on several generations of Viennese. Equally, my Viennese include many of Hungary's so-called 'Great Generation', often born in Budapest, but as familiar with the capital of the empire as with their natal city. In this pre-passports era, thinkers, scientists and writers such as Karl Polanyi, John von Neumann and Abraham Wald shuttled contentedly between Budapest and Vienna, collaborating with the Viennese and sometimes making the Austrian capital their home.

Furthermore, I don't feel any need to claim such figures *exclusively* for Vienna; such was the interconnectedness of central European culture at the time that several cities could often claim them, just as their own intellectual formations would often owe a good deal to multiple destinations. Vienna's Hollywood film directors, such as Billy Wilder and Fritz Lang, owed as much to Weimar Berlin as to Vienna, for example, but I include them here as having been born and educated in Vienna; Lang fought devotedly for the Austro-Hungarian empire during the First World War.

Lastly, as I am dealing principally with Vienna's influence on the world, I have restricted myself to those Viennese whose life and work resonated beyond the city. There are others who glowed brightly enough in the Vienna of their day – such as the satirist Karl Kraus – but who had little discernible impact elsewhere. This is not their story. As I hope the reader will agree, there were still quite enough Viennese whose lives did reverberate outside the Austrian capital city to form the subject of the present book.

The book is divided into three parts. The forging of Vienna as a city of ideas in its golden age up to the First World War is described in Part I. Part II considers the remarkable impact of Red Vienna, and its eventual destruction by Austria's own brand of fascism, followed by the Nazis. Lastly, Part III reviews the influence of Vienna's émigrés and exiles abroad, principally in the United States and Britain, but also in the wider world, towards the end of the twentieth century.

PART I

A Viennese Education: The Rational and the Anti-Rational

The masonry of liberalism: a view of Vienna's Ringstrasse in 1884.

Chapter 1

Growing up Viennese:
An Education in Liberalism

Alone and old, almost petrified in his remoteness, but still close to us and ubiquitous in the great and colourful Empire, lived and ruled the old Emperor Franz Joseph. It was possible that in the misty depths of our souls there slumbered those certainties called instincts, the certainty above all that with each passing day the old Emperor was dying, and with him the monarchy, not so much a fatherland as an empire, something greater, wider, more spacious and all-encompassing than just a fatherland.[1]

Thus, the journalist and novelist Joseph Roth recalled the fading of an era in his elegiac *The Emperor's Tomb*. By the eve of the First World War, when Roth set his novel, very few could even remember life before Franz Joseph, the Habsburg monarch who ruled over 52 million people in the sprawling, multi-ethnic, plurilingual Austro-Hungarian empire, known officially as the Imperial and Royal Dual Monarchy. Born in 1830, emperor from 1848 until his death in 1916 at the age of eighty-six, Franz Joseph remains the sixth-longest-serving monarch in history.

By the time of Roth's novel, for many the emperor was a relic of a bygone age. All mutton-chop whiskers and buttoned-up tunics, he had little time for the era's extraordinary technical and scientific advances, many of which emanated from the empire itself. New-fangled devices were not for the austere and frugal emperor. The Schönbrunn Palace, his official residence, included 1,441 rooms but, it was alleged, no baths, as they were considered a needless luxury; Franz Joseph rose at 4 a.m. every morning to be doused in ice-cold water. The emperor always preferred letters to the telephone, and until his death the rambling Hofburg Palace in Vienna, housing the emperor's private study, was lit by kerosene lamps. He slept on an iron camp bed. Shooting and deer stalking were his only apparent means of relaxation.

In short, at first glance the ageing emperor seemed an unlikely figure to preside over one of the most intense bloomings of European thought and culture since the Florentine Renaissance. This was the Vienna of its 'golden age', the period from the mid-nineteenth century to the start of the First World War, an era that overlapped almost precisely with the reign of Franz Joseph and with which he became closely identified. Yet this was not just a matter of chronological coincidence. Even young and dandyish types, such as Roth, acknowledged that, ironically, it was the supposedly remote and antiquated emperor who guaranteed their liberty to turn the world upside down. In this sense, even amidst rapid social and political change, the emperor's relevance and importance seemed only to increase, rather than dwindle. Pieter Judson, a recent historian of the Austro-Hungarian empire, writes: 'As ideas, both empire and dynasty came to symbolize a reassuring constancy in times of bewildering change; Emperor-King Francis Joseph enjoyed unprecedented popularity . . . [watching] over the progressive transformation of society, moderating social radicalism of the politicians where necessary.'[2]

This chapter charts the intellectual contours of this golden age, so closely intertwined with the new political doctrine of liberalism and the old Austro-Hungarian empire. In particular, we have to understand how the unique circumstances of Vienna produced so many outstanding men and women who were to have such a profound impact on the world, across just three or so generations. Growing up Viennese was an education in itself.

Bourgeois values

Franz Joseph's long reign began in the most inauspicious of circumstances, in the wake of the European-wide insurrections of 1848. After giving a little ground to the revolutionaries, the new emperor reverted to a period of 'neo-absolutist' rule. But the rise of nationalist sentiment, particularly in Hungary, forced the monarchy to change tack, hastened on its way by military defeat in 1866 at the hands of Bismarck's Prussia.

Absolutism gave way to a constitutional monarchy, guided firmly by a rising generation of liberal politicians. In 1867 the Dual Monarchy of Austro-Hungary was founded, to assuage Hungarian nationalists. Thereafter, a benign Franz Joseph ruled with relative equanimity for the following five decades or so, the heyday of political liberalism.

As in other European countries, capitalism and political reform were the cornerstones of Austria's liberal era. The country's traditional guild structures were swept away following the passage of the Trade Ordinance of 1859, liberalising the labour market and creating a (partly) free-market economy. Then in 1867 the emperor proclaimed the December Constitution, which included a bill of rights guaranteeing equality before the law for all of the empire's ethnicities, as well as freedoms of expression, religion and assembly. This was one of the most progressive documents of its time; the bill of rights is still in force today.

Vienna, more than anywhere, was transformed by these changes. An important consequence of the uprisings of 1848 was that the monarchy granted every individual the right to move freely within the empire, encouraging a surge of migration from farms and villages as people looked for better-paid work (and new freedoms) in the rapidly expanding towns and cities. Vienna itself grew rapidly, from

431,000 people in 1857 (including the suburbs) to over 2 million by 1910, making it the fourth-largest city on the continent.

A newly confident and assertive bourgeoisie took an early opportunity to stamp their mark on the city by orchestrating Europe's most ambitious and didactic programme of urban redevelopment. The old medieval city clustered around the Gothic cathedral of St Stephen had been dominated by the churches, aristocratic *palais* and imperial residences of the old order. In 1857, however, the massive fortifications that had encircled the city since the thirteenth century, which had successfully repelled successive Turkish sieges, were torn down to make way for a grand new boulevard, the Ringstrasse (see image p. 8). Over the course of the next two decades or so Vienna's bourgeoisie erected not just a new city but a new civilisation, celebrating 'in architecture', as Carl Schorske writes, 'the triumph of constitutional *Recht* over imperial *Macht*, a secular culture over religious faith. Not palaces, garrisons, and churches, but centres of constitutional government and higher culture dominated the Ring.'[3]

Historicism was the style of the day; each pillar of the liberal order was therefore assigned an appropriate architecture. Classical Greek, of course, was chosen for the monumental parliament building, advertising the empire's new faith in (limited) democracy. The University of Vienna plundered the neo-Renaissance style, proclaiming the triumph of European culture. Neo-Gothic was selected for Vienna's Rathaus (town hall), neo-baroque for the opera and theatre, and so on.

This was bourgeois triumphalism in stone and mortar, built largely by Czech navvies; they were also responsible for the massive, often heavily rusticated four- and five-storey apartment blocks in the streets running off the Ringstrasse. Equally, the Danube was tamed; a new riverbed was dug and a section of the Danube canal straightened. Following London in 1851 and Paris in 1855, Vienna staged its own International Exhibition, or World's Fair, in 1873, to showcase the latest wonders of the empire. Hundreds of new buildings and a fairground were built in the old royal hunting grounds of the *Prater*. In 1897 a giant Ferris wheel, the largest in the world, was added to the *Prater*, in honour of the emperor's golden jubilee. Designed as a symbol of the city's modernity, built by English engineers, it remains one of Vienna's most celebrated landmarks.

'Ringstrasse' was soon being used as shorthand to describe bourgeois liberalism in full flood. These edifices were designed to impress, to intimidate, and they did. One new arrival to Vienna, from the northern Austrian city of Linz, was virtually paralysed in awe. As Adolf Hitler recalled in his autobiography, 'For hours I could stand in front of the Opera, for hours I could gaze at the Parliament: the whole Ring Boulevard seemed to me like an enchantment out of "The Thousand-and-one Nights".'[4] Despite the Führer's ambivalence about the country of his birth, it seems clear that his obsession with building a grandiose new Berlin with his own chief architect, Albert Speer, was rooted in his fascination with the Ringstrasse.

Another overawed young boy was Fritz Lang, who lived in one of the new apartments within the Ringstrasse. 'The director's unique visual style,' writes biographer Patrick McGilligan, 'especially in his epic silent films, was nurtured by his boyhood experience of dwelling in the shadow of gargantuan statues and massive stairwells, steepled churches and huge public buildings.' The young Lang had more incentive than most to reimagine the Ringstrasse so devotedly. His father, a successful building contractor, was responsible for building many of those same vertiginous stairwells, cavernous vestibules and outsized apartments that so impressed his son.[5]

Every European city of the age, however, had embarked on similarly grandiose building programmes. Equally, the other great imperial capitals – London, Paris and Berlin – suffered from comparable inequities and inequalities, of which more in the next chapter. Yet Vienna boasted several exceptional features, creating a unique social and political environment from which would emerge a distinctly Viennese intellectual and cultural tradition.

For a start, Vienna was probably the most multiethnic of the imperial capitals, humming with the vast variety of peoples from the imperial lands who gravitated there from the 1860s onwards. It was thus primarily a city of *immigrants*, often recently arrived. The census of 1910 recorded that only about half of Vienna's residents had 'legal domicile' in the city, usually indicating where a person was born. The rest were domiciled in other parts of the empire, most frequently Lower and Upper Austria, Bohemia, Moravia, Hungary, Galicia, Silesia and the German empire.[6] Although most of the men and women covered in this book were born in Vienna, it was often only their parents, or sometimes grandparents, who had emigrated from the 'provinces' or the 'Crown Lands' (such as Moravia and Bohemia). To a considerable degree, therefore, 'Viennese' came to be an identity in itself. People moved to Vienna to shed their past, to build new, cosmopolitan selves at the heart of an imperial system that was unusually accepting of people from all religious and ethnic backgrounds. Berlin and Paris, for instance, despite their imperial aspirations, remained relatively homogenous. The Viennese mélange of ethnicities was often commented upon and gave the city a particular tinge. One historian has called Vienna and Habsburg central Europe a 'laboratory' for the pluricultural experience; others continue to pore over the empire for clues as to how contemporary politicians might 'cope with the challenges of modern cultural heterogeneity'.[7]

Size certainly played a role. Unlike the other imperial capitals, Vienna was big enough to absorb incomers, yet small enough for everyone to meet and mix, if they chose to, particularly within the confines of the Ringstrasse. It takes less than thirty minutes to cross the inner city at a brisk pace; this was a geographical space that could have been specifically designed to encourage the casual meetings, the meshing of peoples and professions that produced Vienna's close-knit community of infinite varieties. The city's twentieth-century architects might have pioneered international Modernism, but, above all, they esteemed the particular spatial qualities of their native city. Victor Gruen (born Grünbaum), inventor of the shopping mall, spent his professional life attempting to reproduce these aspects of Vienna in America, not entirely successfully. Unusually for a Viennese exile, in later life he bought an apartment in the centre so he could once again enjoy the city of his youth. As he rhapsodised:

> From my residence there I can reach, within a few minutes' walk, places of the most diversified character: the opera; the famous concert hall of the *Musikverein*; the *Konzerthaus* and two theatres; shops and stores of every type and description; elegant restaurants; both elegant and modest cafés; the central market for fruit, meat and vegetables (the so-called *Naschmarkt*) . . . and the art galleries at the *Künstlerhaus* and *Sezession* . . . The residents of the area represent a potpourri of all economic and cultural groups, from modest workmen to millionaires; but the mixture is so small-grained, because no single economic or national stratum overpowers another by sheer numbers.[8]

Of cafés, and football

The Viennese café was the quintessential meeting place of the city, a well-upholstered extension of the public sphere. As one historian of this era writes, the Viennese café 'was an institution of a special kind . . . a sort of democratic club, for discussion, writing and playing cards'.[9] There were about 600 of these coffee-houses in the imperial capital in 1900. Some Viennese conducted most of their work in cafés, often alternating between two or three favourites in a day. One businessman was said to have had his hours printed on his cards thus:[10]

From 2 to 4 o'clock – Café Landtmann
From 4 to 5 o'clock – Café Rebhuhn
From 5 to 6 o'clock – Café Herrenhof.

Each café attracted a particular coterie – of architects, economists or writers, as we shall see. But the fact that anyone could listen to them hold forth merely for the price of a *Wiener Melange* made the latest ideas and speculations, on any subject, accessible to a uniquely broad audience – the 'democratic club'. Equally, any notion of intellectual hierarchy tended to deliquesce in the constant ebb and flow of café society.

Take football. Just like the composers and politicians, the city's clubs adopted their own cafés as well; fans of Rapid Vienna congregated at the Café Holub, Austria Vienna fans at the Parsifal. Here, players, fans and managers mixed, but writers, philosophers, playwrights and mathematicians would weigh in as well, changing football forever. The football journalists mainly gathered with the theatre and opera critics at the Ring Café, the hub of Vienna's intellectualising football culture, described as 'a kind of revolutionary parliament of the friends and fanatics of football'.[11] From being very much a muscular, working-class game imported in the late nineteenth century from Britain, when put through the wringer of the Viennese coffee-house, football emerged as a sophisticated battle of wits, deploying entirely new tactics that demanded a new breed of player.

Of these, Viennese footballers such as centre-forward Josef Uridil and the slight, creative genius Matthias Sindelar, nicknamed *der Papierene* (the Paper Man) for his ability to drift through defences, were lauded in the coffee-houses just as much as the architect Adolf Loos or the composer Arnold Schoenberg. As Jonathan Wilson, the best historian of the game, writes: 'For the importance of tactics to be fully realised, the game had to be taken up by a social class that instinctively theorised and deconstructed, that was as comfortable planning in the abstract as it was with reacting on the field, and, crucially, that suffered none of the distrust of intellectualism that was to be found in Britain.'[12] That team managers began to play with distinct 'philosophies', with no trace of irony, owes much to Vienna. It was an admiring theatre critic, Alfred Polgar, after all, who described Sindelar as having 'brains in his legs'.

It was no coincidence, therefore, that the heyday of Austrian football – the interwar years – overlapped with the last, glorious flourish of Viennese coffee-house intellectualism. The irresistible clamour for Sindelar to be included in the national team, affectionately known as *das Wunderteam*, began over the roasted beans in the Ring Café. Managed by the famous Hugo Meisl, *das Wunderteam* subsequently beat Scotland (a 5–0 thrashing) in 1931, Germany 6–0 and then finally England in 1936. Meisl's team reached the semi-finals of the World Cup. Other European teams, notably Italy, were watching closely. From this point on continental football rapidly left the rugged, long-ball game of its English homeland far behind.

The culture of *Bildung*

Austria Vienna football club, originally founded in 1910, was closely associated with the city's Jewish bourgeoisie, and the club's rapid upward trajectory closely mirrored that of the Jewish community as a whole. For of all those who, from 1867 to 1914, hastened to the city to recast themselves as Viennese citizens, Jews were amongst the most numerous, and certainly the most successful.

Thousands moved from the east of the empire to the inner suburbs of the city. The district of Leopoldstadt, dominated by the textile trade, was their favoured destination, separated from the inner city only by the Danube canal. The entirety of Leopoldstadt was much bigger than its Jewish quarter, and non-Jews outnumbered Jews. Nonetheless, by the 1920s the district still housed a third of the city's Jewish population, and served as a shorthand for Jewish Vienna.[13] From here, new arrivals could begin the complementary processes of economic, social and cultural assimilation that might one day afford them an apartment on the other side of the waterway. Jewish people were the principal beneficiaries of the Habsburg monarchy's liberal reforms of the nineteenth century; they gained the right to reside in Vienna after the 1848 revolutions, and were granted full civil rights in 1867. In that year, the Vienna census registered 6,000 Jews, but this number grew to about 180,000 by 1936. This was about 10 per cent of the city's population; among Europe's capitals only Warsaw and Budapest had higher proportions.

This Jewish component of Vienna's population has been exhaustively analysed, as has the degree to which Vienna's culture and thought were specifically 'Jewish'. As the historian Steven Beller shows, some disciplines and professions, such as psychoanalysis, philosophy and literature, were heavily dominated by Jews (the novelists Roth and Zweig, for example), others, such as economics or visual arts, much less so.[14] There were wealthy Jews living in opulent palaces on the Ringstrasse, but many more lived in extreme poverty, crowded into Leopoldstadt.

In short, it is almost impossible to generalise about Vienna's Jews, assimilated or not. A salient point, however, is that within the middle and upper-middle classes of Vienna, people of Jewish *and* non-Jewish background were intricately linked by a shared belief in *Bildung*, the German tradition, dating back to late eighteenth-century Weimar Classicism, of intellectual self-improvement, focusing on the personal growth of mind and spirit over the acquisition of wealth or worldly status (although many Viennese in these pages managed to combine all three). Weimar Classicism was most strongly associated with the poets Friedrich Schiller and Johann Wolfgang von Goethe, revered by the Viennese as much as by their own compatriots.

Prussia and the northern German states had led the way in this respect during the first half of the nineteenth century. Austria, and particularly Vienna, were relatively slow starters, but from the 1840s the capital of the Habsburg empire began to outstrip its northern rivals in enthusiasm for the fresh intellectual values of *Bildung*. Subtle differences, however, emerged between the German and Viennese concepts of this, yielding, over time, significant differences in the formation of rival intellectual traditions.

In Germany, the term *Bildungsbürger*, an 'educated citizen', carried with it distinct overtones of class and innate intelligence. *Bildung* was often thought of as a process of self-realisation, of finding and expressing an individual genius, the product of breeding. The Viennese concept of *Bildung*, by contrast, came to be much more democratic. The Viennese believed that intellectuals were primarily formed through education and experience. The Viennese tradition of *Bildung* was therefore more accessible to those born *outside* the apparently rigid ethnic, class, religious and gender hierarchies of the mid-nineteenth century. This favoured Jews, for instance, and Protestants, as we shall see below, and later, women. One historian, David Luft, has written of Austrian *Bildung* as a 'secular, emancipatory vision', almost like a religion in itself.[15]

During the 1848 upheavals in Austria, which lasted from about February to July, the students at the University of Vienna were among the most forceful opponents of the old order, demanding an end to the clerical stranglehold on education and learning that had prevailed since medieval times. A strong commitment to the virtues of free and open enquiry, of *Bildung*, was therefore entwined with the new liberal era. One of the intellectual leaders of this generation of students, the art historian Rudolf Eitelberger, proclaimed in September 1848, as the dust settled on months of street violence: 'The position adopted by the university in the March days belongs to one of the most dazzling epochs of Austrian history . . . old Austria fell, and the new era, with its hopes and wishes, its enthusiasms and passion, broke in all the more forcefully.'[16]

Despite the monarchist reaction against the revolutionary spirit of 1848, the intellectual apparatus of the state was gradually reformed, if only to draw the sting from the revolutionaries. The old medieval privileges of the universities were dismantled and they became state (that is, Crown) institutions. Chairs and departments were founded in new disciplines such as physiology, geography and physics.[17] A commitment to the academic freedom necessary for *Bildung* was enshrined in the liberal constitution of December 1867. Article 17 of the bill of rights stipulated that 'Knowledge and its Teaching is Free'. This started to unfetter learning and education from the Church, just as Article 14 guaranteed 'complete freedom of conscience and creed'.

Further legislation in 1868 abolished the supervision of public primary and secondary schools by the Catholic Church. Among the other changes this spurred was a steep decline in the numbers of clergy involved in secondary education. In 1861, 62 per cent of teachers in the *Gymnasien* were in Catholic religious orders; by 1871 this was only 36 per cent.[18] Intimately woven into Vienna's particular belief-system of *Bildung* was a fervent commitment to education as a public good, and the liberal governments of the 1860s and 1870s set about one of the most rapid and impressive expansions of educational attainment in nineteenth-century Europe. A free, secular primary education was mandated for all boys and girls from the ages of 6 to 14. Textbooks were centralised at all levels, to give all children access to the same knowledge; these were often written by the leading minds of the empire, such as the physicist Ernst Mach. The number of *Gymnasien*, the famously academic secondary schools, and *Realschulen*, their more scientific and vocational equivalents, quadrupled from 101 in Austria in 1851 to 432 by 1910, far outstripping the rate of population growth.[19] Indeed, after the 1880s governments were more concerned with trying to *restrict* secondary-school numbers 'to deter lower-middle-class youth from aspiring to professional and bureaucratic careers that few could ever realise'.[20]

An important consequence of this huge increase in the number of well-educated teenagers was a commensurate increase in the numbers enrolling in higher education. Before the 1860s Austria had been a conspicuous laggard in this respect, but by the early twentieth century the situation had been reversed. By 1900, 1.06 per cent of all Austrians aged twenty to twenty-four years old were studying at university or an equivalent institution, compared with 1.02 per cent in Italy, 0.92 per cent in France, 0.89 per cent in Germany and just 0.79 per cent in Britain. Only Switzerland, an outlier, surpassed Austria, with 1.40 per cent.[21]

As we shall see, enrolment at a *Gymnasium* was in itself no guarantee of intellectual sophistication, let alone achievement.

Nonetheless, it is clear that the seriousness with which the liberal reformers took their duty to improve access to education, and to inculcate the virtues of learning in as many people as possible, had a great deal to do with the extraordinary flowering of intellectual and cultural talent during Vienna's golden age. Proportionally, of course, the numbers of the population as a whole benefiting from an élite education at the University of Vienna remained tiny – but still large enough to encourage many families to at least contemplate such an education for their sons and, later, daughters.

The idols of *Bildung*

For Viennese, the idols of the continental European enlightenment were German, and bore down on Viennese youth at every turn, both figuratively and literally. Consider this *mis-en-scène* from the childhood of the architect Richard Neutra, in his autobiography *Life and Shape*:

> My elder brothers . . . were living in quarters which were highly respected by my unerudite parents. Their study bedroom was equipped with 'the bookcase', a globe standing on it, and more books on a board; on the opposite wall were small white plaster busts of Mozart and Beethoven, again, as well as bronze-plated busts of Goethe and Schiller . . . a 'lexicon' or world encyclopedia in many volumes was in the glass-doored bookcase. I was told it held everything there was to be known in the world.[22]

This particular quartet – Mozart, Beethoven, Goethe and Schiller – surpassed all others in esteem, except perhaps for the philosopher and mathematician Gottfried Wilhelm Leibniz. They were held to enshrine through their poetry, prose and music a universal order, secular, rational and liberal, that transcended petty nationalisms and religious obscurantism. Later, Richard Wagner and Friedrich Nietzsche would be allowed into the pantheon. It was a powerful, beguiling vision, and provided the central intellectual framework for the Viennese bourgeoisie and the Habsburg monarchy, passed down from generation to generation, gathering mass as it went. Even in the dog days of the liberal era, Gustav Klimt's celebrated *Beethoven Frieze* provided yet another extravagant expression of this vision: a rich, sensual tribute to Richard Wagner's interpretation of Beethoven's 9th Symphony, the 'Ode to Joy', from a poem of 1785 by Schiller. Klimt's pictorial climax, *The Kiss*, references Schiller's line 'This kiss to all the world'. The *Beethoven Frieze* was originally painted to complement an exhibition in 1902 of a statue of the master as a

Klimt's Beethoven Frieze *in situ.*

22

naked Olympian deity by the German sculptor Max Klinger. At a private view of the Klimt and Klinger Beethoven exhibition, Mahler conducted a specially arranged version of the chorus to 'Ode to Joy' for six trombones only. It was the *Bildung* of universal values incarnate.

Learning was particularly revered by the Jews, so they slipped easily into Vienna's levelling culture of *Bildung*. Religious study had always been taken very seriously, and this intent was simply transferred to secular learning. 'What mattered,' writes Steven Beller, 'was not so much a religious education, but any education, otherwise you really were a nobody.'[23] It should also be added that an advanced education offered Jewish immigrants to Vienna the most reliable means of economic and social advancement. Medicine, in particular, could provide the newly qualified doctor with a good income in private practice at a relatively young age. Jews therefore gravitated towards the medical faculty of the University of Vienna in greater numbers than anywhere else.

But the most assured means of assimilation through *Bildung*, for Jews and other minorities, was to enrol in the city's *Gymnasien* and *Realschulen*. Unsurprisingly, therefore, the Jewish minority secured a significant overrepresentation at Vienna's schools relative to their population (and the same was true throughout the empire). By 1910, Austrian Jews were enrolling in academic secondary schools at more than three times the rate of the Catholic majority, relative to their population. Already by 1875 Jews might have accounted for a small proportion of the city's population but they made up almost a third of its *Gymnasien* students. Slavic and Protestant minorities were also over represented; the Protestant minority was drawn particularly to the *Realschulen*, displaying a strong interest in science and technical subjects.

It was the same story in Austria's eight universities, only more so. By 1910, 'Jewish representation relative to population among Austrian university students . . . was more than four and one-half times as great as that for all Catholics in Austria and two and one-third times that for all Protestants.'[24] At the height of the golden age, between the 1870s and 1910, Jewish students accounted for up to one-fifth of Austria's university enrolment, and the proportion was even higher in the faculties of the University of Vienna. This preponderance of ethnic and religious minorities in the empire's schools and universities did not go unnoticed, and was already a source of considerable resentment among the Austrian Catholic majority by the turn of the century.

Some Jewish families converted to Protestantism, the religion of the German enlightenment, or aspired to shed any vestiges of religion altogether. The *Gymnasien* and the University of Vienna were, by the standards of the day, relatively cheap and thus socially mixed, which added to the appearance of social inclusivity. Austrian universities granted half or full exemptions on fees to up to one-third of all students.[25] Even so, some 'assimilated' Jewish children noticed that they always tended to bunch with their own at school or university; there was an inescapable feeling that they were always different. Generally, however, within the educated middle class, Jews and Gentiles mixed fairly easily, even when they hailed from the farthest corners of the empire. The newspaper of choice for this middle class was the famous, rather solemn *Neue Freie Presse*, another shared reference point. It staggered on until just before the Second World War, only succumbing to fascism in January 1939.

So powerful was the hold that this German enlightenment culture exerted over Vienna's assimilated Jews and other minorities that many remained blind to the fact that this same pantheon of poets, composers and writers could be claimed by others to represent something altogether quite different, namely a specifically German ethno-nationalism, as was increasingly the case from the late nineteenth century onwards.[26] Vienna's Jews acquired their knowledge of German culture through books, and, as has often been pointed out, it was thus almost impossible for them to believe, as proved to be the case, 'that the Germany of real life was not that of Schiller'.[27] To a degree, therefore, the Viennese came to see *themselves* as the real guardians of German high culture, even more so than ethnic Germans themselves.

Moreover, it would be wrong to think that it was only the assimilated Jews who struggled, and often failed, to comprehend how *their* German enlightenment had been usurped by ethno-nationalists. Take the economist Friedrich von Hayek, nominally a Roman Catholic but raised in the same secular, enlightenment tradition. In Britain at the beginning of the Second World War, eager to show fealty to his adopted country, he wrote to the newly established Ministry of Information with some suggestions for 'Propaganda in Germany'. Plaintively, he proposed that the best way of combating the 'political principles of the Hitler regime' would be 'to show that it is Great Britain and France which now stand for all the principles which were dear to the great German poets and thinkers whose names are still sacred in Germany . . . it is of the greatest importance that so far as possible, German sources should be quoted to explain the ideals for which Great Britain and France are fighting'.

One such source that Hayek singled out was Schiller's renowned historical essay 'The Legislation of Lycurgus and Solon', in which the poet, dramatist and philosopher contrasted the free Athenian republic of Solon with Sparta's authoritarian regime of Lycurgus. The idea of broadcasting Schiller into Nazi Germany must have mystified the authorities; the professor received a polite rejection letter. By 1939 it was rather too late for such nuances.[28]

The educations of a polymath

These enlightenment values, of *Bildung*, were drummed into the offspring of the Viennese bourgeoisie through a deceptively complex educational process – not so much a formal 'system' as an overlapping network of official, informal and domestic pedagogy. Overall, this was virtually unique to Vienna, and contributed in no small part to the city's prodigious output of talent.

On the face of it, a Viennese bourgeois education seemed to be fairly straightforward, in common with the rest of the German-speaking world. Boys attended a *Realschule*, which focused on technical and scientific subjects, or a *Gymnasium*, followed by, for the more academic, three or four more years at the University of Vienna, founded in 1365, then the fourth-largest such institution in the world and one of the most prestigious in Europe. The artistically inclined could go to the Kunstgewerbeschule des k.k. Österreichischen Museums für Kunst und Industrie, or School of Applied Arts, founded in 1867. This progressive institution, far more open to women students, for instance, than the university, offered vocational courses in subjects such as architecture; graduates included the painters Gustav Klimt and Oskar Kokoschka, and the ceramicist Lucie Rie.

A *Gymnasium* education offered a largely classical curriculum: Greek, Latin, German language and literature, as well as history and geography, maths, physics and religion. Some could take French and English as well. The schooling was certainly rigorous, and demanding, with up to eight hours of Latin grammar, vocabulary and literature a week. It was also, by every account, designed to induce *rigor mortis* among the students.

'Nothing but a constant surfeit of tedium', bemoaned the writer Stefan Zweig, born in 1881, in his memoir *The World of Yesterday*. 'School to us meant compulsion, dreary boredom, a place where you had to absorb knowledge of subjects that did not seem worth knowing, sliced into neat portions . . . We sat there in pairs, like convicts in their galley, on low wooden benches that made us bend our backs, and we sat there until our bones ached.'[29]

There was too much rote learning, and little fraternisation between the children and the Dickensian Gradgrinds in the senior common room. The management theorist Peter Drucker recalled that few teachers at his 'famous classical Gymnasium' were of 'even low-level competence. Most bored their students most of the time, and themselves all of the time.'[30] They demanded, pompously, to be addressed only as 'professor', a practice sanctioned by imperial decree.[31] Unsurprisingly, there was a high drop-out rate; at one point only one-third of those who had started at a *Gymnasium* were finishing the whole eight years. Those who survived the ordeal then had to sit a notoriously arduous exam, the *Matura* (or, officially, *Reifeprüfung*). Science was almost entirely neglected, sport even more so. The *Realschulen* were slightly more pedagogically adventurous, but not by much.

Such a passive, infantilising experience could never have produced such a wealth of ferociously bright and inquisitive minds, and indeed it did not – most of that was done at home. For the real work of forging the city's intellectual and cultural élite was taking place behind the elegant facades of the Ringstrasse's apartments, particularly when it came to science. *Bildung* started, and sometimes finished, at home.

The city's musical and literary salons were renowned, hosted by wealthy families such as the Wittgensteins. Less well known is the fact that Vienna's spacious middle- and upper-class homes often accommodated as many amateur zoos, herbariums and laboratories as bedrooms and bathrooms. Karl Przibram, a physicist, recalled this environment from his own childhood:

The dominant spirit of my paternal home was that of the educated Jewish bourgeoisie of the liberal era, with its unconditional faith in progress and its open-mindedness for all achievements in art and science ... My father himself, incidentally a gifted poet and full of deep social feeling, was very much interested in technical applications of the sciences. He took part in the invention of a galvanic battery, by means of which in the beginnings of the 1880s he illuminated our flat.[32]

Not to be outdone, the young Karl installed his own laboratory at home where he replicated some of the experiments on electricity carried out by the inventor Nikola Tesla, himself a one-time youthful tinkerer from another part of the Austrian empire. But it was the aspiring naturalists who really taxed their parents' patience. Around 1900, a craze swept the German-speaking world for families to house increasingly large aquariums and terrariums, tended by children as young as five. The world's first club for aquariums and terrariums had been founded in 1882 in Gotha, Germany, and by 1911 there were no fewer than 284 such associations. The first Austrian club, called Lotus, was set up in 1895 – others soon followed.

All the most famous Viennese biologists and zoologists started out by nurturing animals in their own homes. Karl von Fritsch and Konrad Lorenz (together with a third honouree) shared the Nobel Prize in Physiology or Medicine in 1973; the former had a small zoological garden in his bedroom as a pre-schooler, whilst the pubescent Lorenz kept an extraordinary menagerie of animals in the garden (and rooms) of his parents' summer house in the village of Altenburg, just outside Vienna. The mature Lorenz eagerly complied with a request to keep certain animals in the house in order to restock Vienna's zoo after the Second World War, and consequently a large tiger prowled up and down in a cage in his study. Other inmates of the Lorenz family home included a baby hippopotamus, a parent of the hippo resident in Vienna's zoo today.[33]

Or consider Paul Kammerer, an experimental biologist. Born in 1880, by his teenage years the boy who would become one of Vienna's most celebrated scientists was already keeping more than 200 species in his parents' apartment at Karlplatz, just off the Ringstrasse (there were no private gardens in inner-city Vienna). Young Paul started off innocently enough with the usual guinea pigs and squirrels. These were soon joined, however, by two large American alligators, tropical marsh turtles, Australian snake-necked turtles, salamanders, a variety of frogs (including two species imported from Singapore, the first of their kind brought to Europe), as well as a huge collection of stuffed animals, including a Nile crocodile and 3,400 types of insect. History does not relate exactly how big his apartment was, but we do have a very accurate inventory of Kammerer's collection by virtue of his own accounting and various articles by awestruck journalists. They must have been dispatched to the Kammerer household by sceptical editors to verify this unlikely tale.[34]

Paul's ability to look after all these animals probably owed much to his father. From an assimilated Jewish family, Karl Kammerer was a wealthy entrepreneur who had founded and half-owned the only Austrian business producing and selling optical instruments. He sold his products to observatories and other scientific institutions around the world, so may well have provided some expert help in building the glass tanks and cages that were needed to prevent the alligators from terrorising the neighbours. For the future course of biology, the major significance of Kammerer's home zoo is that the precocious teenager started experimenting with his animals' environments. He connected each animal house to a gas appliance to deliver heat, and also developed his own ventilation device to change their air regularly. By his own account, these were his 'first shy attempts' to change and regulate the environment of his wards, 'in order to indirectly influence [their] living conditions, possibly the forms themselves'.

Even those young Viennese who did not mature into Nobel Prize-winning zoologists and physiologists were profoundly influenced by the all-consuming interest in science and experimentation. Hayek, for instance, was reared in an apartment overflowing with his father's extensive botanical collection of live and dried plants, photos and prints, and a herbarium of up to 100,000 sheets. The elder Hayek was a district physician in the city's health office by profession, but his real passion was botany; eventually he was to gain an unsalaried professorship to teach the subject at the university. He took an ice-bath every morning to tone up mind and body for the day ahead and regularly took his son to meetings of the Vienna Zoological and Botanical Society. Every other Thursday, Hayek senior would host an informal gathering of botanists and other scientists in the family apartment to discuss the latest developments in the field.[35] Unsurprisingly, the young Friedrich, who developed an extensive insect and plant collection of his own, was tempted to become a botanist himself. He did not, of course, but being instilled with the methodology of scientific enquiry from such a young age certainly informed most of his subsequent thinking about economics.[36] His two brothers would both become professors in the natural sciences (anatomy and botany).

To return to more formal educational paths, the pedagogy at Vienna's famous university could be just as conservative as that of a *Gymnasium*. The university, however, redeemed itself on several counts. First, it offered an intoxicating breadth of intellectual enquiry. A prospective student took a general exam to enter, and was then allowed to roam pretty much at will before settling on a final subject in which to be examined for a degree. Students therefore had plenty of time to seek out the professors who interested and inspired them, a common experience for many in this book.

Like other German-speaking universities, that of Vienna had only four faculties: Medicine and Anatomy, Theology, Law and Philosophy (which after 1900 was the largest). Most other subjects were taught in one or other of these last two faculties, meaning that interdisciplinary boundaries were porous, if indeed they existed at all. Economics, for instance, was taught in the Law faculty, natural sciences in the Philosophy faculty. There were no arbitrary divisions between 'science' and 'humanities' – all was 'philosophy', in its purest sense, the study of fundamental questions. A student was encouraged to shape his or her own epistemology, and thus fortified, the university's alumni would continue to do so for the rest of their lives.

Take Hayek again. As we have seen, he trained at home as a botanist to a quasi-professional level; he then graduated in law, received a doctorate in political science from the university, but by his own account spent most of his time there studying psychology, all before becoming a revered economist. As he remembered later, 'The decisive point was simply that you were not expected to confine yourself to your own subject . . . Nominally I was studying law, but still it left me time . . . [to] shift from subject to subject, readily hearing lectures about art history or ancient Greek plays.'[37]

Such an education tended to produce extraordinary polymaths. Hayek was to write professionally on economics, psychology, political science, political theory and more. His range of expertise, however, was quite narrow compared with some of his Viennese contemporaries. Take Ludwig von Bertalanffy, born in 1901, later the founder of General Systems Theory (GST). Also equipped with a small laboratory and dissection table at home, he at first specialised in zoology and biology, his interests stirred by a neighbour at his mother's estate in the Viennese suburbs – one Paul Kammerer. Very soon, however, he was ranging over almost all the natural and physical sciences, making useful contributions to physical chemistry, psychiatry and the diagnosis of cancer. Over the course of publishing more than 250 articles and papers during his life, he also wrote on mathematics, the philosophy of science (and history), as well as the origins of the mail service in Renaissance Italy.

Bertalanffy attempted to discern the common principles underlying such diverse fields of enquiry. Hence his development of GST, which rests on a belief that all complex systems share such principles, and that they can be modelled mathematically. Some historians have speculated that such integrative thinking was a hallmark of Viennese intellectuals because of the particular circumstance of the Austro-Hungarian empire. 'Nowhere else in Europe,' writes the historian William M. Johnston, 'did such discordant values and standpoints collide daily as in the streets of Vienna, Prague and Budapest. The sheer irreconcilability of the forces in evidence prodded thinkers to synthesize in imagination what external events left divided ... It was the Austrian Empire's very inability to furnish a *raison d'être* that incited her intellectuals to ponder unity amid diversity.'[38]

An intellectual hinterland

As well as being required to embrace a vast diversity of subject matter, students also benefited from an unusually wide range of people from whom they could learn. Besides the relatively small number of salaried professors (*Ordinarien*) at the University of Vienna, with whom students had little contact, there were also

Privatdozenten. These were individuals with a higher degree who were, for the most part, paid directly by the students to deliver classes at the university. They were not, however, on the permanent staff. Many of Vienna's most celebrated names, such as Sigmund Freud (for a while) and the economist Ludwig von Mises (throughout his time in Vienna), were *Privatdozenten,* as was Bertalanffy.

Students were thus exposed to the most brilliant minds in the city while the occasional lecturers had an opportunity to burnish their reputations and gather followers – or not. Vienna's most illustrious mathematician of the interwar years, Kurt Gödel, could not get a salaried position at the university, so was forced to give classes as a *Privatdozent* instead. It was not a happy experience. Gödel, a nervous personality who was to suffer from spells of mental instability later in life, spoke very fast, chalk in hand, facing the blackboard, leaving even his most enthusiastic students utterly lost. By the end of one semester, what had begun as a full lecture room was reduced to one student, a doggedly dedicated Polish logician. For his entire term's work Gödel was paid enough money to buy just two beers.[39]

Gödel aside, this system of private tuition with the *Privatdozenten* had considerable benefits. It blurred the boundaries between formal bastions of knowledge – such as the university – and the wider, richer hinterland of knowledge production that lay beyond. Indeed, the *Privatdozenten* often led their own seminar, or *Kreis* (circle), that was usually more stimulating than any of the formal university lectures. Freud's Wednesday Psychological Society, which started in 1902 (and which was to evolve into the Vienna Psychoanalytic Society), was a case in point, as was Mises's *Privatseminar,* which started in 1920 and became the fulcrum of the 'Austrian School' of economics during the interwar years. For many of the participants, these private seminars were the formative intellectual experiences of their lives.

Many of these *Privatdozenten* would also hold forth at a particular café, usually at an appointed time and even at a certain table, as did anyone else of a certain intellectual standing: architects (including Loos), writers, journalists and would-be revolutionaries (among them the young Leon Trotsky). An evening at the cafés Central, Landtmann or Prückel could thus be quite as instructive as a day at the university or an afternoon at the *Privatseminar*. Zweig remembered sitting in his favourite coffee-house 'for hours every day', imbibing all the latest trends in art, philosophy and literature.[40]

Furthermore, later in the evenings there was the cabaret, another education all of itself, frequented by bohemians, paupers and prostitutes, a gathering place for the more *outré* elements of liberal Vienna. Poets, writers and artists, such as Kokoschka, presented their works in between skits and sketches satirising self-righteous politicians and clerics. Many Viennese, such as Lang and Gruen, devoted a lot of their youth to the cabaret; the latter was a member of *Politisches Kabarett*, a theatre group that toured venues performing socialist slapstick skewering the hated old aristocratic-clerical establishment. If that wasn't enough, there was always the satirist and polemicist Karl Kraus, who from 1899 to 1936 turned out, almost single-handedly, 922 issues of his little magazine, *Die Fackel* (The Torch), in which he gleefully roasted all the leading businessmen, politicians, journalists and churchmen of the empire, sprinkling his scintillating prose with the aphorisms for which he was best known. His particular targets were the serious press, and the latest fads, for which Vienna provided easy pickings. Reading Kraus, almost forgotten today, was a tutoring in its own right.[41]

A truly Viennese education, therefore, was as much informal as formal, a rich tapestry of pedagogies and 'teachers' in the widest sense of the term.[42] It was a culture where the coffee-house could afford as rigorous an education as the classroom, and the *Privatseminar* or family home could offer as stimulating an environment as any university course. Equally, this process of acquiring knowledge respected, and encouraged, an easy flow between the professional world and academia, and an equally fluid exchange between disciplines. A Viennese education was hardly systematic, but it was

certainly comprehensive; the dead hand of specialisation had yet to intrude. Such an extraordinary intellectual upbringing was also, essentially, organic – flowing as it did from a multitude of initiatives: imperial, domestic and private.[43]

Mach one: Vienna, science and literary Modernism

Of all the disciplines, a great emphasis on science marked out the intellectual life of Vienna. This was a vital component of Viennese (particularly assimilated Jewish) middle-class society, and has often been overlooked. The Imperial Academy of Sciences had been founded in 1847, and the subsequent decade or so saw the creation of similar institutions, as well as overseas expeditions, across almost every field of scientific endeavour.[44] Science, and particularly medicine and the natural sciences, were absolutely central to the city's overall intellectual production.[45] The presiding geniuses of this scientific culture, deferred to by one and all, were Ernst Mach and Ludwig Boltzmann, of whom the first was by far the more important.

Born in the city of Brno, now in the Czech Republic, in 1838, Mach's contributions to physics were impressive enough. His work on shock waves, which he first photographed successfully in 1886, was groundbreaking. His name was consequently given to a measure of the speed of a body relative to the speed of sound, and much else besides; less well known are the Mach crater and asteroid. But it was for his advocacy of a modern, scientific worldview that he became a hero to scientists, philosophers and writers alike. For them, he was an archetype of the adventurous Viennese intellectual spirit.

After a professorial career at Prague's Charles-Ferdinand University, Mach became the first physicist to be appointed to a chair of philosophy in Europe at the University of Vienna in 1895. From this provocative blend of disciplines, Mach founded the

(opposite) Ernst Mach, an inspiration to scientists, philosophers and writers alike.

entirely new field of the philosophy of science. Albert Einstein, for one, who clashed frequently with Mach, still wrote of him: 'I believe that even those who consider themselves opponents of Mach are hardly aware of how much of Mach's way of thinking they imbibed, so to speak, with their mother's milk.'

Mach was probably most responsible for carving out Vienna's distinctive intellectual tradition in the German-speaking world.[46] With a long flowing beard and sharp, deep-set eyes, from his perch at the university the ebullient, effervescent Mach waged war against the metaphysics of German idealism, then the dominant school of philosophy in northern Europe. Herein lay his importance for Vienna. Mach defined a great dividing line between a rigorously scientific approach that the Viennese developed across all disciplines, and what he dismissed as the often obscurantist and epigrammatic disposition of German idealism, which he regarded as 'pseudo-science', the most damning epithet in the Viennese lexicon.

Mach took aim at the entire canon of German philosophy – Arthur Schopenhauer and Nietzsche particularly – but reserved most of his scorn for Immanuel Kant, the high priest of German idealism. Kant had argued that objects could exist independently of observation – the famous concept of the 'thing-in-itself'. Mach, on the other hand, regarded this as a useless abstraction. For him, as the contemporary Viennese mathematician Karl Sigmund has admirably summarised it, 'All knowledge had to be grounded in experience, and all experience grounded in perception, hence in "sense-data", which is to say, sensations.' These would include temperatures, sounds, pressures, time and so forth. Mach's philosophy of phenomenalism, as it was called, was 'all-encompassing'.[47] The economist Ludwig von Mises wrote in his memoirs of growing up in a Vienna that Mach and his acolytes had *liberated* from German idealism: 'The air in Austria was free of the spectra of Hegelian dialectics. In Austria, one did not feel it was his national duty to "overcome" the ideas of Western Europe. In Austria . . . hedonism and utilitarianism were not precluded, but studied.'[48] This was a defining feature of the Viennese tradition. Time and again, the Viennese ranged themselves against what the art historian Ernst Gombrich would later call the 'metaphysical fog' of idealism.

Mach exerted an extraordinary influence, and not just on professional scientists. He had a direct bearing, for instance, on many of Vienna's younger novelists, poets and playwrights, and through them the creation of literary Modernism. Under his spell the guiding praxis of Vienna's writers was to deploy the latest developments in science – more specifically, medicine, psychology and Freudian psychoanalysis – to provide a deeper, more multidimensional account of human motivation, in which the erotic (Mises's 'hedonism') would now play a large role.

For some of these writers, the links to Mach were very immediate. Robert Musil, for instance, author of *The Man Without Qualities*, a long meditation on the fall of the Habsburgs, wrote his dissertation on Mach's philosophy of science.[49] His father was a professor of mechanical engineering, and the younger Musil studied the same subject before moving on to experimental psychology and philosophy at university, a distinctly Viennese *mélange* of the empirical and 'humanities'.

Mach exercised an equally strong pull on the 'Young Vienna' group of writers, the main pioneers of Modernism in the city. Hermann Bahr, an essayist and the main spokesperson for the group, did most to popularise Mach's scientific philosophy with the publication of *The Unsalvageable Ego* in 1903. Here, Bahr extended the arguments in Mach's seminal *The Analysis of Sensations* (1886), where Mach had proposed that the ego was 'not a definite, unalterable, sharply-bounded unity', but rather a bundle of sense impressions of the world. That is, we cannot *know* the world, only our sense impressions of the world.[50] Bahr connected the art of the French Impressionists, for instance, to the style that Modernist writers would attempt to create on the page.

Another member of 'Young Vienna' was the playwright and short-story writer Arthur Schnitzler, born in 1862, who at one point was trying to compose an opera with Mach.[51] More than any other of Vienna's writers, Schnitzler's literature was applied science. His father was a renowned laryngologist, and the young Schnitzler consequently trained as a doctor; his brother was a surgeon, and his sister married a professor of laryngology. Schnitzler had already begun work at Vienna's General Hospital before giving up medicine as soon as his father died, an act of oedipal rebellion. Nonetheless, his medical background permeates his oeuvre. One of his best plays, *Professor Bernhardi*, is set in a hospital and focuses on a confrontation between a doctor and a priest.[52]

The particular sciences that fascinated Schnitzler as a medical student were psychology and, later, psychoanalysis. He worked in the clinic of Theodor Meynert, Freud's teacher, becoming an expert on hypnosis, even publishing a paper on the subject.[53] From here he became interested in dreams, telepathy and, like Freud, the erotic as unconscious drivers of human behaviour. These pepper his writing, so much so that he was often branded a pornographer by his contemporaries, particularly for his notorious 1897 play *La Ronde*, since made into countless films and TV dramas.[54] Freud, for his part, recognised a fellow-traveller in Schnitzler, hailing him as a 'colleague' in the investigation of the 'underestimated and much-maligned erotic'.[55] This aspect of Schnitzler's work ensured a select but deliciously scandalised readership across Europe, even decades after his death in 1931.

Hugo von Hofmannsthal, a 'Young Vienna' poet, attended Mach's lectures and referenced him in his own doctoral dissertation. More naturally, philosophers were drawn to Mach. William James, the American founder of the philosophy of Pragmatism, read Mach carefully and sought him out, eventually meeting the great man in Prague.[56] As we will explore later, Mach was also the main inspiration for the 'Vienna Circle' of logicians.

So when the Ministry of Culture commissioned Klimt, then at the height of his fame, to design and execute three ceiling frescoes for the ceremonial hall of the University of Vienna in 1894, the authorities chose for 'Philosophy' the very Machian theme of 'the triumph of light over darkness'. Perhaps they were expecting something akin to Raphael's *School of Athens* in the Vatican, with a robed Mach holding forth centre-stage. Consequently, when Klimt instead produced a painting of coiled nude bodies apparently floating in a void, there was outrage among the professoriate. The image was considered shocking not so much for the nudity, but because it seemed to owe more to German metaphysicians than to Mach and Viennese rationalism. Klimt's concept, it seemed, came out of that same metaphysical fog that so appalled the Machians, provoking a monumental row. The professor who led the charge against Klimt, one Friedrich Jodl, a progressive liberal of the best Viennese kind, objected to a 'dark, obscure symbolism which could be comprehended by few'.[57] Klimt's painting for 'Medicine' was even more offensive in their view; 'Jurisprudence' still worse. In the end, after a long confrontation, the panels were never installed; they are believed to have been tragically destroyed by the retreating Germans in a fire in 1945. It was, above all, a victory for Vienna's self-conception of itself as a home of science and rationalism. A disillusioned Klimt never accepted an official commission again.

Vienna also differed noticeably from the continent's intellectual mainstream in one other important respect, namely the city's attitude towards the hottest scientific topic of the day: Darwinism and evolution. After the publication of Charles Darwin's *On the Origin of Species by Means of Natural Selection* in 1859, evolution was a pervasive intellectual concern of the late nineteenth century, akin to climate change today. Broadly speaking, increasingly dogmatic interpretations of Darwin swept through Europe, particularly Germany.[58] Vienna, by contrast, emerged as a centre of Darwin-scepticism. This was significant because the Viennese school of evolutionary biology, as opposed to the 'central dogma' of Darwin's inheritance theorem, was intimately linked to the aspiring middle-class concept of progress, *Bildung* and, ultimately, free will.

In particular, Viennese scientists challenged those who maintained that the Darwinian mechanisms of 'natural selection' and 'survival of the fittest' could *fully* explain *all* of the bewildering variety of the world's flora and fauna. In 1901, the influential paediatrician Max Kassowitz convened a series of discussions at the University of Vienna entitled the 'Crisis of Darwinism'. He and another influential Viennese professor of botany, Richard von Wettstein, acknowledged the broad principles of Darwinian evolution, but argued that other evolutionary mechanisms must exist, namely an adaptation over generations to the environment.

This idea had originally been proposed by the French biologist Jean-Baptiste Lamarck. By the late nineteenth century the 'inheritance of acquired characteristics' was known as neo-Lamarckism.[59] Dogmatic Darwinists (but not necessarily Darwin himself) believed that life was essentially predetermined, whereas many Viennese biologists and thinkers were convinced that neo-Lamarckism gave them a scientific rationale for the exercise of free will *and* a progressive politics, that the poor, malnourished and ignorant could be physically transformed over generations with cleaner air, an improved diet, better sexual hygiene, and so on. This was the 'bio-politics' of Viennese progressivism, a faith shared by most of the middle class and championed by Red Vienna after the First World War. This transformative belief in scientifically grounded human progress characterised almost everything that the Viennese attempted in Austria and later in the West.

The sounds of music

As Richard Neutra's account of his childhood quoted above suggests, an essential marker of the new aspiring middle class in Vienna was a deep knowledge of, and expertise in, music. Neutra's own household was fairly typical; his two elder brothers played the violin to a high standard, whilst he learned the piano for five years. Neutra's father, according to his son, had never been taught an instrument, having tuned his childhood ears on cowbells. Nonetheless, Neutra *père* sensed that *Bildung* demanded rather more effort. Richard recalled, 'Both my parents seemed to take musical education as a natural requirement . . . Listening to Haydn, Mozart, Beethoven and Schubert was second nature to me, and I knew where to find all their busts in the city.' One of his brothers 'mingled with Arnold Schoenberg and his pupils'.[60]

Few of the young Viennese went on to become professional musicians, however. The Neutra brothers, for instance, eventually became engineers, psychiatrists and architects. Yet the classical canon remained central to their lives, with evenings dominated by incessant visits to the opera and concert halls. The Vienna Court Opera was presided over by Gustav Mahler, another immigrant from the imperial provinces, in his case Iglau, a town on the border of Bohemia and Moravia. Sensationally appointed director of the Opera in 1897 at the age of just thirty-six (for which he had to convert from the Judaism of his birth to Catholicism), Mahler's prestige confirmed Vienna as the centre of the musical universe. As well as elevating Vienna's operatic repertoire, these were also the years when Mahler was developing a new musical language in his symphonies; the startlingly modern Fifth was composed in 1901–2. He only resigned his post a decade later, in part to take up a similar, but much better paid, position at the Metropolitan Opera in New York.

By then, however, he was also exhausted by the constant infighting and often puerile controversies that afflicted opera in Vienna, to say nothing of the rising tide of anti-Semitism (he died in 1911). For the Viennese preoccupation with 'der Mahler', and music more generally, was obsessive, even pathological. Neutra recalled a suitor of his sister, one Schvodransky, a 'Russian nihilist', who had heard *Tristan und Isolde*, standing up, score in hand, no fewer than seventy-four times at the Imperial Opera. Some highly cultured Viennese, maybe most, kept diaries, or 'opera books', where they would record their trips to the city's many venues. These make for astonishing reading. One Anglicised Viennese, George Newman, a music publisher, examined his cousin Anne's diary while writing his own memoir of Vienna, *Finding Harmony*. For the season of September 1910 to August 1911, the eighteen-year-old went to seventy-three performances, including twenty operas and nineteen concerts. The following season she picked up the pace, going out on ninety-three occasions – a rate of several times a week.[61] Karl Menger, the economist and Wagnerian, remembered the 'remarkable atmosphere' at concerts and the 'almost religious devotion' to the yearly series of Beethoven quartets.[62]

The philosopher Karl Popper was another young Viennese reared on music, 'a dominant theme in my life', as he acknowledged in his own memoir, *Unended Quest*. His mother played the piano 'beautifully', as did her sisters, one of them professionally. Popper was unusually modest about his own musical accomplishments, but recounts that for about two years in the early 1920s he was thinking 'quite seriously' of playing professionally himself. All of his cousins were excellent musicians, and one boy played first violin in 'an excellent quartet'.[63] One young woman who performed music with the Poppers was an English resident of Vienna, Tess Simpson. Working in the city from 1928 to 1933, she happened to be an exceptional violinist. Playing chamber music in Vienna, she later recalled, was so taken for granted that it was 'like cleaning your teeth'.[64]

Popper's *Unended Quest* is, for the most part, a fairly dry resumé of the author's philosophical accomplishments and confrontations, laced with a few catty put-downs. However, on the question of musical preferences, Popper is roused to a rare degree of passion. He loathed Wagner, but Bach, Schubert and Brahms were all acceptable, as well as the 'twelve-tone' composers Schoenberg and Alban Berg.

His great rival, Ludwig Wittgenstein, was a scion of another intensely musical family. The sumptuous Palais Wittgenstein in the Alleegasse was famed for its musical salons, held in a specifically designed room complete with a small organ. Two generations of Wittgensteins cultivated Vienna's most renowned composers and performers, including Richard Strauss and Clara Schumann. The family's relationship with Johannes Brahms was particularly close. Ludwig himself believed that music had stopped with Brahms, exhibiting none of Popper's taste for the contemporary. He was an accomplished clarinettist and, more whimsically, a virtuoso whistler. His elder brother, Paul, was a renowned concert pianist. Music remained the most important topic of family conversation throughout their lives.

From his notebooks, it is clear that Wittgenstein (like Popper) mused on the connections between music and philosophy; for a man concerned primarily with the boundaries of human language and expression, in the broadest sense, it would be strange if he had not. Yet on this subject, as on so much else, he remains elusive and fragmentary. In the midst of writing the *Tractatus Logico-Philosophicus* in February 1914, he recorded: 'Musical themes are in a certain sense propositions. Knowledge of the nature of logic will for this reason lead to knowledge of the nature of music.'[65] Yet nowhere in his published works does Wittgenstein refer to music, unlike Popper. Perhaps, though, this was not for want of trying, but of facility. In 1949, as he was working on the *Philosophical Investigations*, published posthumously, he confided mournfully to his friend Con Drury, 'It is impossible for me to say in my book one word about all that music has meant in my life. How then can I hope to be understood?'[66]

If, as it seems, the Viennese's profound knowledge and understanding of music at least helped them in their work, if only as an analogous reference point to philosophical enquiry, it also served as a firm bond between them in exile. Certainly, the fact that so many scientists, philosophers, mathematicians, painters and more were steeped in music gave them a shared hinterland and perspective. The Viennese were equally passionate about theatre. Zweig famously wrote of the last performance at the old Burgtheater in 1888, before it was demolished, that when the curtain came down for the final time the whole audience swarmed onto the stage to pry away 'a relic of the boards upon which the beloved artists had trod'. These splinters would be preserved, like holy relics, in the living rooms on the Ringstrasse.

The Secession of art

As suggested by the Wittgenstein salon, patronage of the arts was an essential marker of the Viennese upper-middle class, and a vital expression of *Bildung*. Indeed, a musical salon was commonplace among Vienna's middle classes more generally, hosted even by families who evinced no other discernible interest in music. More daringly, however, the Viennese haute-bourgeoisie was also keen to support and sponsor all that was new and avant-garde in the arts, and in the sciences as well. This allowed them to forge their own identity, as distinct from the conservative, tradition-obsessed court and the older Viennese aristocracy. Consequently, it was often the patronage of the newly rich, assimilated Jews that sustained and encouraged Viennese experimentation and innovation through to 1934. Through such patronage these Jewish families sought to build a more modern, integrated and multiethnic Viennese identity.

This new wealth was often the result of fortunes made in industries such as iron and steel. Karl Wittgenstein, Ludwig's father, is an obvious example. He worked his way up from being a draughtsman in a rolling mill to preside over one of the most successful industrial conglomerates in Europe. By the time Karl gave up his day job in 1898, his family was one of the wealthiest on the continent, 'the Austrian equivalent of Krupps, the Carnegies, or the Rothschilds'.[67] Thus it was that in 1897 the ageing Karl Wittgenstein came to pay for most of the construction of the Secession Building, with its iconoclastic golden cupola perched on top of a plain white cuboid, designed by the young rebel Joseph

Maria Olbrich. This was perhaps the formal starting-point of Viennese Modernism.

Wittgenstein and other such patrons were guided in their taste by a prominent Jewish art critic called Berta Zuckerkandl. Married to a professor of anatomy at the university, Zuckerkandl helped to cultivate that taste through her own celebrated salon, which featured most of Modernist Vienna, including Klimt and Mahler as well as Schnitzler, Hugo von Hofmannsthal and Zweig. Zuckerkandl very much believed that the Secession movement could be 'a shared cultural platform for rapprochement between the city's Jews and Gentiles'.[68] Advised also by his eldest daughter Hermine, Karl Wittgenstein became probably the most influential backer of Secessionist artists, those who rebelled against the stultifying conservatism of the official 'Society of Fine Artists' to found their own movement. The fifty or so Secessionists included the architects Olbrich and Otto Wagner, the designers Josef Hoffmann and Koloman Moser, and their first president, Klimt. The latter also mentored the younger Egon Schiele, who would show his work at later Secessionist group shows. Klimt, in particular, was very close to the Wittgensteins; the painter liked to refer to the steel magnate as 'the Minister of Fine Art'. When Karl Wittgenstein's daughter Margarethe ('Gretl') married in 1905, the family naturally turned to Klimt to paint her portrait.[69]

The Habsburg monarchy's ministers embraced Modernism as well, even if for their own political reasons.[70] They hoped that art, and especially Modernism, would act as a unifying force, transcending ethnic and national differences in the empire as a whole. As the Minister of Culture, Ernest von Koerber, argued: 'Although every development is rooted in national soil, yet works of art speak a common language, and, entering into noble competition, lead to mutual understanding and reciprocal respect.'[71] Even the emperor, a confirmed philistine, gave his personal imprimatur to the Secession, attending its first exhibition.

Just as important as the Wittgensteins in the development of Viennese Modernism were the Waerndorfer family, textile magnates and also assimilated Jews. The young Fritz Waerndorfer was another backer of the Secessionists and played the crucial financial role in setting up the Wiener Werkstätte in 1903, an art and design workshop that would produce many of the most memorable examples of the Austrian *Jugendstil* – Viennese art deco, in glass, metal, ceramics and paper.[72]

Inspired by Victorian Britain's Arts and Crafts movement, the Werkstätte was co-founded by the two Secessionist designers Hoffmann and Moser. Their goal was to apply the highest aesthetic standards to the implements of everyday life, thus restoring beauty to ordinary homes. Their aims were expressed in the ideal of *Gesamtkunstwerk*, or 'total work of art'. The concept had been popularised by Richard Wagner to propose the unity of drama and music, exemplified by his *Ring* cycle.

The crowning moment of their work was a public exhibition in 1908, called simply *Kunstschau* (Art Exhibition). The pavilion was designed by Hoffmann, and Klimt gave the group's statement of aims in his opening address: 'The progress of culture consists only in the ever-increasing permeation of all of life by artistic purposes.'[73] Like William Morris before them, Moser and Hoffmann wanted to reach as many people as possible with the new art. But the beautiful, intricate glassware, cutlery, postcards, books and textiles produced by the hundreds of dedicated Wiener Werkstätte (WW) craftsmen and women proved to be far too expensive for the vast majority of households; it only survived with the patronage of a few wealthy families.

Most of those were, again, assimilated Jews, including the Ephrussi, bankers originally from Odessa. But other patrons also stepped in. A Catholic banker, Otto Primavesi, and his wife Eugenia commissioned several important Klimt paintings as well as houses and interiors from Hoffmann. Their family hailed from Olmütz, now Olomouc in the Czech Republic. The mansions that many of these rich Viennese families built for themselves near the Ringstrasse were also important sources of work for the Modernist designers, although the finest achievement of the WW, the Stoclet Palace, was built for the railway magnate Adolphe Stoclet in Brussels. With its distinctive, richly decorated tower, the Stoclet Palace was indeed a total work of art. No expense was spared. Every detail was designed in the WW's trademark style by Hoffmann and a mosaic frieze by Klimt adorned the dining room.

For the empire, to the end

This, then, was the culture of *Bildung* that united the Viennese middle class of this era. Vienna's dynamic cultural and intellectual life was a space in which the assimilated Jewish families could meet on more or less equal terms with their peers, be they Catholic, Protestant or, more rarely, secular. Many of the Jewish community, in particular, fiercely resisted the ethnic, nationalist and political labels that others (among them, but not only, the Nazis) would always persist in attaching to them. The art historian Ernst Gombrich was vehement on this point, arguing that identifying his peers as Jews or Gentiles, Aryan or otherwise, was best left 'to the Gestapo'.[74] His close friend Popper famously rejected Jewish nationalism as much as German (or any other) nationalism, in favour of 'uncompromising cosmopolitanism'. A colleague of Victor Gruen's would always say of the architect, born in the city in 1903, 'Victor was much more of a Viennese than a Jew or a Socialist.'[75] Neutra recalled Vienna very emotionally, as 'that cultural metropolis to which we belonged with our hearts'.[76] Most of the Viennese middle classes considered themselves to be simply Viennese, understanding exactly what this self-identification meant.

Cultural *Bildung* acted as a strong centripetal force in the empire against the countervailing centrifugal currents of nationalism and ethnicity. But there were other such centripetal forces at work as well. A law passed in 1868 made young men in the empire liable for military service, although by no means everyone was called up in any given year. Those who were not, served in the reserves. This system gave the Austro-Hungarian reserves 'a far greater social and religious diversity (and a much higher percentage of Jewish officers) than in neighbouring Germany or Russia, where the officer corps remained bastions of aristocratic social exclusivity'. The language of command was German (in its Austrian form), but elaborate care was taken to use and incorporate those languages that were most familiar to the men serving in any given unit or regiment. Every recruit thus had to familiarise himself with a common language, and some standard empire-wide customs and beliefs.[77]

Above all, it was the emperor who was the staunchest defender of the liberal constitution, especially when it came under strain from the new political forces of anti-Semitism and nationalism in the 1890s. Admirably, Franz Joseph, a devout Roman Catholic, made a point of visiting – and worshipping – at the temples and churches of all denominations within the empire, including synagogues. For several years he refused to allow the first explicitly anti-Semitic mayor, Karl Lueger, to take up his office in Vienna after winning election in 1895. He also personally helped to force the University of Vienna to admit women.

Thus, on the outbreak of the First World War the mood in Vienna was slightly different from other European capitals. As elsewhere, the hostilities provoked a surge of jingoism, but in Vienna this was tinged by a particular loyalty to the Habsburgs, especially amongst the Jewish middle classes. This was a chance to prove their loyalty, and to repay the emperor for his protection. As the monthly magazine of the Austrian-Israelite Union commented in August 1914: 'In this hour of danger we regard ourselves as fully entitled citizens of this state . . . We want to thank the Kaiser for making us free, with our children's blood and with our worldly goods, we want to prove to the state that we are its loyal citizens, as good as anyone . . . There must be no anti-semitic enticement after this war and all its horrors.'[78] Indeed, it was partly because of their high regard for the emperor himself, and all that he represented, that however clever, cultivated, avant-garde, Jewish or Gentile anyone was in 1914 Vienna, the young men and women of the empire for the most part willingly rallied to the imperial cause on the outbreak of the First World War.[79] Overall, the empire raised an astonishing 8 million soldiers to fight the Great War.

Contrary to Vienna's *fin-de-siècle* reputation for decadence and ennui, therefore, these young recruits, almost without exception, made unusually dedicated, well-motivated and fearless soldiers. Many were honoured by the state for bravery. By contrast, many British liberals, and certainly socialists, opposed their country's entry into the war. The young men and women of the progressive Bloomsbury Group, for instance, perhaps the nearest equivalent to Vienna's liberal middle class, passionately objected to the conflict. They were certainly not inspired to fight for an idea.

All three Wittgenstein brothers distinguished themselves, including Ludwig. A grievous wound rarely dissuaded anyone from returning to the fray. Paul Wittgenstein, for example, lost his right arm fighting in the first months of the war. A concert pianist, he could have been forgiven for retiring from the fray, but Paul badgered the army until they allowed him back to the front lines. Fritz Lang, for his part, was repeatedly praised in official accounts for his courage under fire. As a reconnaissance officer, obliged to crawl close to enemy lines in order to bring back first-hand accounts of their deployments, Lang was often in mortal danger. He distinguished himself at the battle of Cholopieczy against the Russians in June 1916, his military file stating that: 'It was mainly due to his exemplary reports that a strong enemy did not gain ground.' During twelve hours of heavy fighting Lang was wounded slightly in the shoulder, but he suffered more substantial injuries a week later. This time he was hospitalised, but still volunteered to return to the front, where he was wounded and decorated yet again. By this stage of the war the Austrian army was running out of horses and so, family legend has it, the young lieutenant persuaded his father to buy him his own horse. Damage to an eye forced Lang to wear a monocle, or sometimes a patch, for the rest of his life. As things turned out, he turned this misfortune to his professional advantage: a monocled Lang – with polka-dot scarf accessory – was instantly recognisable in Hollywood.[80]

Such was liberal Vienna's investment in the imperial cause – it was as if everyone sensed how quickly it could all crumble away. This process duly began in November 1916 with the death of Franz Joseph. His demise, amidst a third year of an unimaginably brutal war, was not by itself fatal to the cause, but was nonetheless deeply unnerving and demoralising, even though he was swiftly succeeded by his great nephew Karl. Lang later recalled clearly the moment of Franz Joseph's passing in 1916: 'With the death of the old Kaiser, a strange emptiness began in me and the other officers of the Austrian army. Of course, we swore an oath to his successor, but that strange love we didn't really have for Kaiser Karl as we did for the old Herr. This love was unendurable.'[81]

Given their depth of feeling for Franz Joseph, many – perhaps most – Viennese remained nostalgic for the monarchy long after it had been swept away. That nostalgia only increased, of course, as Austria began its post-war descent into fascism. Thus, Franz Joseph became an unwitting symbol of better times, of *The World of Yesterday*, as Zweig entitled his own elegy, composed in the years before the novelist committed suicide, in exile in Brazil, in 1942.[82] The economist Joseph Schumpeter was another royalist in mourning, never entirely comfortable in the post-war world and forever lauding Britain's constitutional monarchy. Years later, he would tell a lecture audience: 'I liked those times [before the war], but since there is no use in wishful thinking, I realize that that world is dead and buried and there is no way back to it.'[83]

The author of *The Radetzky March*, Joseph Roth, descended into a parlous state of alcoholic despondency; he, more than most, anticipated what dark forces the end of the Habsburgs might unleash. He wrote to a friend, Otto Forst de Battaglia, in October 1932, a year before leaving Nazi Germany for permanent exile in Paris: 'The most powerful experience of my life was the war and the end of my fatherland, the only one I ever had: the Dual Monarchy of Austria-Hungary. To this date I am a patriotic Austrian and love what is left of my homeland as a sort of relic.'[84] Roth died of drink and despair in Paris in 1939. He was only forty-four.

Dr Karl Lueger.

Chapter 2

Black Vienna and the Birth of Populist Politics

here was another education available during Vienna's golden age, however, which was to prove just as significant – and much more devastating – as anything offered by Mach and the city's pluralistic liberalism. For at the same time, in direct opposition to that tradition, there developed a political disposition that we would now identify as 'populism'. This divisive, discriminatory and anti-democratic ideology found its modern voice in Vienna, expressed by demagogues, rabble-rousers and elected politicians. Long before it was fashionable to do so, Schorske wrote of these Austrians that they pioneered 'a post-rational politics', with 'a mode of political behaviour at once more abrasive, more creative, and more satisfying to the life of feeling than the deliberative style of the liberals'.[1]

This was the milieu in which Hitler matured before the First World War; he lived in Vienna from 1907 to 1913, when he left for Munich, enlisting in the German army in 1914. By that time, most of the ideas and prejudices that shaped him were already fully formed in his mind, either developed in his hometown of Linz or

(opposite) Reinventing politics: Karl Lueger, a role model for Hitler.

the product of intense reading, bitter disappointment and emotional turmoil during his years as a dismal drop-out in pre-war Vienna. Germany's defeat in 1918 and subsequent humiliation at the negotiating table only nourished what he had picked up in Vienna. Hitler's Austrian precursors were political disruptors, dedicated to tearing down the apparently solid edifice of Viennese liberalism – but they also proved to be all too creative in building a well-crafted, multidimensional worldview, drawing on many of the same new intellectual disciplines as the liberals did. This gave them a ready-made action plan – legislative as much as coercive – for when they seized power in Germany, and Austria after 1938.

Hogarthian Vienna: life beyond the Ringstrasse

That the wealthy scions of liberal Vienna of the last chapter and the illiberals of this one barely ever encountered each other was due, in part, to the geography of Vienna. People might have mingled freely in the centre, yet beyond the splendours of the Ringstrasse and its sumptuous apartments were the slums, lodging houses and tenements that housed most of the city's growing population. This was the physical environment in which a new politics could flourish, where late nineteenth-century liberalism seemed to offer few benefits.

Living conditions here were wretched, famously chronicled by the economist Eugen von Philippovich. He described families squeezed into one-bedroom apartments that had neither running water nor light (natural or artificial); their miserable occupants had to use outdoor toilets that served as many as 120 people. Often, interior squalor was hidden from the street by deceptively grand facades replete with the same ornaments and motifs that might grace a middle-class apartment. One contemporary Viennese diarist noted:

> the complete contrast here between the shabby interiors of the needy inhabitants and the exterior of their dwellings. The stranger

is surprised by how ... individuals and groups looking like a Hogarth caricature peer from the windows, and that surprise grows to astonishment when he observes how balconies supported by artfully executed caryatids are adorned with shabby laundry put out to dry.[2]

The living conditions of Vienna's poor therefore afforded little relief from working the seven-day, seventy-hour weeks that were still common into the 1880s.[3] It was not unusual for factories to employ children, and only after 1883 were employers mandated to give everyone twenty-four hours of rest on a Sunday. Women, meanwhile, received considerably less pay than men for the same work: many were forced into prostitution to make ends meet.

The outer city walls were only demolished in 1894, finally allowing some integration of the outer working-class suburbs into the city as a whole. Nonetheless, the festering resentments of Vienna's poor and marginalised remained, and could occasionally turn violent. There was widespread rioting provoked by hunger and inflation in the working-class district of Ottakring in September 1911. School buildings and streetcars were set on fire, barricades went up, 'the troops fired on the people, and behind the frenzied crowd the lumpenproletariat plundered shops'.[4] The anarchy briefly spilled over into the central quarter before being contained by soldiers with fixed bayonets.

These were the immediate circumstances of anger, bitterness and discontent that a new breed of politician could identify and exploit – a side of the city that has been called Black Vienna (as black was generally the colour of fascism). The emotional spasms that coalesced into a coherent ideology of fascism in the late nineteenth century might have come out of more ancient prejudices deeply rooted in European history, but they were certainly intensified by opposition to the bourgeois hegemony of liberal Vienna.

One strand of this opposition was 'pan-Germanism'. The creation of the German empire in 1871 after Bismarck's victory in the Franco-Prussian war, incorporating all the southern German states adjoining

Austria, gave an enormous fillip to the cause of pan-Germanism. Bismarck had specifically excluded Austria from the original confederation of German states in 1866 after the Austro-Prussian war. But from 1871 onwards the creation of a unified and geographically-bounded German identity to the north of Austria persuaded many ethnically German Austrians that they had an equal claim on the glories of what was now continental Europe's strongest power. Thus, just as the Austro-Hungarian empire enjoyed a last bloom of multi-lingual, multiethnic politics, so those countervailing forces gathered strength, redefining 'German' not as a universal enlightenment culture but as a specifically nationalist and Aryan identity, reified magnificently – so they claimed – in the operas of Richard Wagner.

In Austria, this insidious new spirit was embodied by Georg von Schönerer, the founder of a novel brand of aggressively divisive politics. Born into an impeccably bourgeois family in Vienna in 1842, from his early twenties he was convinced that the Austrian exclusion from the German empire was but a temporary aberration, and that an *Anschluss* (meaning in English a connection, or joining) of Austria's German part was inevitable. Bullish in body as well as spirit, as a parliamentarian Schönerer became the leader of Austria's pan-Germans, usually quoting Bismarck at his rallies: 'That which is German, will sooner or later return to Germany.' He always reassured his devoted audiences that 'the Germanic way of viewing the world and life shall once again blaze the trail'.[5]

From the 1880s onwards Schönerer's admirers founded a plethora of pan-German associations and organisations, and ensured that German-language schools were available in mixed-language areas. Hence German nationalist rhetoric acquired an institutional structure. Schönerer also turned his campaign for the 'German people' into a battle against Jews and Slavs – the Other. 'We German nationals view anti-Semitism as a keystone of the national idea,' he announced, 'as a main support of a true folkish mentality.' One of his slogans was 'Through Purity to Unity'. In short, to be German, you could no longer be Jewish.

Equally, social democracy was identified as a specifically Jewish politics, and capitalism as a Jewish conspiracy. Schönerer mounted a campaign in parliament against the financial power of Baron Rothschild. He roused those artisans and small shopkeepers who had lost out to the economies of scale achieved by capitalism, directing their anger at Jews. In 1882, he poisonously told the Austrian Reform Union that he was declaring war on the 'sucking vampire . . . that knocks . . . at the narrow-windowed house of the German farmer and craftsman'.[6]

Even his opponents had to acknowledge that the perpetually furious and emotionally unbalanced Schönerer was nevertheless a powerful, charismatic speaker. 'Physically [he] is short and stocky, and his fat, red beer face with its fat eyes does not leave a pleasant impression,' recorded one. 'Yet when the man speaks, he looks different. Then those otherwise weary eyes begin to glow, his hands start moving, and his features become very lively, while his words reverberate from his lips throughout the room.'[7]

Many young Austrians were heavily influenced by Schönerer, including Hitler. The jobbing artist probably never met his first idol, but that did not stop him referring incessantly to Schönerer and his abhorrent ideas for the rest of his life. Having moved to Vienna, Hitler failed (twice) to enrol in the Academy of Fine Arts, thereafter scrimping a living as a postcard painter. Living in hostels, an embittered, destitute itinerant in Vienna's 6th District, Hitler absorbed the shrill, xenophobic and racist literature that was circulating in the city at the time, much of it inspired by Schönerer. One particularly chilling text, published in 1900 by an anti-Semitic priest called Joseph Scheicher, looked forward to an Austria in 1920 that had been 'cleaned' of its Jews by the country's new ruler, one Karl Lueger, of whom more below (see image p. 52). Thousands of Jews, Scheicher fantasised, had been hanged and the rest driven out. Scheicher's 'dream', as he called it, was later parodied by the writer Hugo Bettauer as *The City Without Jews*; Bettauer imagined a dystopian city unable to function, instead of Scheicher's grim utopia.[8]

Ugly Karl

Schönerer is mentioned several times in *Mein Kampf*, and in many ways 'the demagogue of Rosenau', who referred to himself as 'Führer', was Hitler's first and most influential role model. But Hitler reserved his most effusive praise for Karl Lueger, Austria's (and one of Europe's) most notorious turn-of-the-century politicians. He was mayor of Vienna from 1897 until his death in 1910, and a founder and leader of the Christian Social Party. Lueger was the first recognisably 'populist' political leader of the modern era, mobilising new constituencies of voters to forge a fresh political project. In particular, the 'Lord God of Vienna', as his supporters liked to call him, was probably the first open anti-Semite to be elected to an official position in Europe, just as the Christian Social Party was the first to elevate anti-Semitism into a doctrine of government.

Hitler first heard Lueger speak in 1908. After admiring Schönerer so much, Hitler was ready to be disappointed. Instead, he was transfixed: 'I felt compelled to admire him; he had absolutely outstanding talents as an orator.'[9] One witness described Lueger as he worked an audience:

> The roar of applause releases off his talents . . . in the quickfire attack that befits his temperament, he overruns reason and proof, stamps great meanings into the ground, and then holds up trivialities with a single word so rapidly that they appear the pinnacle of truth. He is happy to adopt the insults of the street, voice the stupid phrases of old superstitions, and use clerical gestures that have long been abandoned in the pulpit – but all this only makes him more effective . . . his power over the Viennese people is that they all speak through his mouth.[10]

Here was the antithesis to the rhetoric of liberal politics, a prototype for all who would follow him. Lueger, born in 1844, had originally been an acolyte of Schönerer's, but later split away to fashion a coherent political programme out of his mentor's overheated rhetoric and incongruent prejudices. Lueger founded a Viennese brand of 'municipal socialism', for the first time shifting the centre of political gravity from the liberal individualism of the nineteenth century towards a more collectivist model, based on an ambitious programme of public works funded by long-term domestic loans and foreign debt.[11]

His greatest achievement, lauded to this day, was to look beyond the imperial grandeur of the Ringstrasse and create a modern, interconnected metropolis that embraced the outer districts of the city.[12] Gas, water and electricity services, previously in the hands of private owners, were all municipalised, extending these utilities to hundreds of thousands of new homes. Horse trams made way for an electric streetcar system, by many accounts the best in Europe. Otto Wagner, originally appointed to his post in 1894, oversaw the design of the stations for the new metropolitan railway system, connecting the city centre with the suburbs. Wagner's elegant green and gold *Jugendstil* constructions remain amongst Vienna's signature buildings.

But Lueger's public works were accompanied by demagogy and divisiveness. Taking his cue from Schönerer he declared that 'Vienna is German and must remain German'. 'Handsome Karl', as the blue-eyed Lueger was dubbed by his female cheerleaders (the self-declared 'Lueger's Amazons'), therefore took measures to limit immigration to Vienna. From 1890, new citizens had to swear to 'uphold the city's German character as far as possible'.[13] The Christian Socials governed as an explicitly anti-Semitic party; indeed, they kept their original designation of 'The Anti-Semites' in the party's official title. 'Greater Vienna must not turn into Greater Jerusalem', declared Lueger. So offensive was his anti-Semitism that when he first won an election for mayor, in 1895, not only did the scandalised emperor refuse to appoint him, but the liberal *Neue Freie Presse* even warned that 'the dregs' of Vienna were rising to the surface.[14] Two years later, however, even the emperor bowed to the democratic will of his people (and, it is said, the personal intervention of the pope), and Lueger moved into City Hall.

A self-declared 'tribune of the people', he promised to look after the 'little man' against the supposedly exploitative (Jewish) upper-middle class of bankers and 'profiteers'. The electoral franchise was extended to include the lower-middle classes, and this became his core constituency. Women had not yet been enfranchised, but he went out of his way to court their good opinion, convinced that they had a marked bearing on the way that their husbands voted. He was also careful to keep the powerful Catholic Church on side, as well as the pan-Germans. He skilfully wove together his new 'base' with the stitch of anti-Semitism.

Along with his policies, the mayor's personal style was also mould-breaking. Lueger was a flamboyant showman, attending to the theatre of politics with processions, set-piece rallies, extensive entertainments, lots of dressing-up and oceans of press coverage. His relentless self-promotion reached a peak for his sixtieth birthday celebrations in October 1904. These included a torchlight procession through the city, and all Viennese schoolchildren received a *Festschrift* devoted to Lueger, given away for free by the School Board.[15] Unmarried, it was said that Lueger was solely devoted to his beloved Vienna. The same would be claimed for Hitler, who studied his new hero closely, and his own beloved Third Reich.

Lueger had been ill for a long time with diabetes and kidney disease, among other ailments, before he died in March 1910. The stoical manner in which he bore his pain and disabilities only added to his mythic status. The Christian Socials declined as a political force after Lueger's death, but, nonetheless, he had blazed a trail for ethno-nationalist, anti-Semitic and anti-capitalist politicians throughout Europe. Tragically, Austria's defeat in the First World War, followed by the country's immiseration, only increased the appeal of the new politics.

Specifically, defeat prompted the Christian Socials and conservative Catholics into advocating more radical policies for what was diagnosed as a growing Jewish problem. As we will see in the next chapter, the influx of Jewish refugees from the east during the war gave anti-Semitic politicians a pretext to advocate ever more discriminatory policies. As early as 1920, during a debate in the federal parliament, Christian Social politicians argued for Jews to be 'interred' in 'concentration camps, without delay', or expelled. The influential German-born journalist Joseph Eberle expressed mainstream, Catholic anti-Semitism at this time through the pages of two journals that he edited, first *Das neue Reich*, a title that needs no explaining, and from 1925 onwards a weekly magazine *Schönere Zukunft* (roughly, Brighter Future). Frequently raging against liberalism and socialism as products of a bankrupt enlightenment, in 1919 he advocated 'defensive measures' to be taken up by Christians 'against Jewry's demonic drive to conquer them'. He called for the 'restriction of Jews in all branches of culture and business to a percentage corresponding to their number in the general population' and 'setting the Jews under a special set of laws'.[16]

De-rationalising society

For their part, liberal, and thereafter social democratic, Viennese were fatally ambivalent towards the menaces of rabid anti-Semitism and ethno-nationalism. When organised anti-Semitism had first emerged with Schönerer, one response had been to accept and acknowledge that even the most acculturated Jews would never be accepted by Gentiles. It was therefore logical to look to a separate Jewish homeland. This was the vision of the dandyish anglophile Theodor Herzl, as articulated in his political pamphlet *Der Judenstaat*, published in 1896, the founding text of Zionism. Ironically, for the man who broke the Jewish consensus on assimilation, his conception of the new state was immaculately Austro-liberal. His vision was to reproduce a truly liberal Vienna, governed by a benign, English-style aristocracy. As a true son of Vienna's *Bildung* he was inspired by a particularly passionate performance of Wagner's *Tannhäuser* to feverishly sketch out his bold plan for a Jewish state, feeling, perhaps, the Wagnerian revolt of the young against the old, the romantic against the rational.[17]

At the time, however, few of Vienna's assimilated Jews were listening to Herzl, who died in 1904. By 1913, Herzl's movement could count on just 1,300 fee-paying Zionists, a minority's minority.[18] Even Herzl's close friends, such as Stefan Zweig, assailed the segregationist spirit of Zionism. The liberal and socialist assimilationists optimistically hoped that anti-Semitism would just melt away in a socialist society, together with the class struggle and other such unpleasantries. Not least, they believed, because the Jews *themselves* would have shed Judaism on the path to socialism, thereby becoming of no more consequence to their opponents. This was more of a pious hope than a well-grounded expectation, but it was symptomatic of the many ways in which the Social Democrats badly underestimated the intensity and appeal of Schönerer, Eberle and the mystical, *völkisch* Richard Kralik, another hero to the right.

Writers like Karl Kraus dismissed these anti-Semitic propagandists as cranks, but they commanded huge followings, and not just amongst the vagrants and thugs who inhabited Hitler's various hostels. Over time the nationalist right developed a historically grounded and philosophically coherent ideology that permeated élite academic and intellectual circles as well as the street. The *Reichspost* and *Das neue Reich*, papers in which this new ideology got a good airing, were among the best-selling highbrow publications in interwar Europe. The historian Janek Wasserman has calculated that about a fifth of the contributors were university professors, mostly from Vienna, and two-fifths had some form of advanced degree.[19]

The most compelling proto-fascist intellectual in Vienna after the First World War was himself a professor at the university. Othmar Spann, born in 1878, was appointed in 1919, and although he is seldom remembered today, in the 1920s and 1930s he was probably the most celebrated academic in Vienna. Spann's landmark book

Der wahre Staat (The True State), published in 1921, quickly became the bible of Austria's right-wing nationalists.

Spann attacked the entire intellectual edifice of liberal Vienna, arguing that the consequences of nineteenth-century 'individualist' social theory had proved to be entirely negative, leading to capitalist exploitation, plutocracy and societal divisions exacerbated by a mass democracy that had encouraged atomisation and anarchy. In its place Spann argued for a 'universalist' social theory where everyone was bound to each other by reciprocal obligations. Values and politics would emerge from the 'whole' of society, not just competing parts of it. He specifically argued for a period of 'de-rationalisation', on the grounds that modern science had sundered the old bonds of feudal society, which now had to be carefully restored.

Der wahre Staat was a blueprint for Austro-fascism, an ideology that governed Austria from 1934 to the *Anschluss*. The author himself joined Austria's nascent National Socialist Party, originally formed as the German Workers' Party. A charismatic lecturer, Spann packed the room (as well as the adjacent corridors) when he took to the lectern. He drew many young Viennese into his orbit, including, briefly, Hayek. On purely academic grounds he probably deserved his cult status; as a committed and enthusiastic teacher, about 90 per cent of all law students during the first republic took at least one course with Spann. He was also an energetic promoter of his acolytes to positions at the university, a group of loyalists known as the *Spannkreis*. These ultras served 'as a linchpin of Viennese culture and Central European radical conservative politics. The most influential intellectual group in interwar Vienna was also its most conservative.'[20]

In the Bear's Den: the university and the rise of anti-Semitism

The prominence of Spann was symptomatic of the fact that, ironically, nowhere did this 'post-rational' politics take hold more strongly than at the University of Vienna itself, home to Mach and

Vienna's liberal, scientific tradition. By the years leading up to the First World War, for many professors the defence of liberalism had ossified into a defence of privilege, and specifically male, Aryan and Catholic privilege, seasoned with pan-Germanism. By the 1920s the venerable old university was less a pinnacle of learning and open-mindedness than a bastion of prejudice and exclusivity. Furthermore, it was a bastion vigorously policed by the professors themselves, often dedicated anti-Semites, Christian Socials or worse.

The full details of the extraordinary and deeply dispiriting story of how the university became an enforcer of Black Vienna's politics have been unearthed only in the last few years, principally by the scholar Klaus Taschwer. From 1919 onwards the university's old guard rallied its forces against the rising tides of socialism and feminism, backed up by successive German-nationalist or even proto-Nazi politicians at the federal Ministry of Education.

The ringleader of the right-wing professoriate was a palaeontologist called Othenio Abel, appointed to a full professorship at the university in 1917. He clearly exerted considerable power within the institution, claiming no fewer than twenty-four rooms for his extensive collection of bones, fossils and taxidermy specimens. A German nationalist, Catholic and virulent anti-Semite, Abel made it his job to corral like-minded colleagues into resisting what they regarded as the increasing incursion of Jews, socialists and women into the university. Reporting to a sympathiser in early 1923, he wrote: 'We bound together our anti-Semitic groups at the University so firmly, that we are building a strong phalanx.' This work Abel considered to be just as 'necessary . . . as writing books'.[21]

This 'phalanx' contained about nineteen professors, an all-male cabal that held regular, clandestine meetings in Abel's paleo-biology seminar room, surrounded by the remains of extinct primeval animals, including a cave bear – hence the conspirators' own name for their group, the Bear's Den. Mostly from the humanities, these professors were often members of the ultra-nationalist German Club, a proto-Nazi group that met at the Hofburg Palace, and various anti-Semitic associations. Assimilation, however diligent, was no defence against the aggressive anti-Semitism of the Bear's Den; anyone with the faintest hint of Jewish heritage, or even close connections with Jewish colleagues, was almost certain to have their application for a post at the university, however humble, turned down. As Taschwer writes, 'Prior to the forming of the Bear's Den, researchers of Jewish descent still had some chance of a career in the faculty of philosophy . . . but by 1923 that was over except for a very few exceptions.'

Well before the Austro-fascists took over in 1934, therefore, and the Nazis in 1938, careers were being stunted and ambitions frustrated by the highly organised institutional racism at the university. With little expectation of any paid jobs, academic career options for bright young Jewish men and women, particularly of the left, were severely curtailed. Moreover, as well as preventing their opponents from taking up any new positions at the university, the Bear's Den also made it their business to identify, and 'out', their existing colleagues of Jewish backgrounds, with devastating results. Lists of Jewish teachers were published in the right-wing press. These lists probably formed the basis for the very speedy expulsion of those few Jews who were left at the university, and similar institutions, once the Nazis took over after the *Anschluss* in 1938.

Furthermore, many students took their political cues from the professoriate. The all-male student fraternities at the university had always been notoriously alcoholic, rowdy and violent, encouraged by the fact that the sacred autonomy of the university prevented any interventions by the police. By the early 1920s, however, these fraternities had also become heavily politicised. All those student groups of a clerical-conservative, German-nationalist character belonged to an umbrella organisation called the *Deutsche Studentenschaft* (German Students' Federation). They too circulated blacklists of objectionable professors and lecturers.

The proto-Nazi students ruthlessly targeted anyone deemed to be among *die Ungeraden* (literally translated as 'the odd ones'). Those identified as 'Judeo-Marxist teachers' would have their lectures interrupted or broken up by well-prepared, thuggish students wielding clubs and chanting anti-Semitic slogans. To Stefan Zweig, these nationalist mobs 'established an unparalleled, violently terrorist regime, under cover of academic immunity . . . their faces battered, drunk and brutal, they dominated the university hall'.[22]

Julius Tandler, an anatomy professor (of whom more in the next chapter), was particularly exposed, as not only a Jew by birth, but also a socialist and a prominent politician on the city council, in charge of health reform. Violently confronted by the full menace of Black Vienna at his place of work, understandably Tandler grew disillusioned with the city and the prospects of meaningful social change. Increasingly, his assistants took his lectures. As well as professors like Tandler, Jewish, Slavonic and even Italian students were picked out, leading to mass brawls. Victims of the nationalist students were, according to one witness, 'dragged out of classrooms and severely beaten'. Ambulances were often called, and even the fire brigade had to be summoned on occasion, to help students escape out of the windows.[23] There is a graphic photograph in the university archives of students, including several women, fleeing down ladders from the open windows of a lecture room in the Institute of Anatomy as a mob rampages inside. This may have been the occasion of one particularly notorious assault on a Tandler lecture by Nazi students brandishing steel rods, whips, brass knuckles and knives. Fifteen were injured, including three Jewish-American students. This, at least, resulted in an official protest from the American legation in Vienna.[24]

The university had to be evacuated regularly due to anti-Semitic riots, but in truth the authorities seem to have done little to forestall the perpetrators. The *Deutsche Studentenschaft* was even given permission by the rector to set up a shooting range on the university premises.[25] Zweig lamented that the police could only watch 'helplessly from the sidelines as these cowardly thugs went on the rampage. Police officers had to confine themselves to carrying away the injured and bleeding who were flung down the steps.' To protect themselves, Jewish students and other potential targets armed themselves with whatever came to hand. One young medical student, Benno Weiser Varon, much later an Israeli diplomat, carried around a bundle of large metal keys, affording quick access to the anatomy department's bone collection should the odd femur or tibia be needed as weapons. In one particular fight, in 1932, he rescued a fellow Jewish student by cracking the skull of one Nazi with two of his outsized keys while thirty more such Nazis watched from the upper floors. He considered this to be his own rite of passage, proving that 'Jews are no cowards'.[26]

The poisonous politics of the university and the generally enervating and conservative culture of what was left of Austria had significant consequences for Vienna's intellectual life in general, and dramatically shaped the intellectual output of Red Vienna in the post-war city. With so many formal academic careers at the university thwarted by the unofficial ban on those identified as Jews, leftists, and women, many looked abroad, contributing to a brain drain from Vienna that began as soon as the First World War was over, as we shall see later. One aspiring academic who received no joy from the university hierarchy, almost certainly due to his Jewish background, was jokingly comforted by a friend in verse:[27]

It is forbidden by church and state
To be a genius in this land.
Search another homeland for your mind
Here only idiots are assigned.

For those who stayed, many could only develop politically and intellectually outside the established educational bureaucracy. This had profound consequences for the remarkable achievements of the post-war generation of Viennese intellectuals, scientists and others who were part of Red Vienna, the subject of Part II. One historian has described all these biologists, mathematicians, philosophers, artists, radiologists, economists, psychoanalysts, political philosophers and more, who were to make such a contribution to the West in the interwar years, as constituting a 'counter-culture'.[28] This term exaggerates; many were conservative by disposition or politics, and sometimes closely linked to the establishment networks of Vienna and Austria. More to the point, they all became increasingly *identified* as representing a hateful and 'alien' culture by ethno-nationalists and National Socialists. Tragically, despite the obvious hostility towards them, this generation rarely gauged the depth and intensity of that hostility, nor could they possibly imagine the savagery and barbarism that would follow. They knew little of Black Vienna, too dazzled, perhaps, by the exhilarating churn of ideas in their own immediate milieus to peer far beyond them.

PART II

The Rise and Fall of Red Vienna

Wien XIX. Karl Marx-Hof

135

The Karl-Marx-Hof, Europe's biggest public housing estate
and an abiding symbol of Red Vienna.

Chapter 3

The New Human

In stark contrast to Lueger, Spann and the other ideologues of Black Vienna, those Viennese who were responsible for the last great flourishing of the city's intellectual and culture life during the interwar years were the legatees and beneficiaries of liberal Vienna. The scientific method, empiricism and the pedagogy of rational deliberation that they inherited from the golden age guided their lives and politics as they attempted to create a new civilisation amidst the economic chaos and political debris of the First World War. As a new generation, they often interrogated and questioned their precursors, but they never rejected them wholesale.

The era of Red Vienna, when the city was ruled by a new breed of socialist politicians from 1919 to 1934, is often skated over by historians and commentators. Tony Judt, a foremost chronicler of modern Europe, dismissed Red Vienna as 'a brief socialist municipal experiment'.[1] In fact, the significance of Red Vienna can hardly be overestimated. For the first time, socialists won a mandate at the ballot box (unlike the communists in Russia) to transform an entire society according to the most advanced, 'scientific' theories of the day.

Indeed, Red Vienna's goals of personal and political transformation were wildly more ambitious than anything of which the pre-war liberal generation could have conceived. This was the 'radicalisation' of the *fin-de-siècle* era, and from this radicalisation flowed much of Vienna's influence on the world. For those younger Viennese, often born on the cusp of the new century, who worked for or lived through Red Vienna, it was an exhilarating period, especially for young women. Red Vienna was the most ambitious democratic political project in the world of its time.

Let Marie Jahoda, a founder of social psychology, and one of the best of their number, sum this generation up, looking back in 1986: 'In Vienna we lived with the great illusion that we could be a generation of fulfilment, that our generation would establish democratic socialism in Austria. Our whole lives were based on this fundamental idea.'[2] This chapter looks at the aims and politics of Red Vienna, while the following chapter looks at the interlinked intellectual culture that prospered during this remarkable period.

The spectre of defeat

For Austria, more so than for any other combatant country, except perhaps Russia, the First World War was a humiliating disaster. It marked a radical disjuncture in the country's history, and the Viennese of this new generation, of Red Vienna, in stark contrast to the pre-war generation, had to live with the terrible consequences of war, defeat and economic ruin for much of their young lives. This was the essential context of Red Vienna.

Military incompetence certainly played a part in the defeat of the Austro-Hungarian forces. Even the withdrawal of Russia from the war in 1917 scarcely seemed to make any difference to the litany of losses and setbacks on the battlefield. But, above all, it was hunger that undermined the Austro-Hungarian empire, with lasting consequences into the 1920s. The loss of Galicia to Russia in 1914 was an early and devastating blow. The province contributed one-third of all the empire's farmlands, thus exerting pressure on food supplies from the start. The Allied naval blockade squeezed the empire still further. Rationing had to be introduced as early as 1915, and those rations were gradually reduced throughout the war; by 1918 there was no milk to go round. Vienna suffered far more in this respect than other European cities. Paris, for instance, rationed only two items, sugar and then bread, beginning in 1917; London did not introduce any rationing at all until 1918. Physicians in Vienna estimated that starvation was a direct cause of between 7 and 11 per cent of deaths during the war, and a contributing factor in a further 20 to 30 per cent of deaths where a postmortem was carried out.[3] The war of 'waiting in line' for dwindling supplies of potatoes provoked riots and protests. In the empire more widely, by 1918 hunger had provoked waves of industrial strikes which quickly evolved into demonstrations for an end to the war and political reform.

With the empire unable to fulfil a basic obligation, to feed its people, so 'the powerful sense of reciprocal relations that had linked the state to its citizens disintegrated . . . this failure in turn produced a general indifference to the fate of the empire'.[4] In late October 1918, regional nationalist authorities representing ethnic Czechs, Poles, Serbs, Croats, Serbians and others began to usurp power, emboldened by the almost-victorious British, French and American governments vowing to recognise the successor states of Czechoslovakia, Poland and Yugoslavia. One by one the new nationalities declared their independence, beginning with the Poles on 15 October, followed by the south Slavs and then the Czechs and Hungarians on 28 October.

There was little quibbling from Vienna, even though these new 'countries' would prove to be every bit as ethnically unstable as the empire they replaced, precipitating the outbreak of the Second World War and the Balkan Wars in the 1990s. Recognising the hopelessness of the situation, the new Emperor Karl effectively resigned the imperial throne on Armistice Day 1918, ending the Habsburgs' dynastic rule. The very next day a Provisional Assembly proclaimed a new country. Eventually, the Social Democrat Karl

Renner was proclaimed as chancellor of the First Republic of Austria in September 1919 after Allied negotiators at the Paris peace conference rubber-stamped the new facts on the ground. The Treaty of Saint-Germain officially dissolved the empire.[5] In November 1921 the British, with long experience in such matters, were given the task of sailing the last Habsburg emperor, like Napoleon before him, into permanent exile, on the Portuguese island of Madeira. Karl died there of pneumonia the following year, at the age of just thirty-four.

The new Austria that emerged from the war was a rump that nobody had wanted, willed into being by foreign politicians in far-away countries. A despondent Zweig wrote of this moment: 'The Czechs, Poles, Italians and Slovenians had taken back their lands, leaving a mutilated torso bleeding from its arteries.'[6] Clemenceau, prime minister of France and one of those primarily responsible for the dismemberment of the old empire, put it most pithily, if harshly: 'L'Autriche, c'est ce qui reste', roughly translated as 'Austria is just what's left over'. Vienna itself, previously at the geographical centre of a vast empire, was now stranded on the eastern fringe of a small republic.

The city underwent dramatic change, accentuating further the differences between this cosmopolitan centre and the rest of the country. As thousands of Czechs, Slovenians, Croats and others streamed out of the city in a process of reverse migration to their newly independent homelands, so thousands of Jewish refugees filled up the city from the east, shifting the ethnic mix. This process had begun in 1915, mainly to escape Russian pogroms. The influx of economically poor Jews from the Galician *shtetls* bought the total number of refugees, according to the interior ministry, up to about 125,000. The visibility of these so-called 'Eastern Jews' provoked a backlash from nationalists and anti-Semites, as we have seen. This was the beginning of the end of Vienna's 'homogenised heterogeneity'. By the early 1920s the distinctively Jewish character of Vienna as opposed to the rest of Austria was even more marked than before the war; by 1923, whereas Jews made up about one-tenth of the capital's population, the proportion throughout the rest of the country was just 0.64 per cent, making them dangerously isolated and exposed in Austria as a whole.[7]

The economic consequences of defeat were devastating. Cut off from its former markets and sources of wealth in the old empire, Austria's plight in the immediate post-war period was desperate. Within the space of five or so years Vienna had been transformed from a rich, glittering metropolis into a dirty, disease-ridden city facing starvation. Between 1919 and 1921 one-third of Austria's children were evacuated abroad to afford them a better chance of survival.[8] With the economy collapsing, inflation quickly spiralled out of control. From 1919 to 1922, like their contemporaries in Weimar Germany, Viennese were reduced to carrying knapsacks stuffed with enormous wads of virtually worthless banknotes to buy a loaf of bread. The Austrian *krone* depreciated to about one 140th *of 1 per cent* of its pre-war exchange rate.[9] Middle-class savings were wiped out. Many of the post-war generation, such as Karl Popper, would remember their home city more for its abject poverty than for the delights of the coffee-house.

A lucky handful were able to access hard currency. The Freuds and their circle, for example, encouraged clients from America and Britain, bearing dollars and pounds, to visit Vienna for analysis or training. For those who made the trip, however, it could be a disheartening experience. The American psychoanalyst Esther Menaker trained with Anna Freud. Treated largely as a cash-cow by the Freud family, she later wrote a sour, scathing memoir of her Viennese years, remembering the city mainly for its beggars, poverty and condescension.[10] For his Austrian clients, meanwhile, Freud would on occasion trade a session on the couch for sacks of potatoes.

Zweig vividly recalled the chaos, scarcities and occasional absurdities of the city's immediate post-war years in *The World of Yesterday*. Brought up in a comfortable bourgeois family himself, he felt the new privations keenly. 'A man who had saved for forty years and had also patriotically put money into the war loan became a beggar, while a man who used to be in debt was free of it . . . There were no standards or values as money flowed away and evaporated; the only virtue was to be clever, adaptable and unscrupulous, leaping on the back of the runaway horse instead of letting it trample you.'[11]

Living just outside Salzburg, where he had bought a large house during the war, Zweig recorded that every foray into the city was a 'distressing experience . . . For the first time I saw, in the yellow, dangerous eyes of the starving, what famine really looks like. Bread was nothing but black crumbs tasting of pitch and glue, coffee was a decoction of roast barley, beer was yellow water . . .'. The only beneficiaries of Vienna's hyperinflation were the tourists who came to live like kings on their hard currency or, as Zweig put it, to 'feed off the twitching corpse of the old Austrian currency'. The snobbish Zweig even claimed, although it has been hotly disputed, that the poshest hotel in Salzburg, the Hotel d'Europe, was booked out by 'unemployed members of the English proletariat, who could live here more cheaply than in their slums at home, thanks to the generous benefit they received'.[12] Even if these English chancers were phantoms of Zweig's imagination (his memoirs include plenty of embellishment), the anecdote captures the Austrians' sense of resentment and helplessness as their country, so recently an epicentre of European wealth and civilisation, lay prostrate. Like the rest of Vienna, the university could not heat its premises. One medical student, returning from the hardships of war in 1919, found that the dissecting rooms were so freezing that students and professors alike developed frostbite on their hands.[13]

The poverty and subsequent lack of opportunities persuaded many young Viennese to leave for richer pastures, principally Germany, but also America. Hence the start of Vienna's interwar brain drain, encouraged by the vigorous talent-scouting of the Carnegie and Rockefeller Foundations. The latter, established in 1913 with capital of about $3 billion in today's money, was dedicated, tellingly, to the 'Well-being of Mankind Throughout the World'. It was particularly active in defeated central Europe and, as we shall see, started the transatlantic careers of many Viennese during the 1930s and 1940s.[14] For some Viennese, these were Zweig's vultures feeding off the Austrian corpse – although Zweig was probably unaware of the fact that American aid, in the shape of the American Relief Administration, also fed hundreds of thousands of starving Austrian children for several years, thus stopping a disaster from turning into a complete catastrophe.[15] Overall, Austria became the fourth-largest beneficiary of Allied aid in the immediate post-war period, after Germany, Poland and Belgium. At least, unlike Germany, Austria was spared war reparations; it was deemed too poor to pay anything.

A small red dot

This, then, was the old empire's bequest to the new Vienna. The moment marked an equally radical disjuncture in the city's politics. In the municipal elections of May 1919 the Social Democrats won an absolute majority of 54 per cent of the vote and 100 out of 165 seats on the city council, ousting the right-wing Christian Socials, who had run the city continuously since Karl Lueger's appointment as mayor twenty-two years previously. On 22 May the first socialist mayor of Vienna, Jakob Reumann, was elected by the council. Vienna's Social Democrats, founded in 1888–89, benefited immensely from a new suffrage law that was passed in 1918. Now, all Austrians over the age of twenty could vote, including, for the first time, women. Buoyed by the votes of Vienna's working-class men and women, the Social Democrats kept their council majority through to the end in 1934. For just a year, from 1919 to 1920, the social-ists, who won 43 per cent of the vote at the national elections in 1919, participated in a federal coalition with the Christian Social Party and in this brief period they managed to push through several other equally radical measures, including the abolition of noble titles and privileges.

Despite the success of the Social Democrats in Vienna, after the collapse of the coalition government in 1920, for the rest of Austria the picture was very different. Federal politics was dominated by their opponents on the right, particularly the Christian Socials, who appealed largely to rural, Catholic and nationalist sentiment. They occupied the presidency and the national ministries, in a series of coalitions with pan-German and conservative forces. From 1927 onwards, for most elections this coalition was called the *Einheitsliste*. The leader of the Christian Socials, the Catholic prelate Ignaz Seipel, was its principal political figure, serving as chancellor in 1922–24 and 1926–29 and afterwards as foreign minister. Seipel's prominence suggests the close connection between the rise of ethno-nationalism, anti-Semitism and Catholicism, which in Austria was 'particularly inflexible and reactionary'.[16] It was Seipel who coined the term Red Vienna in the first place, as a pejorative to denigrate his socialist opponents; *Rotes Wien* was used almost interchangeably with 'Jewish Vienna'.

Physically hemmed in by their opponents, the relatively small area over which the Social Democrats presided shrank further in 1921 when the city of Vienna was divorced from its surrounding province of Lower Austria, thereafter becoming a state in its own right. Vienna, to all intents and purposes, became an independent socialist fiefdom. The Social Democrats had planned to transform *all* of Austria, but now Vienna alone would have to do.

The founder of Austria's Social Democrats had been Victor Adler, who died on Armistice Day in 1918. More important, however, was the group of intellectuals who developed the Social Democrats' particular brand of politics known as Austro-Marxism. The most important of these were Otto Bauer, Karl Renner (chancellor of the First Republic in 1918–20) and Max Adler. They were mostly scions of liberal Vienna, and often assimilated Jews. In the post-First World War period, mostly by virtue of the fact that all other parties were, to varying degrees, overtly anti-Semitic, the Social Democrats attracted strong Jewish support; about 75 per cent of the country's Jews voted for the party, just as it is estimated that 80 per cent of socialist intellectuals were Jewish.[17] The social democratic leaders also hailed from many different parts of the empire. What made Austro-Marxism distinctive is that its leaders attempted to harness the intellectual rigour and empiricism of liberal Vienna to Marxism, leading, so they hoped, to a peaceful, democratic and gradual transformation of society in all spheres: cultural, ethical, sexual and economic. Most of the surviving great names of liberal Vienna, with varying degrees of enthusiasm, were cajoled into helping, or even guiding, Red Vienna's great project, swept up in the rational exuberance of the whole undertaking. Freud, and even more so his great psychoanalytic rival Alfred Adler, were both enrolled. So, too, the architect Adolf Loos and a score or so of Otto Wagner's pupils, as well as many other leading social scientists, doctors and biologists.

Their mission therefore extended beyond the usual socialist aspiration to improve the material conditions of the industrial working class. They wanted to create what Max Adler called *die neuen Menschen* (new humans), men and women for a fresh, post-imperial age, transcending race and religion, and above all governed by reason, or what Popper more precisely termed 'critical rationalism'. Bauer spoke of a 'revolution of souls'. In order to accomplish this, Red Vienna set out to utilise all the latest techniques and insights from social science, biology, economics, psychology, psychoanalysis and mathematics, forging an exceptionally close relationship between theory and practice.[18]

This was a new brand of socialism and a new style of politics, steering a middle way between the destructive determinism of communism and the restrained, incremental reformism of the Fabians in Britain. Importantly, democracy, for the Social Democrats, was never a bourgeois smokescreen, as the communists argued. For Red Vienna, power won at the ballot box would be more durable than the violent attempts of several other contemporary European cities and provinces to impose socialisation by fiat. As Bauer

commented, socialism in Austria would be achieved 'solely by creative legislative and administrative work'.[19]

The anatomy of a movement

Burnishing the links between theory and practice, many of the city councillors and activists who actually implemented the policies of Red Vienna were academics or theorists themselves. The two most significant were Julius Tandler and Otto Neurath. The first was a prominent anatomist and physician, a professor at the university and dean of the prestigious faculty of medicine during the First World War. As Health Care Councillor for Vienna from 1920 to 1934 he led the city's revolutionary health reforms, but still continued to lecture at the university throughout. Now largely forgotten, his influence on Red Vienna, and on mid-century European socialism, was immense, earning him the popular moniker of 'the medical pope of social democracy'.

Whereas most of the social democratic leaders were middle-class intellectuals, Tandler, born in 1869, was himself working-class. Austere, self-disciplined and ferociously hard-working, he chose medicine for his degree. From a Jewish background, at the age of thirty he converted to Catholicism. The University of Vienna was a world leader in the study of anatomy during this period, partly due to the easy availability of corpses,[20] and it was in this field that he made his major contribution to medicine. But, typically for Red Vienna, Tandler saw no distinction between his medical studies and his politics. His greatest academic legacy, a *Textbook of Systematic Anatomy*, published in four volumes from 1918 to 1924, pioneered a new, more accessible way of studying the human body. The illustrations in his textbook were not the two-dimensional representations of corpses that predominated in

(opposite) Julius Tandler, socialist and political anatomist.

other anatomical atlases. For the first time, he presented three-dimensional schemas of living people, *die neuen Menschen*. Avoiding the usual engravers of anatomy books, Tandler hired a Prague-born landscape painter to produce his images, derived from the new x-rays as well as more traditional sources.[21] As a committed neo-Lamarckian, Tandler believed that health reforms could transform people physiologically. His anatomical drawings provided a more realistic and detailed scrutiny of the human body, from which, he hoped, health reformers would profit.

As the founder and editor of the academic *Journal for Applied Anatomy and Constitution*, Tandler directed and encouraged research that helped to understand the human body, in all its detail, and how the human 'constitution' might be strengthened over time. In practice, in his role as the city's health-care czar, this vision entailed Tandler sending out a newly raised army of health-care and social workers to delve 'into the innermost reaches of life in the private sphere – an expansion of the notion of culture to encompass the worker's total life, from the political arena and workplace to the most personal and intimate settings.'[22]

Tandler also worked tirelessly to make advice and information on hygiene and physical well-being more accessible to the working class. To overcome problems of illiteracy, Tandler thus pioneered visual and pictorial health education, in tandem with the other dominant figure of Red Vienna, Otto Neurath. Born in 1882, Neurath was the quintessential central European polymath, bought up in a scholarly home, as he later recalled, surrounded by books, 'and the impression thus gained accompanied me throughout my life'. As a child he took to counting the volumes in his father's library, mostly arranged two rows deep, and 'reached a peak number of 13,000'.[23] But Neurath was no desiccated bookworm. Thrice-married, he was an exuberant, generous-hearted bear of a man in constant motion. More than anyone, Neurath was the presiding genius of Red Vienna, integral to just about everything that the socialists tried to achieve.

He was also incurably optimistic, a valuable characteristic as the bitter disappointments of mid-century socialism crowded in. Neurath began studying mathematics and physics at the university, but soon switched to economics, history and philosophy. His interests ranged over graphic design and linguistics as well. Over the course of his life he made lasting contributions to many of these fields, eventually publishing over 400 books, pamphlets and articles. Moreover, he was an energetic and resourceful practitioner as much as a protean thinker.

Neurath's most important early theoretical work was on the appropriate 'system of socialisation' that should replace capitalism. In particular, Neurath was an early advocate of an 'in-kind', or *natural*, economy, that would abolish money as a unit of calculation. By the end of hostilities in 1918 Neurath was arguing that the sort of limited central planning that had been key to fighting the war provided a model of a transitional state that would lead towards yet more extensive planning. This would eventually bring about, almost by stealth, a fully socialist economy, to be run by a 'central economic administration' that would direct all production based on reams of statistical information from banks, industries, economic-control councils and the like. All this was to be compiled and curated by 'experts' – people like himself – who would thus organise all aspects of the economy.[24]

Briefly, Neurath took on just such a role, accepting an invitation to head the Central Economic Administration of the short-lived, revolutionary Bavarian Soviet Republic, declared unilaterally in April 1919 as Germany's government disintegrated after the war. For a few heady weeks, Neurath was given free rein to implement his ideas, proposing legislation to take over the press, farms and the mines. But his fun was over almost as quickly as it had begun. Government troops swiftly crushed the putative revolution and Neurath was arrested and convicted of high treason. He was deported back to Austria only after the intervention of Otto Bauer, then the country's foreign minister.

Back in Red Vienna, an unrepentant Neurath held a series of positions helping the city council implement its programme. Above all, he became the most forceful advocate of harnessing Vienna's scientific and empirical tradition to the implementation of socialism – to him, they were one and the same, a guiding leitmotif of the era. Neurath 'trusted firmly in the power of science. Not science on its own as an abstract system of thought, but science in the hands of the social technician, who can "orchestrate" the different systems of knowledge to build new social orders.'[25]

Always on the look-out for such expertise and scientific research that would deepen and strengthen the socialist praxis of the city council, Neurath, Tandler and another Austro-Marxist reformer, Otto Glöckel, ran their own politico-intellectual hothouse out of

Otto Neurath, the presiding genius of Red Vienna.

city funds. It was set up in 1922 in a grand neo-Renaissance building, the Palais Epstein, which fronted directly onto the Ringstrasse. Appropriately enough, it was the former home of a wealthy banker who had lost his fortune (and the house) in a stock market crash in 1873. The 'Vienna School Authority', as the building was officially known in the 1920s, housed several research organisations specifically to advise the reformers on best practice in education and housing.[26] Thus, Red Vienna set up its own intellectual infrastructure, specifically to blend theory and praxis. This officially sanctioned reformist, intellectual environment fed equally into a wide array of other circles, groups and institutes in Vienna.

In sum, of Neurath's generation of Red Vienna, some were fully fledged Marxists, most were at least socialists, but they were certainly all *activists*, in the sense that they believed they could change the world for the better through the application of scientific methodology. In part, this was a conscious reaction against what one writer has characterised as 'the artifice and the shallow passion for display' of the pre-war generation. For the generation that lived through Red Vienna, theirs was less a leisurely *fin-de-siècle* saunter through the salons and opera boxes of the pre-war city, more a hectic blur of socialist summer camps, marching songs, adult education lectures and utopian politics. Underlying it all was a grave seriousness of intent. Hayek later remembered of this era:

What struck me most was a radical passion for truthfulness in everything . . . It meant much more than truth in speech. One had to 'live' truth and not tolerate any pretence in oneself or others. It sometimes produced outright rudeness and certainly, unpleasantness. Every conversation was dissected and every conventional form exposed as a fraud.[27]

Americans and British often commented on the Viennese émigré's 'directness' of speech. For those caught unawares, it could be extremely disconcerting.

Housing for all

There was little in Austro-Marxist theory, however, that prepared the Social Democrats for the immediate task of staving off disaster as the empire fell apart in 1918. The Spanish influenza was ravaging Vienna, as elsewhere, killing thousands, including Klimt, then in his mid-sixties, and the younger Egon Schiele. The already over-burdened health service took a full month to set up special isolation wards, allowing plenty of time for the epidemic to circulate.[28] The most pressing crisis, however, was homelessness and vagrancy.

Even before the end of the war, thousands of refugees, alongside impoverished Viennese, had occupied open land on the peripheries of the city, building makeshift shacks and growing their own vegetables. Conditions were primitive. By 1918 there were more than 100,000 people living in these shanties.[29] They soon began to organise their own self-governing councils, not so different from the revolutionary soviets of Russia, Bavaria and Hungary. Collectively, they were called the *Siedlerbewegung*, or 'settlers' movement', and from the start many of Vienna's young, middle-class, left-wing activists were drawn to supporting and helping the *Siedler*. This spontaneous show of solidarity jump-started Red Vienna's commitment to radical action. The settlers were seen as a genuinely proletarian movement by Vienna's idealistic, socialist youth. Many of the city's intelligentsia became involved, pledging to help the settlers build their own permanent homes, with proper gardens, in place of their shacks.

Otto Neurath, of course, took control of the Settlements and Allotment Gardens Association, the umbrella organisation set up to coordinate this work. Neurath's close friend, the designer and architect Josef Frank, was enlisted to help build some of the new settler housing estates on the fringes of Vienna, together with a young Margarete Lihotzky, the first woman to practise as an architect in Austria. Their mentor, Adolf Loos, an early and enthusiastic advocate for the settlers, provided technical assistance. From 1921 to 1924 Loos had a more substantial role as chief architect to the official federal body in charge of the settlement building. He himself designed four *Siedlungen*, together with other architects.

For the first few years, at least, theirs was a genuinely revolutionary endeavour, expanding the possibilities of how houses could be designed, built and inhabited. With money scarce, at least until limited federal funds became available in 1921, Neurath was forced to improvise as he went along. Frank's settler houses had to be simple, as the new owners were required to contribute up to 2,000 hours of labour to their own home, constituting the equivalent of about a third of the total costs.

To help them, Neurath opened a school where he, Frank, Lihotzky, and occasionally Loos, gave informal classes on building techniques. One good example of Frank's work was the *Hoffingergasse Siedlung*, 286 identical three-bedroom houses in rows. Vitally, and uncharacteristically for Vienna, each cottage-style dwelling was provided with a little garden and shed, to house livestock. Neurath, in particular, romanticised the settlers as 'urban gardeners', providing 'every kind of food that other cultures have long had'.[30]

But with the end of the immediate housing crisis, the *Siedlung* movement lost its support from the council. As more money became available with Vienna's eventual recovery from the war, mainly with the help of foreign loans, so the Social Democrats began to plan for their real mission, to rebuild the living environment of the urban proletariat. To fund this, Hugo Breitner, the council's immensely able finance officer, levied new taxes on middle-class goods and property, denounced as 'tax sadism' by his opponents. In September 1923 the council embarked on a five-year housing programme to build 25,000 'healthy' homes. This huge undertaking marked an abrupt change in emphasis. Frank's and Neurath's cottage-style *Siedlung* houses were abandoned in favour of huge, dense housing estates, the *Gemeindebauten* (translated as 'community buildings') – a symbol of Red Vienna to this day, and the most visible reminders of the political moment.

Frank, in fact, was involved in building two prototypes of these *Gemeindebauten*, the Winarsky-Hof and the Wiedenhofer-Hof, containing 247 apartments. With their innovative building techniques, severe Loosian facades and boxy appearances, these two housing complexes became the prototype for a new style of mass public housing, copied around the world. The kitchen, for the first time, became a focus of attention, as we will see in Chapter 5.

In the decade after 1924, scores of large *Gemeindebauten* went up all over the city. About 200 architects were involved, many of them former students and followers of Otto Wagner. They were not necessarily socialists, but the work was welcome regardless. The apartments themselves were well organised, if relatively small. In compensation for their size, however, chores that took up space – such as the washing – were relocated to communal facilities. Most *Gemeindebauten* had a central laundry. The spacious green courtyard (*Hof*) in the middle of the estates also contained kindergarten schools, childcare centres, meeting rooms, refuse facilities and playgrounds.

One of the first such estates, designed by Hubert Gessner, a former student of Wagner, was the Reumannhof, named in honour of the first mayor of Red Vienna. This had 485 apartments and looked out onto a public garden that doubled up for sports and outdoor gymnastics. The Reumannhof was the most prominent of a cluster of such buildings built between 1924 and 1927 along a main boulevard called the Margaretengürtel, a few kilometres to the south-west of the centre. A proud social democratic mayor, Karl Seitz, hailed this as the 'Ringstrasse of the Proletariat'.[31] Admirers and detractors alike called them 'Peoples' Palaces'.

Yet the Reumannhof was a minnow compared to the colossal Karl-Marx-Hof, rightly described as 'the central monument of Red Vienna' (see image p. 70). Squeezed into a thin, awkward strip of land between a train station and a hillside, this continuous structure of over a kilometre long, punctuated by huge pedestrian archways, remains, by some accounts, the longest single inhabited building in Europe, and possibly the world. Built between 1926 and 1930 to a design by Karl Ehn, the building is a small town all in itself, encompassing an area of over 150,000 square metres; 5,000 people still live here in 1,382 apartments, sharing two big central laundries, communal bathing facilities, dental and maternity clinics, post offices, pharmacies, schools, several playgrounds and acres of outdoor space. It is big enough to have four tram stops. The epic quality of the Karl-Marx-Hof was reinforced by enormous flagpoles and sculptures: part proletarian fortress, part commune. Henceforth Vienna became a mecca for Europe's aspiring socialist planners and the *Gemeindebauten* inspired similar estates in Berlin, Hamburg, Frankfurt, Dessau and even Leeds in the UK (the Quarry Hill Flats, for a long time the largest housing complex in the country, demolished in 1978).

Overall, in roughly ten years the socialist administration achieved a remarkable citywide transformation. Almost 64,000 apartments were built in nearly 400 municipal housing complexes, as well as 5,000 settler homes. Before a new rent law was passed in 1922, working-class families had faced arbitrary eviction by capricious land-lords. For the first time, families in the *Gemeindebauten* could regard an apartment as their own, to decorate and furnish as they chose.

A holy mission: healthy bodies, healthy minds

The insistence on light, space and air in these new apartments reflected the overarching concern of Red Vienna with mental and physical health. Here again, the approach was nothing if not radical. Rather than targeting specific categories of need for attention, as other contemporary social reformers did (the poor, unemployed or elderly, for instance) Tandler advocated a holistic approach, arguing that only by improving the health and welfare of *all*, from the cradle to the grave, could the scourges of ill-health and stunted physical development be avoided.[32] Tandler called the care of Vienna's citizens the 'administration of the organic capital of society'. As he wrote: 'Welfare is more than accidental aid, more than provision

of material help, more than social service; it is psychological investigation, mental influence, true education and becomes a HOLY
MISSION especially where people are still educable.'[33]

Here again, theory, in the portly, immaculately well-dressed shape
of Alfred Adler, was closely linked to practice. Adler, the second of
seven sons, born to a poor Jewish family in a village on the western
fringes of Vienna, was Sigmund Freud's great rival in psychoanalysis.
Whereas Freud was better known internationally at the time, Adler
attracted more attention in Vienna. He was lionised by the Social
Democrats for his doctrine of 'individual psychology', over which he
had broken with Freud in 1911. In 1927 he was to coin the term
'inferiority complex'.

'Individual psychology' is poorly named, as it means exactly the
opposite. Whereas Freud continued to believe that all neurosis was
fundamentally linked to one's sexuality, only curable by individual
analysis, Adler widened the causes of neurosis, pointing out the
self-evident truth that people were also heavily influenced by the
wider society and communities in which they lived. This was, essentially, the psychological rationale for Austro-Marxism. He lectured
extensively, both in and beyond Vienna, becoming probably the most
popular propagandist for Viennese socialism. His followers contributed to the cause in a very practical manner by setting up twenty-eight
free child-guidance clinics across the city from 1919 onwards, all
attached to schools in the poorer neighbourhoods of the city.
A peroration to one of his speeches, on the importance of 'social
feeling' to humans, captures the essence of Adler. Arguing for
improved economic conditions, he concluded on a visionary note:

Thus it will no longer be necessary for an individual to be
condemned to an unhappy fate simply because he originated in
an unfortunate family, or hereditary, situation. Let us accomplish
this alone, and our civilisation will have taken a decided step in
advance! A new generation will grow up courageously conscious
that it is master of its own fate![34]

90

In a huge step forward for maternal and infant health, these were now subjects of enthusiastic political attention. Before the First World War, the University of Vienna had established itself as a world leader in paediatrics, so, once again, there was a great deal of expertise at hand to inform the city council's vigorously interventionist approach. Particularly important in this respect was the aristocratic Clemens von Pirquet, professor of paediatrics at the university (and also, briefly, at Johns Hopkins University). Pirquet was essentially an immunologist, who in 1906 had coined the term 'allergy' to describe hypersensitive reactions of immunological origin. He also worked on the diagnosis of tuberculosis, but his primary contribution to public health reform was to pioneer the study of nutrition in a systematic, scientific manner and to analyse in detail the links between malnutrition and stunted growth.[35] He served as director of the University Children's Hospital in Vienna before his double suicide with his wife in 1929.

For the first time parental and maternity clinics (*Mütterberatungsstellen*) were set up across the city, which provided all new mothers with counselling, blood tests and free layettes. 'No Viennese child shall be born on newspaper!' declared one advertising poster for these clinics. Child welfare centres ran dental and tuberculosis services. A plethora of schemes, clinics and devices were introduced to relieve the burden on working-class mothers. The council opened 120 new *Kindergärten*, often located in the *Gemeindebauten*. All children enrolled were given three free, or at least cheap, meals. Overall, the results were impressive. The death rate dropped by 25 per cent; child mortality by half compared with pre-war levels. The rate of tuberculosis fell markedly.

Sex and sexuality were also taken seriously. For the Austro-Marxists, these were pressing issues of public health. Gonorrhoea and other sexual diseases were rife in the city. It has been estimated that about one in ten women in Vienna had been reduced to prostitution and were therefore at risk, as were their clients. Centres were established to give frank advice on sexual matters from both a hygienic and emotional perspective.

Aside from sex education, the council's adult welfare policies focused on physical activity, organised games and sports. This was integral to the evolution of *die neuen Menschen*, if only to prepare physically for the inevitable class conflicts ahead, and even armed struggle; the Social Democrats maintained their own paramilitary defence force, the several thousand-strong *Schutzbund*. Working-class Viennese had traditionally fled in the summer to spend alcohol-charged weekends swimming on the upper Danube, known locally as the 'proletarian Riviera'. Now the city council embarked on a crash programme of constructing full-size pools in the city itself, also partly because the new flats did not have bathrooms. The crowning glory was the sumptuous, highly ornate Amalienbad, built between 1923 and 1926, which remains the most successful synergy of form and function in modern Austrian architecture. The 33-metre-long pool came with diving boards, Turkish steam baths, hot tubs, hairdressing salons and shampoo cubicles.[36] Twenty-three open-air pools were also built for children.

The model of the socialist-athlete was Matthias Sindelar, the graceful, brilliant playmaker for Austria Vienna, probably the most admired footballer of his generation. He made no secret of his social democratic sympathies, and the success of the national team, inspired by Sindelar, seemed to justify the new emphasis on sport and athleticism. Sindelar famously refused to play for the 'united' German team after the *Anschluss*, and was found dead in his flat on the Annagasse in suspicious circumstances in January 1939. His death rapidly became a symbol of the end of an independent, democratic Austria; 40,000 people attended his funeral, and the Austria Vienna club received over 15,000 telegrams of condolence. 'The good Sindelar,' wrote one obituarist, 'followed the city, whose pride and joy he was, to its death.'[37]

Football apart, the climax of Red Vienna's fetishistic idolisation of the worker-athlete was the 'Workers' Summer Olympiad' held in Vienna in July 1931 (following the winter version held in the mountains of Austria a few months before). This was the second iteration of the Workers' Olympics, started by the Socialist Workers' Sport International in 1925 (the last was held in 1937 in Antwerp). Founded to rival the official Olympics, which were regarded as élitist and anti-Semitic by socialists, these games accepted all competitors, regardless of ability, and played down national rivalries in favour of working-class solidarity.

Red Vienna's sports supremo was Julius Deutsch, who also founded the *Schutzbund*. For Deutsch, athletic prowess, good health and the physical defence of the working class were all one and the same thing. He genuinely wanted to foster 'peak performances', but not through a bourgeois obsession with records and placings. This was merely a pathology of capitalism, so he argued, in which 'the stronger triumph over the weaker and are rewarded with honour, fame, and riches . . . [fostering] particularly, unrestrained *egotism*'.[38] With hindsight, it is hard to gainsay Deutsch and his colleagues. In 1936 the Nazis staged the notorious Berlin Olympics, specifically to advertise the supposed superiority of the Aryan races over all others. It proved to be the nadir of the official Olympic movement. Not a particularly impressive athlete himself, Deutsch later went on to be a general in the Republican forces fighting fascism in Spain from 1936 to 1939.

The Viennese edition of the workers' Olympics was a massive affair, involving 37,000 athletes, or 100,000 if the mass-gymnastic events are included. It was watched by about 250,000 spectators, more than saw the 1932 Los Angeles Olympics. Red Vienna lavished money and attention on their showcase event, building a brand new 60,000-seat stadium in the Leopoldstadt district in just twenty-three months. Originally called the Praterstadion, it has since been renamed the Ernst-Happel-Stadion and remains the largest in Austria. On the last day of the 1931 games, all 100,000 participants marched in ranks across the inner city in the style of a proletarian vanguard.

Minds, as well as bodies, were attended to, although in the field of education Red Vienna made less of an impression. This was not for want of trying, but the reformers were frustrated by the administrative-political demarcations of the Austrian state; the control of secondary schools and universities was under the purview of the federal ministry of education, controlled by the Christian Socials. The socialists therefore devoted their energies to reforming primary schools and setting up 'workers' libraries', often situated in the *Gemeindebauten*. They also ran adult education courses. A who's who of Vienna's progressive intelligentsia graced this programme with free lectures and classes. Workers' clubs and associations were supported to encourage pastimes and hobbies of every conceivable description, from cycling to political cabaret, from angling to chess, from hiking to poetry readings.[39] Nothing, it seemed, was to be left to chance.

Too bossy. . .

Red Vienna attracted visitors, admirers and imitators from all over Europe, dazzled by the city's audacious slum clearances and pioneering welfare clinics. Even the sceptics were impressed. One visiting English journalist wrote in the *Spectator* that Vienna's achievements in this regard put his country to shame, exposing 'our own national lethargy'.[40]

Yet for its critics, and in particular for many of the supposed beneficiaries of Red Vienna's utopian planning, the socialist city became the epitome of what would later be known as the 'nanny state'. To keep the vast, communal *Gemeindebauten* shipshape, for instance, life was micro-managed by government-appointed concierges who enforced an extraordinary variety of rules and regulations. Times were set aside specifically to beat rugs, deposit rubbish and use the laundry. Children had to keep off the grass and all residents were to keep quiet after 10 p.m. There were rules on the appearances of hallways, stairways and balconies, all backed up by a monthly inspection. The famous communal laundries were tightly managed by supervisors who allotted monthly 'wash days' to families.

The residents themselves had little say in formulating these rules. They were merely on the receiving end of the 'expert' advice handed down to them at the new clinics, kindergartens and consultation centres. 'Small wonder, then,' writes the historian of Red Vienna, Helmut Gruber, 'that municipal socialism was often viewed as regimentation from the top by its beneficiaries themselves, a condition that workers were already subjected to in full measure at the workplace.'[41] Little has changed to this day. The sturdy, well-built *Gemeindebauten* have survived remarkably well, and provide relatively inexpensive living in a major European capital. But supervisors in the block are still paid to keep a weather-eye on the residents; most of the signage is restrictive, prohibiting residents from skateboarding, cycling and playing football in the common areas, just as there are restrictions on pet ownership.

Red Vienna, as we have seen, was devised and run almost entirely by earnest reformers from liberal, middle-class Vienna; well-meaning men, but with little knowledge of the realities of working-class, or women's, lives. The priorities of Red Vienna often reflected their own tastes and preferences, rather than those of the people they were trying to help. Take culture, for instance. Reared in the honourable tradition of *Bildung*, few could see beyond the end of their Beethoven and Goethe, with a detour via Marx. They were usually tone deaf to the new mediums of film and radio, regarding these as merely unwelcome diversions from the realities of class struggle. They gave no funding to film, yet it quickly became the most popular form of entertainment. Equally, having spent big sums of money on new libraries, the Social Democrats then bossily restricted the choices available, banning, for instance, cowboy books by the German-born Karl May, the best-selling author of the day (and a hero to readers as diverse as Fritz Lang and Hitler). May's pulp fiction, it was decided, contributed nothing to building class-consciousness. Unsurprisingly, the council bureaucrats later discovered that the number of workers taking out books was actually quite small.

Bitter resentments were stirred in particular by the new foster-care system. In the interest of better child rearing, health officials were empowered to take a child away from its mother if they were convinced that she would be unable to bring up the child herself, due to poverty or homelessness. The children were removed to what was considered to be superior accommodation, but at the cost of grieving and traumatised families. Moreover, in moving everyone into small apartments, however clean, airy and efficient, the reformers broke up those extended families, living cheek-by-jowl in mutual interdependence, which had sustained working-class life and culture in the past. Thus, an *organic culture* had been supplanted by a *planned society*, with often disastrous consequences, precipitating sometimes violent conflicts between workers and welfare officials bent on enforcing the rules.

There was an economic critique of Red Vienna as well. Housing about 200,000 people in new dwellings between 1919 and 1934 seemed impressive, but despite the new taxes on consumption and middle-class wealth, there was not enough money to house everyone, and corners inevitably had to be cut. There were never enough laundries and washing facilities, for example; many tenants were forced to shower in *Gemeindebauten* far from their own, or in the municipal baths. Meanwhile, the private housing sector was crowded out by the enormous scope of the municipal housing programme, leaving people little alternative but to wait for council apartments, if they ever became available. By and large, people had to accept what they were given. In short, Red Vienna, for all its achievements, was grist to the mill for all those economists and sociologists who were to argue that, in practice, the loss of individual freedom was too high a price to pay for such 'socialisation'.

Or too feeble . . .

An alternative, and equally influential, critique held that rather than being too bossy, too overbearing, in fact the socialists had been too weak in the face of the challenges from the political right – the proto-fascists of Black Vienna and Austria more generally.

For certain Viennese on the left, the rot set in as early as July 1927, when the Social Democrat city council had apparently allowed the police to gun down eighty-nine of their own supporters. These people had been protesting against a court verdict releasing three right-wing paramilitaries who had killed two of their own in an ambush. In retaliation, the protestors stormed and set fire to the city's Palace of Justice, provoking the police into their murderous assault. As well as the dead, another 500 or so were injured. The Social Democrat mayor, Karl Seitz, had tried to persuade the demonstrators to disperse before the police charged in, but to no avail.

Even at the time, the bloody events of 15 July appeared to many to be a fork in the road. Take Ilona Duczynska, for instance, the wife of the socialist journalist and economist Karl Polanyi. Born near Vienna to Hungarian and Polish parents, up to that point she was a fervent supporter of the Social Democrats. Holidaying at a Danubian resort on the day, she hurried back to the city as news of the massacre spread. Using a press pass to cross police lines, Duczynska was appalled by the devastating scenes, akin to the Peterloo Massacre, and was equally dismayed by the 'total irrelevance' at this vital juncture of the social democrat leadership and their failure to immediately mobilise the *Schutzbund* and issue arms to protect the working class. For Duczynska the debacle set an unhappy precedent of constant retreat by the Social Democrats before the more ruthless and determined forces of the right. 'The powerful potential of the Austrian workers' movement,' she argued, was 'frittered away in a long drawn-out process of yielding one position after the other.'[42] One modern writer has called this process social democracy's 'serial failure of nerve'.[43]

Others drew similar conclusions. The radical psychoanalyst Wilhelm Reich dashed from his consulting room as the demonstrators poured past his window. He witnessed the massacre on the streets and the blaze at the Palace of Justice as it was torched by the protestors. For Reich, this was the day when the conciliatory ways of social democracy proved their inadequacy against the repressive forces of the right. In Marxist terms, the Social Democrats had privileged the corrupt procedures of the bourgeois legal system over the interests of the working class. 'I saw, in short,' Reich wrote later, 'that the real life of the working masses is lived on a completely different level from that on which the tumult of politicians and party politics rages.'[44] In *The Mass Psychology of Fascism* he offered a scathing critique of social democracy, imprisoned within a conservative, bourgeois straitjacket. 'Without intending to, it helped fascism, for the fascism of the masses is nothing other than disappointed radicalism plus nationalistic "petty bourgeoisism" . . . I come from these circles and know them well. I am happy to have rid myself of their influence.'[45]

In the final analysis it seemed to the likes of Reich and Duczynska that the Social Democrat leaders, products of an older, liberal, bourgeois Vienna, lacked the steel to deploy the full resources of the working class to fight against the Austro-fascists and later the National Socialists. Tens of thousands strong, the *Schutzbund* had been created out of the old workers' guards. There remain stirring photos of the *Schutzbund*, well-drilled and armed, marching proudly through the streets of Vienna in the early 1930s, a seemingly unconquerable vanguard of working-class intent. Yet at every moment of confrontation with the paramilitary forces of the right, the *Heimwehr*, the Social Democrats hesitated to throw the *Schutzbund* into action.

The final test came in 1934, when the *Heimwehr*, together with the army and police, manufactured the opportunity finally to crush the remnants of the *Schutzbund* and the workers' movement. Yet such was the ingrained passivity of the social democratic leadership that the left crumbled before the onslaught. Foreign Minister Otto Bauer himself acknowledged the failure:

The working masses awaited the signal to fight . . . We might have been able to prevail at that time, but we shied away from the fight. We dodged the fight because we wanted to spare our country the disaster of a bloody civil war . . . This was a mistake, the most fatal of our mistakes.[46]

While it lasted, however, whatever its faults there is no doubt that the specific political methodology of Red Vienna, its close links between theory and practice, provided a powerful stimulus to the intellectual production of the interwar years. Red Vienna shaped that production in many ways, giving rise to an intellectual culture particular to the city, with long-lasting consequences.

The Looshaus, flashpoint of architectural modernism.

Chapter 4

Fresh Thinking for a New Era: The Birth of the Knowledge Economy

The thriving intellectual culture of interwar Vienna was made up of an interlocking grid of institutes and research centres, formal and informal discussion groups, as well as the celebrated circles (*Kreise*). Some survived from the pre-First World War era, such as Freud's Psychoanalytic Society. Many, however, were creations of the post-war years and shared the political ethos of Red Vienna; all were shaped, in one way or another, by the politics of the city at this time.

This chapter looks in more detail at the intellectual Petri dish of Red Vienna. Compressed into a small geographic space, the various clusters of institutes and *Privatseminare* followed a very similar modus operandi, marking the specifically Viennese contribution to the history of ideas. For at the same time as research was being carved up into carefully policed and self-limiting academic disciplines elsewhere in Europe, the Viennese consciously encouraged a clash of ideas and methodologies, as we have seen. Eager to dissolve boundaries between biology and mathematics, psychology and art, sex and endocrinology, or mathematics and philosophy, the Viennese consequently sparked off and delineated entirely new fields of study. They were not necessarily aiming to invent new disciplines, but that was nonetheless the natural result of their intellectual style.

In order to mediate these (often ferocious) clashes and collisions, the Viennese privileged methodological rigour above all else. The mathematician Kurt Gödel referred to Vienna's commitment to 'truly exact thinking and truly exact methods'. This usually involved applying the latest scientific techniques to what most people had previously considered to be merely childhood hobbies – such as rearing hundreds of exotic animals in crowded Ringstrasse apartments – or new fields of activity that had previously been subject to mere conjecture or idle curiosity. Finding out how listeners chose which shows to listen to on the radio, how consumers decided what to buy in a shop, or how people really reacted to prolonged bouts of unemployment, were all increasingly urgent and relevant questions to which the Viennese intellectual community now applied such 'exact thinking', generating new disciplines – such as communications research and consumer motivation research – along the way.

The management guru Peter Drucker, a scion of Red Vienna, born just outside the city in 1909, famously described this process as the 'knowledge economy' in his book *The Age of Discontinuity*, published in 1968. In Drucker's terms, the Viennese were making knowledge 'productive', through the 'systematic and purposeful acquisition of information and its systematic application'. This is what Red Vienna very consciously set out to do, and the Viennese of this generation were uncommonly good at it; the politics of the era *demanded* it. *Fin-de-siècle* Vienna might have produced pure knowledge, in an abstract, intellectual sense, but the successor generation succeeded in the 'systematic application' of such knowledge. As Drucker wrote,

> When the intellectual says 'knowledge' he usually thinks of something new. But what matters in the 'knowledge economy' is whether knowledge, old or new, is applicable, e.g. Newtonian physics to the space program. What is relevant is the imagination and skill of whoever applies it, rather than the sophistication or newness of the information.

The Bühlers and Lazarsfeld(s): a new psychology

A striking example of Drucker's dictum was the Vienna Psychological Institute, set up in 1922 by two Berliners, Karl and Charlotte Bühler. They stimulated many of their students to develop new statistical and mathematical techniques that were applied not only to psychology but a wide range of other fields, often well outside the academy. It is barely remembered today, yet the Institute provided a key link between Red Vienna and many of the city's intellectual groupings of the interwar years. It was supported by a ten-year grant from the Rockefeller Foundation.

The Bühlers were imported from Berlin directly by the Social Democrats to help with the politicians' educational reforms. Karl, several years older, was awarded a professorship in psychology, whilst Charlotte followed in 1929 with an assistant professorship. Charlotte had been one of Karl's students; the two married in 1916 after a whirlwind romance. Glöckel was instrumental in securing the Bühlers ten rooms for the new Institute of Psychology in the council's policy hothouse at the Palais Epstein, where it remained until 1934. This was very much Charlotte's domain.

One of the main ideas behind school reform at this time was, as the historian of the institute, Mitchell Ash, writes, 'to have a child-centred pedagogy, as they called it, instead of rote learning and memorisation ... [they] wanted to professionalise pedagogy by making the teacher's certificate equivalent to a university degree and to reorganise teacher training on a scientific basis'.[1]

Charlotte, born in Berlin in 1893 to Jewish parents, was already an acknowledged expert in child psychology; her 1918 book on *The Mental Development of the Child* fitted neatly into Glöckel's reform scheme. As well as being head of the Institute of Psychology, Charlotte was also made director of the psychological work undertaken at Vienna's publicly funded child welfare office (*Kinderübernahmestelle*), the first of its kind in Europe. Here she had a two-room suite, attending to those children who were in need of care or even adoption, all overseen by Tandler. Thus, as the historian Edward Timms wrote, across all these areas she 'bridged the gap between theory and practice, bringing her professional expertise directly to bear on questions of social policy'.[2]

Interwar Vienna has often been described as 'the capital of child analysis', a reputation that owed much to Bühler, as well as Anna Freud, daughter of Sigmund. Unlike the younger Freud, however, Bühler eschewed an exclusively psychoanalytic approach to child development in favour of close observation and empirical testing. While in Vienna, Bühler established a series of tests, for cognitive development, manual dexterity and visual coordination, in order to measure a child's progress. At best, these youngsters were supposed to be able to perform progressively more complex activities as the months passed. As Timms comments, 'all this may seem rather obvious, but this is because Bühler's response-testing techniques have now become standard practice'.[3] She set out what have become known as the 'Bühler baby tests' at length in a groundbreaking book translated into English as *Testing Children's Development from Birth to School Age*. She is regarded as one of the main founders of modern developmental psychology.

The Institute of Psychology was close to the university, but operated at arm's length from it. As well as being a scientist of the first rank, Charlotte Bühler was also a brilliant talent-spotter and mentor, particularly to young women frustrated by the lack of opportunities elsewhere. Her role in this context will be examined in more detail in the next chapter.

The Bühlers were also central to another vital cog in the city council's quest to harness theory to (socialist) practice, the Pedagogical Institute, another brainchild of Glöckel's, also housed in the Palais Epstein. He amalgamated the city's previous teacher-training schools into his new institute in 1923 and opened it himself. Several of Red Vienna's luminaries lectured there in the 1920s, including Adler, but always central to the new institute's curriculum were the Bühlers. The institute published its own journal, *Die Schulreform*.

These institutes were something of a cross between an intellectual proving-ground and dating agency for a whole generation of Viennese. Another distinguished student at the Pedagogical Institute was Karl Popper, who met his future wife Anna Henninger ('Hennie') while studying there from 1925 to 1927. Popper earned his doctorate at the Pedagogical Institute, subsequently taking up teaching posts in maths and physics. Another young man to flourish under the Bühlers was the aspiring zoologist Konrad Lorenz. In the 1930s he worked up his theories of animal behaviour, later developed into the new discipline of ethology, under their leadership.

The most important of the Bühler protégés, however, was probably Paul Lazarsfeld, born into a prosperous, left-leaning Jewish Viennese family in 1901. More than any other of the Bühler students, Lazarsfeld, armed with a degree in applied mathematics, sought to link mathematics and empirical research to a broad study of society. For a time, in the late 1920s, he worked directly as Charlotte Bühler's research assistant on statistics.[4]

As the academic Peter Simonson and others have suggested, Lazarsfeld owed much of his astonishing success throughout a long career to his collaboration with very bright and well-educated women, several of whom he met as fellow students of the Bühlers, two of whom he subsequently married.[5] He certainly had a model for strong, intellectual women in his own mother, Sophie, a formidable advocate of women's rights who trained in psychology with Adler. Lazarsfeld's first important research partner was the Bühler student Marie Jahoda, born to liberal Jewish parents in 1907. She became his first wife in 1927; they divorced in 1934. Later, Herta Herzog took Jahoda's place as Lazarsfeld's 'collaborating spouse' in America.

Lazarsfeld, Herzog and Jahoda were typical examples of the youthful idealism of Red Vienna. At the tender age of sixteen, Lazarsfeld co-founded the Socialist Association of High-School Students. One of his main jobs was to organise the socialist summer camps, designed to build *die neuen Menschen* through fresh air, organised games, communal eating and endless theoretical discussion. He was tasked with laying on suitably rousing talks by outside speakers. Many of those who worked with Lazarsfeld in Vienna and later in America had participated in the events he set up at these summer camps. Jahoda also helped to organise them, while still in high school. At the age of just eighteen she was picked as one of the speakers at the city council's May Day celebrations in Vienna, to give voice to socialist youth.

Having served his apprenticeship with the Bühlers, in 1931 Lazarsfeld felt confident enough to establish his own Research Centre for Economic Psychology, the prototype for many similar outfits founded by Viennese émigrés and exiles abroad, including Ernest Dichter and Herzog, amongst the principal founders of the modern advertising industry in post-war America. Methodologically, the centre owed much to the Bühlers; their institutes and Lazarsfeld's new creation often worked in tandem, sharing the same personnel. Both were rigorously academic in their approach, yet operated at arm's length from the University of Vienna. Similarly, they were both politically engaged with Red Vienna and the development of public policy.

Lazarsfeld's centre was novel in one important respect, however. In order to fund its more academic and political research work, the centre used the same empirical techniques and psychological insights on behalf of large companies as well. This constituted a further significant dissolving of boundaries. As Jan Logemann writes, the centre was 'tasked explicitly to study the psychology of markets, understand consumer behaviour, assess public social programs, and generally improve the conditions of economic life in Austria'.[6] What is now the huge mainstream business of consumer research was then a daring new undertaking.

The board was made up of industrialists and businessmen, alongside university professors and public officials, at that time an unusual blend of expertise. Over the course of its brief life the centre conducted dozens of studies of consumer markets, from shoes to stockings, men's suits to water heaters, for scores of businesses and clients in Austria and abroad. Such activities not only brought in money but also allowed the centre's researchers to hone their skills and theories in practical fieldwork. In probing consumer behaviour in this way, Lazarsfeld, Herzog and others developed the new techniques of 'depth interviewing': hours-long, structured interviews with consumers that were designed to reveal the motivations for purchasing one product over another – then called the *focused interview*, and later focus group. These new techniques also allowed them to branch out into new and surprising forms of political work, such as analysing working-class consumption habits.[7]

The centre's most famous work, however, was a study of long-term unemployment in the town of Marienthal, twenty miles south-east of Vienna. This came about at the suggestion of Otto Bauer. Marienthal had been heavily dependent for its economic vitality on a textile mill, but this had been forced to close after the collapse of the Austrian banking system in 1931 and the subsequent depression. The report, *Marienthal: The Sociography of an Unemployed Community*, was published in 1933. Lazarsfeld, Jahoda and Hans Zeisel were credited as the authors, but others at the centre also contributed to the unprecedented amount of fieldwork involved.

For the first time researchers embedded themselves in a community over a relatively long period. Jahoda, and another young Bühler student, Lotte Danzinger, stayed with some households for months. Danzinger distributed clothes to a hundred families, giving her access to their homes for research. She arranged a dressmaking pattern design course, so as to chat twice a week with about fifty women, and started a girls' gymnastics course, to meet young adolescents. The researchers compiled time-flow charts of daily behaviour. Jahoda and Danzinger combined the 'use of numerical data with immersion into the situation . . . [to] learn the smallest details of their daily life'.[8] By measuring walking speeds, for instance, they discovered that the women were more purposeful and busier than the newly unemployed men!

The report was highly innovative. It still makes harrowing, some-times distressing, reading, as the authors chronicle the disintegration of lives under the remorseless impact of enforced idleness. The report's conclusion, at least for starry-eyed interwar Marxists, was sobering, and worrying. Rather than producing revolution, as they might have expected, long-term unemployment produced only apathy and disillusion. As the report concluded:

> Anyone who knows how tenaciously the working class has fought for more leisure ever since it began to fight for its rights might think that even amid the misery of unemployment, men would still benefit from having unlimited free time. On examination this leisure proves to be a tragic gift . . . the workers of Marienthal have lost the material and moral incentives to make use of their time.[9]

The invention of the orgasm, 1927

Charlotte Bühler admonished her students for going anywhere near the new and exciting discipline of psychoanalysis. The tough empir-icist regarded Freud's work as a pseudo-science, essentially untestable and unverifiable. She was not the only one; Popper regarded it, in his own terms, as 'unfalsifiable'. Despite these reservations, from the start, as we have seen, psychology and psychoanalysis were integral to Red Vienna.

Adler was ensconced as one of the leading theoreticians in these fields, and he collected his own coterie of equally committed followers. These included the young Viktor Frankl, who was paid by the Social Democrats to run youth counselling centres in Vienna while he was still a medical student. In particular, he counselled teens and students at risk of suicide. His methods were apparently so successful that, famously, by 1931 not one student took their own life; as a result he was transferred to the female suicide ward at the state hospital, Am Steinhof. Soon after, he evolved his own school of psychotherapy, 'logotherapy'.[10] A survivor of the Holocaust, his book *Man's Search for Meaning* was a post-war best-seller.

Adler believed that psychotherapy should be free to those who could not afford it, not merely an indulgence of the upper-middle classes. His former mentor, Freud, was certainly no socialist, but even he had to make the odd bow to the spirit of the age. In a speech in Budapest in 1918, he acknowledged that Freudians had to create 'institutions or out-patient clinics . . . where treatment shall be free'. In an unlikely peroration, the staunch liberal predicted that 'the conscience of society will awake and remind it that the poorest man should have just as much right to assistance for his mind as he now has to life-saving help offered by surgery'.[11] So began the story of Freud's free clinics. Starting in 1920, with the Poliklinik in Berlin, Freud's followers founded several such institutions across Europe; Vienna's followed Berlin's in 1922, joined later by similar institutions in Budapest and London.

Vienna's free clinic, the Ambulatorium, was opened shortly after Freud's sixty-fifth birthday. Eduard Hitschmann was the first director of the clinic, and he was joined by several younger Freudian psychoanalysts who all volunteered their time. These included Wilhelm Reich as the deputy director, and Annie Pink, who married Reich the same year that the clinic opened. Helene Deutsch and Edmund Bergler also worked there. The clinic operated out of a conspicuously unglamorous building next to the general hospital.

This 'second generation' of psychoanalysts had a radical, socialist vision that took the Ambulatorium far beyond anything that Freud might have imagined. The historian of the free clinics, Elizabeth Danto, has described their work as 'a challenge to conventional political codes, a social mission more than a medical discipline'. Danto quotes Helene Deutsch, that they were 'drawn to everything that is newly formed, newly won, newly achieved'.[12] But Reich was the circus-master for these younger Freudians, and largely responsible for the most memorable features of their work.

Born in 1897 in what is now western Ukraine, Reich was a psychoanalyst, but his principal interest was in sexology, and his life was to become another excellent example of how this interwar generation of Viennese radicalised and repurposed the intellectual breakthroughs of the city's golden age. Reich's precursor of that era was the German-born Richard von Krafft-Ebing, successively a professor at the universities of Graz and Vienna. His book *Psychopathias Sexualis*, published in 1886, is usually credited as the founding text of sexology, a discipline that sought to use the application of science to rob the Church of its monopoly of wisdom on sexual affairs. The relatively slim volume expanded through many later editions until the author's death in 1902. Rarely can any one book have spawned so many words and phrases in common usage. His taxonomy of sexual behaviour included homosexuality, masochism, paedophilia and fetishism, all coined or given their modern meaning by Krafft-Ebing. He made Vienna a European centre for sexology.

Reich organised informal seminars on sexology at the university, but these became so popular that he turned them into a more strategic course of talks on how the study of sexuality could be informed by disciplines such as biology, endocrinology, physiology and of course Freudian psychoanalysis. The master had already written extensively on the sexual component of neurosis, most strikingly in his 1905 book *Three Essays on the Theory of Sexuality*. Under these influences, during his work at the Ambulatorium and the regular contact that this afforded with working-class, homeless and unemployed 'patients', Reich developed his belief that sexual suppression – for him a primary cause of neurosis – was symptomatic of bourgeois, capitalist society. Neurosis and sexual problems, he argued, arose directly from 'social conditions rooted in the bourgeois social order'.

This was the root of the 'Sex-Pol' movement that he founded in the late 1920s, a marriage of Freudianism to Marxism expounded in his most celebrated book *The Mass Psychology of Fascism*, published in German in 1933. Here, he fingered the bourgeois family unit as a principal reason for Germany's turn to Nazism:

> From the standpoint of social development, the family cannot be considered the basis of the authoritarian state, only as one of the most important institutions which support it. It is, however, its central *reactionary germ cell*, the most important centre for the reproduction of reactionary men and women and conservative individuals. Originating and developing from definite social processes, it becomes the most essential institution for the preservation of the authoritarian system that shapes it.[13]

Reich allied these insights to a more *activist* form of psychoanalytical and medical interventionism. Beginning to use the phrase 'social work', rather than just passively waiting for patients to come to the Ambulatorium he resolved to take his services, and message, out to those who needed it most. He created a form of community-based social service, setting up six free 'Sex-Hygiene Clinics for Workers and Employees', and at the weekends drove a van into working-class districts to dole out sex-education pamphlets and contraceptives door-to-door, usually accompanied by a fellow Sex-Pol worker Lia Laszky. He would also use these opportunities to deliver earnest homilies on 'the sexual misery of the masses under capitalism'.[14] Thus, as the historian Britta McEwen writes, 'whereas *fin de siècle* sexology sought to classify and heal individuals ... this shift refocused sexual knowledge away from sexological taxonomies ... and towards advising heterosexual, reproductive couples.'[15]

Reich's own wife, Annie Pink, endured her own measure of sexual misery with the libidinous and possibly abusive Reich, as did many other women. Laszky was by no means the only one with whom he had an affair, to which he considered himself perfectly entitled despite his marriage. As his daughter remembered, 'He had lots of affairs, and he felt that if you didn't go along with that you were just clingy and neurotic. This was totally different if women cheated on him . . .'[16]

Reich became a passionate exponent of sexual expressiveness, which would vanquish both neurosis *and* patriarchal capitalism (and also, usefully, justify his own permissiveness). For Reich, the measure of this 'expressiveness' was the orgasm, on which he came to focus most of his research. Treating his patients at the Ambulatorium, he developed the theory that 'enabling the patient to achieve orgasm was the measure of successful therapy', and he collected a mass of data at the clinic to support it. He published *The Function of the Orgasm* in 1927, a book that was rediscovered in 1950s America with momentous results. The subsequent search for 'orgiastic potency' formed the rest of his life's work.

Reich remains an ambivalent figure, even in the socialist utopian carnival of Red Vienna. On the one hand, he campaigned for a host of progressive reforms in the laws and customs that controlled sexual behaviour, laws that are now commonplace. He advocated for the right to free abortion, for free contraceptives, the abolition of any legal distinctions between the married and the unmarried, treatment rather than punishment for sexual offences, and the lifting of all laws against homosexuality. He campaigned for women to enjoy orgasms just as much as men. Reich, more than anyone, rationalised a new sexual permissiveness, what he termed 'the Sexual Revolution', the title of the English edition of his book *Die Sexualität im Kulturkampf* (Sexuality in the Culture War), published in German in 1936. This was probably the first time that the phrase 'sexual revolution' was used.

But his increasing obsession with the orgasm to the exclusion of almost anything else alienated many, including Freud, who broke with Reich completely in 1930. A mop of unruly, vertical white hair atop an intense, brooding face suggested to many the epitome of a 'mad scientist'. Annie Pink described him as 'angry, paranoid and suspicious'; others thought him clearly psychotic. Ostracised by the mainstream psychoanalytic community, and then by the

Austrian and German communist parties, he drifted off to the margins of politics before having to escape the onset of Nazi rule by leaving for Norway.

Less well-known than Reich, but also central to the history of social work and psychoanalysis in Vienna and beyond, was August Aichhorn, one of the first people to work therapeutically with delinquent youth. On his own initiative, Aichhorn, formally an elementary-school teacher, set up a home for such miscreants, the Jugenderziehungsanstalt at Ober-Hollabrunn, a project supported by Social Democrats on the city council, perhaps the first of its kind in Europe. The site had originally been a refugee camp. Aichhorn challenged the idea that rogue teenagers were a product of hereditary degeneration, arguing instead that they could equally be victims of their upbringing and social environment. In particular, he looked at the baleful consequences of arrested development arising from the disruption of early child–parent relationships.

His social work was encouraged by Freud and particularly by Freud's daughter Anna, whose later work on child development was influenced by Aichhorn's ideas. Freud *père* himself wrote the introduction to Aichhorn's seminal book on delinquency, *Wayward Youth*, published in 1925. Aichhorn subsequently trained as a psychoanalyst with him. Unusually for these circles he was not a socialist or a radical. Nonetheless, recognising that he had an enormous empathy with young men, the Social Democrats put Aichhorn in charge of training the new breed of municipal social workers.

Atonalism for socialists

Like Adler and Reich, the radical composer Arnold Schoenberg was also close to Red Vienna and intimately involved in the city council's cultural didacticism. Just as Reich radicalised the work of Freud, so Schoenberg radicalised the work of his own idol, Mahler. This extended to all aspects of music, from composition to performance. In order to decouple music from the commercial and aesthetic demands of the bourgeoisie, for example, Schoenberg founded his own Society for Private Musical Performances in November 1918. Its purpose, as expressed by his disciple and fellow composer Alban Berg, was 'to give artists and music lovers a real and exact knowledge of modern music'. Critics were banned, performances free to members. The programmes were kept secret so as to ensure that every concert had an equal chance of being well attended.[17]

By 1918, however, Schoenberg was already adept at upsetting the old order. Born in 1874, he had initially scandalised Vienna's bourgeoisie with his unsettling *Two Songs for Voice and Piano*, composed in late 1907, followed by *The Book of the Hanging Gardens* in 1908. In both works he began to reject the hierarchical tonal order of the European musical canon. In his own words, he called this the 'emancipation of dissonance', fundamentally a means of shaking the bourgeois order out of its comfort and complacency. In what amounted to a manifesto of the new music published in 1911, called, prosaically, *Theory of Harmony*, Schoenberg directly contrasted the 'comfort' of the old order with those 'searching' for the truth of the new.

Indeed, Schoenberg spent the two years before the First World War working on a large symphony explicitly to celebrate the 'death of the Bourgeois God'. Described by the music critic Alex Ross as 'sharp-witted, widely cultured [and] easily unimpressed', the youthful Schoenberg had just the personality to take the Modernist crusade into the concert halls. A thick skin was required to survive the 'seat-rattling, whistle-blowing, and ostentatious walkouts' that greeted performances of his provocatively experimental music, not to mention the full-scale rioting at the so-called *Skandalkonzert* in 1913, an evening of the latest Viennese expressionist music conducted by Schoenberg that had to be ended prematurely. Ross persuasively compares the shock of Schoenberg's early music to the release of the punk band the Sex Pistols' *Anarchy in the UK* in 1976.[18]

It was only after the war, however, that Schoenberg constructed his serial, or twelve-tone, system, whereby no tones are repeated until a twelve-note sequence has been repeated in its entirety. Thus was born the 'Second Vienna School', resetting all subsequent classical music. In 1921, his followers and friends were invited to his house on the outskirts of Vienna to learn of the master's breakthrough with dodecaphony. Despite the obvious inaccessibility of the music, at least to untutored ears, the anti-bourgeois intent of Schoenberg meant that the exponents of the Second Vienna School were swept up by Red Vienna.

Like Berg, Anton Webern was another pupil of Schoenberg's, a shy, cerebral and militantly anti-populist composer; indeed, unlike almost all of his peers he was a pan-German nationalist, sympathetic at first to Hitler and the Nazis. Yet he made an oddly successful director of the Vienna Workers' Choral Society, a mixed-voice amateur choir, many of whose members could not even read music. Despite the professed amateurism, the society's events drew large crowds. At the May Day celebrations in 1931, the organisers claimed that the festival of the Workers' Choral Society involved 4,700 singers, accompanied by a symphony orchestra of 120 and a troupe of 100 dancers, all performing in front of 50,000 people. Webern was also a conductor and curator of some of the events in the Workers' Symphony Concert series, originally introduced in 1905.[19]

For the ideologues of Red Vienna, Webern's concerts represented the mass democratisation of high culture. The instigator of such events was David Josef Bach, head of the Social Democratic Arts Council, founded in 1919, and so effectively the city's culture czar. A close friend and staunch supporter of Schoenberg, Bach's job was to try to make 'high' culture more accessible to the working class, which included providing reduced-price tickets to the opera and theatre. Bach believed, as the academic Julian Johnson writes, that 'social and aesthetic progress' could go hand in hand, and that 'radical art might complement rather than oppose a radical politics'.[20]

Bach made Schoenberg virtually the official composer of Red Vienna, organising a celebration of the composer's fiftieth birthday in 1924, hosted by the mayor himself. Equally enthusiastic about

Schoenberg's shift to atonal music was the musicologist and composer Paul Amadeus Pisk, a board member and sometime pianist at the Society for Private Musical Performances. He and Bach considered the advances in Viennese music to be similar to the moves towards abstraction in art. In 1924, the first Music and Theatre Festival was held, directed by Bach, the forerunner of the Vienna Festival, first held in 1927.[21] It lapsed during the Second World War, but was refounded in 1951 and continues to this day.

In promoting Schoenberg so energetically, Bach had to deflect the inevitable accusations of middle-class cultural élitism. Bach tried to present Schoenberg as the glorious successor to the dependably popular Mozart and Beethoven. Bach's critics on the left, however, demanded more authentic 'proletarian' fare, such as folk music and workers' marching songs. Some younger, more leftist Viennese composers such as Hanns Eisler, another pupil of Schoenberg's, came to reject the teacher's Modernist complexity completely. A communist, Eisler took his own music directly into the halls and bars of Berlin's working-class neighbourhoods, drawing 'shouts of approval whenever he banged the piano keys with a balled-up fist'.[22]

Perhaps Red Vienna's councillors could never have hoped to please everyone. There is no doubt, however, that their attempts to popularise atonal Modernism afforded this difficult music an importance that it would otherwise not have had, thereby establishing it as the dominant musical innovation for the rest of the century. Schoenberg escaped the rise of fascism by emigrating to New York and subsequently Los Angeles, where one of his most enthusiastic students was a young John Cage. He took Schoenberg's dissonance even further with his three-movement *4'33"* piece, first performed in 1952, the year after Schoenberg's death. Cage's composition was quickly nicknamed the 'silent piece', with good reason. David Tudor, the pianist, came on stage, opened the piano lid and did nothing, only closing it again at the end of a 'movement'. The duration of the non-performance was four minutes and thirty-three seconds.

The magic circle

The 'Vienna Circle', as it became known, was perhaps the best known of the interwar clusters. Comprised principally of philosophers and mathematicians, it met from 1924 onwards and collectively developed the philosophical school of logical positivism. Despite publishing a manifesto in 1929, suggesting that the Circle readily agreed on a collective view, in truth it was much less homogenous in its outlook than is often thought. This is hardly surprising given the disparate cast of strong-willed characters involved. Nonetheless, its broad outlook, its fundamental intellectual disposition, was to be extremely influential.

The Circle had its roots in a small discussion group formed before the First World War by, inevitably, Otto Neurath, the physicist Philip Frank and the mathematician Hans Hahn, all friends from university. Neurath married Hans Hahn's sister Olga, who lost her sight at a young age. She was a gifted mathematician in her own right and also a member of what is sometimes referred to as the 'First Vienna Circle'.[23]

Their efforts were revived after the war under the new leadership of Moritz Schlick, a German philosopher who took over Ernst Mach's former chair at the University of Vienna in 1922. He organised and inspired the new circle, which began meeting in 1924 on every other Thursday at 6 p.m. in a dingy room next door to Hahn's cramped study at the university.[24] As well as taking in members of the 'First Circle', Schlick also recruited the young German-born philosopher Rudolf Carnap. Other members included the mathematicians Karl Menger, appointed professor of geometry at the university in 1927 and son of the *fin-de-siècle* economist Carl Menger (of whom more below), and Kurt Gödel, as well as philosophers Herbert Feigl and Friedrich Waismann, and Felix Kaufman.

Much divided these intellectuals, in particular Neurath and Schlick. The ebullient, politically committed Marxist could not have been more different from the modest, diffident and punctiliously polite academic. Always groomed and well turned out, unlike the unruly Neurath, Schlick appeared to be the least revolutionary person possible. Most other participants, however, such as Carnap, were at least sympathetic to Red Vienna, and Gödel, it would seem, completely apolitical. But they were united (almost) in their heroes, and even more so in their villains.

Amongst those heroes, the most obvious was the venerable Mach. Broadly, every member of the Vienna Circle sought to apply Mach's scientific method to philosophy, allowing them to hack away at what they regarded as philosophy's accumulated muddles and distractions. Indeed, most of them were officers of the Ernst Mach Society, founded to valorise the great man's legacy. 'Verbal sedatives' were the enemy. As Menger later recalled in his memoirs, above all they 'fervently believed in clarity. Nothing was more odious to them than a hazy expression of presumed truths . . . Metaphysical depth raised in them a strong instinctive distrust even before logical analysis revealed that it was not depth that characterised such speculations, but emptiness of cognitive content.'[25]

The Vienna Circle's manifesto, published in 1929, owed its inspiration to Mach's anti-metaphysical thinking.[26] Entitled *The Scientific World Conception: The Vienna Circle*, the slim pamphlet was written principally by Neurath, and it can equally well be taken as an exposition and defence of Red Vienna's worldview. Given the Circle's differences of opinions, Neurath bounced some of his less didactic colleagues into accepting it. Nonetheless, the authors declared that the Circle was devoted to elucidating a 'scientific worldview' that, as the introduction continued, 'knows no unsolvable riddles. Clarification of the traditional philosophical problems sometimes leads to their unmasking as pseudo-problems, and other times converts them into empirical problems, which can thereby be subjected to the methods of experimental science.'

The manifesto was presented to their fellow philosophers and mathematicians at a congress in Prague that same year. Hans Hahn gave the opening address on 'The Significance of the Scientific World View, Especially for Mathematics and Physics'. His talk amounted to a definitive summary of the Circle's core beliefs:

[We] confess our faith in the methods of the exact sciences, especially mathematics and physics, faith in careful logical inference (as opposed to bold flights of ideas, mystical intuition, and emotive comprehension), faith in the patient observation of phenomena, isolated as much as possible, no matter how negligible and insignificant they may appear in themselves (as opposed to the poetic, imaginative attempt to grasp wholes and complexes, as significant and as all-encompassing as possible).[27]

Mach had been a great admirer of William of Ockham, the medieval friar who advocated a simplification, an economy of thought, to deal with fundamental problems – an epistemological device thereafter known as 'Ockham's razor'. Members of the Circle followed the same method. Another hero, for most of the Circle, was the enigmatic Ludwig Wittgenstein. His *Tractatus Logico-Philosophicus*, written largely during his war service and published in 1921, seemed directly to continue the toil of Ockham and Mach by taking a razor to language itself. The slim volume was subjected to a forensic, line-by-line reading in the Circle. Schlick, in particular, was enthralled. Neurath, however, was a dissenter. He regarded the haut-bourgeois Wittgenstein with the same scorn that he reserved for Freud; they were both 'pseudo-scientists' incarnate.

However, all would have agreed with Wittgenstein when he opined, 'Bad philosophers are like slum landlords. It's my job to put them out of business.' Of those classified as 'bad', the most egregiously awful were advocates of metaphysics, the peddlers of Mach's 'pseudo-science'. Thus, the Circle extended Mach's quarrels with German idealism, and in particular with the contemporary philosopher most identified with that school, Kant's vicar-on-earth

Martin Heidegger. The German had given his own defence of metaphysics in a public lecture (published as *What is Metaphysics?*) only slightly before the Circle brought out their manifesto in 1929. In 1932 Carnap published an essay solely devoted to dismantling Heidegger's lecture. As it turned out, Heidegger proved to be a National Socialist, notoriously praising the movement just four years later in a speech he gave as the rector of the University of Freiburg. He was banned from teaching for a period immediately after the war, and despite ample opportunities to do so never fully repudiated his earlier publicly stated views.

Yet excluding any consideration of what the Circle derided as the idle speculation of German metaphysics came at a cost. Morality and ethics, in particular, were thus largely cut out from their considerations, on the grounds that it was impossible to say anything *meaningful* about these subjects. By the mid-1930s, however, as the political situation darkened in Austria and Germany, this position looked increasingly untenable. Surely philosophers, above all, could not pass over in silence the descent into a new age of barbarism and mass-murder?

It was Menger who bravely took up the task of applying some of the Circle's intellectual rigour to the real world. In his own words, he tried to produce a new 'theory of ethics – an application of exact thinking that would bear to traditional ethics a relation somewhat comparable to that of mathematical to traditional logic'.[28] Nonetheless, Menger still resisted the notion that, as he aimed at 'strict objectivity', he could assign such words as 'good' or 'evil' to any norms or codes of behaviour. This was a major weakness of the Circle's thinking, especially in the context of the 1930s; they themselves, and their families, would be the victims of an all-too tangible evil. Part of Menger's slender book, published in 1934 as *Morality, Decision and Social Organization: Toward a Logic of Ethics*, is in the form of a dialogue with an imaginary friend, who compares a value-free ethics without any concepts of good and evil to a zoology that ignores animals. It was an apt comparison.[29]

Nonetheless, through its tightness as a group and the clarity of its aims, for a time at least the Vienna Circle exerted a huge influence on contemporary and subsequent philosophy, refining what was to become the dominant school of 'analytic' philosophy in post-war Anglo-American universities. This was no accident, for the members of the Circle were not content merely to debate the finer points of logic in Vienna. Inspired mainly by Neurath, who did his utmost to push his colleagues in the direction of something akin to a coherent movement, they devoted considerable energy to publicising their agenda beyond Austria.

As well as publishing a manifesto, the Circle also took over an existing philosophy journal and converted this into a house journal, renamed *Erkenntnis* (Knowledge), which for years was required reading amongst philosophers. Over the next few years, most of the main Circle members would get an airing in *Erkenntnis*; it was also the first journal in which Karl Popper published. Frank and Schlick also edited a book series, *Schriften zur wissenschaftlichen Weltauffassung*, or 'Writings on the Scientific World Conception'.

The Circle spread its message abroad by organising, or co-organising, international conferences, and by inviting suitably qualified foreign visitors to sit in on its proceedings. The first such conference took place in Prague in 1929, on the subject of the 'Epistemology of the Exact Sciences'. Subsequent meetings were held in Paris, Copenhagen and Königsberg. The last was in Cambridge, Massachusetts; the Second World War broke out on the first day of the conference.

Of the Circle's foreign visitors, the most important, as it turned out, was a young and combative English philosopher, A.J. ('Freddie') Ayer. He attended meetings of the Circle over the winter and spring of 1932–33 and in 1936 published the most readable summary of the Circle's thinking, his surprising best-seller *Language, Truth and Logic*. Famous, in particular, for its exposition of the Circle's 'verification principle', a formula for identifying a statement as 'meaningful' (or otherwise), this text was the main conduit for the Circle's thinking to the English-speaking world. Ayer also left behind an indelible image of Neurath as 'A large man, running to fat in middle-age, with a white puffy skin, reminding me of a marshmallow.'[30]

From America, the most significant visitor turned out to be a young graduate student called Willard Van Orman Quine, usually considered to be one of the most important philosophers of the twentieth century. Already interested in logic and in William James's theory of pragmatism, Quine won a travelling study fellowship to Europe and attended Schlick's lectures as well as several meetings of the Circle. Undaunted, apparently, he even gave a lecture to the group on his doctoral thesis. Together, Ayer and Quine were to be the main emissaries of logical positivism to the Anglo-Saxon world. When Quine was first appointed a lecturer at Harvard, he taught what he himself described as a 'philosophy course along Carnap's lines'.[31]

Most of the Circle, being essentially sympathetic to the city council's policies, actively supported and lectured at the newly founded adult education centres, the *Volkshochschulen* – sometimes called the 'people's university of Vienna'. Neurath, Hahn and Feigl all taught regularly at the centres, on philosophy, mathematics and economics. Here again, theory was deployed in action.[32]

A new language, in pictures

The restless Neurath had not only the Vienna Circle to occupy him; in 1925 he founded the Museum of Society and Economy, for the study of town and city planning along socialist lines. This was an integral part of his campaign for the scientific worldview, and was to produce his most important and instantly recognisable legacy. Less a traditional museum, the institution would be, in his own words, 'a means of education, a schoolbook on a grand scale', offering a glimpse into the socialist nirvana using a new methodology – the pictorial representation of statistics, from which are descended today's omnipresent infographics.[33]

Courtesy of the city council, the main part of the misnamed 'museum' was situated on the ground floor of City Hall. The museum became one of Red Vienna's most powerful propaganda tools, with exhibitions on the council's achievements in housing, health ('social hygiene'), employment and more. Neurath, in partnership with the German graphic artist Gerd Arntz and designer Marie Reidemeister (later his third wife), was the first to deploy data and statistics in an easy and accessible manner, thus creating what he regarded as a universal language. In his own words, the aim was to 'create pictures that can be understood without words if possible ... We have to create symbols that can be "read" by all of us, just as we can all read letters, and just as experts can read musical notes. This requires the creation of a set of hieroglyphs which can be used internationally.'

Neurath's primary innovation was both breathtakingly simple and devastatingly effective – to show quantity by repetition, not enlargement. As he put it, 'A sign is representative of a certain amount of things; a greater number of signs is representative of a greater amount of things.' Neurath called his new visual language the 'Vienna Method of Pictorial Statistics', but it was Reidemeister who came up with the name by which it was to be better known, ISOTYPE, an acronym for 'International System of Typographical Picture Education'.[34]

After the Austro-fascist takeover of Vienna in 1934, Neurath and his team were forced into exile, first in The Hague, and later in Britain. By this time, the Vienna Method had begun to attract international attention. In 1931 Soviet Russia founded the 'All-Union Institute of Pictorial Statistics of Soviet Construction and Economy', more easily digestible as plain 'Izostat', to proclaim the advances of Stalin's Five-Year Plans. This was clearly based on Neurath's Viennese museum, and the Soviet authorities invited Neurath, Arntz and others from Vienna to Moscow to improve the output of Izostat. Neurath and his team travelled to Moscow to assist regularly between 1931 and 1934, by which point Neurath had had enough of the institute's nakedly propagandist output.

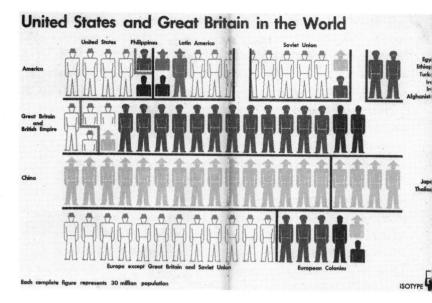

Neurath at work: an isotype from 1943.

As opportunities closed in Soviet Russia, so they opened up in America. In the early 1930s several Americans started working together to introduce the Vienna Method into the United States. Interest in Neurath's work spread quickly, producing a frenzy of early infographics. Neurath was commissioned, for example, to make charts for the Museum of Science and Industry in Chicago, and he visited America for the first time in 1933. He caused a stir wherever he went – 'The Big Man who created the Little Man is with us', proclaimed one magazine. New Deal organisations began to commission charts and diagrams from an American offshoot of Neurath's museum called Pictorial Statistics, Inc., run by another Viennese called Rudolf Modley. Cheap imitators sprouted up everywhere, and by 1938 one writer was warning that 'The pictograph from Vienna has started a real vogue for pictorial charts in this country. This vogue promises to engulf the public and the educator with a deluge of "Americanised" pictographs produced by the trial and error method.'[35] Further international acknowledgement of his work followed; he helped to found the Museum for Science and Industry, a replica of his Viennese institution, in Mexico City.

He also started the Unity of Science movement, an attempt to forge an international language of science that would provide countries and communities with the methodological tools for common progress towards, in effect, socialism. Neurath's interest in 'universal languages', whether through infographics or science, was a common theme of interwar Vienna. Perhaps, as we have seen, it was as much a consequence of the old empire's search for commonalities to unite a vast diversity of peoples – through Secessionist art, for instance – as of Red Vienna's quest to unite the working classes. Certainly, this was a common reference point, identifiable as the beginning of theoretical Modernism. 'Words divide, pictures unite', was Neurath's pithy slogan for his museum. The film director Fritz Lang harboured the same ambition for his own visual medium. Writing from Berlin in the 1920s, Lang argued that 'the internationalisation of filmic language will become the strongest instrument available for the mutual understanding of peoples, who otherwise have such difficulty understanding each other in all too many languages'.[36] Unfortunately he was writing just before the invention of talkies.

Some ornaments must stay: architects at war

Inventing an 'international language', as Neurath attempted to do, *was* a quintessentially 'Modernist' project. But Viennese Modernism, if there was such a beast, can be deceptive. It developed in a very local fashion during this era, perfectly illustrated by the city's architectural tradition. Like the Vienna Circle's philosophy, it evolved, in part, in contradistinction against German meta-narratives. This was hardly surprising, as there were close connections between the Vienna Circle and the city's architects. For another dedicated socialist deeply involved in Vienna's quarrel with German metaphysics was Neurath's close friend and frequent collaborator, Josef Frank.

As a designer and architect, Frank was also grappling with the issues of universal styles and, as we have seen, he was also closely involved in the politics and practice of Red Vienna. He was also tightly connected to the Vienna Circle; as well as his friendship with Neurath, Josef's elder brother Philipp Frank, a mathematician, physicist and close friend and biographer of Albert Einstein, was a co-founder of the 'First Circle'. These relationships again demonstrate how the Viennese regarded their apparently disparate disciplines as intertwined, and all subject to the same 'exact thinking'.

Josef Frank followed the Circle's work and attended their discussions. Like many of their number, the Frank brothers were assimilated Jews, sons of a determinedly upwardly mobile father born in Heves, a province in north-east Hungary. Ignaz Frank migrated to Vienna as a young man and quickly prospered in the textile business. By the time Josef and Philipp were born in the mid-1880s, the family was extremely wealthy; one uncle was an engineer, another made a fortune manufacturing early car batteries. The young Franks were thus brought up firmly in the mainstream of cosmopolitan, aspirational, middle-class Viennese life. Their Judaism was little more than a footnote.

Through the agency of Neurath and his brother, Josef Frank was listed as one of several 'closely connected authors' in the Circle's roster of members. These like-minded few were described as working on the 'basis of the scientific world view and are in personal and scientific contact'.[37] This was particularly so in Frank's case, as by the late 1920s he was also fighting the Circle's war against German metaphysics and the looming threat of totalitarian thinking, not in philosophy but in architecture and design. Indeed, so woven into the Circle's main contentions in philosophy were Frank's concerns about the state of his own profession that he was invited to give the very first public lecture under the banner of the Vienna Circle, entitled 'The Modern Worldview and Modern Architecture'.

Just as the Circle forged their philosophy in a dialogue with Mach, so Frank and his fellow architects had developed their ideas on architecture and design with their own Viennese precursors, namely Otto Wagner (1841–1918), and Adolf Loos. Frank attended Vienna's Technische Hochschule to complete his formal training in architecture, but like many others he probably learned just as much from the informal gatherings at the Café Museum presided over by Wagner, as well as Josef Olbrich and Josef Hoffmann.

Frank, like many of his contemporaries, was also mesmerised by the impromptu lectures offered up by the intemperate and icono-clastic Loos, the doyen of the younger generation of Viennese architects. Many of those had already left Vienna by the mid-1920s, but Frank, by contrast, fought this generation's battles over art and design in Vienna itself, before emigrating to Sweden in 1933 and taking citizenship there in 1939, courtesy of his Swedish wife.

What were these battles, and why did they matter? Otto Wagner, who became professor of architecture at the Academy of Fine Arts in Vienna in 1894, was the most important of the *fin-de-siècle* gener-ation of architects. He was the first to break decisively with the historicism of the Ringstrasse, publishing his celebrated manifesto, *Moderne Architektur*, in 1896, in which he argued that 'new human tasks and views called for a change or reconstitution of existing forms'. He aligned himself closely with the Secession movement, applying the latest art nouveau motifs to his buildings, such as the Postal Savings Bank in central Vienna and the glorious Kirche am Steinhof in the grounds of a mental-health hospital on the outskirts of the city. Wagner was the first architect to dignify the hardwiring of a modern industrial environment with style and design.

However, the truly disruptive figure was Wagner's own pupil, Loos. Whereas Wagner had opened up a war on one front, against the historicism of the nineteenth century, so Loos, inspired partly by his early exposure to America on a trip to New York and Chicago, brazenly opened up a war on two fronts, against both historicism *and* Vienna's own *Jugendstil* and Secessionists. His campaigns came to a head in one notorious building, now called the Looshaus, one of the very few commissions that he actually completed (see image p. 100). He was invited to submit his plans by the tailors and outfitters Leopold Goldman and Emanuel Aufricht in Michaelerplatz, right opposite the recently finished (in the historicist style) entrance to the Hofburg, the imperial palace. The site could not have left him more exposed, but it was here, in the words of Christopher Long, that the arrogant thirty-eight-year-old decided to mount his 'challenge to late historicism and the *Jugendstil* – to what he deemed a misguided revivalism on the one hand and a contrived and inauthentic modernism on the other'.[38]

Given its prominent location, the Looshaus was bound to attract scrutiny. Indeed, it caused a storm, as artistic controversies often did in Vienna. In its own time the lugubriously historicist opera house had provoked equally strong opinions, so much so that the architect responsible had hanged himself after the Emperor himself criticised the design. The main offence of the Looshaus, as intended by the architect, was its radical lack of adornment – the famously plain facade of the upper storeys, punctuated (at least at first) by nothing but the windows.

Loos had declared his intentions quite plainly in his polemical lecture 'Ornament and Crime', given to various audiences in Vienna and Berlin in 1909–10, and later published as a pamphlet. Conservatives, and in particular the Christian Socials, attacked Loos viciously, denouncing the building as a sin against the monarchy and the traditions of the city. Critics derided it variously as a 'dung crate', a 'grain store', or 'the house without eyebrows'. Indeed, so severe was the criticism that the city planning department, as well as Goldman and Aufricht, wilted. As a gesture of appeasement, bronze window boxes were added to the upper-storey windows, taking the edge off the blank facades. To this day, the window boxes miserably undermine the intended effect of the whole.

With hindsight, it is clear that the Looshaus controversy was a significant waystation in the increasing tensions between the younger, more radical, often Jewish, generation, which largely supported Loos (himself a Catholic), and an increasingly hostile establishment. For Loos himself, the consequences were grim; the constant rows over the building made him ill, pretty much for the rest of his life, and he never worked on a large building again. In 1928, he was convicted of child molestation; the full, more shocking details of the case have been revealed only recently. The episode gave the conservative press further opportunities to assail him. By the time of his death in 1933, Loos was a broken man.

The Looshaus, and its accompanying pamphlet, 'Ornament and Crime', are often quoted as the founding works of Modernism. They were certainly very influential in the development of European – and American – art and architecture. But the important point as far as the evolution of Viennese design was concerned, is that the Looshaus was never as revolutionary as it seemed.

High Modernism, as developed by architects such as the Swiss Le Corbusier, the German Mies van der Rohe and the Bauhaus school, particularly in the 1920s, took Loos's maxim on ornament to logical extremes, stripping out all decoration, superfluous motifs and historical references until a building was reduced to a square box, regardless of its function or location – the International Style. But the most striking feature of the Looshaus is that *form* is still following *function*; it is a building very much in two halves, reflecting its actual purpose and the lives of the people who would be using it. The tall, classical, green marble columns of the bottom half of the Looshaus allowed for display windows and a suitably arresting entrance to a high-end tailor's, akin to the gentlemen's outfitters on London's Saville Row. The very different upper half of the building, however, contained apartments, which only needed the windows looking onto the street. The real importance of the Looshaus is that rather than slavishly following dogma, Loos advocated an architectural language appropriate to the people who would actually use the building and live in it, almost leapfrogging Modernism at the same time.[39]

The Looshaus thus set up a distinctively Viennese opposition to international Modernism; it was in this Viennese tradition that Josef Frank and Loos's other acolytes, especially those who went to America, were operating, with important ramifications for the city's influence abroad. For by the time that Frank gave his lecture on behalf of the Vienna Circle in April 1929, the International Style, as developed in Germany, the Netherlands and elsewhere, had become such a cast-iron doctrine, nurtured by an obsession with the machine age, that Frank, for one, feared that the likes of Walter Gropius and Ludwig Mies van der Rohe were abandoning any rational perspective on architecture – and how ordinary people might actually want to live their lives – for a sort of metaphysical belief in oversimplified machine forms, and, ultimately, the box. This was probably very much the argument that he worked up in his Vienna Circle lecture, and one that he developed at greater length in his full-on critique of what he called the radical moderns, published in 1931 as *Architecture as Symbol: Elements of German Modern Architecture*.

Frank argued instead for an *organic* approach to design and architecture, allowing that it was fine to borrow from the past, particularly as 'numerous household objects' represented 'perfected types' that had been developed over many years. By way of illustration, he contrasted his own rounded, softly shaped door- and kitchenware handles with those sharp, angular and entirely impractical handles churned out by the Bauhaus – 'poorly adapted to be grasped by hand', as Frank put it. These were the early prototypes of the aggressively contemporary teapot that is impossible to pour and the cup that is impossible to hold, however dexterous one's fingers.

Frank's book *Architecture as Symbol* was one of the first to rehearse all the most penetrating criticisms of Modernism that were to become familiar over the following decades. For a start, Frank observed that the whole project was deeply flawed politically. It was already evident that the proletariat, in whose name the Marxist Modernists claimed to be labouring, were unimpressed by the exciting new workers' estates into which they were being herded, with their poky rooms, limited facilities and crabby fixtures and fittings. Quite simply, many did not like living in them.

The aspirations of the working class, Frank argued, were not focused on simplicity, but on getting and enjoying all the amenities that they had long been denied. The best modern building, therefore, was one 'that can accommodate everything vital in our time and yet at the same time remain an organic, living creation . . . Modern German architecture may be objective, practical, principally correct, often even attractive, but it remains lifeless.'[40] As the 1930s progressed, Frank's attitude towards the Bauhaus and the German designers hardened, until he ended up with a critique of architecture very similar to Hayek's of economics, suggesting that Modernism in design and architecture stemmed from the same authoritarian instincts that produced Five-Year Plans and corporatism.[41]

Accusing the Modernist avant-garde of totalitarianism, in essence, was hardly likely to endear him to Mies van der Rohe and the other German, French and Dutch pioneers who dominated the International Style. They held the Viennese in low regard anyway, highly suspicious of what they regarded as Vienna's enduring love of frippery. When their unofficial leader, the Swiss architect Le Corbusier, and others started to corral the Modernists into their own thought-collective in 1928, founding the *Congrès Internationaux d'Architecture Moderne* (CIAM), Frank was the only Austrian invited to join, and he lasted just two meetings before resigning in despair. The split in the Modernist ranks was now open, with Vienna very much in the minority.

The arguments that raged in the interwar years between Vienna's architects and the German-led High Modernists therefore mirrored those of the Circle. Just as Frank, supported by Neurath, opposed the totalising system of the Bauhaus, which excluded any deviations from a set of rules ordained by Gropius and Mies van der Rohe and enforced by CIAM, so the Circle's mathematicians and scientists battled the same dispositions in philosophy – namely German metaphysics. In both cases, the Viennese were arguing for an open-mindedness, the continued application of reason and exact thinking that were slowly being squeezed in the darkening intellectual and political environment of central Europe.

On incompleteness

Even more so than the Vienna Circle and Josef Frank, it was the economists, or more accurately political economists, of 1920s Vienna who were working against the grain of creeping totalitarianism and metaphysics. As distinct from those who gathered round the Circle, however, the economists evolved into the principal Viennese critics of the social and political goals of the socialist city council. However, a bridge of sorts between the Circle and the economists was provided by the Mathematics Colloquium, founded by Karl Menger. A kindly, gentlemanly figure, unusually so by the standards of the day, the other 'Handsome Karl' was well suited by temperament to play the role of linkman between the various clusters of rancorous intellectual rivals and opponents.

The mathematicians were, for the most part, naturally apolitical. The principal figures in the Mathematics Colloquium were Menger himself, Gödel, Abraham Wald and Oskar Morgenstern.[42] John von Neumann, a Budapest-born mathematician, also attended when he could. It met once every two weeks in the university. From 1931 onwards, the group published a journal containing a selection of papers presented at the meetings. The Colloquium lasted until 1937, when Menger left for America.

Gödel, a hypochondriac prone to regular bouts of depression and ill-health, was the star. He was, arguably, the most eminent logician, and perhaps also mathematician, of the twentieth century. Born in Brno, Moravia, in 1906, entering the University of Vienna in 1924 he attended the meetings of the Colloquium regularly and was helped through his frequently difficult life by the close friendships that he maintained with Morgenstern, Wald and Neumann, especially after all of them emigrated permanently to America in the

1930s. The murder of his close friend Schlick, in 1936, plunged him into a cycle of despair from which he never really recovered. Thereafter, he developed a particular fear of being poisoned, insisting that only his wife Adele could cook his food.

Gödel was closely involved in the central mathematical enquiry of the era, the search to ground the discipline in a bedrock of consistent mathematical logic that would ultimately yield coherent answers to all mathematical puzzles. This quest was known as the 'foundational debate', or even 'crisis' in German (*Grundlagenkrise der Mathematik*). The call-to-arms had been issued by the great German mathematician David Hilbert in 1900 at the International Congress of Mathematicians in Paris. Hilbert had challenged his peers to come up with a 'finite number of purely logical processes' that would ensure the 'solvability of every mathematical problem'.

'We hear within us,' Hilbert continued, 'the perpetual call: There is the problem. Seek its solution. You can find it by pure reason, for in mathematics there is no *ignorabimus*, nothing unknowable!'[43] In 1928, Hilbert issued some more specific challenges at a similar congress in Bologna: that mathematicians should prove the consistency of mathematical systems, containing no contradictions; that they should demonstrate the completeness of any mathematical statement, so that it could be derived entirely from basic axioms; and that they should outline the complete system of first-order, or predicate, logic. All this, he believed, was within their grasp.

The young Gödel, still working on a PhD thesis, dutifully set out to advance Hilbert's programme, only to discover in the process that the master's quest was, in reality, futile. Gödel demonstrated that much would, in fact, have to remain 'unknowable', thereby transforming mathematics, and the more general field of scientific investigation, thereafter. He first announced this, almost casually, at the very end of a discussion at a conference in Königsberg in 1930, with a single sentence: 'One can even give examples of propositions . . . that while contentually true, are unprovable in the formal system of mathematics.'

Gödel's 'incompleteness theorem' showed, indeed, that there were mathematical propositions that could *neither be proved, nor disproved*. In short, the entire, immodest pursuit of a general theory to explain all mathematics was a chimera. It was truly a eureka moment, and recognised as such by the excited members of the Mathematics Colloquium. His mentor, Menger, was in America when he heard of Gödel's theorem and interrupted a lecture to give his bemused students the news. 'Thus the mathematicians at Rice Institute were probably the first group in America to marvel at this turning-point of logic and mathematics', he later recalled.[44] Gödel published the proof for his incompleteness theorem the following year.

With hindsight, it is clear that Gödel's breakthrough ranks with Einstein's Theory of Relativity in terms of its transformational effect on mathematics, physics and science more generally. At the time, however, it took a while for the implications of his work to sink in – indeed, they are still being debated. The consequences for artificial intelligence, for instance, were profound. Rather than regretting his apparent subversion of mathematics' claims to omnipotence, Gödel, as his latest biographer writes,

> believed that his proof was profoundly encouraging for human activity. Humans will always be able to recognize some truths through intuition, he consistently maintained, that can never be established even by the most advanced computing machine. A machine that can literally duplicate the reasoning, learning, planning, and problem-solving ability of the human mind will be forever impossible if Gödel was right about what he believed to be the more far-reaching implications of his theorem.[45]

Even more influential was Gödel's actual *proof* for the incompleteness theorem, which involved assigning numbers to every logical statement (called 'Gödel numbering') and then manipulating them according to the rules of mathematics. With his 'coding' in place, he then produced what can best be described as a primitive algorithm that would speed up the process of decoding the (often very high) numbers back into logical statements. It was his friend Neumann who immediately spotted the profound repercussions of this – that Gödel had, in effect, 'written a computer program long before any machine capable of running it would exist. He had dissolved in one fell swoop the rigid distinction between syntax and data.'[46]

Gödel showed that it was possible to devise a rigorous system in which logical statements (that were very much like computer commands) could be rendered as numbers. Alan Turing, the Cambridge mathematician, was, like Gödel, also working on Hilbert's challenges a few years later when he produced his famous paper describing an imaginary 'universal computing machine' that could write, read or erase such Gödelian symbols.[47] Turing was working with Neumann at the Institute for Advanced Study (IAS) at Princeton in the mid-1930s before returning to Britain where he joined the codebreakers at Bletchley Park during the war. Meanwhile, Neumann used Gödel's 'coding' and Turing's abstract idea for a computing machine as the foundations upon which to program one of the world's first electronic computers at the IAS.

There were other themes to emerge from the Mathematics Colloquium, such as applying mathematics to economics, particularly in the field of what came to be known as general equilibrium theory. This was the particular domain of Wald and Morgenstern, who presented their first papers on the subject to the Colloquium in the mid-1930s. Wald's work, on probability statistics, was especially innovative. From the ideas partly developed at the Colloquium, Wald, Morgenstern and Neumann developed the new discipline of 'game theory', which was to have an intellectual impact well beyond economics (see Chapter 9). Wald, who was originally from Kolozsvár (now Cluj, in Romania), emigrated to America with the help of Morgenstern in 1938.

The Austrian School

Wald and particularly Morgenstern also worked closely with the economists of what came to be called the 'Austrian School'. During the interwar years, this consisted mainly of Ludwig von Mises, Friedrich von Hayek, Gottfried Haberler (born 1900), Fritz Machlup (1902) and Morgenstern himself. Their collective identity was defined principally through membership of the fortnightly meeting of Mises's celebrated *Privatseminar*, or *Mises-Kreis* (Mises Circle), presided over by the man himself. With the benefit of hindsight, it is clear that this was the most important *Kreis* of them all.

For Mises himself and the other economists of the Austrian School, their own founding father was the leading economist of the *fin-de-siècle* generation, Carl Menger, the father of the Vienna Circle's Karl. Like Ernst Mach, Menger had been a pillar of Vienna's late nineteenth-century liberalism; he had also received a useful leg-up early in his career by being appointed private tutor to the Crown Prince, Rudolf. A professorship at the University of Vienna, in the personal gift of the emperor, soon followed.

Working in the 1870s, Menger had overturned previous concepts as to what constituted the value of a product in the capitalist system. The hitherto prevailing 'labour theory of value', as Marxists termed it, inherited from the notion of 'natural' prices from classical economists such as David Ricardo, had insisted that the value of any product was the sum of the *inputs* required for its production, primarily the cost of labour. Menger, however, argued that it is *the worth that buyers attach to a product* that determines its value, and thus price, in the marketplace. 'Value,' Menger asserted in his most famous work, *Principles of Economics*, 'is nothing inherent in goods, no property of them. [Value] is a judgement economizing men make about the goods at their disposal for the maintenance of their lives and well-being. Hence value does not exist outside the consciousness of men.'

This was the so-called 'marginalist' revolution in economics. A few other contemporary economists, notably the Englishman

William Stanley Jevons, had reached similar conclusions independently, but from Menger onwards it was the Austrian School that was to be most closely associated with this revolution in economic thinking. His principal acolyte was Eugen von Böhm-Bawerk, a finance minister in the 1890s, and Menger's successor as economics professor at the university. Here he proved a highly influential teacher to Mises and Joseph Schumpeter, among others.

Another follower of Menger was Friedrich von Wieser, who taught Hayek. Wieser's book, *Natural Value*, included the best contemporary exposition of Menger's ideas. 'Value is determined not by inputs, but solely according to the demand for and supply of goods of all sorts,' he wrote. Thus, Menger's tablets of free-market wisdom were handed down, and refined, through the Viennese generations.[48]

Böhm-Bawerk died in 1914 and Menger in 1921, after which leadership of the Austrian School passed to Mises, born to Jewish parents in what is now the city of Lviv, in western Ukraine, in 1881.[49] A kindly face belied a combative, cantankerous and notoriously inflexible nature. Fearless and rude in debate, he had a highly elevated opinion of his own importance, and was not afraid to share it: 'I was the economic conscience of post-war Austria', he recalled in his memoirs.[50] Even friends and colleagues crossed him at their peril; after Machlup dared to question Mises's views on the gold standard, he was blanked for three years. Some thought he mellowed slightly in later years after he married – others strongly disagreed. Many people, even those sympathetic to his political views, disliked him intensely; others forgave him much because of the discrimination that he had likely suffered in Vienna. It has never been proved conclusively, but he was probably a victim of the prevailing anti-Semitism at the university, for Mises never got a full-time academic post there. Instead, in 1909 he became chief economist for the Lower Austrian Chamber of Commerce and Industry (*Handelskammer*), later known as the Vienna Chamber of Commerce, working there for twenty-five years before taking up an academic position in Geneva.

For all his prickliness, and despite having no formal teaching position, Mises exerted an immense influence over the younger generation of economists through his seminar and his intellectual leadership. From October through to May, every other Friday at seven in the evening, by invitation only, a score or so of men (and occasionally a woman) gathered in Mises's expansive office at the Chamber of Commerce, opposite the war ministry and just around the corner from Otto Wagner's *Jugendstil* Postal Savings Bank. Their purpose was to discuss 'important problems of economics, social philosophy, logic, the epistemology of the sciences of human action'.

The location in the Chamber of Commerce was important, as the historian Quinn Slobodian has pointed out, for, from the start, Mises's young economists were accustomed to being 'actually involved in practical activity – the application of economic knowledge – getting their hands dirty in advising business, drawing up charts and gathering statistics'.[51] His protégés such as Haberler got some of their first paid employment assisting Mises on his very practical work at the Chamber. Furthermore, the participants in the seminar were always encouraged to think in the widest possible perspective, on a global scale. 'For the liberal,' Mises reminded his followers, 'the World does not end beyond the borders of the state . . . His thinking encompasses the whole of mankind.' [52]

Mises presided over his Circle sitting at his desk, often accompanied by a sizeable box of chocolates that he would pass around. A talk was followed by three hours of heated argument and discussion. Participants then adjourned for dinner at an Italian restaurant, Ancora Verde (The Green Anchor), to pick over some 'finer points of theory'. From 11.30 p.m. into the small hours, the men (only the men) slinked off to the Café Künstler for relaxed drinks and, finally, conversation of a 'lighter tone'. They might even end with a song – the lyrics would set some aspect of economics to a

(opposite) Doyen of the Austrian School, the irascible Ludwig von Mises.

popular drinking tune, although they do not, perhaps, bear up to the passage of time. Mises himself recalled of his creation: 'We cultivated neither school, nor community nor sect. It was through contradiction rather than agreement that we supported each other.'[53]

The Mises-Kreis was the first of hundreds of subsequent iterations of Austrian School communions, such as the Mont Pelerin Society, that survive to this day – if without the singing. Graduates of Mises's circle included all the Austrian School economists of the day, and the wide-ranging discussions would prepare them well to situate their economic arguments for free-market economics in a wider social and political context. This compulsion to think more widely about economics as just one component of a larger reflection on the nature of the good society was a hallmark of the Austrian School, and very much a consequence of Vienna's particular intellectual tradition. One modern critic has gone so far as to suggest that we abandon calling the members of the Mises-Kreis economists at all, as it comprehensively fails to capture the breadth of their analysis – better to think of them as 'Viennese Students of Civilization'.[54]

Of all those who benefited from Mises's patronage and encouragement, the most significant was undoubtedly Hayek, born to bourgeois, nominally Catholic parents in 1889. Both of his grandfathers had been scholars; his father, as we have seen, was an eminent amateur botanist and a second cousin was Ludwig Wittgenstein – so an academic career seemed to be almost predestined.

After serving on the Italian front during the war, Hayek enrolled in the Faculty of Law at the University of Vienna. On the recommendation of his tutor he was sent off to help Mises at the Chamber where the elder man was then working for the government on the economic aspects of the Treaty of Saint-Germain. Hayek joined the inner sanctum of the Austrian School, the Mises-Kreis, in 1924. So began their lifetime's collaboration and friendship, with Mises eventually passing the leadership of the Austrian School to Hayek in the 1940s. Mises's circle was exhilarating company for the young

Hayek. 'Nothing could be more exciting,' he later recalled, 'than Vienna of the 1920s and early 30s.'

It was Mises who set up Hayek at another important institutional base for the Austrian School in Vienna, the Institute for Business Cycle Research. This was founded at the instigation of Mises and largely financed by the Rockefeller Foundation. Hayek was director of the institute from 1927 to 1931, before being recruited for a professorship at the London School of Economics. The particular Viennese methodological innovation at the institute was to compile and analyse statistical data from around the world for the purpose of economic forecasting. This was a whole new discipline, provoking some fractious disagreements among the Austrian School as to whether such forecasting was even possible. Morgenstern was the second professional to be hired to work at the institute.

A leap in the dark: the debate of the centuries

Mises's intellectual leadership was just as important as his patronage. In 1920 he established his reputation as one of the world's pre-eminent critics of Marxism with the publication of a momentous article, 'Economic Calculation in the Socialist Commonwealth', followed up two years later by a book titled *Socialism: An Economic and Sociological Analysis.*[55] At the time, especially amongst the younger generation coming to maturity after the war, as we have seen, socialism and Austro-Marxism had swept all before them in the clamour to build a new republic out of the ruins of war and defeat. Mises's lifelong task was to disabuse such progressives that their ambitions were even theoretically possible, let alone practical politics.

As Mises conceded in the introduction to his book, 'Socialism is the watchword and catchword of our day. The socialist idea dominates the modern spirit. The masses approve of it, it expresses the thoughts and feelings of all; it has set its seal upon our time.'[56] Even Hayek emerged from the war as a fashionable Fabian socialist, eager to rebuild his country on scientific principles – this was a major reason for him to study economics in the first place. But now, for the first time, Mises pushed such young idealists onto the back foot by arguing that as socialism had no theory of economics, it was doomed to failure. This was the most powerful critique of socialism yet developed, kicking off the 'socialist calculation debate'.

Mises, of course, was taking on an entire ideology, but he had a very particular human target in mind as well, Otto Neurath. Both Mises and the great ideologue of Red Vienna had been taught together by Eugen Böhm-Bawerk at the university, and for Mises, at least, this had been a painful and irritating experience. He waspishly remembered the seminars: 'Unfortunately babblers sometimes abused the freedom to speak that was allowed to participants. Especially disruptive was the nonsense which Otto Neurath presented with fanatical fervour.'[57]

Mises nurtured a contempt for Neurath and all his works for the rest of his life, an *animus* subsequently inherited by Hayek, though apparently not reciprocated by Neurath himself. Nonetheless, these personal antagonisms would spice up a dispute that was to shape and define political and economic debate for the rest of the century.

Neurath, as we have seen, was an early proponent of a 'natural' or 'in-kind' economy, abolishing money as a unit of calculation. By 1918–19 he was arguing that the sort of limited central planning that had been accepted as necessary to prosecute the war provided a model for a fully socialised economy directed by his 'central economic administration'. In practice, as the 1920s progressed, Neurath's socialist colleagues on the city council never implemented his wholesale socialisation schemes, preferring a more centrist approach, but Mises and his allies were not to know this in the early 1920s. Given Neurath's prominence and his involvement in the Bavarian soviet uprising of 1918–19, merely his theorising in the vital years immediately after the war seemed dangerous enough.

As it was, it was one of those theoretical articles, 'Through War Economy to Economy in Kind', published in 1919, that specifically provoked Mises's first rebuttal of Neurath the following year.[58] Mises's aggressive opening paragraph of 'Economic Calculation in the Socialist Commonwealth' set the tone: '[Socialists] invariably explain how, in the cloud-cuckoo lands of their fancy, roast pigeons will in some way fly into the mouths of the comrades, but they omit to show how this miracle will take place.'[59] Broadly, Mises argued that only the price system under capitalism could ensure the efficient allocation of scarce resources. Under capitalism, the subjective value of any goods, that is, how much they were in demand from people, was indicated by the price of those goods (the 'price mechanism'). But under socialisation and the government control of the means of production, interference with the normal calculus of demand and supply would necessarily distort prices to such an extent that they would become useless in conveying any information to planners about how to allocate resources. 'Everything,' Mises famously declared, 'would be a leap in the dark. Socialism is the renunciation of rational economy.'[60] As he continued, 'Where there is no free market, there is no pricing mechanism; without a pricing mechanism, there is no economic calculation.'[61]

For those who cared to look, Mises had abruptly punctured all the inflated dreams and expectations of a generation that had sought to employ socialism to build a more just and better world. Using all the Viennese intellectual rigour at his disposal, Mises tried to show that full-blown socialism was simply unworkable. The effect on some of those younger, mildly socialist optimists, such as Hayek, was explosive. He later recalled that Mises's 1920 article 'shocked our generation, and only slowly and painfully did we become persuaded of its central thesis'. It was Hayek who might have been the very first to introduce the socialist calculation debate to an English-speaking audience, writing to *The Times* in April 1925 to alert readers to Mises's 'most searching criticism of the economic programme of the Socialists yet attempted'.[62]

In retrospect, Mises, quite intentionally, and Neurath, somewhat unwittingly, thus became the principal theoretical protagonists of

Red Vienna, and by extension the principal antagonists in a debate over the merits of planning versus the market that has never abated. Neurath, unfairly, has receded into semi-obscurity, but he had certainly served a purpose. 'If today,' remarks the Neurath expert Thomas Uebel, apparently without irony, 'we are somewhat better informed about what advantages a market economy does and does not possess, it is due in part to the stimulus of Neurath's early socialisation plans.'[63]

But there was a third participant in the original socialist calcu- lation debate, whose contributions at the time have often since been overlooked. His long-term influence, however, was to prove every bit as decisive as that of the other two Viennese theorists. Karl Polanyi was a Hungarian by extraction, but Viennese by birth (in 1886). His father was a successful and wealthy railway entrepreneur who maintained an apartment in the city as well as a large house in Budapest. After serving as a cavalry officer in the Hungarian army during the war, the young Karl moved to Vienna to recuperate, having contracted typhus and almost been crushed to death when his horse tripped and fell on him.

In Vienna, he met his Polish-Hungarian wife Ilona. A revolu- tionary Communist, always some way to the political left of her husband, she had also been born in the city.[64] The couple would live for most of their time in Vienna in a small flat in Leopoldstadt. An assimilated Jew, the gentle, scholarly Polanyi was a quintes- sentially cosmopolitan product of the Austro-Hungarian empire. His siblings were equally remarkable: Michael, for one, was a renowned scientist and philosopher, particularly close to Hayek during the 1940s.

Karl Polanyi had graduated from the University of Budapest as a Doctor in Law, but his main interest was in political economy. In 1924 he was made a senior editor of Vienna's most prestigious economics and current affairs journal, *Der Österreichische Volkswirt*, then central Europe's equivalent of London's *The Economist* news- paper, on which it was modelled. From this vantage point Polanyi commentated on all the major doctrinal debates in economics and politics until he was forced to leave the city in 1934.

As a leftist progressive, Polanyi naturally admired the attempts of Red Vienna's politicians, many of whom were his personal friends, to create *die neuen Menschen*. By the same token he also became increasingly critical of the Austrian School, hence his interventions in the socialist calculation debate in 1922, and later in 1925. If Mises and the Austrian School sharpened their intellectual weaponry on the whetstones of Neurath and Red Vienna, so, in turn, did Polanyi on Mises.

Polanyi's contributions to the socialist calculation debate set the tone for all his later thinking, and indeed for what is now called 'Polanyian economics'. The originality of Polanyi lay in the fact that he criticised *both* the command economy, for the loss of freedoms and the precision in allocating resources that it entailed, *and* the market economy. In other words, it was not a question of either/or, as Mises would have his admirers believe, for the market economy contained some fundamental theoretical flaws as well. Most tellingly, Polanyi argued that although the price mechanism was undoubtedly useful, it could not provide any information on what we would now call 'externalities', those more opaque effects – such as the consequences for the climate – of economic transactions.

This failure, he argued, had come about by mistaking the origins of the market economy. The Austrian School conceived of the market as a natural process of interaction between individuals to create prosperous societies, whereas Polanyi saw the market as an abstract theoretical construct existing outside and beyond the real concerns and needs of society. A key word that Polanyi would use later was 'embedded'; he argued that the economy should therefore be embedded in society, to serve people and the environment, rather than the other way round. At the time, in 1922, Polanyi advocated a sort of Guild Socialism as a third way between Neurath's command economy and Mises's freewheeling market capitalism.[65] A short debate was joined between Mises and Polanyi in the pages of the journal *Archiv für*

Sozialwissenschaft und Sozialpolitik; unsurprisingly, Mises was keener on Polanyi's critique of central planning than the market.

It took another twenty years for Polanyi to fully work out his ideas for an alternative to market capitalism, the subject of his most important work, *The Great Transformation*, of which more in Chapter 9. But the origins of the lasting debate on how to organise modern societies were to be found in this initial joust between the trio of Viennese thinkers in the pages of an obscure academic journal in 1922 during the years of Red Vienna. Few people were paying much attention at the time; millions more would in the future.

Chapter 5

The Muse Has Had Enough: Feminism and Socialism

ntering the University of Vienna through its imposing entrance on the Ringstrasse, a short walk takes you straight into the main courtyard, the *Arkadenhof*. This is the architectural heart of the institution, and within its arcades is a memory vault: the busts and statues of over 150 of the university's most august personalities dating back to 1888, as chosen by the professors themselves. A stern and unbending Sigmund Freud gazes out from one corner, Karl Popper looks suitably sharp and quizzical in another. Up until 2016, however, the university's Valhalla, as it is known locally, included just one woman, and she had to make do with a wall plaque.

It was only in 2005 that the university authorities deigned to start rectifying this glaring occlusion. Four years later the artist Iris Andraschek inserted an inlay of anthracite-coloured granite, 'Nero Assoluto', into the stone floor of the courtyard. It forms a giant female silhouette, an anonymous shadow to contrast with the physically memorialised males in the arcades. *The Muse Has Had Enough*,

(opposite) Lise Meitner, the Viennese physicist responsible for the discovery of the element protactinium and nuclear fission.

it is pointedly called. The first seven busts and artworks commemorating female scientists only appeared a further seven years later, in a shamefully late gesture of catch-up.

Despite their almost total erasure from the official chronicle of Vienna's intellectual history, I strongly suspect that these women would still have been opposed to inhabiting a chapter specifically on their contributions to Red Vienna and its intellectual hinterland. As we saw in Chapter 1, the Viennese were often deeply averse to being categorised, as socialist or conservative, Jew or non-Jew, German, Galician or Czech; 'identity politics' was anathema. They were just Viennese, a descriptor which embraced the plenitude of their era. The same goes for gender. Those very few women of this generation who were ever asked whether there was a specifically feminist story to be told resisted the notion, politely but firmly.

Take Herta Herzog, for instance. Pressed by one putative biographer, an American academic, she replied briefly: 'Gender has never played a role in my professional life. I am not a feminist, but understand if others are.' An immigrant to America, she conceded that almost all her colleagues were men during her time in the notoriously macho world of New York advertising in the 1950s and 1960s, when she was probably the most prominent woman in the entire business, but again she said, 'to my knowledge there were no gender-related problems for them, or me'.[1] Given the working environment on Madison Avenue in the 1950s and 1960s, evident in the TV show *Mad Men*, this argument seems scarcely credible. Did Herzog choose steadfastly to ignore all the gender politics, or was she just extraordinarily naïve? The latter seems unlikely. Her close colleague Marie Jahoda, one of the few chosen to take up her place in 'Valhalla' in 2016, was asked by one interviewer in which 'community' she felt most at home. 'If I want to be high falutin,' she replied, 'I can say "I am a world citizen". But if I want to be true, oh, I'm just a rootless refugee.'

Yet, as has often been argued, historians cannot allow the subjects they study to define the terms in which they can be understood. Despite the resistance of men like Gombrich or Popper to be considered as Jewish, it has always been clear that a more comprehensive account of Vienna (or Germany) and the socio-political forces that led to the Holocaust is only available if Jewishness *is* studied. As the historian Leora Auslander argues, 'Part of the scholar's job is, in fact, to determine how gender, race, or Jewishness may have mattered even when the subjects of research thought that it didn't.'[2]

Thus, despite the resistance from beyond the grave, I suggest that any account of Vienna's influence on the twentieth century is much richer for a specific account of how women came to play such a significant role. Historically, they were the first cohort of women to be educated at the same élite educational institutions as men, so theirs was a pioneering generation. All the more so in Vienna where they were consequently able to make a more telling impact on the city's intellectual and cultural production than they might have achieved elsewhere. Moreover, it was the very presence of women across a whole range of disciplines that most distinguished the generation of Red Vienna from the *fin-de-siècle* generation. More often than not, this was precisely the radicalising element in Vienna's intellectual life, shaping the city's influence abroad in particular ways.

Furthermore, their contributions to the Viennese story, as more generally, have usually been ignored or downplayed by later generations because they were women – hence the scandal of the *Arkadenhof.* The account that follows is therefore, to an extent, a reckoning. Last, but not least, in a few respects Viennese women of the Red Vienna generation colonised some fields of study in higher proportions to men than is even the case today. There is much to learn from Vienna's pioneer generation.

The poisonous legacy of Otto Weininger

The achievements of this female generation are all the more remarkable as Viennese women in the late nineteenth century faced as much resistance to any improvement in their circumstances as anywhere else in Europe, if not more. The historian of the Austrian women's movement of this era, Harriet Anderson, has identified three focal points of anti-feminism in the last decades of the Habsburg monarchy.

Most obviously, conservative, male opinion, embodied by Karl Lueger and his Christian Social supporters, strove to uphold the patriarchal order. Lueger might have been a radical in much of his municipal politics, but on this he was quite unflinching. The demagogues of Black Vienna were quick to demonise any woman who, in their considered opinion, dared to question the status quo of gender politics. For example, one of the most prominent and vocal of these anti-feminists was Joerg Lanz von Liebenfels, an occultist, mentor of Hitler and self-proclaimed *Mannesrechtler*, roughly a 'champion of men's rights'. He regarded the female feminist as oversexed, exhibiting an unnatural appetite for power. In his racist and sexist worldview, the entry of women into politics, or the professions, would invite a precipitous national decline.[3]

Such views were buttressed by the cod-science of male academics and writers. The most notorious of these was Otto Weininger, author of the highly influential *Sex and Character*, published in 1903. The depressive and academically brilliant Weininger was born in Vienna, to a Jewish goldsmith, although he himself later converted to Protestantism. He committed suicide at the age of just twenty-three, shortly after the publication of his one and only book (although another was published posthumously). Many men regarded such a death as a grand, romantic gesture, befitting a youthful genius, especially as Weininger wittingly took his life in the house where Beethoven had died. They subsequently elevated Weininger, and his book, to almost mythical status. Twenty-five reprintings of *Sex and Character* were churned out in German in the following twenty-two years.[4]

The book was not only rambling and inchoate, indeed almost unreadable, it was also deeply misogynistic and anti-Semitic. Setting out to resolve what he called the 'woman question' (*Frauenfrage*),

Weininger started with the relatively progressive notion that every person has a mix of masculine and feminine traits. However, deploying algebra, biology and philosophy, Weininger went on to argue that whereas masculinity is supposedly dynamic, ethical, conscious and logical, femininity is passive, sexual and illogical. The sacred duty of the male, therefore, armed with reason and ambition, was to strive for genius – 'which he regarded as the highest form of consciousness'[5] – an intoxicating proposition for the highly educated, restless and self-regarding male scions of Vienna's haute bourgeoisie. Hence the book's popularity amongst them.

Ludwig Wittgenstein, for one, was a devotee; he regarded *Sex and Character* itself as a work of genius, and recommended it to friends. Indeed, so troubling for Wittgensteinians is their master's deep admiration for Weininger that six scholars have devoted a volume of essays to the connection between the two Viennese. The most charitable interpretation they can put on Wittgenstein's infatuation is that the philosopher of language drew a general ethical inspiration from Weininger, 'the passionate commitment to the pursuit of honesty, [and] self-knowledge'.[6] Wittgenstein was but one fan, however. August Strindberg, Franz Kafka and many more were also avid readers.

Consequently, as well as having to deal with the Victorian, conservative reflexes of the older generation, women also had to contend with the fact that many of the younger, male writers and artists of *fin-de-siècle* Vienna were also very ambivalent, and often hostile, to women's 'forced entry into the male sphere'.[7] These men might have been bold enough to challenge and undermine the hypocrisies of contemporary bourgeois sexual morality, but as far as women were concerned, any progress was to be confined to the private sphere. This was, as Brigitte Hamann has written, 'the flip side of the sexual permissiveness glorified by Viennese modernism'.[8]

Gustav Klimt, for one, echoed Weininger in his painting, particularly the fountainhead's suggestion that woman was 'universal sexuality', her goal merely to 'use the sexual act to rob creative man – who was equipped with reason – of his creative power and to ruin him'.[9] Klimt produced reams of images trying 'to capture the feeling of femaleness', as Carl Schorske has written, drawing heavily on Weininger's erroneous taxonomy. In exploring the erotic so viscerally, Klimt was assuredly challenging his bourgeois elders, but also expressing his successor anxiety that the overt, released sexuality of the female would threaten the male. Some of Klimt's most renowned paintings deal with the themes of decapitation and castration: *Judith and the Head of Holofernes*, of 1901, depicts a sexually sated, voluptuous Judith clutching the obscured head of her victim.

Many of the most 'progressive' of the *fin-de-siècle* generation subscribed to these troubling views, and they were often carried over to the interwar years as well. The youthful Stefan Zweig was honest enough on this point in his memoirs: 'Going out with girls seemed to us a waste of time, since in our intellectual arrogance we regarded the opposite sex as intellectually inferior by their very nature, and we didn't want to spend our valuable time on idle chatter.'[10]

Sigmund Freud was a shameless example of this contemporary misogyny; many of his views on women were only a few shades less regressive than Weininger's. The Vienna Psychoanalytic Society remained resolutely, notoriously, all male, and Freud's immediate acolytes carried their exclusiveness over to America and elsewhere after being forced into exile. The rebellion against Freudian orthodoxy in America was partly fuelled by his feminist critics, who subsequently contributed to the 'second wave' of feminism from the 1960s onwards. Similarly, the Vienna Circle of philosophers was virtually all male. Only one woman attended regularly, Olga Hahn-Neurath, 'always smoking a big cigar'.[11] Mises's *Privatseminar* of economists was slightly better in this respect.

Bildung for girls, and the patriarchy

To a degree, the interest in *Sex and Character* reflected the fact that the 'woman question' was already a subject of heated debate and political protest in Vienna by the turn of the century, as it was in other European capitals. A movement for full civil and political rights for women had begun in Vienna in the 1860s. Local agitations and campaigns were eventually given a national framework with the founding of the League of Austrian Women's Associations in 1902, led by Marianne Hainisch.

From the start, Hainisch and others put a woman's right to equality in education at the heart of their demands. The assimilated Jewish middle class put a strong emphasis on emancipation through education – *Bildung* for girls, as well as for boys. In 1871 a *Höhere Bildungsschule* was opened for women but, more momentously, in 1892 the first girls' school along the lines of the boys' *Gymnasium* opened, the *Gymnasiale Mädchenschule*. This was the first of its kind in the German-speaking world. Lacking its own building, classes were held in the Natural History Museum. Initially, there were just twenty-eight girls, but such was its popularity that by 1904–05 it had the same numbers as an equivalent boys' school. Initially, the *Gymnasiale* was not recognised by the state, and not until later did it win the power to set its own exams – the *Matura* – although they still had to be physically sat at the boys' schools. However, with no government subsidies, this form of girls' education was only available to the upper-middle class; it is estimated that 35 to 40 per cent of those attending the school were Jewish.

The University of Vienna had never allowed women to sit for a degree, but with the support of a few prominent professors such as Mach and Theodor Gomperz, pressure mounted for change. That came in 1897, when the Faculty of Philosophy finally accepted women. It wasn't until 1900 that, reluctantly, women were allowed to enter the medical and pharmaceutical faculty. In 1907 Elsie Richter became the first *Dozentin* (lecturer) at the university. A telling indicator of the pent-up demand for higher education amongst the young middle-class women of Vienna in the decade or so before the First World War is the quick increase in the proportion of female students at the university. In the academic year 1897–98, just 37 women were enrolled, making the ratio of women to men 1 to 183. By 1914 there were 796 women, forcing the ratio down to 1 in 12. In 1903, Olga Steindler became the first woman to take a dissertation in physics at the university.[12]

Nonetheless, despite these grudging signs of progress at the university, the Bear's Den and their all-male allies put up a fierce, organised resistance to women taking up any sort of teaching job, let alone becoming professors. The fact that many of this first generation of educated women were assimilated Jews put them at a double disadvantage, for they suffered the same anti-Semitic discrimination as their male Jewish peers. So, the university patriarchy remained largely intact, with significant consequences for Vienna's intellectual life. Blocked and frustrated by the university (as well as much of the official Austrian bureaucracy), most women in this story flourished only in the informal, often privately funded intellectual hinterland of Red Vienna.

As well as the campaign for civil and political rights, and equal access to education, some Viennese feminists embraced a more ambitious and radical transformation of society altogether. They argued, as Auguste Fickert did, that the 'women's movement . . . is the bearer of new moral ideals and it expects women's entry into public life to bring the moral regeneration of civilised humanity . . .'.[13]

Fickert, a teacher by profession and founder of the General Austrian Women's Association, focused on the appalling plight of working-class women and prostitutes in Vienna, thus yoking feminism to broader campaigns on social inequality and exploitation. There were 2,400 registered prostitutes in Vienna in 1896, and probably over ten times more unofficial ones, in a population of 1.5 million. Most were desperately poor, out-of-work actresses or chorus-girls, often very young and vulnerable. The law provided little protection.

The same was true for domestic servants, an occupation that accounted for one-eighth of all women in Vienna. The few flimsy regulations that did exist dated back a century, with the result that domestic staff were often ill-treated and abused. Young men of middle-class households were known to take advantage of servants to have their first sexual encounters, if, that is, a prostitute was not procured. The fear of catching a sexual disease in the process, as some men inevitably did, also 'fundamentally influenced their images of women . . . and contributed to the general contempt for them'.[14]

The campaigns to ameliorate the condition of maids and prostitutes bore directly on the questions of labour regulations, working conditions and equal pay – all bread-and-butter issues for the Austro-Marxists. From an early stage, therefore, Viennese feminism was yoked to the politics of Red Vienna. Raising the status and improving the working conditions of women became a vital contribution to the overall creation of *die neuen Menschen*.

Several women who had fought for women's rights before 1919 were closely involved with the politics of Red Vienna, such as Sofie Lazarsfeld. Social democratic luminaries such as Julius Tandler and Otto Glöckel were strong supporters of women's rights. For the first time in Europe, therefore, a commitment to improving women's lives was at the top of a major political party's agenda, a vindication for years of campaigning by feminists *and* socialists. On taking office in 1918, as we have seen, the city council immediately set about trying to lift the 'triple burden' of household chores, paid work and child-rearing on working-class women.

The close bond forged between feminists and Red Vienna was not only ideological, it was also a matter of practical politics. After the Social Democrats had pushed their bill for universal suffrage through the national parliament in November 1918, granting men and women equal voting rights (although registered prostitutes were excluded until 1923), the support of women at the ballot box was integral to the party's hold over the city council. By now about a third of party members were women. With voting rights and formal representation in the national parliament also came campaigns on specific issues, such as making abortion legal. The change in women's status was one of the most obvious indications that post-war Vienna was a very different place from the pre-war imperial city. It was often remarked upon in the 1920s and early 1930s, as were the subtle shifts in sexual politics. Professionally, the gains made in education yielded far more, and far more varied, career choices, as we will see below. But women also won much greater autonomy in their sexual and emotional lives.

For the alternatives confronting a young woman, however wealthy and well-connected, were hardly enticing in pre-war Vienna. As Stefan Zweig reflected, they had little chance of normal sexual experiences. While the young men were often encouraged to have their first sexual encounters with prostitutes, 'the young girls were placed in airtight compartments under the control of their families, sealed off from life, their physical and intellectual development stunted'.[15] If they were very lucky, they might make a good match at an early age. By their mid-twenties, however, young women were considered to be 'old maids' by their families, and a Jewish father with means might give his daughter over to a marriage broker, a *Schadchen* (from the Yiddish), to find a match, any match. Such unions could be disastrously unhappy, the wife only spared any further agony by the premature death of an often much older husband.[16] After the war, however, women won much greater autonomy and independence in making their own choices.

These were signs of a new, more general frankness and honesty about sexual matters in post-war Vienna. Symptomatic of this atmosphere was the appearance of Vienna's first erotic lifestyle weekly on Valentine's Day, 1924, *Er und Sie: Wochenschrift für Lebenskultur und Erotik* (Him and Her: Weekly Magazine for Lifestyle and Eroticism), edited by the fearless and provocative journalist Hugo Bettauer. Best known as the author of *The City Without Jews*, Bettauer was already notorious as a serial breaker of taboos, and his new magazine was no exception. It dwelt at length on matters of sex, love and women's rights, all linked to the new pedagogy on sexual and emotional health. Every issue therefore featured a column by a psychiatrist or a specialist in women's health. Bettauer himself assumed the role of an agony uncle, responding to readers' questions in a column called 'Life's

Problems'. Radically, for the time, he argued that everyone had a right to the 'private enjoyment' of masochistic, flagellistic and other sexual behaviour, as long as it was consensual.[17] For the first time *Er und Sie* also carried personal ads, a chance for both women and men to meet each other on their own terms, unencumbered by the expectations and demands of family and society. As the historian Lisa Silverman points out, judging by the fact that the number of ads rose from just 14 in the first to 123 in the fifth and final issue, this new form of dating proved to be popular.

Naturally, Bettauer, a Jew who had converted to Protestantism, was denounced as a 'pornographer' by his Christian Social opponents. Bettauer was tried, and acquitted, of public indecency, but *Er und Sie* was still forced to close. Undeterred, Bettauer continued publishing the personal ads in another of his papers, *Bettauers Wochenschrift: Probleme des Lebens* (Bettauer's Weekly: Life's Problems). Here, many aspects of the 'New Woman' were covered; bobs, women wearing trousers, smoking and the campaign for the legalisation of abortion. 'By the time of his death [in 1925] Bettauer was receiving 200–300 letters per day from readers asking for advice and commenting on his articles.'[18]

The women of Red Vienna

But for all the talk of emancipation and sexual fulfilment, it should be remembered that within the ideological framework of Austro-Marxism, women's lives were still significantly prescribed. In place of the 'triple burden', the all-male, more strait-laced Austro-Marxists assigned just two overriding roles to women in their ideal state, neither of which allowed for the sorts of wide-ranging freedoms and creativity enjoyed by their male peers. The first was to become a more competent, efficient and dedicated mother, deemed essential to creating the *neue Menschen* – 'population politics', in the jargon. The second was to be a more dedicated party member, in order to build socialism.

A multitude of ingenious ways were therefore devised to free up women's time so that they could devote themselves to these heroic tasks, from the radical 'rationalisation' of domestic work, reflected in new kitchen designs (of which more below), to the building of central laundries equipped with all the latest steam irons and presses. One experimental housing block in the early 1920s, the Heimhof on Pilgerimgasse, even did away with individual kitchens altogether, installing a big single kitchen block and dining-hall instead. For those who tired of the etiquette of making small talk to strangers, meals could also be delivered to individual apartments. (This particular block also had roof terraces for 'regular exercise under expert guidance'.)

Feminist historians have tended to criticise these policies as the 'redomestication' of women after a brief period of essential participation in the workforce during the First World War.[19] Even at the time, there were some fierce debates amongst the post-war generation of predominantly leftist women, many from assimilated Jewish backgrounds, about exactly what the New Woman in a socialist republic should be.

For the male politicians of Red Vienna, the ideal woman was 'modern, open, bold, relaxed, independent, hygiene conscious and athletic' – an almost impossible combination to maintain in a small apartment with a growing family. No matter; the socialists liked to contrast Vienna's New Woman with decadent, capitalist American 'flappers'. In particular, the Viennese fashion for bobbed hair – practical, unpretentious and easy to manage – was taken as the abiding symbol of the modern, athletic socialist woman. Reflecting such optimism, Marianne Pollak, an editor, wrote enthusiastically of the confluence of personal style, clothes and revolutionary potential in the mid-1920s:

The current fashion truly corresponds to the demands of the times. How splendid it is that our young women can run and jump in their short skirts! How much easier it is when they can clean and care for their hair more thoroughly! How practical it is to have a bobbed haircut on the sports field, at work, and in the kitchen! How pleasant it is for the working woman to bend and turn without strings and hoops pressing into her stomach! . . . And no forces of reaction wanting to force women back into the church, the kitchen, and the corset will rob us of this freedom of the human body![20]

But whatever the politicians of Red Vienna had in mind, women had their own ideas as to what the New Woman might be. Beyond the tramlines of Austro-Marxist ideology, there was a wider feeling of emancipation in the air, of women reacting against traditional roles and expectations in every sphere, even when it came to shaping Red Vienna's own politics. As so many of the council's more radical policies were devoted to improving the lives of women, so it was only natural that women should hold prominent posts on the council. Equally, many women were recruited with special expertise to help craft the council's groundbreaking policies, few of which had ever been tried before. Three of the most prominent were Käthe Leichter, Margarete Lihotzky and Charlotte Bühler. They were very different personalities, from very different backgrounds. But they all matched the new feminist politics with the Viennese hallmark of scientific rigour, with long-lasting consequences.

Of the three, Leichter was the activist and politician. She was born Marianne Katharina Pick in Vienna in 1895 to liberal Jewish parents. She was one of the first women to study political science at the University of Vienna. An ardent socialist and pacifist, she was a rare opponent of the frenzied rush to war in 1914. In 1921 she married a fellow activist, Otto Leichter, editor of a prominent socialist newspaper, *Die Arbeiter-Zeitung*. When the new republic was founded, she worked briefly for the federal government, but from the early 1920s she worked exclusively for Vienna's city council. From her perch as the head of what was, in effect, the female labour unit of the department of labour, Leichter roamed over the entirety of women's issues in Red Vienna from 1925 to 1934, promoting legislation to protect working women, household servants and home workers. She pushed tirelessly for equal pay for equal work.

To persuade the city council (and her critics) of her arguments, Leichter systematically collected statistics and data on every aspect of women's work and lives in Austria, publishing her findings in four comprehensive studies between 1927 and 1933.[21] They are still regarded as models of sociological research and used as standard works on the living conditions of women during the interwar period. The most famous of these was *How Do Viennese Homeworkers Live? An Investigation into the Working and Living Conditions of 1,000 Viennese Homeworkers*, published in 1928.

As one biographer has written, 'choosing to combine an academic with a "non-academic" commitment to those whose working and living conditions she wrote about, Leichter tried to bridge scientific research and political principles – an institutionally and discursively innovative approach.'[22] Leichter and her husband led a faction within the Social Democrats that chided male colleagues for not being radical enough; she herself constantly battled sexism within the party itself, and complained vociferously about how women were often relegated to lowly bureaucratic positions.

This courageous pioneer had a brutal fate. After the *Anschluss* in 1938, her husband and children escaped from Austria, but she was betrayed to the Gestapo by an informer and compelled to give herself up. In 1940 she was deported to Ravensbrück concentration camp and murdered two years later, along with 1,500 others at the Bernburg Euthanasia Centre.

The contribution of Margarete Lihotzky (later Schütte-Lihotzky) to Red Vienna was no less impressive than that of Leichter, especially in the context of the city's building programme. She was the youngest of the trio and the first woman to complete her architectural training at the Kunstgewerbeschule, Vienna's School of Applied Arts, receiving her diploma in 1919. Before then it was impossible for women to study architecture at either the Kunstgewerbeschule, founded in 1867, or the Technical University. She subsequently became the first woman to practise as an architect in Austria.

After a short time in Holland, she returned to Vienna in 1920 and quickly caught the eye of several architects involved in the Siedlung movement, including Adolf Loos himself and Josef Hoffmann, a former tutor at the Kunstgewerbeschule. An ardent socialist, as we have seen, she was intimately involved in the social and architectural movements of Red Vienna from the start, specialising in domestic interiors and in particular the kitchen space. Lihotzky's work on the kitchen was revolutionary. There is no record as to whether she was assigned to work on the kitchen specifically because she was a woman; whatever the case, she made the kitchen her own architectural domain.

When Lihotzky started work, few questioned the traditional role and importance of the *Wohnküche*, the standard kitchen/living room of the Austrian (and European) working-class dwelling. However, in a very Viennese fashion, from 1921 onwards Lihotzky applied the latest science and sociological methodologies to modernising this space. In particular, she used the time and motion studies of scientific management pioneered by the American Frederick Winslow Taylor, and used to great effect on America's early industrial production lines.

Her mission was to lift the load on the overtaxed housewife. So, after careful study of traditional patterns of work in the *Wohnküche*, she decided to separate off most of the tasks involved in cooking and washing into a separate area, which at first she called a *Wirtschaftsnische*, meaning, roughly, 'work niche'. This could be screened off from the *Wohnküche* by a curtain, and within it, for the first time, all the 'units' – sinks, cupboards, working surfaces, drawers – were joined up and manufactured together to make optimal use of the available space. Furthermore, as Eve Blau writes, 'Spatial relationships were also carefully calculated. For example, cutlery could be taken with the left hand from the work surface above the tub, rinsed in the sink, and returned to the drainboard, without the dishwasher having to stretch or pass anything from hand to hand.'[23]

So was born the 'fitted kitchen'. The first was installed in one of Red Vienna's new housing blocks in 1924. Quickly Lihotzky introduced a range of labour-saving devices and other innovations to make this new dedicated kitchen/work space as efficient as possible. Foldaway ironing boards were introduced, as were dish drainers, movable light fixtures and a cutting table with a waste catcher. The great advantage of this new design was that it could be mass-produced, and thus easily installed throughout the new housing estates, and not only in Vienna. In 1926, Lihotzky went to work for the Frankfurt city council, which had embarked on a similar housing programme. Given more time to develop the new kitchen concept, she eventually produced a fully developed prototype which was then mass-produced. The Frankfurt council installed about 10,000 of these prefabricated kitchens in their new workers' apartments. The 'Frankfurt kitchen', as it was known, remains a design icon.

Some women complained that the kitchens were too small, and of course the design was hard to modify in order to suit particular needs. Nonetheless, after the Second World War the popularity of the fitted kitchen boomed; by 1968, up to 40 per cent of all flats in Germany, for instance, had built-in kitchens. Furthermore, by this point the fitted kitchen had become an indispensable propaganda weapon in America's Cold War arsenal. Whereas the Soviets liked to show off Sputniks, and even a nuclear ice-breaker, at the various Cold War trade fairs, the Americans countered with the latest in consumer goods and domestic technology, most memorably the lavish General Electric versions of Lihotzky's fitted kitchen. The lemon-yellow kitchen on display at the 1959 American National Exhibition in Moscow was paradigmatic, especially as vice-president Richard Nixon made sure that he was on hand to demonstrate it all to the Soviet premier Nikita Khrushchev. Nixon argued that this was a supreme example of the benefits of Western consumer capitalism. The so-called 'kitchen debate' caught the headlines; the *New York*

Times suggested it was 'perhaps the most startling personal international incident' since the end of the war.[24]

The Bühler school

Charlotte Bühler's path to Red Vienna was very different. As we saw in Chapter 4, she and her husband were specifically imported from Berlin to support and develop the city council's educational reforms. Unlike the politically engaged Marxist Leichter, Bühler remained studiously academic throughout her time in Vienna, a 'proper German mandarin', in the words of one admirer. Yet while she might have maintained a critical distance from the intellectual maelstrom around her, she was also clearly a compelling and inspirational teacher, particularly for women; some switched courses solely to be taught by her. Consequently, much of Red Vienna's young female talent was either educated by her directly, at the Institute of Psychology and the university, or passed through her sphere of influence at some point. Her impact on this generation was immense. The consequent impact of the Bühler students alone deserves a book.

Bühler was instrumental in opening up new horizons for her women students in every respect. Arriving in Vienna in 1923, she was already a renowned expert in her own field of psychology, a profession that was still largely male-dominated. Yet Charlotte seemed to be a living refutation of Weininger's absurd theories about professional women. At twenty-nine years old, she was still relatively young for a senior academic, and strikingly handsome, not afraid to dress and behave as a fashionable woman. This was a powerful combination. It was certainly disconcerting for her male peers, and even some of her female students. One of them later remembered her shock when attending her first Bühler lecture, as Charlotte entered sporting red nail varnish.

It is possible to reimagine the impact that she must have had amongst the mutton-chop whiskers at the Faculty of Philosophy by strolling round the *Arkadenhof* today. In contrast to the male busts, Bühler's sculpture portrait, by Thomas Baumann, is original and arresting. With her trademark pearls and a dazzling ruff of silver surrounding her intelligent, open face in a blaze of glamour, she certainly does not look intimidated by her male confederates.

Charlotte Bühler presides over her peers in the University of Vienna's Arkadenhof.

Intellectually, Bühler opened up exciting areas of study for those that she mentored, sometimes related to subjects of particular interest to women. Always, she encouraged her students to apply the latest techniques in psychology and the social sciences to their chosen specialisations, including statistics and 'depth interviewing', with enduring results. Two of the most inventive such research projects were studies of pre- and post-pubescent working-class schoolgirls carried out by two of her star graduates, Margarete Rada and Hildegard Hetzer. Rada's report was particularly revealing as it showed how knowledgeable these young girls were about sexual matters – including pre- and extra-marital affairs. They picked this up from their daily experiences in overcrowded apartments, particularly the shared bedrooms. In short, summarises the historian Helmut Gruber, unlike their middle-class peers, 'for these girls, sexuality was a matter-of-fact part of their daily lives, which was a cumulative part of their experience from the earliest years'.[25] This evidence for early sexual maturation startled many of the reports' priggish Austro-Marxist readers.

Another star pupil of Bühler was Herta Herzog. Born in 1910 to a Viennese middle-class family rendered almost destitute by the post-war inflation, the remarkable Herzog later described how she endured post-war Vienna by living off 'a kind of turnip [that] doubled for most regular food, which was scarce and severely rationed'.[26] Precociously bright, she enrolled at the University of Vienna in 1928 to study Greek, Latin and Archaeology, but switched to Psychology after encountering the Bühlers in her first year.

Under their guidance she started applying psychology and linguistic analysis to the nascent field of audience research for radio and films. Her PhD thesis, investigating how radio listeners could determine the main characteristics of individuals from their broadcast voice alone, involved the first mass-audience research project in Austria. After recovering from polio, which left her with a lame right arm for the rest of her life, she worked at the Institute of

Psychology from 1932 onwards, and participated, albeit only tangentially, in the Marienthal project with Paul Lazarsfeld, whom she married and moved to America with in 1935. There she helped to found the field of communication studies and pioneered the use of 'depth interviewing'.[27]

Herzog, like most of the Viennese women of this era, was not given to introspection and did not write an autobiography. Neither, unlike her male contemporaries, did she go out of her way to help others record her life, despite her manifold achievements (she worked into her nineties and died at 100). Self-effacing to a fault, she was thus occluded from the standard accounts of several fundamental methodological developments in sociology and market research for which she was in fact largely responsible, notably the creation of the 'focus group'. This controversy, and her role as one of the founders of the modern advertising industry – 'the most powerful woman on Madison Avenue', as she was dubbed – will be discussed further in Chapter 10. Her formative role in the industry was acknowledged, if not very flatteringly, with a walk-on part in the television series *Mad Men*; in the first series she is thinly disguised in the figure of the rather sinister Dr Greta Guttman.

She conceded that she had not been 'very good . . . at integrating personal and professional life',[28] a trait that she shared with many of the Viennese of her generation. In both her marriages, to Lazarsfeld and later to an American academic, family and personal time was relegated solely to the weekends. If her generation of Viennese middle-class women did not conform to the Austro-Marxists' prescribed role for them, as mothers of *die neuen Menschen*, many went to the other extreme and buried themselves in their new professions. Another of those seven women belatedly added to the university's Valhalla was Marie Jahoda, the Bühler student who had worked on the Marienthal project. She was equally self-effacing, despite being one of the founders of modern empirical sociology.

A further Bühler protégée was the psychologist Else Frenkel. Born in Lemberg, Galicia (now Lviv, Ukraine) in 1908, she studied under Karl Bühler at the University of Vienna and was research assistant to Charlotte from 1931 to 1938, before escaping to America where she married another alumnus of the Bühlers, Egon Brunswik. He had taken up a research post at the University of California at Berkeley the previous year and Else moved there with him.

Frenkel was an integral part of the research team, including the German sociologist Theodor Adorno, that produced *The Authoritarian Personality* in 1950. Drawing on her work with the Bühlers, Frenkel-Brunswik contributed to the quantitative side of the work, conducting interviews to delve into the family backgrounds that tend to produce such a personality. In fact, she might well have done most of the work on this much fêted book herself; Adorno, to whom the book is often attributed, contributed relatively little.[29] Published in the shadow of Nazism and the Holocaust, *The Authoritarian Personality* was one of the most influential sociology texts of the time.

New science, new woman

With normal career paths in research and academia often blocked by misogyny and anti-Semitism at the university, so this first generation of well-educated women gravitated towards those more independent institutions, such as the Bühlers' Institute of Psychology, which embraced them. For the same reason, they also tended to plunge into newer, more experimental disciplines, such as physics and biology. These sciences lacked the long-entrenched male hierarchies of philosophy or medicine. In the first year of female undergraduate enrolment at the university, one-third of the new intake chose mathematics and physics.[30] Fortunately, Vienna had institutions beyond the university to scoop up female talent, run by scientists who welcomed and nurtured the contributions of women. The most impressive in this respect was the Institute for Radium Research, specialising in the study of radium and uranium, leading onto nuclear physics.

These were relatively new disciplines, which encouraged a more imaginative approach as to how they were studied, as well as *who* studied them. The Radium Institute was endowed in 1908 by a wealthy lawyer called Karl Kupelwieser, another instance of Jewish bourgeois patronage of the sciences during this era. Kupelwieser had studied law at the University of Vienna, and had subsequently married Bertha Wittgenstein. Kupelwieser was the legal adviser to her father, and himself bought a rolling mill in Bohemia. Having amassed a fortune, he proceeded to give much of it away, supporting a variety of social and scientific projects before putting up the money for the Radium Institute, with premises on Boltzmanngasse.

During the interwar years, the institute was one of Vienna's most prized possessions. There were only four similar research laboratories in the world: that of Marie Curie in Paris; those of Ernest Rutherford in Manchester and Cambridge; and the Laboratorium Hahn-Meitner (as it would later be called) at the Kaiser Wilhelm Institute for Chemistry in Berlin.

Vienna was well-placed to share the lead in this field – apart from anything it enjoyed easy access to Europe's only source of uranium pitchblende for experimental work, at the Joachimsthal mines in Bohemia. These provided plenty of residue to the Curies, which they used to identify polonium and radium. As researchers at the time had little notion of the adverse side-effects of working with radium, so the Viennese institute (like the Curies' laboratories in Paris) could be a hazardous place to work; four grams of the stuff was stored with few precautions in the basement.[31] The windows were left open in contaminated laboratories, but that was about the sum of the safety measures. Consequently, fingers and hands could often be severely burned. The (usually) friendly rivalry between these research centres produced most of the early advances in nuclear physics, leading, after the Second World War, to the dawn of the atomic age. Some of the most important work, though, was done by the women graduates of Vienna's Radium

Institute. The city council was a strong supporter of the institute's work too, as the anatomist Tandler grasped the contribution that radiology could make to improving medical treatment in the city's hospitals.

In the first instance, however, the institute's success owed much to two men, the physicists Franz Exner and Stefan Meyer. The former was a scion of one of the Austro-Hungarian empire's most important academic families, a pioneer in many fields, including radioactivity. One of his assistants was the Nobel Prize-winning Erwin Schrödinger. By 1910 Exner was the grand old man of his subject and a natural choice to be the first (rather hands-off) director of the institute, although he soon handed over this duty to his former student, the youthful, brilliant Meyer.

Apart from their other attributes, both men were consistent advocates of integrating women into the very male world of experimental physics, and science more generally. Every Saturday night, Exner hosted a salon – called 'Exner's Circle' – for the younger physicists, and every day at the Radium Institute, at 4 p.m. precisely, he presided over a convivial teatime gathering where men and women were made to feel equally welcome. Meyer was just as encouraging; the institute was even designed with women's toilets, a rarity at the time. Meyer, who wrote the first German-language book on radioactivity, was himself Jewish, so was also supportive of Jewish women working at the institute. Consequently, the Radium Institute was as much a haven as anything. About a third of its scientists were women, an extraordinarily high proportion not only for the time – but since.[32] Maria Rentetzi's comparison with Rutherford's Cavendish laboratory is instructive. In 1921, the Cavendish group photo of researchers shows one woman out of twenty-three people, and in 1932, just two out of thirty-nine. One of those female researchers who joined Vienna's institute in the 1930s was Berta Karlik. After the war she became the director, a post she held until 1973. She was also the first woman to gain a full professorship at the University of Vienna, as late as 1956.

171

Several women from the institute made groundbreaking contributions to their fields. Elizabeth Rona, for example, born in Budapest, joined in 1924 to work on radioactive isotopes. Her earlier work encouraged the later mass spectrographic and heavy-water studies performed by other scientists. She became the leading expert on dealing with polonium, and her work was later used in the official American studies on the effects of radiation poisoning.

Marietta Blau, born in 1894, developed ways to visualise the paths of high-energy nuclear particles and atomic events using special photographic emulsions. The images so produced helped launch the field of particle physics, and in particular enabled scientists to study reactions caused by cosmic-ray events. Yet before taking up her post at the Radium Institute, Marietta Blau tried to get a lectureship at the university and was told baldly to her face: 'You are a woman and a Jew and together this is too much.'[33]

The most important alumna of the Radium Institute, however, was Lise Meitner, born in 1878, a daughter of Leopoldstadt, to whence her parents had come from Moravia (see image p. 148). A precocious talent, in 1905 she became the first woman to earn a doctorate in physics, under the supervision of Exner, from the University of Vienna (and by some accounts only the second in the world). Close to Meyer, she worked at the Radium Institute for a few years before moving to the Kaiser Wilhelm Institute for Chemistry in Berlin, where she became the first female professor of physics in Germany, working closely with the physicist Otto Hahn. Their primary achievement was to conduct the research that led directly to the process of nuclear fission, by bombarding thorium with neutrons to produce different isotopes. It was Meitner, together with her Viennese nephew, Otto Frisch, who first described this process in a paper that they co-authored for the journal *Nature* in February 1939. They gave it the name 'fission', a term that Frisch borrowed from biology; 'binary fission' is a form of asexual reproduction whereby a single organism divides into two independent organisms.

Once outlined, this principle led directly to the subsequent manufacture of the first atomic bomb. Frisch was visiting at the University of Birmingham when the Second World War broke out, thus preventing a return to his post in Copenhagen. In 1940, together with another émigré scientist, Rudolf Peierls, and with war in mind, he outlined for the first time how, in practice, an atomic bomb could be detonated. The 'Frisch–Peierls Memorandum', as it was known in Whitehall, kick-started Britain's project to build a bomb, codenamed 'Tube Alloys', later superseded by the Anglo-Canadian-American Manhattan Project. Frisch was an integral part of both ventures, responsible for calculating the exact amount of enriched uranium that was needed to provoke reactions in Fat Man and Little Boy, the atomic bombs dropped on Nagasaki and Hiroshima. He returned to Britain in 1946 to take up the post of head of nuclear physics at the government's new atomic research centre at Harwell, whilst also teaching at Cambridge University for the next thirty years.

Aunt Lise, however, had a more difficult time than her nephew after their theoretical breakthrough. As a Jew, she was forced to flee from her Berlin laboratory in 1938. To the consternation and anger of many of her friends, it was her colleague Otto Hahn who was awarded the 1944 Nobel Prize in Chemistry, specifically for *her* description of nuclear fission. Her biographer, Ruth Lewin Sime, has chronicled in detail why Meitner was overlooked; petty jealousies and interdisciplinary nit-picking told against her, but misogyny almost certainly played a role as well.[34] She was nominated for a Nobel Prize in Physics more than twenty times up to 1965, but to no avail. Marietta Blau was also nominated several times for a Nobel Prize in both physics and chemistry, but never won.

None of this seemed to trouble Meitner, at least not outwardly. If she did quietly crave a bit of fame, she was amply rewarded by a trip to America immediately after the end of the war where she was celebrated, unnervingly, as the 'Mother of the Atomic Bomb'. Meitner eventually retired to Britain to live near her relatives, including Frisch, and died in Cambridge in 1968.

The scandalous Lady Bluetooth

Not all those who made lasting contributions to science were formally trained, or worked at well-funded institutes. This was certainly true of the extraordinary Hedy Lamarr, the film actress and inventor. Or, in the order she would have preferred, inventor and film actress.

Far ahead of her time, Lamarr defied all the gendered conventions of her age, regularly slipping the bonds of the fixed roles of wife and studio starlet prescribed for her by society. Dubbed 'the most beautiful woman in the world', she enjoyed fame, but always regretted that her work in films overshadowed her more substantive achievements in science. 'Any girl can be glamorous,' she once remarked dismissively. 'All you have to do is stand still and look stupid.' Inventing was another matter entirely. She was fortunate, however, that she lived long enough to glimpse how her work on radio waves would transform the world, even if she never received the credit that she deserved, nor made any money from it.

Hedwig Kiesler, as she was born, was an admirable example of the scientific autodidact, a product of all those childhood laboratories and amateur tinkerers on the Ringstrasse. Her father was an assimilated Jew from Lemberg, now Lviv, a successful banker who also took an avid interest in new technology. He passed this enthusiasm on to his daughter during their long walks together around Vienna as he explained all the city's latest gadgets and innovations.

Lamarr always wanted to act, though, and spent her teenage years in small films in Vienna after being taken on by the theatrical producer and film director Max Reinhardt. She moved to Berlin, where in 1933 she first broke convention by appearing, very briefly, semi-naked in a mainstream film. Lamarr was only seventeen when she appeared in *Ecstasy*, by a Czech director, and later claimed to have been duped into the nude scenes. Her appearance was hardly pornographic, as her biographer argues, 'but sensational for the time'.[35] Her father was inevitably upset, but the role made her instantly famous, not to say notorious.

The next convention she broke was marriage, when she ran away from a ghastly husband, something that became a habit. Friedrich Mandl, the first of six spouses, was the third-richest man in Austria and a right-wing arms manufacturer. Lamarr was expected to play a new role, that of trophy wife, which filled her with boredom. 'He had not married me, he had collected me, exactly like a business prize,' she later recalled.[36] So, she absconded to London.

Here, in 1937, she met film producer Louis B. Mayer, head of MGM, who recruited her for the studio, changing her screen name to Hedy Lamarr. She was soon appearing with many of Hollywood's biggest names in a series of modest successes (*Algiers*, *Ziegfeld Girl*), alongside some more forgettable offerings.

Crucially, the money allowed her to indulge a youthful passion for science. Breaking convention again, instead of socialising with the cast and crew between takes on set, she studied in a laboratory that she had set up in her trailer. Often lonely, she would spend the evenings in the drawing room of her house where she had installed an 'inventor's corner', with drafting table and lamp. The tycoon (and her sometime lover) Howard Hughes was one of the very few who appreciated her scientific side, especially after she successfully helped to redesign the wings of his flying boat.

Frustrated at being typecast in films, after 1940 she determined to contribute to the Allied cause at her drawing board. With the war at sea going badly, particularly in the Atlantic, she focused on the problem of torpedo guidance technology, aware that it was proving too easy for the enemy to jam Allied torpedoes and send them off course. At this point in the war American torpedoes were especially feeble. Normally, torpedoes were directed on a single frequency, which was simple to use, but easy to interrupt. Instead, Lamarr proposed a new 'frequency-hopping' signal. Thus, if a radio transmitter and receiver were synchronised to change their tuning simultaneously, together hopping from frequency to frequency apparently randomly, then the radio signal passing between them would be much harder to jam. Lamarr's system envisaged eighty-eight possible frequencies.

A few inventors, such as Nikola Tesla, had described this process before, but only partially. Lamarr, together with a friend – avant-garde composer and pianist George Antheil – developed the idea into a working mechanism. They consequently filed a patent for what they called a 'Secret Communication System', which was granted number 2292387A in 1942.[37] The Navy, however, never used it, partly, it seems, because Lamarr had filed the patent under her birth name, Hedy Kiesler, and the Navy was suspicious of any ideas from an 'enemy alien'.

Nonetheless, 'Spread Spectrum' technology, as it is known, was subsequently used for a variety of military applications, including secret communications systems. Furthermore, in the mid-1970s, manufacturers jumped at the obvious commercial applications of the idea. Bluetooth, a short-link radio technology designed for portable devices, applied frequency-hopping spread spectrum (FHSS) to equipment from the late 1980s onwards; the first hands-free mobile phone headset appeared in 1999. Direct sequence spread spectrum (DSSS), a development of the more basic FHSS, was used for wi-fi, or wireless local area network (WLAN) technology, designed to replace cabling in various fixed electronic devices such as desktop computers. The Global Positioning System (GPS) also uses DSSS technology, as do unmanned aerial vehicles.

In 2009, Microsoft published a study of the economic value of *just* spread-spectrum wi-fi in homes, retail and hospitals, arriving at a sum of between $16 and $37 billion a year. This, they calculated, was only about 15 per cent of the potential market.[38] For her part, Lamarr received no money from the technology that she had helped to invent, as her patent had lapsed in 1959.

After the war she started to struggle in Hollywood. She had one enormous hit in 1949, playing opposite Victor Mature in *Samson and Delilah*, directed by Cecil B. DeMille. But, breaking convention again, she co-founded her own production company to develop scripts with more interesting parts for women. She starred in a few successes, but after losing millions of dollars on her own productions, she increasingly retreated from the business. Despite her numerous marriages, she spent the last thirty-five years of her life single and died in 2000 at the age of eighty-five, secluded, virtually penniless and totally unrepentant. She continued to invent, for instance suggesting design modifications for Concorde. Her ashes were scattered in the Vienna Woods. Only in 1997 did her scientific contribution begin to be recognised with induction into the United States National Inventors Hall of Fame.

Anna Freud and children's rights: the discreet revolutionary

Another, more formally trained, female scientist in the Austrian capital was Anna Freud. Often regarded as merely a terrier-like guardian of her father's reputation, this assessment scarcely does her justice. As her biographer Elisabeth Young-Bruehl and others have shown, she was remarkably significant in her own right, even if always within the broad parameters of Freudian orthodoxy. Determined, fine-looking, generous and good-hearted (unlike her father), Anna Freud is an outstanding example of how the interwar generation of Viennese applied the scientific innovation of liberal Vienna to such a wide variety of fields, yielding long-lasting and, in this case, humane results.

As we saw in the last chapter, Anna Freud was an integral part of the group of radical 'second-generation' psychoanalysts, such as August Aichhorn and Wilhelm Reich, who pulled the discipline in fresh and unexpected directions. Anna Freud's two most important works of that period, *An Introduction to the Technique of Child Analysis*, of 1927, and *The Ego and the Mechanisms of Defence*, published in 1936, both owed much to this younger coterie of Viennese psychoanalysts.

However, it was only after she arrived in Britain in 1938 that she started to flourish in her own right, especially after being released from the duty of care to her father (he died the following year after a long illness). The house that Freud's London followers had found

Much more than an orthodox Freudian: Anna with her father.

for him, 20 Maresfield Gardens, in Hampstead, remained Anna's base for the rest of her life.

Her principal achievements were threefold. Firstly, she did much to feminise psychoanalysis, a discipline that up to that point had been dominated almost entirely by rather grand central European men. Consequently, she helped to refocus the discipline on child-rearing, child psychology and development in particular. As one expert on Viennese culture, Edward Timms, wrote, she successfully brought 'Freudian theory down to earth, helping to reverse the patriarchal assumptions that had shaped psychoanalysis for fifty years and to shift the focus towards adequate mothering'.[39] Secondly, bravely, she ventured beyond the confines of orthodox psychoanalysis to combine it with direct observation of people's behaviour, in order to form a more rounded diagnosis of a patient's condition. One modern writer on Anna Freud, Nick Midgley, has called this the 'double approach'.[40] Lastly, in the 1970s, towards the end of her life, in conjunction with the Yale Law School in America, Freud co-wrote several groundbreaking texts on children and the law. In all three areas, Freud's views were, in their day, considered to be highly contentious, nay heretical. Now they are considered commonplace.

Many of her ideas were developed in the succession of nurseries that she ran in Vienna, and later in London. In the last year or so of her time in Austria, Anna Freud had set up an experimental nursery paid for by her American friend Edith Jackson, after whom it was named. The nursery was innovative on two counts; it encouraged the study of children under two years of age, which was unheard of at the time, and, secondly, it depended on close observation and meticulous record-keeping, much more Bühler's style of work than traditional Freudianism allowed. The children were mostly from poorer families, also unusual for the time; their parents were only too happy for the free childcare.

Her work was carried over to Britain where she set up the famous Hampstead War Nursery in 1940, mainly for orphans from the

Blitz, or young children separated from their parents for long periods by the exigencies of war.[41] As it turned out, these were ideal circumstances to study child–parent bonding and what is now called attachment theory. For the first time, children's reactions to extended periods away from their parents were carefully documented on index cards, forming the raw data for the nursery's publications.

This methodology owed much to the Bühler students who worked for Freud. Ilse Hellman, for example, had been a research assistant to Bühler. Hellman knew little of psychoanalysis, but her close observational work later confirmed beyond all doubt that inadequate, poor parenting during a child's earliest phases would result in 'irreversible damage'.[42] Other Bühler trainees who had escaped Vienna with Freud included Josefine Stross. Unusually, she had trained as a paediatrician and psychoanalyst in Vienna, and had looked after the sick and elderly Sigmund Freud during his flight from Vienna. She also spent thirteen years as paediatrician to a group of children who had been flown to England from the concentration camp at Terezín, of which more below.

Early on, Anna Freud realised that the policy of evacuating children to 'safe' spaces – like the nursery, or the countryside – might spare them one kind of danger, but it also caused 'broken attachments' with parents. The Hampstead Nursery thus did as much as possible to encourage parents to visit their children. Unlike typical British nurseries of the day, which had remarkably limited 'visiting hours', she gave her children's mothers and fathers free access, day and night. She also recruited male conscientious objectors to the nursery in the place of absent fathers, acknowledging men's important, but often overlooked, contribution to child rearing.

One of these recruits was James Robertson, a Quaker who became the chief social worker at the nursery. Based on his own experiences there, he went on to revolutionise children's hospitals, drawing on Freud's work to show how damaging the separation of children from their parents in hospital could be. Shockingly, at the time London's biggest teaching hospitals, such as St Thomas's, only allowed parents to see their children *asleep*, from 7 p.m. to 8 p.m., while St Bartholomew's permitted visits only on Wednesdays, between 2 p.m. and 3.30 p.m.[43] Based on his Bühler-inspired observational training, Robertson formulated a celebrated theory of children's responses to being hospitalised without a mother, progressing through a three-step cycle of protest, despair, followed by denial and detachment.

His insistence on prioritising the well-being of children in hospital angered the medical profession, which resented the interference in what they regarded as their own clinical domain. To overcome such resistance, Robertson (and a colleague, John Bowlby, who had written a widely-read report on maternal deprivation for the World Health Organization) made a half-hour film on a shoestring budget about the experiences of a child (Laura) spending a week on a ward for an operation. *A Two-Year-Old Goes to Hospital*, released in 1952, chronicles Laura's despair and emotional deterioration as she endures the intrusions of an ever-changing cast of unfamiliar and apparently insensitive doctors and nurses. The film was a devastating critique of the standard practices of the time and proved seminal in changing access to paediatric wards and in highlighting the importance of bonding between parents and children more generally.

After more hard years of campaigning by Robertson, Bowlby and others, a government report of 1959 finally recommended parental visiting for over-fives and living-in for under-fives, after which Robertson wrote that any hospital that didn't follow these guidelines was guilty of 'cruelty'.[44] It was a major and often overlooked step towards a more humane society. By 1964, 80 per cent of British hospitals were allowing daily visiting compared to just 23 per cent in 1952. The British reformers in this area were also influential in shifting attitudes further afield, in America, Australia, Canada and Europe.

The work of Anna Freud and colleagues at the nursery thus had a profound practical impact on the rights of children in society generally, and more particularly in professional care. Freud constantly pressed to apply psychoanalysis to different fields, such as paediatrics, always with an eye to the real-life results of her work. In London, for instance, she held a regular workshop with many of the capital's leading paediatricians to discuss how psychology and psychoanalysis could inform the care of children on their hospital wards. Like Reich and her other Viennese contemporaries, Anna Freud firmly believed that psychoanalysis could help to change the world for the better and that as many people as possible should benefit from its insights.

These attitudes were very evident in her last great campaign, to promote the rights of children in family law, a natural extension of her efforts to promote children's mental and emotional health in medicine. In 1961, already in her mid-sixties, Anna Freud was visited by the dean of the Yale Law School, Eugene Rostow, who invited her to join the faculty as a visiting lecturer. This she did, teaming up with two other professors – Joseph Goldstein, who was already interested in the application of psychoanalytic ideas to law, and Al Solnit of the Yale Child Study Center. This collaboration produced three jointly authored books that were to transform the standing of children in America's, and later Britain's, legal systems.

The first of the trilogy, *Beyond the Best Interests of the Child*, was the most consequential, and has been described as 'the most discussed book on law and family ever published'.[45] It considered the appropriate guidelines that the courts should employ to decide on child placements, while the second volume, *Before the Best Interests of the Child*, focused on the issue of whether the state was justified in modifying parent–child relationships. Perhaps the most controversial proposition in these books was that the courts should pay more regard to what they called a 'psychological parent', the person:

who, on a continuing, day-to-day basis, through interaction, companionship, interplay, and mutuality fulfils the child's psychological need for a parent, as well as the child's physical needs . . . this may be a biological, adoptive, foster or common-law parent, or any other person. There is no presumption in favour of any of these after the initial assignment of birth.

Thus, they maintained that placement decisions had to be based on the child's need for continuity of relationships, rather than the rights of a parent. Of course, real-life custody battles would rarely be clear-cut, which is why they contended that the guiding principle for family law decision-makers should be what was 'least detrimental . . . for safeguarding the child's growth and development'.[46] They also argued the case for children to have legal representation in their own right.

As Midgley argues, many of these ideas have 'entered common practice', particularly putting children at the heart of the family law process. Anna Freud died in 1982, and was cremated at Golders Green Crematorium where her ashes were placed next to those of her parents in 'Freud Corner'. Here, the funerary urns of many members of the Freud family came to be deposited. In 1986, as Anna Freud had requested, her London home was converted into the Freud Museum. Overwhelmingly, it commemorates her father. Even in death, filial piety overshadowed her own accomplishments.

For all Anna Freud's achievements, however, and the lustre of her name, she certainly did not have the field of psychoanalysis to herself in Britain. In many ways she was overshadowed by another Viennese immigrant to Britain, Melanie Klein. The tussles between Freudians and Kleinians have largely defined psychoanalysis ever since.

Klein had been born into a Jewish family in 1882. She married early and suffered from depression after having children, which persuaded her to go into psychoanalysis. It was while observing her own children that she developed her 'play technique' of therapy for youngsters, arguing that this was akin to using the 'free association' technique with adults. She was one of the first to apply the theories of psychoanalysis to very young children, from the age of two onwards. Her paper on 'early analysis', presented a number of times in 1924, marked, as Edward Timms writes, a 'decisive shift in the development of psychoanalysis; the emergence of a female perspective' and a new interest in child analysis.[47]

Klein moved to Britain in 1926, where her theories diverged increasingly from Freudian orthodoxy. Whereas Freudians believed in a chronological psychosexual development in five stages, from the oral to the genital, Klein posited a 'psychic-position' theory, whereby young children as they grew up oscillated between certain positions such as the 'paranoid-schizoid' and 'depressive'.

Given these differences, there was bound to be a clash when the Freuds arrived in Britain in 1938. They brought with them the complete German edition of Sigmund Freud's writings, and this 'gave the Viennese the feeling that they were stewards of truth and orthodoxy in psychoanalytical theory and practice'.[48] Klein, however, was a bold and feisty adversary, and the British Psychoanalytic Society quickly developed into two camps. Kleinians and Freudians tried to thrash out their differences in a series of debates in London from 1942 to 1944 called the 'Controversial Discussions'. In sum, these debates attempted to answer many of the same dilemmas that worried the Viennese economists and mathematicians during the same period, mainly concerning methodology. Klein emphasised the role of 'unconscious fantasies', and free association – regarded by many as inherently untestable and unverifiable – whereas she had little time for Anna Freud's double approach employing close observation.

These wrangles had one very practical consequence. The two sides eventually agreed to disagree, thus splitting formal psychoanalytic training in Britain into opposing camps, each with their own protocols. Later, a third independent (or middle) group emerged, which became more dominant. Generally, the Freudians congregated institutionally at the various iterations of Anna Freud's Hampstead

Nursery, the latest of which is the Anna Freud Centre in Islington, London, while Kleinians clustered at the Tavistock Clinic, originally founded in 1920 and now the Tavistock and Portman NHS Foundation Trust.

Art as therapy and the Theresienstadt drawings

If Anna Freud campaigned for children's rights in a legal and medical context, more Viennese women developed the use of art and drawing as an important therapeutic tool for children, and later adults as well. Three Viennese-born women were mainly responsible for the evolution and popularisation of art therapy, namely Emmy Zweybrück, Friedl Dicker-Brandeis and Edith Kramer. Zweybrück and Kramer both became famous in America for books and courses on children's art and art therapy.

All three benefited from the pioneering work of the Secessionist artist Franz Cizek, a professor at the School of Applied Art. Significantly, as in the case of nuclear physics at the Radium Institute, the school's staff – especially Cizek – were less hidebound by tradition than elsewhere, teaching new disciplines to new cohorts of students, including women. Generally, they were keen to experiment as they went along, and this was certainly true of Cizek. He was born in northern Bohemia in 1865, came to Vienna when he was aged nineteen and died in the city in 1946.

Cizek was the first to systematically apply the liberating potential of art to children – by turning art on its head. Rather than merely using it as a medium to push children into the adult world, through imitative drawing and art historical research, Cizek explored line and colour to encourage playfulness and creativity. Only a child, he argued, could show adults 'revelations of elemental creative power, *ur*-primitive art'. Children aged five to nine years old came to his classes once a week 'to express themselves'.[49] This famous Juvenile Art Class was available free of charge to all Viennese children.

Zweybrück, Dicker-Brandeis and Kramer were all inspired by Cizek's pedagogy. Zweybrück, born in 1890, studied under Cizek and set up her own school employing his techniques in 1915, running it until forced to emigrate to America in 1934. She was also a skilled children's book illustrator, and in Vienna produced toys and art products as well. This stood her in good stead in her adopted country, where she took a job from 1939 to 1956 as the artistic director of the American Crayon Company, the dominant manufacturer of crayons, chalk, blackboards, pencils and much else. From this innocuous-sounding perch, she popularised the benefits of art for children in a stream of best-selling texts, such as *The Stencil Book*, published in 1937, and *Hands at Work*, from 1946.[50]

Dicker-Brandeis was also taught by Cizek, in a textile class.[51] Born in Vienna in 1898, Dicker-Brandeis went further than her mentor, combining his teaching on children and art with her own deep interest in psychology and Freud's new discipline of psychoanalysis. She studied in Vienna at the private school of the Swiss modernist painter Johannes Itten, who shared her dual interests. An ardent communist and political activist, she followed him to the Bauhaus school in Germany where she also studied bookbinding, typography and printmaking. Returning to Vienna, in the spirit of Red Vienna's educational pedagogy she taught kindergarten teachers how to teach art to children, as a medium of self-expression rather than as a technique to be mastered.

Dicker-Brandeis married her husband, Pavel Brandeis, in 1936, and after several years teaching art to children in Prague they were both rounded up as Jews by the Nazi occupation army. In December 1942 they were deported to the town of Terezín (Theresienstadt in German) in Bohemia, now in the northern Czech Republic. The previous year the town had effectively been turned into a Jewish ghetto, to serve as a transit camp for central Europe's Jews; from here about 87,000 would eventually be taken to the gas chambers in the east. But Terezín had a more insidious purpose. It was also designed by the Nazis as a 'show camp', to fool Red Cross and other human-itarian visitors into believing that the prisoners of the Reich were held in tolerable conditions and that the rumours of death camps were just that, rumours. The hoax succeeded all too well.

Almost all that Dicker-Brandeis managed to take with her to the camp was a suitcase of crayons, art materials, and dyed sheets, to use as costumes and scenery in children's plays. On arrival at Terezín, she was duly assigned to help with the youngsters. Split up from her husband, she lived in an all-female barracks. It was on her own initiative that the doughty Dicker-Brandeis started giving undercover art lessons, as formal 'school' was not allowed by the Schutzstaffel (SS) guards. Art classes, with a student posted as a look-out, were mainly held in the attics of her building, where there was less danger that the SS would suddenly burst in.

Generally, Dicker-Brandeis used art in this context to make the girls and boys feel as emotionally secure as possible amidst the trauma, despair and starvation around them.[52] 'She wanted us to get away and into a nice world,' recalled one of her pupils.[53] They formed a group which they called a *Maagal*, a community of peoples in the Jewish lexicon. 'To enter the Maagal,' remembered another of her students, 'we tried to be good, tolerant, considerate, orderly and clean – we strived for perfection.'[54] This alone sustained many through years at the camp.

In her only known statement about what she was trying to achieve at Terezín, written as a lecture given to other teachers in 1943, Dicker-Brandeis expressed her approach as follows:

To insist on the correct form of expression is not the way to go because it is the spontaneous drawing that matters, and although children need to be guided, the main thing is to provide opportunity for their own expression and to wait to see what will come about. As children independently choose, find, and work at their form, they gain courage and truth and unfold their imagination, power to judge, ability to observe, endurance, and later (very much later), taste.[55]

Sometimes, though, the children were allowed 'free art', when they could draw what they wanted. Then the more sinister pencil images would emerge of hangings, and prisoners burying their dead.

Dicker-Brandeis herself was transported from Terezín to be murdered in Auschwitz in October 1944. Before leaving she managed to pack about 5,000 of the children's drawings in two suitcases and leave them with a trusted friend. She always insisted that her pupils sign their pictures, and it is deeply affecting that they did so, for of the nearly 660 authors of the drawings, 550 were killed in the Holocaust. Of the 15,000 children who passed through Theresienstadt during the war, only about 1,000 survived. After the war, the suitcases were delivered to what remained of the once-flourishing Jewish community in Prague; thanks to her care, the drawings are now mostly preserved in the Jewish Museum there.

Together, they form one of the most moving and poignant records of the Holocaust. They detail, for instance, the obsessive interest in food among the inmates of Theresienstadt as the meagre rations were steadily reduced. 'I went to see my uncle in [his] barracks,' remembered one young prisoner, 'and I saw them throw out potato peelings and ten people threw themselves on the little pile and fought for them.'[56] About 34,000 people in the camp, mainly the elderly, died of malnutrition and starvation. Epidemics of typhoid, tuberculosis and infectious diarrhoea spread through the camp as well.

These celebrated drawings, which have since been exhibited around the world, are not, however, Dicker-Brandeis's only legacy. Her main pupil and disciple, Edith Kramer, born in Vienna in 1916, managed to flee to America after the *Anschluss*, taking her teacher's pedagogy with her. Kramer had trained under the 'passionate and temperamental' Dicker-Brandeis from the age of fifteen, so was thoroughly familiar with her mentor's work. She settled happily into New York; as she later recalled, 'The bohemian environment of Vienna . . . in 1938 was not so different from Greenwich Village of 1938, so it was not such a terrible culture shock when I moved here.'[57] Her parents were outré even by the bohemian Viennese standards of the day. They were both Marxists and enjoyed an open marriage.

As Kramer wrote. 'When I began to work as an art therapist in 1950 with underprivileged, traumatized children of greater New York, I applied what I had learned as an assistant to Friedl in her work with children in Prague.' At first Kramer worked with children and adolescents at the Wiltwyck School in New York, a residential institution for juvenile delinquents. From her own experiences in New York, she herself wrote the two foundational texts on the subjects, *Art Therapy in a Children's Community* and *Art as Therapy with Children*, published in 1958 and 1971, respectively.[58] She died in 2014, aged ninety-seven, having kept alive the convictions of her mentor beyond the camps and into future generations.

After the Anschluss, *students performing the Nazi salute before a lecture at the University of Vienna, 1938.*

Chapter 6

The War on Science and the End of Vienna

H *igh Noon* is one of the best Westerns ever made – some rank it behind only John Ford's *Stagecoach*. However, this celebrated example of a quintessentially American genre, starring the archetypal American movie star, Gary Cooper, was directed by a Viennese immigrant, Fred Zinnemann. It was his first, and last, Western. Why, asks one of Zinnemann's biographers, would an urbane, highly educated European want to direct a Western in the first place?[1]

The plot of *High Noon* is straightforward. A newly-wed marshal, Will Kane, is about to leave town for his honeymoon when news arrives that a vicious outlaw whom he had sent to prison is arriving on the noon train, bent on revenge. His fiancée begs him to leave, but out of a sense of duty to the townspeople he stays. His attempts to round up a posse to confront Frank Miller, however, fail; old friends and sympathisers all proffer excuses to back out of the fight. In the end, Kane is forced to confront the enemy on his own.

At the time it was made, in 1952, many critics interpreted *High Noon* as an allegory of the blacklisting in Hollywood of former communist actors and screenwriters, shunned by their erstwhile colleagues. John Wayne, the star of *Stagecoach*, turned down the role of Kane precisely because of the screenplay's political implications –

the deeply conservative actor was actually in favour of blacklisting. And certainly, the screenwriter himself, Carl Foreman, had been a member of America's communist party years earlier.

Zinnemann, however, saw the script differently, as he recounted in his memoirs:

> To me it was the story of a man who must make a decision according to his conscience. His town – symbol of a democracy gone soft – faces a horrendous threat to its people's way of life. Determined to resist, and in deep trouble, he moves all over the place looking for support but finding that there is nobody who will help him; each has a reason of his own for not getting involved. In the end he must meet his chosen fate all by himself, his town's doors and windows firmly locked against him. It is a story that still happens everywhere, every day.[2]

Zinnemann was born in Rzeszow, now in south-east Poland just over the border from Ukraine. His assimilated Jewish family moved to Vienna early in his life and he graduated with a degree in law from the University of Vienna in 1927. Before moving to Berlin, and afterwards to Hollywood in 1929, Zinnemann had stayed long enough in Vienna to experience the city's worsening anti-Semitic intimidation and discrimination at first hand. 'Boys came to school with swastikas in their lapels,' Zinnemann remembered. '"Aren't you ashamed?" I asked one. "I'm proud of it," he said.'[3]

By the time *High Noon* was in production, Zinnemann had discovered that both his parents had been murdered in the Holocaust. For him, the message of the film was clear: that people – and countries – have a duty to stand together in solidarity against evil, or evil will triumph. In the film (spoiler alert), Marshal Kane is lucky, his fiancée returns in the nick of time, turning the tables. But when it's all over he flings his marshal's star in the dust, disgusted by those who have sheepishly emerged to thank him for risking his life on their behalf.

Looked at in this light, *High Noon* is the story of the end of Vienna; the European democracies, gone soft, looked the other way as the Nazis marched in, cheered on by many citizens who now turned savagely on those who had added so much lustre to the city's reputation. A particular target of both Austria's own Austro-fascists (who ruled from 1934 to 1938) and then the Nazis was the intellectual culture of interwar Vienna, which they considered to have been responsible for the 'aberration' of Red Vienna. This chapter explains why the political right had to destroy the scientific worldview of Vienna during this period, and how it came to be obliterated so comprehensively. Very few of the victims, if they survived the war at all, ever returned. For them, the greatest metropolis in Europe had been reduced to a city of ghosts.[4]

The battleground of eugenics

Given the demand from many Austrians to be included in Germany after the dismemberment of their empire in 1918, the prospect of a weakened Austria's incorporation into a greater Reich hung over much of the country's post-war politics. For many Germans, too, it was only logical that the smaller state should be folded into Germany even before Hitler came to power in 1933.

Nonetheless, there were other, more specific, reasons, as to why the Nazis should have wanted to end Austria's independence. Red Vienna and its nexus of institutes and research centres were perceived by fascists to be firmly in opposition to National Socialism, and to be irredeemably Jewish. Of course, these sentiments were shared by many right-wing ethnic Germans in Austria itself. So, even before the *Anschluss*, emboldened by the accession of the Austro-fascist Kurt Schuschnigg to the chancellorship of the country after the assassination of Engelbert Dollfuss in 1934, these forces were beginning to assail the intellectual hinterland of Red Vienna that had flourished so remarkably in the 1920s. After the Nazi military occupation, the process was brutally accelerated.

But the ground had been well prepared beforehand by the Austrians themselves.

Probably the most important point of difference between liberal Vienna and German National Socialism was their contrasting attitudes towards Darwinism and eugenics. 'National Socialism is nothing but applied biology,' Hitler's deputy Rudolf Hess is supposed to have declared in 1934. Certainly, for the Nazis, no subject was more significant. Austria boasted its own distinguished lineage of research in the field; the monk, mathematician and biologist Gregor Mendel, founder of the modern science of genetics, was born in Silesia (now part of the Czech Republic) in 1822 and studied at the University of Vienna under, among others, the physicist Christian Doppler (of the Doppler effect).

Mendel's now famous experiments on pea plants in the 1850s established many of the rules of heredity, including the concepts of 'recessive' and 'dominant' genes (although he himself did not use the word 'gene'). His work was little understood at the time, and was only rediscovered decades later, notably by the English biologist William Bateson. He, and others, merged Mendelian 'genetics' with Darwin's theory of natural selection to produce a solid account of evolutionary biology based on genetic inheritance, later called the 'modern synthesis', or 'central dogma', of evolution.

Despite the rediscovery of Mendel, however, the city council of Red Vienna, as we have seen, was more interested in the theories of Lamarck – which were usually taken to be in opposition to the 'modern synthesis' – and used a neo-Lamarckian interpretation of evolution to rationalise its socialist policies. National Socialism, by contrast, drew heavily on a singular interpretation of Darwin and the central dogma developed by two Victorian Englishmen, both idolised by the Nazis: Francis Galton, a scientific polymath who first coined the term 'eugenics' in 1883, and Houston Stewart Chamberlain.

The latter was particularly insidious. Born in 1855, Chamberlain was an avid Wagnerian who married the composer's daughter, Eva von Bülow. Like Hitler, Chamberlain cultivated his own fervid anti-Semitism in Vienna, during a prolonged stay in the 1890s. Chamberlain was central to Nazi ideology because he was one of the first to develop a full-fledged racial theory of history, published in two volumes as *The Foundations of the Nineteenth Century*. Here he worked up the dominant Nazi eugenicist narrative at length, arguing that all the greatest advances in modern civilisation were attributable to the 'Aryan' race, which was now under mortal threat from interbreeding with 'lesser' races. The book was highly influential in pan-German *Völkisch* circles in the first decades of the following century. Chamberlain himself became a naturalised German and was revered by Hitler, who visited him on his deathbed in Bayreuth, of course, in 1927.

The Nazis' favourite text on the subject, however, was not Chamberlain's but a voluminous tome first published in 1923, the appropriately-named *Foundations of Human Heredity and Racial Hygiene,* written by three German biologists: Erwin Baur, Eugen Fischer and Fritz Lenz.[5] This trio were the leading German eugenicists of their day, and Lenz, in particular, commenced hostilities with Vienna's neo-Lamarckian biologists. In particular, he paid special attention in the *Foundations* to the 'degeneration' that would follow from mingling the superior Nordic with other races. 'The half-breeds resulting from such unions should be of the inferior type mentally and morally', he argued. Warning that the Nordic race was squandering its 'biological mental heritage', Lenz finished with a call to arms: 'It will not be many generations before we cease to be the superiors of the Mongols. Our ethnological studies must lead up, not to arrogance, but to action – eugenics.'[6]

In a chapter on 'Morbid Heredity Factors', Lenz devoted considerable space to an attack on the inheritance of acquired characteristics – 'there is no such thing', he declared. The biologist continued archly that 'a noted clinician' maintained that such inheritance was indeed possible, but, he continued, 'those who voice such views show a lamentable failure to understand the difference between biological inheritance, on the one hand, and the hand-ing-down of the acquirements of civilisation on the other . . . The microscopic study of human reproductive cells has not told us anything new about human heredity.' He conceded that environ-mental factors could 'help or hinder the flowering of hereditary factors', but no more. Only a strict regimen of breeding from the same superior gene pool – 'racial hygiene' – could maintain the superiority of the Nordic races.[7]

Inside the Vivarium

The noted clinician who had so provoked Lenz was Paul Kammerer, the scientific prodigy of the Ringstrasse. By the early 1920s, the idiosyncratic and gifted Kammerer had become probably Europe's leading scientific exponent of neo-Lamarckism, chiefly through his experimental work at the Vivarium, a vital, but now half-forgotten, bastion of Vienna's interwar scientific community. The Institute for Experimental Biology, to give its formal title, was founded in 1902. Kammerer's views were considered heretical to conventional Darwinists, and even more so to National Socialists, for he, and the Vivarium more generally, challenged their central doctrine – that the characteristics of the Nordic race were immutable. Hence Lenz's attempts to debunk Kammerer in the *Foundations*.[8]

A prime example of Vienna's entrepreneurial intellectual spirit, the founder of the Vivarium was Hans Przibram. Barely twenty-eight years old at the time, he financed the project out of his own family's considerable fortune, taking over a large pseudo-Renaissance building that had been constructed as an aquarium for the World's Fair in the Prater. The aquarium had never succeeded in making money, so the building, renamed Vivarium, had been given over to an indoor zoo – exhibiting, among other treats, what it claimed to be the largest reptile collection in the world, featuring sixty giant snakes. The building was destroyed at the end of the Second World War. All that remains of this extraordinary institution today is a small plaque on a fence marking its original location, a few minutes' walk from the Prater's famous Ferris wheel.

Przibram despaired of the usual approach to biology in university departments at the time, which mostly consisted of simply recording and classifying (dead) animals and plants. The University of Vienna, where he had been trained, was a case in point; its laboratories were also notoriously cramped and ill-equipped. Przibram's ambition, in his own words, was to 'transform biology into an exact science', by applying mathematics to biology.[9] Furthermore, the Vivarium was founded with an explicitly didactic purpose, to test scientifically whether the theories of Lamarck were correct. As we have seen, the debate over Darwin's theory of evolution was a central intellectual preoccupation of the era, so the work of the Vivarium assumed enormous importance, especially during the 1920s when Julius Tandler was in the town hall. Przibram was joined in his enterprise by two colleagues, from very similar backgrounds, who shared his ambitions for biology; Wilhelm Figdor, the eldest of the triumvirate, and Leopold von Portheim, whose family came from Prague. Both were botanists, and also, like Przibram, the scions of wealthy Jewish families on the Ringstrasse.

From the start, the Vivarium stimulated innovation. It encouraged theoretical speculation combined with the close observation of, and physical experimentation on, live animals. Its staff, enthusiastically led by Przibram himself, went on research trips abroad to capture these unfortunate creatures, which were then shipped back to Vienna; previously biologists had concentrated mainly on killing and then preserving the animals that they wanted to study.

Towards the end of the nineteenth century, several research stations had been set up in Europe to study the nascent sciences of evolution and embryology, but these were all on the coast, concentrating on marine biology. The Vivarium, however, not only brought the facilities of a research aquarium to the heart of a city, but also

provided the facilities to test how animals – primarily rats, but there were hundreds of other species at the Vivarium – adapted over generations to different levels of heat or cold, light or darkness. To this end the building itself became a totally controlled, artificial environment, with, effectively, the world's first purpose-built air-conditioning system. This allowed experiments to be conducted at anything between 5°C and 20°C. Humidity could also be adjusted. To replicate conditions at sea in the Vivarium's huge fish tanks, saltwater was brought in barrels by train from the seaport of Trieste.

Kammerer was one of the first recruits to the Vivarium, hired for his expertise in handling animals. The Vivarium allowed him to study changes in the form of an animal exposed to a variety of external atmospheric environments over time. Picking up from where he had left off in his bedroom, Kammerer was in the forefront of providing experimental evidence for the inheritance of acquired characteristics. During the 1920s and 1930s those working at the Vivarium made huge strides in genetics, plant biology and particularly endocrinology (the study of the endocrine system and its hormonal secretions).

Kammerer was a eugenicist, too, but of a very different hue from Lenz and his German colleagues. Kammerer (and Tandler) believed that rather than reproducing as many as possible of one (Nordic) type at the expense of everyone else, by changing the environment in which all young children were raised the genetic stock could be improved more evenly. Those improvements could slowly but surely be passed on to subsequent generations, as he sought to prove experimentally at the Vivarium. Everyone stood to benefit. This school of thought has often been called 'positive' eugenics, for as the historian Paul Weindling writes, these eugenicists 'discussed positive measures based on social welfare to improve the biological

(opposite) The most controversial scientist of his day, Paul Kammerer of Vienna's Vivarium.

Paul Kammerer's laboratory space in the Vivarium.

status of beneficiaries, as opposed to "negative" measures, such as birth control, sterilization, castration, and institutional custody to prevent procreation'.[10] Kammerer's positive eugenics emphasised 'the value of raising fewer more completely developed individuals in ways that did not sacrifice anyone'.[11]

As we shall see later, there were plenty of negative eugenicists in Vienna as well, closely allied to the nationalist, Catholic politics of Black Vienna. The cluster of biologists and health reformers around Tandler and the Vivarium, however, represented a distinctly Viennese approach that has often been lost in the rush to lump the city in with 'Greater German' eugenics.[12] In fact, in advocating positive eugenics, Kammerer represented perfectly the Vivarium's very unique and advanced school of 'developmental plasticity', a way of thinking across all the natural sciences – botany, biology and zoology – which emphasised the possibilities of change over stasis.

The biopolitics of a midwife toad

By giving people better housing and maternity services, Kammerer's theories in action would, so the Red Viennese hoped, eventually produce *die neuen Menschen*. Kammerer's views amounted essentially to socialist eugenics, sometimes called 'reform eugenics'. As the historian Stefan Kühl writes, socialist eugenicists 'demanded that one must first equalise the environmental conditions for all people . . . By systematically planning for reproduction under the best social conditions, so went the utopia of the socialist eugenicists, a society of genetically and socially valuable humans could be created.'[13]

At the time, Kammerer, a natural showman, was one of the most famous scientists in Europe. Partly influenced by his work in Vienna, several of the rising generation of British scientists, most prominently J.B.S. Haldane and Joseph Needham, had become socialist eugenicists. In 1926 Kammerer was invited by the Soviet Union to establish his own institute in the biology department of the Communist Academy, to lead Russian research into reform eugenics. Negotiations for the position had been completed, his library had even been shipped ahead of him, when in September of that year Kammerer took a train to Puchberg, a health resort south-west of Vienna, wandered into the woods with a pistol and put a bullet through his head.

His exact motives for committing suicide remain obscure. Kammerer, as his photos suggest, was possessed of a tense and febrile personality; nowadays he might have been diagnosed as bipolar. He was emotionally erratic, often swept up in dramatic love affairs – most notoriously with Alma, widow of Gustav Mahler, who briefly worked as his assistant at the Vivarium. He threatened to shoot himself on her late husband's grave if she didn't marry him. But the more immediate cause of his suicide may have lain elsewhere, in his lingering despair at the bitter controversy surrounding his most notorious experiment, one that went to the heart of the profound biopolitical differences between Viennese socialists and Germany's National Socialists.

Kammerer's work at the Vivarium with the European midwife toad, conducted before the First World War, had gone a long way to establishing his fame. In two sets of experiments, utilising the Vivarium's specially designed air-conditioning system, Kammerer had bred the toads normally but had then altered the environment in which their offspring would develop, to test whether there would be differences, and whether those would be passed on.

The second series of experiments was crucial, focusing on the development of nuptial pads – rough, black swellings between the forearm and the thumb of most male frogs, which help them grasp the females when they mate in water. Male midwife toads generally do not have these. By increasing the temperature in the laboratory, Kammerer persuaded the normally landlocked midwife toads to move to the water and mate there instead, to cool off. Female midwife toads deposited their eggs directly in the water, rather than on land as they usually did. After several generations, the male toads could no longer grasp and carry the eggs, as they were slippery. Kammerer reported, however, that male individuals from the new generations had developed rough nuptial pads to better seize females when mating, thus, apparently, proving that Lamarck was correct.

Other biologists, such as the German Richard Semon, had already outlined sophisticated theoretical arguments as to how a Lamarckian process of evolution might work, but Kammerer's supposed 'proof' caused a sensation. For the *New York Times*, he was the 'new Darwin'. But for all his fame, many fellow scientists distrusted his methods, and, more relevantly, the midwife toad experiments also made Kammerer a hate figure for racial hygienists. Because of the dramatic biopolitical implications of the midwife toad experiments, Kammerer's work was subjected to intense scrutiny. Much turned, it seemed, on the nuptial pads of the Vivarium's toads.

It was, therefore, with some relief amongst the racial hygienists that, after years of controversy, the American herpetologist Gladwyn Kingsley Noble, having examined one of Kammerer's last specimens in Vienna, wrote in the journal *Nature* in 1926 that the fingers of Kammerer's toad had, in fact, been injected with Indian ink, *so as to create an artificial resemblance to nuptial pads*. Kammerer protested his innocence, but stood accused of scientific fraud nonetheless. A scandal of unlikely proportions ensued, covered both in the specialist and general press. It was not long after the article in *Nature* that Kammerer took his life.

Tellingly, the whole sorry episode divided Europeans largely along biopolitical lines. Socialist eugenicists tended to believe that Kammerer had been framed to discredit his theories, suspecting that someone had gained access to his laboratory and injected the ink. The Soviets even turned around a quick feature film based on this premise, called *Salamander*, in which a professor experimenting on animals gets bumped off by a sinister cabal of reactionary clerics and aristocrats. National Socialists, however, and racial hygienists like Lenz, were only too happy. In the second edition of the *Foundations* he added a footnote ridiculing Kammerer for faking his toad experiment, arguing that the fraud had proved Lenz right all along.[14]

The Case of the Midwife Toad, the title of an investigative book by the Hungarian-born journalist Arthur Koestler, published in 1971, remains one of the twentieth century's most tantalising scientific mysteries. Did Kammerer inject the ink himself, or was it a case of scientific sabotage? The story has attracted plenty of writers besides Koestler. The latest to delve into it is the Viennese Klaus Taschwer, who points a finger firmly at Othenio Abel, the palaeontologist and convenor of the Bear's Den at the University of Vienna. We know that he was bitterly critical of Kammerer's work, and blocked his promotion at the university. Abel had every incentive to damage Kammerer's reputation, and equally the reputation of what he regarded as the overly Jewish Vivarium. Familiar with the biologist's work, he would have been able to brief a perpetrator very easily on how to inject the ink.[15] We will never know for sure.

Glandular revival, or getting Steinached

Another thorn in the side of National Socialists and racial hygienists was the other star of the Vivarium, Eugen Steinach. Despite his worldwide reputation, Kammerer's fame might even have been surpassed by that of Steinach who, in one caricature of the time, was grouped with Freud and Einstein at the summit of the scientific world. Born in the Tyrol in 1861, he pioneered the new field of endocrinology. Most of his greatest experimental work was completed before he arrived at the Vivarium in 1921, where he headed his own department. Nonetheless, his work there was to help enormously in the development of hormone glandular surgery, sex-change procedures and hormone replacement therapy. With a long-flowing, square beard and a suitably furrowed brow, Steinach looked every inch the scientific eminence that he was. He was nominated for the Nobel Prize in Physiology six times during his Vivarium years, but never won it. Like Kammerer, his work was deeply opposed to the central tenets of National Socialism and the denizens of Black Vienna.

Just as Kammerer and Tandler stressed the flexibility of human biology, so did Steinach's neuro-endocrinology. Until his work, the supposed sexual qualities of men and women were rigidly defined by the apparent physical characteristics of their sperm and eggs; sperm were active and competitive; eggs, by contrast, passive and nurturing. So 'the sexual attributes of men and woman became projections of their gametes, dictating even mind and personality'.[16] All very Weiningerian.

Steinach, however, undermined such neat categorisations by adopting the theory, first proposed by two French physiologists, that there were in fact two separate types of cell in the gonad, one responsible for sexual development and libido, composed of interstitial cells, the other strictly for reproduction. By transplanting the gonads of pigs and rats, and observing the results for years afterwards, Steinach demonstrated that the sex hormones estrogen and testosterone influenced sexual behaviour in both men *and* women. In his own account of his work, published in 1940 as *Sex and Life: Forty Years of Biological and Medical Experiments*, he gave this summary:

Perfect specimens of one single sex are in reality theoretical details . . . it is possible to detect in every man some, though possibly minute, traces of femininity, and in every woman some slight attribute of masculinity . . . Between a real man and real woman there are innumerable others.

Many considered his discoveries to be as important as Freudian psychoanalysis in determining new approaches to sexuality, and indeed life as a whole. Homosexuality, for instance, could no longer be characterised as merely a symptom of immorality. As Cheryl Logan writes, 'The reproductive endocrinologists of the Vienna School had replaced a sexual biology of degeneracy with a flexible biology of development.'[17]

Sex reformers, in particular, took notice, notably the great German physician and sexologist Magnus Hirschfeld. Homosexual himself, Hirschfeld campaigned tirelessly to end the legal and cultural discrimination against homosexuality both in Germany and abroad from the late nineteenth century onwards. He always tried to argue his case on a scientific basis, so followed Steinach's experiments and publications closely. Even before the Great War, he had visited Steinach in his laboratory in Vienna and published appreciative accounts. The motto of Hirschfeld's campaigning body, the Scientific-Humanitarian Committee, was 'Justice through Science'. Much of the science came from Steinach.

'Their relationship,' writes the academic Chandak Sengoopta, 'was to reinforce the work of each other. Hirschfeld's clinical work . . . was part of his broader political program for the emancipation of homosexuals, and he used Steinach, in effect, as a political ally.'[18]

One of the main vehicles for Hirschfeld's concept of sex reform through science was the World League for Sexual Reform, of which he was president, and the body's fourth congress was held in Vienna in 1930, attracting 2,000 participants and guests. The event was enthusiastically backed by the city council (Tandler spoke), lasted a week and attracted a lot of comment, not all of it favourable.[19] Steinach did not speak, but his work was fêted, alongside that of Freud. Delegates were invited to tour Steinach's laboratory at the Vivarium. Together with Hirschfeld, Steinach now helped to pioneer gender reassignment surgical procedures, carried out at the German's clinic in Berlin. The first complete gender reassignment operation, from male to female, was carried out at the Institute for Sexual Science as early as 1931.

Steinach's main claim to fame – and later notoriety – during the interwar years, however, rested on another aspect of his work. It was already widely suspected that senility might be caused by a decline in the sex gland functions, so, Steinach conjectured, if one could stimulate the proliferation of interstitial cells the advance of senility might be arrested. He attempted to achieve this by destroying the germinal (reproductive) cells in a vasectomy-type operation, giving more room to the interstitial ones to grow. He tried this procedure on rats in 1912, and reported great success, especially in the recovery of their sexual prowess: 'Some hitherto decrepit animals were now tireless sexual performers, having intercourse as many as nineteen times in fifteen minutes.'[20] A colleague of Steinach's performed the first such operation on a man in 1918. News of the operation, and the subsequent improvement in the patient's physical attributes, strength, and sexual vigour, spread quickly around the world.

It was hardly surprising that this part of Steinach's work provoked endless fascination and publicity. In the early 1920s, the idea that a body's chemicals and glands could be manipulated to restore, and possibly prolong, life was thrilling. Doctors (and quacks) throughout Europe and the Americas cashed in on the craze for glandular therapy with a wide range of treatments, some of them based on

Steinach's research, some not so much. In New York alone there were supposed to be 100 surgeons offering the treatment. The fad produced novels, plays, farces and films, and Steinach was in the middle of it all; by many accounts, Vienna became a byword for exotic glandular rejuvenation.[21] Hearing of his plans to come to America at one point, the *New York Times* announced in a headline 'Dr Steinach Coming to Make Old Young'. His name was turned into a verb to describe the vasectomy-like procedure that the Viennese performed – 'Steinached'.[22] Freud and the Irish poet W.B. Yeats were amongst the many celebrities of the age to be Steinached. The sixty-nine-year-old Yeats was very happy with the results, enjoying, according to his own assessment, a revival of his 'sexual desire' and a renewal of his creative powers. The sixty-seven-year-old Freud, stricken with cancer, was less convinced.

The efficacy of the Steinach operation, however, was questioned by many at the time, and has been ever since. By the 1940s it had already fallen out of vogue. Many doctors argued that any effects from being Steinached were the result of the power of suggestion, although champions of the operation retorted that identical results had been produced in patients who had been Steinached without their knowledge, during the course of another operation. Steinach himself lamented the fact that so much of the press attention focused on the sexual aspect of the operation, whereas he was more concerned with the wider health benefits. He also despaired at the use of the term 'rejuvenation' to describe his work, implying that he had discovered the secret to eternal life. He tried to replace rejuvenation with 'reactivation' or 'restitution', but the terms never caught on. He was not the last scientist to watch helplessly as a complex scientific procedure was butchered in the press.

The reckoning

Given the importance that the Nazis attached to race theories, once they had taken power in Germany they moved swiftly to enshrine those theories in legislation. As well as drawing on the racial hygiene theories of men like Lenz, they also drew heavily on American jurisprudence. For the bald fact is that Hitler's race laws were directly informed by the latest legislation from America (as amply documented by the historian Stefan Kühl).[23] In a chilling statistic, no fewer than thirty-two American states had passed laws from the early 1900s onwards allowing the forced sterilisation of those who were considered to be mentally unfit and defective, so as to 'protect' the Nordic race. These categories were also used as a pretext to disproportionately target Mexicans and African-Americans.

In particular, the Nazi 'Law for the Prevention of Offspring with Hereditary Diseases', passed in July 1933, which sanctioned the sterilisation of those deemed unworthy of reproducing, was based largely on a close reading of the 'Model Eugenical Sterilization Law' drafted by the American eugenicist Harry Laughlin in 1922. This provided a template for similar laws passed by American state legislatures as well as for the Nazis, who by 1945 had forcibly sterilised 400,000 people throughout occupied Europe. Laughlin's definition of the feeble-minded and defective in his 'Model Law' was sweeping, including the 'mentally retarded, insane, criminal, epileptic, inebriate, diseased, blind, deaf, deformed and economically dependent'. In similar fashion, the Nazis turned to American precedent for the notorious 'Law for the Protection of German Blood and German Honour', one of the so-called Nuremberg Laws passed in 1935. This legal ban on 'race mixing' between Jews and people of 'German or related blood' was informed by long debates over American jurisprudence on racial mixing, at a time when many US states forbade racially mixed marriages.[24]

As well as legislating against 'inferior races', the Nazis moved swiftly against the loci of scientific resistance against them. An early target was Magnus Hirschfeld. Just four months after taking power, Nazi thugs and the *Sturmabteilung* sacked his clinic in Berlin and beat up the staff. All the books in Hirschfeld's enormous library, mainly about sexology and biology, were removed and publicly burned, together with many other collections deemed to be 'un-German'. Hirschfeld fled to Paris, and then to Nice, with his partner; he died there in 1935. Hirschfeld was Jewish, as were most of the senior scientists at the Vivarium and many of the sex reformers. From the beginning, racial hygienists argued that for Jews, disinterested, objective science was but a smokescreen; the apparently Jewish preference for the evolutionary theories of Lamarck was seen as part of a sinister plot to become more German.

Vienna had reared its own share of 'racial hygienists'. They had been working with the National Socialists for years to fight back against what they perceived to be the degenerate, leftist neo-Lamarckians who had hijacked the city council. In 1925, for instance, the Viennese branch of the Deutsche Gesellschaft für Rassenpflege (German Society for Racial Welfare) was founded. It accepted no Jewish members. The influence of such organisations was felt particularly in provincial Austria, beyond the capital.[25]

After the Austro-fascists came to power in Austria in 1934, Vienna's own Nazi-style racial hygienists started to reverse Tandler's dominant strand of reform eugenics. One significant turning-point came just a year later when the Natural History Museum staged an exhibition on 'Heredity Research on Healthy People', which seemed to align Austria more closely with Hitler's sterilisation laws.[26] The Bear's Den at the university and other nationalist groups circulated lists of Jewish and socialist, or just anti-Nazi, academics, researchers and teachers, as we have seen. Jews were excluded from many aspects of Viennese life from 1934 onwards, part of Schuschnigg's policy to reduce the proportion of Jews in professional circles. Jewish physicians were sacked and the numbers of Jewish teachers severely reduced. By 1935 no publishing house could take on Jewish authors, Austrian films were produced without Jews (so that they could still be shown in Germany) and Austrian sports teams that played Germany could not field any Jewish athletes.[27]

Nonetheless, Germany's race laws, applied to Austria within a single day of the Wehrmacht marching over the borders in the

Anschluss of 1938, signified a quickening of both the pace and compass of state-sponsored Aryanisation. A comprehensive purge of the civil service began, and as the university was a state-run and financed institution, so the remaining non-Aryan and anti-Nazi academics were quickly forced out. In the Faculty of Philosophy, 14 out of 45 full professors had to quit, 11 out of 22 associate professors and 56 out of 159 lecturers. Academics now had to declare an oath of allegiance to Hitler, and lectures started with the Nazi salute (see image p. 190).

The new dean of the Medical School was an anatomist called Eduard Pemkopf, a long-standing opponent of Tandler's who had been a member of the Nazi Party since 1933. He gave his inaugural address in a *Sturmabteilung* uniform, stressing that 'negative' eugenics would now be the preferred ideology of the university, promoting the 'elimination of those who are hereditarily inferior by sterilization and other means'. The medical faculty, home to a higher proportion of Jewish members than any other, purged fully 78 per cent of its staff, including three Nobel Prize winners.[28] Starting in the summer of 1938, restrictions were placed on the number of Jewish students at the university. After Kristallnacht in November – the state-sponsored pogrom against Jewish homes, businesses and synagogues – Jews were banned from entering the university altogether.

However, the Nazi assault on the university, regarded as part of the establishment, paled beside the ruthlessness with which they shredded the remnants of Red Vienna's intellectual hinterland. Take the Vivarium; it was, 'relative to its size, the research institute in Austria and the German Reich with the most victims of National Socialism'.[29] On 17 March, just five days after German troops had initially crossed the Austrian border, one Fritz Knoll, a member of the Austrian Academy of Sciences, to which the Vivarium was affiliated, ordered the temporary closure of the Vivarium and its subsequent 'reorganisation'. At this point, probably, the locks were changed and the directors of the institute shut out of their own offices. As part of this 'reorganisation', of the thirty-three scientists working there in 1938, eighteen were expelled immediately on race grounds, including Przibram and Portheim.

Seven members of the Vivarium were to perish in the Holocaust, including Przibram, who died at Theresienstadt on 20 May 1944. His wife, also in the camp, killed herself the following day. Leonore Brecher was murdered at the Maly Trostenets extermination camp, near Minsk in Belarus, in September 1942. Steinach, fortunately, was abroad at the time of the *Anschluss*, and never returned to Austria. Like most assimilated Viennese Jews of his generation, he struggled to acknowledge that the attacks on his work might have been tinged by anti-Semitism. His attempts to emigrate to America all failed, despite being championed in the United States by the German-born sexologist and endocrinologist Harry Benjamin, later famous for his work on transgender patients. But anti-Semitism probably played a part in the negative reception of his ideas in America, too.[30] An embittered Steinach died in poverty in Switzerland in 1944.

The Institute for Radium Research was also decapitated. Victor Franz Hess, who had worked at the institute from 1910 to 1920 as Stefan Meyer's assistant, carried out most of the research there that won him the Nobel Prize in Physics in 1936, for the discovery of what were later called 'cosmic rays'. A Catholic with a Jewish wife, he escaped the country in 1938 to avoid persecution. Jewish members of the institute lost their jobs, although the institute itself did survive the war. Vienna's renowned health-care system, so painfully built up by Tandler, was decimated. By one estimate, the total number of physicians in Vienna was reduced from 4,900 to 1,700 between March and September 1938, with as many as 3,000 fleeing abroad.[31] Of the 124 former and current members of Freud's Psychoanalytic Society in Vienna at the time of the *Anschluss*, 106 were targeted by the Nazis. The vast majority fled, leaving only five in the city, including August Aichhorn.[32]

The members of the Vienna Circle were another obvious target for fascists and National Socialists. It was the theoretical centre of the despised 'scientific worldview', and some of its members were both Jewish and left-wing. As early as 1934, the Schuschnigg government had closed down the Ernst Mach Society, with which most of the Circle's members were closely associated. The ostensible reason was that the society had been acting politically, on behalf of the Social Democrats. In reality, the new regime was intent on extinguishing any organised centres of dissent.

Members of the Circle, certainly those who were Jewish and socialist, drew their own conclusions. Otto Neurath was out of the country at the time of Schuschnigg's takeover, and relocated to Holland. Many in the Circle had been travelling to American universities regularly since the late 1920s, often on Rockefeller grants, and from the mid-1930s, more conscious than most of what was coming, their emigration accelerated. Feigl, aware that his Jewish background would disbar him from getting any sort of teaching post in central Europe, went off to the University of Iowa as early as 1931. Kurt Gödel settled at the Institute for Advanced Study at Princeton in 1939, shortly before another Viennese-born scientist, Wolfgang Pauli, a pioneer in quantum physics and winner of the Nobel Prize in 1945. Karl Menger emigrated to America in 1937, eventually teaching at the Illinois Institute of Technology. Carnap became a naturalised American citizen. The last meeting of the Circle in Vienna was in 1938, but by then it was already a shadow of its former self.

Due to the academic networks they had established from Vienna, remarkably almost all the members of the Circle escaped, and the interest that philosophers like Quine had shown in their work ensured a warm reception in America. Analytic philosophy became an important strand of Anglo-American academic philosophy through to the 1960s. Feigl even tried to mimic the Circle's Viennese heyday by founding the Minnesota Center for Philosophy of Science in 1953. Inspired by the work of the Vienna Circle, the Universities of Indiana and Pittsburgh likewise founded centres or departments in the same spirit.[33] Thus, at least the Vienna

Circle escaped the decapitation of the city – exiled, but otherwise unscathed.

Nonetheless, one of their number, Moritz Schlick, did not get out in time. Dramatically, he was shot dead in 1936 on the so-called 'Philosophers' Staircase', the grand, ornate entrance to the University of Vienna's philosophy faculty, by a deranged former student. The paranoid Johann Nelböck had been threatening Schlick for several years previously, imagining that his former mentor had not only slept with his girlfriend but had also frustrated his putative career as a teacher.[34] Schlick was the scion of a noble Prussian family, unlike most of his (assimilated) Jewish colleagues in the Vienna Circle, but the reaction to his murder betrayed the poisonous atmosphere prevailing in Vienna by the 1930s.

Nelböck offered several, often contradictory, reasons for his actions, but found it most expedient to defend himself in court as a martyr for Christian, conservative values. He argued that his erstwhile teacher had to be killed for promoting a treacherous form of Jewish philosophy, the so-called scientific worldview. That was exactly what the right-wing press wanted to hear; several newspapers took Nelböck's side. A leading fascist paper editorialised that he was not *born* a psychopath, but became one under the 'influence of the radically devastating philosophy professed by Dr Schlick', the 'idol of Vienna's Jewish circles'. Even if Schlick was not Jewish himself, to the Austro-fascists he was a Jew by association, a *Mussjude*, and to them that was equally objectionable.[35] In the end, Nelböck was sentenced to ten years' imprisonment for the murder, but served only two before being freed shortly after the *Anschluss*.

A frenzied bloodlust

In 1925, Kammerer had warned that the negative eugenics of the racial hygienists had become the home of racial fanatics.[36] Certainly, such fanaticism was on full display in the orgy of unrestrained civilian aggression that was unleased on the Nazis' opponents, predominantly Jews, in the days and weeks following the *Anschluss*. The destruction of the Vivarium and other institutes and organisations should be understood against this background. The years of anti-Semitic, anti-socialist and racist propaganda since the end of the empire had clearly done their work. Viennese set upon Viennese with an uninhibited savagery that was far worse than anything that had occurred in Germany itself.

Why this should be so has been a matter of fierce debate. One factor, no doubt, is that unlike in Germany, where an anti-Semitic government very overtly excluded Jews and other opponents from public life over a number of years, the Schuschnigg government's anti-Semitism had been more discreet, part of a wider policy to preserve an independent Austria and keep Nazism in check. Austrian Jews themselves referred to Schuschnigg's less aggressive discrimination as 'rubber-soled anti-Semitism'. Consequently, the Austrian National Socialists had been forced to bottle up their loathing of socialists, Jews and others for decades, until, like a pressure cooker, the top blew off on 11 March 1938. One Viennese émigrée recounted decades later that when she had gone to the cinema to see a film at 5 p.m. on that day, Vienna had been draped in the red-and-white flags of Austria, yet when she emerged a couple of hours later the streets were festooned solely with swastikas.[37]

Amongst the most ardent anti-Semites were those 10,000 or so Austrian Nazis who had been forced to flee to Germany after Schuschnigg's crackdown on the party following the assassination of Dollfuss. They returned to Vienna from exile bent on revenge. Two such were Otto Wächter and his wife Charlotte, who raced back to Vienna to embrace the *Anschluss*, and, still more thrillingly for them, to witness the arrival of Hitler himself on 13 March to 'reclaim' his home country for the fatherland. Otto Wächter had been born in 1901 in Vienna and had absorbed his pan-German nationalism and anti-Semitism, like so many, at the University of Vienna, where he studied law. By the age of twenty-one he was already participating in anti-Semitic demonstrations in the streets, and had joined Austria's National Socialist party. He was only a peripheral member of the putsch against Dollfuss in 1934, but was obliged to escape to Germany all the same. Here he joined the SS, falling into the orbit of a senior Nazi, the murderous Reinhard Heydrich.

The vivacious and adoring Charlotte Wächter was, if anything, an even more committed Nazi than her shrewd, ruthless and philandering husband. Her diary, revealed many decades later, describes the delirious, almost erotically charged scenes of the Nazis returning to Vienna. As the *Anschluss* beckoned she jumped in a car with similarly euphoric Austrians and drove as fast as possible for Vienna, across a now defunct border. For these fellow-travellers, the following days passed in a dazed rapture: 'Every Nazi felt such joy about this miracle, we all embraced each other. Yes, it was one of the most decisive moments of our lives, and in those of the hundreds of thousands who had fled to Germany and were living as "illegals".' Reunited with her husband in Vienna, looking 'splendid' in his 'black SS coat with white lapels', the couple set off for the climax to the *Anschluss*, the appearance of the Führer himself to speak to some 250,000 adoring Austrians crushed into the Heldenplatz (Heroes' Square). He was due to address them from the balcony of the Habsburgs' old Hofburg Palace.

The Wächters were amongst the select few with reserved tickets to the event, and Charlotte stood only a few metres behind Hitler as he officially announced Austria's absorption into the German Reich. Arriving early in her assigned place, she wrote, she 'suddenly heard a loud cry in the distance, which turned into an overwhelming cry of joy, "Heil Hitler". It approached like a surging human sea, getting closer and louder. The Führer was standing with a raised hand, greeting the crowd, which was shouting excitedly . . . a spontaneous and heartfelt outburst of joy.'[38] One historian has described Hitler's 'tumultuous welcome' in Vienna as 'an outburst of frenzied acclamation seldom seen since the days of the Caesars'.[39]

The consequences of such heightened, fanatical emotions on the streets of Vienna were appalling. Jews were sadistically beaten and humiliated by their fellow citizens, encouraged by the new Nazi state. As one historian of the Vienna Circle, David Edmonds, has drily observed, 'for students of psychology interested in the limits of human depravity, 1938 in Vienna was the time and place to be'.[40] Jews were compelled to goose-step around the city and violently shoved to the ground. They had insulting placards hung around their necks, and previously respected professionals were specifically selected to clean toilets.

Giant swastikas were hung outside Jewish-owned buildings, including Freud's apartment block. An 80,000-strong mob rampaged through Leopoldstadt, pillaging as they went. In October, more systematically, soldiers swept through the predominantly Jewish district burning prayer houses, books, Torah scrolls – any symbols of Jewish life.[41] A new law stipulated that Jews should be separated from other patients in hospitals to avoid the danger of 'race defilement'. In the petty minutiae of anti-Semitic regulations, Vienna's Jewish citizens were banned from sitting on benches on the Ringstrasse, swimming in the city's pools or strolling through the Prater.

Kristallnacht, a pogrom ordered directly by the Nazi leadership on the night of 9–10 November, was more destructive and savage in Vienna than almost anywhere else in what was now Greater Germany. Up to 50 synagogues were burned and over 4,000 Jewish-owned shops looted. About 6,000 people were arrested, of whom at least 27 were murdered. Indeed, so savage was the violence that even Nazi officials in both Vienna and Berlin recoiled from what they themselves had unleashed. The Viennese Economic Office of the new regime cited the 'scandalous scenes that have damaged the reputation of the party and the Reich'.

Hundreds of Jews committed suicide in those first weeks. Altogether 3,741 took their own lives in the year after the *Anschluss*.[42] However, many more of those designated as Jews by the new authorities quickly packed their bags. As has often been noted, perhaps the only benefit of the immediate post-*Anschluss* blood-letting was that there could be absolutely no doubt about the intentions of Vienna's new rulers. In Germany, anti-Semitism had often been cloaked in legal sophistry, lulling too many into a false sense of security. In Vienna, there was no attempt at such artifice.

Thus, over just the spring and summer months, an estimated 100,000 Jews left. A plurality of about 30,000 moved to Britain, slightly fewer to America and 9,000 or so to Palestine. Within just three months of the *Anschluss*, observes the historian Bruce Pauley, the Jews had been thoroughly purged from the public life of Austria. Leading German Nazis, such as Hermann Göring, looked on enviously, complaining that, by contrast, the 'dejewification' of the German economy was progressing too slowly.[43]

The Jews were ushered on their way by the merciless and fanatical Adolf Eichmann, the newly installed head of the Central Bureau for Jewish Emigration in Vienna, with offices located in a requisitioned Rothschild palais. Eichmann was born in Germany but had grown up in Austria, attending the same school (though seventeen years later) in Linz as Hitler, Ernst Kaltenbrunner (another top Nazi, hanged for crimes against humanity in 1946) and Ludwig Wittgenstein.[44] Eichmann's job in Vienna in 1938–39 was to strip Jewish emigrants of as much as money and property as he could before they left. He was so effective that the Nazi leadership in Berlin summoned him to Berlin to oversee Jewish deportation from the entire Reich. Thereafter, Eichmann rose rapidly through the ranks of the SS. The new Nazi-appointed governor of the province of Ostmark, as Austria would now be called, was Dr Arthur Seyss-Inquart, like Wächter another law graduate from the University of Vienna.

Whereas before the *Anschluss*, about 200,000 Jews lived in Austria, the overwhelming majority in Vienna, the census of 17 May 1939 counted only 95,000. By September about 75,000 remained.[45] Barely more than 11,000 survived to the end of the war, 5,000 of them in Vienna itself, of whom about a thousand had somehow hidden underground for the duration. The Nazis' new policies of racial hygiene, supervised by specially imported SS doctors, also targeted other alleged 'inferiors'; thousands were deported from Vienna's mental health hospital at Steinhof, to be murdered in the death camps, while others were killed in the hospital itself.

Like Wächter, Eichmann and Kaltenbrunner, other Austrian or Viennese-born Nazi officers (often university-educated) were deeply involved in the Holocaust. One such was the venomous, sadistic Amon Göth, commandant of the Płaszów forced labour camp: Göth had joined the Austrian National Socialist party in 1925, aged just seventeen. Another notorious 'Austrian' Nazi, born in Trieste, was Odilo Globocnik, an early member of the Austrian SS and Gauleiter of Vienna after the *Anschluss*. A methodical killer, he was mainly responsible for the rounding-up of about 1.5 million Polish Jews in 'Reinhard', codename for the operation that led to the establishment of the extermination camps at Sobibor, Treblinka and Belzec. Much admired by Himmler for his ruthlessness, Globocnik may even have been the officer who first suggested the idea of industrial-scale mass-murder to the head of the SS. A deputy commander of Sobibor was the Austrian Gustav Wagner, nicknamed 'the beast' for his insane brutality.

The historian Bertrand Perz has chronicled the way that Globocnik gathered round him what amounted to a think-tank of Austrian experts, including historians, policemen, architects, agronomists and, of course, eugenicists, to inform and improve every aspect of his inhuman work. Among their number was the police officer Franz Stangl, appointed the commandant of Sobibor and Treblinka; the Viennese architect and Nazi Jürgen Lassmann; and Franz Stanglica, a historian with a higher degree from the University of Vienna.

All this adds up to the fact that, in proportion to their numbers, Austrians played an outsize role in the Holocaust. It has been estimated that they comprised 40 per cent of the staff at the death camps. The Nazi-hunter Simon Wiesenthal calculated that Austrians were responsible for about half (3 million) of the deaths in the Holocaust.[46] Furthermore, the Austrian SS officers were unusually committed, callous and unquestioning. As Perz notes: 'There is not one known case in which an Austrian quit his office because he or she rejected the idea of exterminating humans.'[47] Those who survived the war also remained loyal to each other and, as far as one can tell, to the ideals of National Socialism.[48]

The tangled legacy

Austrians, and Viennese, thus included some of the most remorseless perpetrators of the Holocaust as well as its victims. Perhaps this is not surprising, as most Austrian Nazis had been steeped in Europe's most virulent and sophisticated strain of anti-Semitism since childhood, the consequence of decades of unchecked nationalist and anti-Semitic propaganda, as we saw in Chapter 2.

Furthermore, the Austrian Nazis went about their killing with that same distinctive diligence as their victims exhibited in Red Vienna's intellectual hinterland. After all, they were so often products of the same pedagogy at the University of Vienna and other such institutions; they just applied their methodological rigour and 'exact thinking' to mass-murder rather than abstract philosophy. Globocnik's genocide think-tank was a ghastly perversion of learning and scholarship, but it was still very recognisably a Viennese project, stirring a variety of different disciplines together to produce a terrifying new praxis. The Austrian Nazis were recklessly unafraid to take ideas to their logical extremes.

Given their shared educations and intellectual backgrounds in Vienna, it was inevitable that some of Vienna's most prominent scientists came to an accommodation, or worse, with the Nazis. The most notorious was Konrad Lorenz, later the winner of a Nobel Prize in Physiology or Medicine. As we have seen, he was a scion of liberal Vienna and was himself the son of a famous doctor, a founder of orthopaedic surgery. The younger Lorenz was also extremely ambitious, a professional opportunist who saw a chance after 1938 to gain the funding and facilities from the Nazis that he felt had been denied him during the 1930s. But he was politically motivated as well. As he wrote of one of his fellow scientists on the arrival of Hitler in Vienna, 'I believe we Austrians are the sincerest and most convinced National Socialists after all!'[49] He joined the Nazi Party in 1938, by which time he was already one of Europe's most prominent animal behaviourists. The Nazis must have been only too happy when Lorenz started to back up their racial hygiene theories with his own scientific observations of the geese and ducks at his famous menagerie at Altenberg.

As early as July 1938, at a lecture in Bayreuth, Lorenz made the explicit comparison between the breakdowns in the instinctive behaviour of domesticated animals and the 'signs of decay' in the comportment of civilised humans.[50] Lorenz returned to the theme in two articles he penned in 1940, one for the Nazi biology teachers' journal, *Der Biologe*. This was to do him the most damage decades later after he had become famous through his popular biology books (*King Solomon's Ring* and *On Aggression*). As his most comprehensive biographer, Richard Burkhardt, writes, Lorenz never 'specifically acknowledged that as a scientist in the Third Reich, in promoting ideas of racial hygiene and using a language of "elimination", he had possibly made an indirect or inadvertent contribution to a program that resulted in genocide'.[51]

Another scientist who embraced Nazi eugenics and racial hygiene theories was Hans Asperger, of Asperger's syndrome. Born just outside Vienna in 1906, Asperger became a child psychiatrist, building on the work of Leo Kanner who first diagnosed the condition of autism in a famous paper published in 1943. Kanner, who fought for the Austro-Hungarian empire in the First World War, emigrated to America in the 1920s and is now hailed as the father of American child psychiatry.

Like Lorenz, Asperger was intricately linked to the social welfare policies of Red Vienna. As part of the 'positive eugenics' of Tandler,

Asperger learned his craft at the Curative Education Clinic, which developed the term 'autistic' sympathetically, as a description of children rather than as a pathology. But the historian Edith Sheffer has meticulously chronicled how, like Lorenz, Asperger could so easily put his own leading-edge scientific research on children at the service of the Nazis' murderous racial hygiene programme, again, it seems, partly out of conviction, and partly for professional advancement. As well as writing several papers that seemed to endorse the Nazis' negative eugenics policy, he also co-founded the Vienna Society for Curative Education in 1940 with two of the city's 'top perpetrators of child killing in Vienna', the callous, murderous Erwin Jekelius and Franz Hamburger.

As part of the new Nazi regime, the society's 'curative education' consisted principally of sorting children with physical or mental disabilities (such as Down's syndrome or epilepsy) into those who could be rehabilitated, that is, 'cured', and those who could not. The latter would be 'eliminated' in Vienna's notorious Am Spiegelgrund, a children's clinic where 789 patients were killed during the war years as part of the child euthanasia policy, a programme overseen mainly by Jekelius. Children here were also subjected to torture-like medical experiments. Asperger appears to have been closely involved in the transfer of at least forty-four children to Am Spiegelgrund. He must have known that there could have been only one outcome. As Sheffer writes, 'in order to operate in these spheres, Asperger had to demonstrate initiative and extraordinary reliability. Asperger knew this since, as he admitted later in life, he was fully aware of the euthanasia program. His affiliation with child euthanasia was an active, not a passive, choice.'[52]

It was in this deeply sinister context that he published his own groundbreaking paper on autism in 1944, extending the diagnosis of autism to include particularly those who experience difficulties in social interactions, a key marker for the Nazis to identify children who did not fit into the greater German *Volk*. It was only in 1981 that a British psychiatrist, Lorna Wing, unearthed Asperger's 1944 paper and described what she termed as 'Asperger's syndrome' in her own paper. The term took off.

Cleared of any wrongdoing after the war, partly because he could not be linked to any specific killings at Am Spiegelgrund, Asperger died in 1980 disassociated from his crimes. Details of his involvement in Vienna's child euthanasia only emerged much later, so 'when Asperger's work went mainstream, it was cleansed of its historical context. Or rather, maybe it went mainstream because it was cleansed of its historical context.'[53]

While Lorenz became a global TV star, appearing in cuddly nature shows and documentaries, and Asperger prospered in post-war Vienna, taking over as professor of paediatrics at the university, the worlds of the Vivarium, Kammerer and Steinach were buried. Only recently have their contributions been excavated and reassessed. Today, it is thought that Kammerer's midwife toad experiments could well have been authentic. Some have even hailed him as one of the founders of epigenetics, the new science of evolution that has indeed described physiological mechanisms of cellular change over time.

The term was first used by the English biologist Conrad Hal Waddington in 1947, derived from the Greek term epigenesis. It was only later, however, that epigenetics began to challenge the old 'central dogma' of genetic inheritance, excluding any possibility of Lamarckian inheritance of acquired characteristics.[54] In the 1980s, laboratory work began to show how, in the process of DNA methylation, genes could be switched on and off during development, according to environmental and behavioural factors. The only question now is how big a role epigenetics actually plays in evolution. Be that as it may, these recent advances acknowledge, as the biologist Eva Jablonka terms it, 'multiple inheritance systems'.[55]

Steinach's work, too, is much better known, especially on transgender issues. His colleague Hirschfeld is now acclaimed for his early campaigning on homosexual rights. Steinach's faithful (and often sole) acolyte and supporter in America, Harry Benjamin, went on to write the groundbreaking *Transsexual Phenomenon* in 1966, which first laid out at length the somatic (rather than psychological) explanations for transsexualism. It is widely regarded as the first medical textbook on transsexualism, opening the way for the subject to be taken much more seriously in clinics and medical schools, setting the stage for the more contemporary transgender studies. Benjamin died in 1986. Thus, the work of the Vivarium, of Kammerer and Steinach has continued long beyond their lifespans, despite the Nazis' worst efforts.

To its eternal shame, the post-war Austrian state spent decades privileging the 'victim' narrative over sharing any responsibility for Nazism and the Holocaust. Despite a token attempt at 'de-Nazification' after 1945, many officials were merely reinstated to their posts, and the process of erasing the Vienna of the interwar years continued, by other means. Take the Vivarium. The botanist Fritz Knoll, who had willingly signed the closure order in 1938, was commissioned by the Austrian Academy to write two volumes, published in 1950 and 1957, on great Austrian natural scientists, engineers and physicians. Not one of the Vivarium's scientists, let alone the place itself, merited a mention. This was symptomatic of the nationalistic anti-Semitism that lingered in Vienna for decades, even after the full depravity of the Holocaust was revealed.

Among the worst offenders were, once again, university academics. Although more than half of their number were sacked after 1945 as part of the de-Nazification programme, by 1950 many of them had returned to their posts.[56] Right up to the 1970s, the University of Vienna continued to elect Rectors with clear connections to Austria's fascist and Nazi past. As late as the mid-1970s, the Rector was a neurologist, Franz Seitelberger, a former doctor in the SS who had based his *Habilitation*, or thesis, on the brain specimens of three brothers who had died between 1942 and 1944 in the Brandenburg-Görden killing facility.[57] Despite student-led protests against him, he served his full term. In the specific case of the Vivarium, it was only after the 1990s that the Academy came to admit that its treatment of the institution and its staff had been a 'shameful chapter' in its history.[58]

It was only in November 2021, shortly before I finished this book, that the City of Vienna and the Austrian government inaugurated the Shoah Wall of Names Memorial, in remembrance of all those 64,440 Austrian Jewish men, women and children murdered during the Holocaust.

PART III

Emigrants and Exiles

Hollywood gold: Jack Lemmon and Vienna's Billy Wilder made seven films together, starting with Some Like It Hot.

Chapter 7

Awake, Slumbering Giant!
The Viennese Discover America

In this third part of the book I focus mainly on the influence of the Viennese abroad, beginning with the first immigrants to America and Britain from before the First World War. Naturally, perhaps, the historical focus has usually been on those exiles who were forced to leave Vienna and Austria in traumatic circumstances in the 1930s, particularly after the *Anschluss*; many of those exiles have already been mentioned in the previous chapters. It is often under appreciated, however, how many had left their home city even before the mass migrations that immediately preceded the outbreak of European war in 1939. Many Viennese of this pre-*Anschluss* era, the subject of this chapter, not only saw better prospects for themselves professionally in America, they also sensed an opportunity to mould what they saw as a young, hesitant country in their own image.

These early emigrants from Vienna, even more so than the later exiles, excited interest in the Anglo-Saxon world because of their skills and expertise that had been honed in *fin-de-siècle* – and later Red – Vienna. Moreover, they showed a willingness to apply their skills to entirely new fields of commerce, art and, most importantly, everyday living – a disposition that was, as we have seen, markedly Viennese.

The past is a bucket of ashes

Critically, for the purposes of tracing Viennese influence abroad, many of the younger generation, those coming of age around the time of the First World War, were as captivated by the possibilities of building a new, modern world in America as they were by the idea of creating one amidst the debris of post-war central Europe. In contrast to this generation of young Viennese, most of the older generation – born in the mid-nineteenth century – had scarcely bothered with America. When the country did cross their horizons they often exhibited the lofty disdain common amongst Europe's haute bourgeoisie at the time. In this milieu, such contempt only increased after the First World War, as the Viennese, like many central Europeans, mournfully compared their own impoverished, enfeebled civilisation with the newly assertive, abundantly rich and increasingly powerful behemoth across the Atlantic.

Oswald Spengler encapsulated this rich mixture of envy, resentment and fearfulness in *The Decline of the West*, first published in Vienna in 1918. A few years later, in 1925, Stefan Zweig wrote an excoriating critique of American mass culture in the *Neue Freie Presse* entitled 'Die Monotonisierung der Welt' (The Monotonisation of the World). This was a long, snobbish complaint against what he deemed to be the creeping uniformity of life, which he attributed to the invasion of Hollywood films and incipient Americanisation.[1]

Few of the older generation ever visited America unless they absolutely had to, or until they were eventually forced to find refuge there. Freud's abhorrence of America and all things American was almost unbounded. He referred to the United States as 'Dollaria' and its people as 'savages'. 'America is a mistake,' Freud wrote notoriously, 'admittedly a gigantic mistake, but a mistake nevertheless'. A generally admiring biographer, Peter Gay, a German Jewish refugee to America, can barely hide his dismay at Freud's demented strength of feeling on the subject. 'To hear him talk,' Gay writes, 'the country and its denizens were hypocritical, uncultivated, shallow, enamoured of money alone, and covertly anti-Semitic ... these sentiments run through Freud's correspondence like an unpleasant, monotonous theme.' Bending over to be generous, the best that Gay can do is to surmise that the intensely bourgeois European was 'ventilating some inner need rather than listening to his experience'.[2] Freud visited America only once, with significant consequences, as we shall see in Chapter 10.

Contrast that, however, with the sentiments of the younger Adolf Loos, born in 1870. He set off from Vienna for New York at the age of twenty-three to escape an overbearing mother and a stifling education. He spent the next three years in America, particularly in Chicago, and loved it. As his biographer, Christopher Long, argues, these years 'would become the most important formative experience of his life'. For a budding architect who was to be intricately involved in the evolution of Modernism, he could be expected to admire the steel canyonlands of New York and Chicago. More so, however, Loos appreciated a new energy and spirit abroad in America, as well as a receptiveness and openness to new ideas – and people.

Modernism, Loos came to believe, was nothing less than the American willingness to solve problems (whether architectural or otherwise) on their own terms, without resorting to artifice or merely adapting past models to the present. Long quotes from a letter that Loos wrote to a Viennese colleague explaining his perception: 'We were always told to look back, to adopt some other era as our model. This mountain has been swept from my sight. Indeed, the age in which we are now living is beautiful, so beautiful that I want not to live in any other.'[3] Loos's American years fortified him for his life-long campaign against the prevailing historicist school of architecture in his native city, one that was all about delving into the past to embellish the present.

Fired by their master's enthusiasm, Loos's students and acolytes back in Vienna took off for America at the first opportunity. If his promptings were not enough, they were further encouraged by the celebrated edition of Frank Lloyd Wright's early designs and drawings brought out by the Berlin publisher Ernst Wasmuth in 1910, an enterprise supervised by Wright himself. For the first time, Europeans were exposed to the architect's 'Prairie Style' houses with their plain rectilinear form, devoid of any of the usual clutter of historical motifs and classical allusions. Wright's bold and experimental use of new materials was equally exciting. For Loos's followers, in particular Richard Neutra (born 1892), Rudolph Schindler (1887) and Paul Frankl (1886), Wright's work was a stunning revelation. The trio made their way to his studio in Chicago as quickly as they could.

Both Frankl and Schindler succeeded in doing so before the First Word War, whereas Neutra joined them in 1923, having been called up for military service before he could escape. Schindler had a particularly close, but unrewarding, relationship with Frank Lloyd Wright, effectively running his studio from 1917 to 1921 for little pay and less acknowledgement. He was eventually released to begin afresh in Los Angeles, where he set up a practice with Neutra. Josef Frank (born 1885), another young Viennese architect under the spell of Loos, was similarly wrapped up in admiration for America.

Thus began a profoundly fruitful dialogue between Vienna and America in terms of architecture, design, art and business. These Viennese *chose* America; for Neutra, it was 'the country of my dreams'.[4] They were enthusiastic immigrants, rather than exiles. The dire economic problems in Vienna after the war and the lack of jobs also fuelled youthful emigration, as did frustration with the deadening conservatism of much of Viennese society. The latter was all the more reason to embrace America and explains why, on the whole, the new arrivals wanted to become American citizens. By contrast, many of the post-1933 German exiles were often bitterly critical of the country, importing their Freudian prejudices whole, along with their Marxist anti-capitalist politics. It is telling that the Neutras and Schindlers in Los Angeles, for instance, maintained their distance from the exile community on the West Coast after

1938. The two Viennese architects despaired of the incessant European carping about the freedoms, sun and opportunities. Most of the exiles longed to return to Europe; Neutra and Schindler wanted firmly to be Americans, in every sense possible.[5]

Awake, slumbering giant

The American reality, of course, could be very different from the country of an excited young Viennese's imagination, especially after the First World War. Just as the implosion of the Austro-Hungarian empire in 1918 released an overwhelming burst of intellectual and political energy in central Europe, so the end of the war, by contrast, saw America withdrawing rapidly from the new political and financial responsibilities that it had assumed over the previous few years. On the verge of seizing its destiny, it seemed, America had faltered, adopting a risk-averse approach that was to prevail throughout the 1920s. Certainly, culturally and intellectually, anything avant-garde, or even just slightly out of the mainstream, provoked just as much resistance, or more, as it had done before the war.

Such conservatism puzzled and frustrated the Viennese immigrants. Completing his first tour of America in 1914, Frankl recalled in his unpublished memoir:

My visit to the States has been all I could have wished for and a great deal more. My eyes beheld the beauty that is America. I saw much and learned even more, but my search for new expressions in architecture was in vain. Instead I discovered the greatest country in the world, unaware of its own greatness, copying the meaningless outworn form of architecture of bygone days and bygone countries. A giant, slumbering, waiting to be awakened.[6]

This, then, was the Viennese immigrants' mission – to give America an idiom, a style, that was distinctly, unquestionably American, to express all the energy and excitement that Americans themselves

231

seemed so coy about. Wright had taken a few stuttering steps in the right direction, but only with a handful of houses in the Midwest. As a designer, Frankl's ambition was to bring a new, authentically American style into every home. In 1925, after years of experimenting, often in the bohemian enclave that he gathered around himself in Woodstock, north of New York, Frankl finally stumbled upon the idea of arranging slender bookcases on top of one another to produce what the neighbours quickly dubbed 'Skyscraper' bookshelves. Thus was born 'Skyscraper furniture', the first recognisably Modernist item to permeate the more fashionable American homes, and soon the wider culture too, for it not only featured in innumerable household magazines but also became the butt of endless jokes and cartoons.

Frankl's gallery on New York's 48th Street, hitherto a rather hit-and-miss affair, couldn't get the new style out through its doors quickly enough. Most of Frankl's furniture was still hand-crafted; one unfortunate consequence was that cheap imitations were soon filling up all those living rooms that Frankl himself was too slow to reach. But it didn't matter much, as Frankl had at least made a point. As he himself put it, 'the name "Skyscraper Furniture" told the story. It was tied up with the big city and its tall buildings . . . an expression of our day and age.'[7]

Frankl was probably the most tireless promoter of Modernism in furniture, design and architecture in America during the interwar years. He was the driving force behind the creation, in 1928, of the American Union of Decorative Artists and Craftsmen (AUDAC), the first group determined 'to make the modern style American'. AUDAC evolved out of the informal discussion groups on art and design that Frankl hosted at his gallery after hours.

One important ally in Frankl's endeavours was Wolfgang Hoffmann, the son of Josef, founder of the Wiener Werkstätte. The younger Hoffmann emigrated from Vienna to New York in 1925 with his

(opposite) Inventing America: Paul Frankl's 'Skyscraper' cabinet.

vivacious, talented and brand new wife Pola, who was to make her name in America as a fabric designer (when she was better known as Pola Stout, after her second marriage). They were brought over to help the Modernist cause by an often-overlooked Viennese called Joseph Urban, born in 1872, who had moved to the United States, initially to Boston, in 1911. Tall and portly, with expensive tastes in food and wine, the well-connected and workaholic Urban divided his time in America between a suite at the St Regis Hotel in New York and winter sun in Florida. He also maintained a home in Yonkers, where he unexpectedly bred sheepdogs. Urban was in many ways the most successful, and talented, of all the Viennese immigrants of this era. Principally an architect, the prodigy received his first commission at the age of just nineteen from the young Khedive of Egypt, to create a new wing for the Abdin Palace in Cairo.

However, Urban could turn his hand to almost any aspect of art and design, and he is now remembered principally for his contributions to theatre and film. He was a leader of what was called the 'New Stagecraft', which sought to strip away the clutter and visual distractions from the conventional theatre of the time. Between 1917 and 1933 he worked on fifty or so productions for the Metropolitan Opera of New York, and also combined with the impresario Florenz Ziegfeld to create the visual presentation of the *Ziegfeld Follies* (and for good measure he also built the Ziegfeld Theatre, now destroyed).[8]

But it was his contribution to cinema that was seminal, argues one critic, as Urban was 'the first person in America to create modern set designs for films'.[9] Urban created the lavish and enormously expensive sets for William Randolph Hearst's film company Cosmopolitan Productions from 1920 to 1925. (These silent films, such as *Enemies of Women*, often starred Marion Davies, Hearst's secret lover.) Urban's film sets were *Jugendstil* masterpieces. A devotee of the Wiener Werkstätte, he usually filled his interiors with objects from the Viennese workshops; consequently, they bore striking resemblances to Secessionist-style Ringstrasse apartments.

Urban helped several Viennese designers and artists get a foothold in the American market, including Wolfgang and Pola Hoffmann. He commissioned Viennese to work on the architectural projects with which he became involved, most memorably the grandiose and fabulously expensive 128-room Mar-a-Lago estate in Palm Beach, Florida, designed by the architect Marion Sims Wyeth. As the most flamboyant and innovative designer of his day, Urban was the only choice to oversee the interiors of this vast project, the dream of breakfast-cereal heiress Marjorie Merryweather Post. For four years Urban shuttled between New York and Florida to complete the

The interior of Mar-a-Lago, a fantasy in the sun now owned by Donald Trump.

estate, a preposterous confection of European styles and materials blended with southern comforts, including a golf course.

Mar-a-Lago remains, essentially, a glorified film set, a fitting backdrop for the ostentatious lifestyle of the present owner, Donald Trump, who bought the mansion in 1985. Urban's Viennese colleagues contributed a great deal to Mar-a-Lago; Frankl, for one, designed the tower room, which served as guest quarters. Another Austrian, Franz Barwig, was commissioned as a sculptor on the building.

But however much success Urban enjoyed, even he struggled, like Frankl, to make much headway in diverting mainstream American taste towards Viennese Modernism. Despite advertising the wares of the Wiener Werkstätte in his films, Urban's attempt to sustain a branch of the Viennese workshops in New York failed after just two years.[10] It was only after the financial crash of 1929 that American businesses and manufacturers became more receptive to innovation, desperate to revive flagging sales and reach new consumers.

The Viennese in Hollywood

If Urban created the best sets, the soundtracks to these early movies were often provided by the Viennese Max Steiner, who moved to America via Britain in 1914. A precocious musical talent, Steiner had conducted his first operetta in Vienna at the age of just twelve. Steiner is often referred to as the 'father of film music'; from the 1920s through to the late 1950s he produced over 300 original scores for RKO pictures and Warner Brothers, including such huge hits as *King Kong, Gone with the Wind* and *Casablanca* (the latter was directed by another immigrant from the former Austro-Hungarian empire, the Budapest-born Michael Curtiz).[11]

Steiner's only rival in the Hollywood of this era was the even more talented Viennese Erich Wolfgang Korngold, 'so gifted,' according to one admirer, 'that even before his teens he was producing mature works of genuine worth that the greatest musicians of his time clamoured to perform.'[12] Born in 1897 into a middle-class Jewish family in the town of Brno, now in the Czech Republic, Korngold was often compared by his awestruck contemporaries to Mozart, after whom he took his middle name. At the age of five, little Erich was already playing themes from *Don Giovanni* by ear on the piano; he composed his first ballet (*Der Schneeman*, The Snowman) at eleven; and it was performed at the Vienna Court Opera when he was just 13. Mahler, a close friend of his father's, declared him to be a genius. In Vienna such an endorsement assured Korngold a swift rise through the musical ranks. By 1912 Sir Henry Wood was conducting Korngold's music at the London Promenade concerts.

Although of the same generation as Schoenberg, Korngold's music has best been described as epic romanticism. In other words, for all his sophistication he was resolutely *not* a Modernist; devotees of atonal music often dismissed him as a reactionary conservative. However, what appalled the Modernists certainly appealed to the nascent film industry. He was first brought over to Hollywood in 1934 by Max Reinhardt, with whom he had collaborated frequently in Vienna, to adapt the Mendelssohn score for his lavish production of *A Midsummer Night's Dream*, with the unlikely casting of James Cagney as Bottom and Mickey Rooney as Puck.

Korngold was almost unique amongst the German and Austrian émigré composers of this era for both maintaining his status as an acclaimed international composer, celebrated especially for his opera *Die tote Stadt* (The Dead City), whilst also prospering in Hollywood's dictatorial and frequently demeaning studio system. Jack Warner's studio, intent on producing classier fare than the usual gangster movies, would barely move without him. During the 1940s Korngold was earning an astonishing $12,500 per assignment, more than any other composer in the business.[13]

Given his reputation, the indispensable Korngold was allowed unusual liberty on set. Normally, a composer was merely required to add orchestration to a finished movie. For *A Midsummer Night's Dream*, however, he was allowed an orchestra onstage hidden by artificial shrubbery, experimenting with melodies as the actors spoke their lines. Bard of the swashbuckler, he wrote his first full symphonic score for Errol Flynn's *Captain Blood* and won an Oscar for *The Adventures of Robin Hood* in 1938. Korngold was also responsible for another Flynn extravaganza, *The Sea Hawk*, released in 1940. He was Hollywood royalty, living in the luxurious Toluca Lake neighbourhood near Bob Hope and Frank Sinatra. Yet he became deeply depressed by the fate of Austria during the war, only rallying in the late 1940s to compose a last symphony to celebrate Hitler's defeat. He died in 1957, aged sixty, and has subsequently become something of a cult figure. He is buried in the Hollywood cemetery.

Steiner and Korngold were classically trained, and both wrote an impressive number of symphonies, concertos, string quartets and more on top of their film scores. In being willing to apply their classical techniques to an entirely new medium, they won for film composing 'a degree of respectability that soon drew other international celebrities into the game'.[14] Schoenberg, by contrast, who moved to Los Angeles in 1934, a year after arriving in New York, never embraced Hollywood, despite teaching many film composers. Despite this, Schoenberg took to West Coast living with surprising alacrity, playing tennis with Charlie Chaplin, learning a good deal of American slang and following the football team at UCLA, where he was on the faculty.

After the film composers, came the directors. Fritz Lang moved to Hollywood only in the mid-1930s, but long before that, he already judged much of his work by American standards. Like Frankl, he was similarly transfixed by the sheer possibilities of America. Reared on the mighty Ringstrasse, he nonetheless saw his first acquaintance with New York as a step up. He often liked to tell the story of how, glimpsing the skyline of Manhattan from the sea for the first time in 1924, he instantly conceived the idea for his most famous film, *Metropolis*:

The buildings seemed to be a vertical veil, shimmering, almost weightless, a luxurious cloth hung from the dark sky to dazzle, distract, and hypnotize. At night the city did not give the impression of being alive; it lived as illusions lived. I knew then that I had to make a film about all of these sensations.[15]

The flamboyant, domineering Lang was a great myth-maker, and the origins of *Metropolis* were in fact rather more prosaic; his wife, Thea von Harbou, had actually been working on a script for months before the director had his apparent epiphany. Nonetheless, there is no doubting the visual impact of New York on the film, especially its famed opening sequences where planes buzz around streets dwarfed by the towering skyscrapers, anticipating *Blade Runner* and many other homages.

Indeed, the entire convoluted, dangerous and emotionally fraught production of *Metropolis* in Berlin during the years 1925 to 1926 was essentially a tribute to the scale and ambition of America and Hollywood. Lang's production company, Ufa (the biggest in Europe), had mounted some big shoots before, but *Metropolis* topped them all. It was self-consciously the most expensive and extravagant European film ever made, as the studio's statistics emphasised: 36,000 extras, 750 children from Berlin's slums and a further 750 actors, just in the 'small' roles. Fortunately, the film was well-received in America, where Ufa hoped to recoup most of its vast financial outlay, but only after it was cut by about forty minutes. Lang, of course, was scandalised by the edits, but had no choice.

Berlin was the centre of European film making at this time and therefore attracted most of Vienna's young cinematic and theatrical talent, not only Lang but also Billy Wilder and Fred Zinnemann. The jazz-loving, irreverent Wilder, a German-speaking Jew born in Galicia in 1906, honed his plot-lines and dialogue as a cub crime reporter in post-war Vienna, but moved to Berlin in 1926 to learn screenwriting. Like the architects, the young Viennese filmmakers left their home city with scarcely a backward glance. The more urbane Zinnemann, born in 1907, persuaded his parents to let him have his first look at the American film business aged just twenty-one.

239

On experiencing New York, he later recorded: '[It was] full of excitement, with a vitality and pace then totally lacking in Europe. It was as though I had just left a continent of zombies and entered a place humming with incredible energy and power.'[16] He quickly moved to Hollywood to begin his directing career.

The lordly Otto Preminger, two years older than Zinnemann, followed a different path to Hollywood. Like Zinnemann, he also took a law degree at the University of Vienna, but his first love was for the theatre rather than cinema. He started out as a protégé of the Viennese-born stage director and impresario Max Reinhardt. The latter spent most of his career in Berlin up to 1933, but opened his own experimental theatre in Vienna in 1924, the Theater in der Josefstadt.

The young, besotted Preminger lived around the corner, and from the late 1920s started taking lead roles in Reinhardt productions, eventually succeeding his mentor in charge of the theatre. In 1935, Preminger was invited to New York to direct plays on Broadway, before moving to Hollywood soon afterwards. All these directors were born into Jewish families, and so the migration to America was often forced upon them directly by the Nazi takeover in Berlin in 1933 and the deteriorating situation in Austria. Wilder, for instance, hastily left the German capital just as Hitler came to power; a fellow Galician Jew, Sam Spiegel, later a three-times Oscar-winning producer (also with a law degree from the University of Vienna), fled Germany back to Vienna in 1933 and then later to Mexico. Others, however, had left for America well before it was obvious exactly how devastating the fascist onslaught would be, committed to exploring their new environment with the critical faculties and sharp cinematic eye developed in Vienna.

Preminger, whose grandfather had been a Talmudic scholar, was asked by a studio publicist in the 1940s to clarify why he always seemed to prefer American to European subjects. He replied by quoting a line from the poet, Carl Sandburg: 'The past is a bucket of ashes.' As Preminger explained:

Many times I have been asked to do again in America some of the things that turned out successfully for me in Europe, but I have always said 'No', because I have a horror of going backwards ... For me, Europe is the past and America is the future ... as a new American, intensely interested in every facet of American life, I might just possibly have something new to offer to stories with American settings.[17]

The moral challenge of *Some Like It Hot*

Just as the Viennese designers campaigned to craft a new, modern American aesthetic, so the Viennese filmmakers, led by Wilder and Preminger, engaged in a very conscious assault on conservative American taste on celluloid. Together with Zinnemann, they directed many – perhaps most – of Hollywood's biggest hits over the next few decades. The puckish Wilder, instantly recognisable in his trademark trilby hats and square glasses, was not only prolific but unique in his working style; he co-wrote all the films that he directed. He enjoyed an unusually long string of hits, from *Double Indemnity* in 1945, through *Sunset Boulevard* (1950), *The Seven-Year Itch* (1955), *Some Like It Hot* (1959), *The Apartment* (1960) to *The Front Page* in 1974. Some critics rank him as the greatest director of Hollywood's golden age. All in all, he was nominated for an Oscar twenty-one times, and won six.

Lang flourished in America, but arguably he had already made his two masterpieces, *Metropolis* and *M*, before he arrived. By contrast, Wilder, Preminger and Zinnemann saved their best for Hollywood. They were successful because they were prepared to be flexible. Unlike many others, they were prepared to battle it out within the constraints of the strict studio system, just as they were also prepared to work with a variety of genres, from war films to romantic comedy. But they were also drawn to material that specifically challenged conventional filmmaking, as well as the sexual and societal mores of the time. All three directors chafed under Hollywood's extraordinarily squeamish and strait-laced censorship policy.

Self-censorship had begun in 1927 after a series of scandals both on- and off-screen. An organising body, the Motion Picture Producers and Distributors of America (MPPDA) drew up a list of explicit prohibitions, as well as a longer list of more general moral guidelines that films had to follow in order to be distributed in America. Profanity, 'licentiousness', 'any inference of sex perversion', as well as any references to illegal drugs were all strictly banned, while the sacred institution of marriage had to be closely shielded. No 'sympathy' was to be shown to criminals. This was the essence of the Production Code Administration (PCA) which began to be rigorously enforced in 1934, known as the Hays Code after the head of MPPDA, Will Hays. The more important figure, however, was Joseph Breen, head of the PCA for the first twenty years of the code's life. He enforced it with a fervent conviction that drove directors and producers to despair. All scripts were submitted to the PCA before a shoot, and cuts would be demanded from the start. Sometimes the PCA's initial verdict would be so damning that scripts never went forward into production.

To Viennese such as Wilder, reared on the sexual openness, cabaret and prostitution of Vienna (and Weimar Berlin), the PCA was utterly absurd. To give two examples of Breen's prissy restrictiveness, both from Preminger's work: in arguments over the harmless romantic comedy *Centennial Summer*, Breen pounced on a detail of one female character lightly kissing another on both cheeks. 'It will be well for you to shoot this particular scene with the utmost care,' advised Breen sternly in his script notes, 'in order that it will have about it no possible suggestion of the pervert.' On another occasion Breen seized on the word 'fire' in a Preminger script, and noted: 'Please make certain that the use of the word "fire" be so recorded in your sound-track so as to make certain there will be no shouts or cries likely to upset persons within ear-shot of the theatre, who might hear only the word.'[18]

Wilder, in particular, was battling the code from *Double Indemnity* onwards. Previous attempts to make this film, about the moral ambiguities of criminality, had been scotched by a damning report from Breen, but Wilder took up the story and rewrote a screenplay with Raymond Chandler. So artfully was this done that eventually even Breen could not rationally object to the new film. From the mid-1950s both Wilder and Preminger began to be more brazen and antagonistic in their challenges to the PCA. Preminger's film *The Man with the Golden Arm* was a landmark. A story about the taboo subject of drug addiction, in which a man becomes hooked on morphine in the army then gets clear in prison, it was bound to rile the censors, as indeed Preminger intended. Starring Frank Sinatra, the film was consequently refused a seal of approval by the PCA. As a result, United Artists left the MPPDA and lined up separate showings for the film at some cinemas, despite having to take in a few cuts demanded by state censors.

The huge row over the film undoubtedly weakened the code: the fact that audiences did not all immediately take to heroin seemed to invalidate the self-righteous moralising. Consequently, the PCA itself now softened its own restrictions on drug use on celluloid. Preminger returned to the fray with the courtroom drama *Anatomy of a Murder*, starring James Stewart as a lawyer defending a US army sergeant who is alleged to have killed a man who raped his wife. Preminger's insistence that the courtroom discussion about rape be as realistic as possible – the trial judge in the film was a real attorney – involved him in another long confrontation with the PCA. This particular to-and-fro was a triumph for the director, as he not only got a seal of approval but also achieved his own artistic aims of making his court scenes as visceral as possible. Released in 1959, *Variety* magazine claimed that the film was the very first time that American audiences had heard such words as 'contraception', 'panties' and sexual 'climax' in the cinema.

The PCA was having to relax its standards anyway because of the influx of racy British and French films, which did not have to get PCA approval. But the film that finally ended the tyranny of the Hay's Code was Wilder's peerless *Some Like It Hot*, starring Marilyn Monroe, Jack Lemmon and Tony Curtis (see image p. 226). On the run from the mob, Lemmon and Curtis dress up as women to join Monroe's all-female jazz band. Despite the ensuing hilarity, Wilder took his subject matter seriously, and imported a famous drag queen, Barbette, to advise the two men on the finer points of cross-dressing. Drag comedy, however, was not a subject likely to endear itself to the PCA, so Wilder took the bold step of never sending them a script for approval. The fact that he was not sanctioned for this breach showed how the power of the PCA had waned. He won a code seal anyway, demonstrating Wilder's supreme gift for approaching taboo subjects through innuendo and humour.

But the film's most important contribution to breaking the code was its huge popularity with audiences. It showed the authorities that Americans could in fact handle 'adult' themes, and by the mid-1960s the code was barely being enforced. A new rating system was introduced in 1968. Wilder died in 2002 at the age of ninety-five. Together with Preminger and others he had undoubtedly helped shift America in a more permissive direction.

Inventing California style

Unlike the film directors battling against nationwide film censorship, those Viennese designers and architects who moved to the West Coast of America in the 1920s enjoyed an openness to fresh ideas that enabled them to pioneer a genuinely new, indigenous style, uniquely suited to the seductive climate and environment of Los Angeles. The Viennese, to use Neutra's phrase, found Californians 'mentally footloose', and thus more receptive to 'trying something independent of hidebound habituation'.[19] And in the early days of the Viennese immigration to the Golden State the man most willing to kick against tradition and conformity was undoubtedly Rudolph Schindler, the former assistant to Frank Lloyd Wright.

The bohemian Schindler was, for want of a better phrase, a proto-hippy, all open-necked silk shirts and year-round sandals. Sporting a moustache and a mop of unruly swept-back hair, Schindler, together with his American wife Pauline, a teacher and political activist, were determinedly unconventional. He pioneered a new style of communal, West Coast living with the construction in 1921–22 of his Kings Road House (now preserved as the Schindler House) in West Hollywood.

Although it now appears squeezed in and out-faced by towering duplexes on a residential street, the Schindler House was originally built on an open site with sweeping views in every direction. Schindler wanted to create a new form of living space suited to the particular environment and lifestyle of Los Angeles. In Vienna, even before the First World War, Schindler had written about a new concept of 'space architecture', which would dissolve the distinction between 'the indoors and outdoors'. The Californian climate gave him the perfect opportunity to apply this idea, achieved by using sliding, Japanese-style doors and glass walls to dissolve the boundaries between the rooms and outdoor space, in order to enjoy the temperate climate all year round. The Schindler House suited a new style of informal and flexible living.[20]

The dwelling was designed for two couples, the Schindlers themselves and Clyde and Marian Chace; each man had his own studio, and each couple their own patio garden, but the couples could also meet in the communal kitchen and garden. Schindler blended local vernaculars and materials with Viennese Modernism to create an entirely fresh structure; the concrete walls were inspired by the adobe structures of the New Mexican desert, and they were juxtaposed with Californian redwood beams to give the house its main form. There was no obvious front door; people could enter and leave how they wanted. As Schindler himself explained, 'I introduced features which seemed to me to be necessary for life in California.'[21]

At a time when the domestic architecture of a rapidly expanding Los Angeles was dominated by the Hacienda and neo-Renaissance styles, with a sprinkling of mock-Tudor, Schindler's house was startlingly original. It was also easily mocked; not always very comfortable to live in, the roof was notoriously leaky and the rooms often too hot or too cold. Regardless, the house formed the perfect backdrop to the Schindlers' alternative lifestyles, complete with nude dance shows and plenty of alcohol, even during prohibition. Neither is there any doubting the house's extraordinary influence. Here was the beginning of West Coast Modernism. Some have even argued that the Schindler House was the first identifiably Modernist house built in Europe or America, pre-dating Walter Gropius's Experimental House of 1922–23 and Le Corbusier's Maison La Roche of 1923–25.

Just as significantly, however, like his fellow Viennese architects and designers, he had eschewed the dogmas of the International Style and Bauhaus for a design that was wholly rooted – objectively and personally – in the soil and people of California. Schindler later wrote of his creative journey to the Kings Road:

> I came to live and work in California. I camped under the open sky; in the redwoods, on the beach, the foothills and the desert. I tested its adobe, its granite and its sky. And out of a carefully build up conception of how the human being could grow roots in this soil – unique and delightful – I built my house.
>
> And unless I failed it should be as Californian as the Parthenon is Greek and the Forum Roman. In fact the beginning of a new 'classic' growth drinking California sap.[22]

During the 1920s, Schindler was in demand from several clients interested in contemporary design. From 1925 to 1930, the newly arrived Richard Neutra and his family shared the house with Schindler, and together the two Viennese friends collaborated eagerly. But the more commercially minded Neutra quickly began to outstrip Schindler, both in terms of the boldness of his architecture and his popularity with clients. Feeling overshadowed by

Neutra, the opinionated and sensitive Schindler also felt increasingly neglected and marginalised by the panjandrums of the Modernist establishment in New York.

The Schindlers separated in 1927, but Pauline returned to live in the house in 1938. Schindler died there in 1953, and Pauline in 1977. It is now open to the public, affording a glimpse of how radical, even outrageous, the house and its occupants must have seemed to their fellow LA residents.

Houses for pleasure

It was Richard Neutra, however, who became synonymous with the new American home from the 1920s onwards. Like so many other Viennese who prospered in America, Neutra was heavily influenced by Freud. Not only did the architect spend much of his life in psychoanalysis, at a time when this was still considered to be rather worrying, he had also known Freud and his family well in Vienna. As a school friend of Freud's son Ernst, who also became an architect, the young Neutra was a frequent visitor to the Freud apartment at Berggasse 19. When, later in life, Neutra and his wife needed advice on how to cope with their son who had a mental disability, they turned to Freud. Neutra also knew many of the master's protégés in America. Unsurprisingly, therefore, the new science played a considerable role in Neutra's professional practice, and specifically his conception of what a house, a living-space, should be.

Furthermore, as Freudianism became increasingly acceptable after the 1940s, so the canny Neutra accentuated this aspect of his work. Clients were encouraged to describe their emotional and psychological aspirations for their homes, in order for the architect to understand their requirements in more detail. Those hankering after a Neutra house were asked to fill out detailed questionnaires and to record their daily movements and thoughts in a diary, often over several weeks. One Neutra critic, Sylvia Lavin, has called Neutra's living environments the 'empathic house . . . he deliberately modelled his role as an architect for residential clients on the analyst working with neurotic patients'.[23] Thus, architecture became, according to Neutra, 'applied biology and psychological treatment'.[24]

Far removed from the dominating influence of Mies van der Rohe's severe Modernist aesthetic in New York, Viennese immigrant architects therefore developed something very different in Los Angeles. They imported a Modernist aesthetic, nourished by Loos and Frank Lloyd Wright, certainly, yet adapted it to the local environment and specific needs of the people who would live in their buildings. As Neutra insisted, a 'good house is the fulfilment of the search – in space – for happiness'. Over time, he developed his own quasi-philosophy, 'Biorealism', to describe how structures should adapt to the biological realities of those who inhabit them and to stress 'the inherent and inseparable relationship between man and nature'.[25] This radically people-centric philosophy might have seemed merely quaint on the East Coast, but in California, however, it began to attract not only rich private clients but also school boards and public housing authorities.

This new style has been called 'West Coast Modernism', synonymous with the Hollywood Hills and the then-fashionable neighbourhood of the Silver Lake reservoir in Los Angeles. The founding works were commissioned by the same man, Philip Lovell. He had been born in New York in 1894 to Russian immigrant parents but moved to Los Angeles to practise as a holistic doctor. As an anti-drug 'naturopath', he advocated natural remedies for sickness, which included open-air sleeping, massage, nude sunbathing, vegetarianism and lots of sex. He popularised all this in a column that he wrote for the *Los Angeles Times* entitled 'Care of the Body'. Lovell liked to think of himself as a free-thinker, a radical in his chosen profession, and gravitated towards like-minded souls such as Schindler and Neutra.

Lovell recognised that the two Viennese might be able to express his avant-garde beliefs about the dynamic relationship between the body and nature in steel and concrete. First, Lovell commissioned Schindler to build him a beach house, completed in 1926, while Neutra was invited to construct a large home in East Hollywood. This was the daring and structurally innovative Lovell House, also called the Lovell Health House, built between 1927 and 1929. It required the architect to cut into a hillside and was the first house in America to be built with a steel frame, on stilts, effectively. The residence was entered from the roadside at the top level, where the 'enclosed bedrooms' and sleeping porches were located, with the various floors cascading downwards.

This became the prototype for all southern Californian hillside living, as Lovell had intended. The proud new owner opened his house up for tours after its completion, to advertise what he regarded as a whole new way of life. The result was sensational. Thousands of amazed locals wandered through the expansive, wonderfully light rooms and corridors; for many it might as well have landed from another planet.[26]

The Lovell Health House made its architect famous, virtually overnight. Many architects doodle more than they build; Neutra, by contrast, was almost constantly in demand. Unlike Schindler, Neutra was very aware of his own standing, and could in turn be overbearing, pompous and intrusive. Clients had to be prepared for Neutra and his team to vist their new homes out of the blue if the master wanted another look at some detail or other. But they were prepared to put up with it because they loved, almost literally, their Neutra houses. The architect's career was sustained by his wife, Dione, an accomplished cellist, who totally subsumed her own life to serve her 'genius' husband.[27] By August 1949, such was the vogue for Neutra that his bushy eyebrows, shock of receding white hair and intense, quizzical eyes were staring out from the cover of *Time* magazine, the highest honour in the gift of American popular culture. The caption read, 'What will the neighbours think?', conveying the sense that a Neutra house in the late 1940s was still a provocation, a challenge, even slightly dangerous.

*Libido in the desert: Richard Neutra's famous Kaufmann
House, designed in 1946.*

The apogee of Neutra living is undoubtedly the Kaufmann House in Palm Springs, built in 1945–46 for the same Pittsburgh family that had earlier commissioned Wright's most renowned work, Fallingwater. The iconic photographs of the house by Julius Shulman, with Liliane Kaufmann lounging by the pool in the foreground, were published in the same year as Neutra won his *Time* cover. Shulman brilliantly captured the cool sensuousness of the Kaufmann House, all boulders, water, glass and mirrors, provoking, in the words of Sylvia Lavin, 'actual bodily pleasure', in contrast to Wright's 'moral restraint'.[28]

For the contemporary Neutra fan, however, it is much easier to visit his work in the colony of houses that survive on the shore of Silver Lake, a few of which are still owned by the original families for whom they were built. In all, Neutra completed more than a hundred private houses, six apartment complexes, eight schools, several commercial buildings in Los Angeles, and also contributed towards some of the city's most important housing projects.[29] The old Viennese socialist in him itched to contribute his talents to the public realm and he devoted the same amount of energy, drive and attention to his schools and public apartments as he did to his private palaces – even if none were quite as satisfying in aesthetic terms as the latter. He himself ranked his contributions to California's public sphere as his most important accomplishments. School architecture interested him the most, and he left behind some of the most well-designed examples of the genre in the country. Emerson Middle School in west Los Angeles, opened in 1938, was his finest and most widely imitated.

Neutra's own pupils and acolytes, principally Gregory Ain (born in Pittsburgh and raised in Los Angeles) and Raphael Soriano (born in 1904 of Austrian and Spanish Jewish parents in Greece), in their turn perpetuated the Neutra style through to the 1960s and beyond. Towards the end of his life, Neutra spent an increasing amount of time back in Vienna. He died in Germany in 1970.

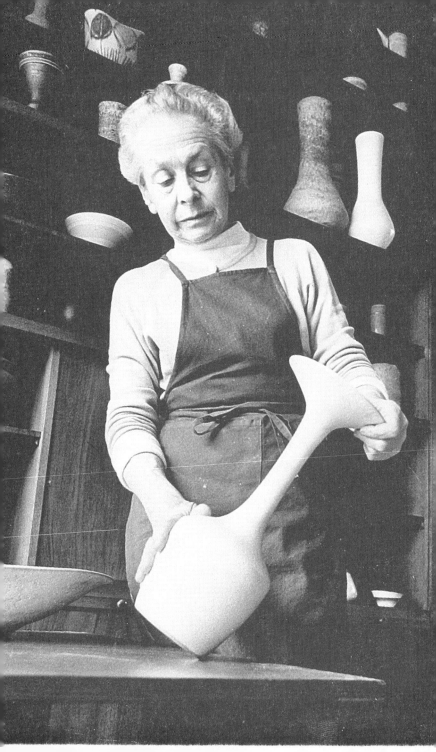

Chapter 8

The Balm of Muddle:
The Viennese in Britain

Whereas America loomed in the Viennese imagination as a sort of *tabula rasa*, an unbounded space of limitless novelty, Britain, by contrast, was often perceived to be quite the opposite – a land of ancient nobility, cosy cottages and genteel customs, about as exciting as the cows that grazed contentedly in its deep green fields. Some Viennese exiles, such as Stefan Zweig, found British life depressingly sterile after Vienna. 'There was sperm in the air', remembered the novelist of his home city as he contemplated the mental pea-souper that was his new London habitat.

Yet most Viennese were nonetheless firm Anglophiles, admirers of Britain's strong traditions of empiricism, liberalism and constitutional democracy. Moreover, many came to relish that very dullness, or more accurately 'conservatism', or even just politeness, after the ceaseless confrontations, incivility and posturing of interwar central Europe. Otto Neurath and his wife Marie Reidemeister, for example, became unlikely converts to British life and culture. After the dogmatism of Germany and Austria, even the tumultuous

(opposite) The ceramicist Lucie Rie in her studio in London.

Neurath found what he called the 'muddle' of his adopted country refreshing. He soon felt, in his own words, part of the 'furniture'.[1]

Furthermore, Britain's very conservatism offered its own opportunities to the younger Viennese. Britain had boasted an intellectual tradition that had outshone even that of Vienna during the country's Victorian heyday. Nonetheless, across many disciplines, by the early decades of the twentieth century Britain's academics and others realised that Vienna had surpassed them. Thus, Britain, like America, hastened to discover the Austrian capital, also encouraging a steady stream of Viennese to cross the continent to London, Manchester and the university cities.

Looking back from the vantage point of the 1960s, the leftist cultural critic Perry Anderson observed this phenomenon with some horror, regarding the 'white emigration' from Europe to Britain as symptomatic of a national culture in decline, robbed of its vitality by the 'cumulative absence of new historical experience', as he put it. 'No matter what the quantum of talent,' sneered the old Etonian, 'any foreign background was an asset in the local doldrums, and might make an intellectual fortune.'[2] Anderson's judgement was harsh, but not inexact; many of these emigrants did indeed make their fortunes, intellectual and otherwise, in Britain.

Even if the British did not have the boundless cash at the disposal of the Rockefeller Foundation, the Viennese intellectual migration was still substantial. For example, the economist Hayek, who arrived in Britain in 1931, was to have a lasting impact on the country, as we shall see in Chapter 11. His distant cousin, Ludwig Wittgenstein, however, was an even earlier émigré to Britain, and he became probably the most famous of them all.

The cult of Wittgenstein

Just as Frank Lloyd Wright's Prairie House designs fired the imagination of Viennese architects and designers before the First World

War, so Bertrand Russell did the same in philosophy with the publication of *The Principles of Mathematics* in 1903. Russell, a scion of one of the wealthiest and most well-connected families in Britain (his grandfather, Lord John Russell, had been prime minister), was to perform a similar role as mentor to Wittgenstein and Vienna's young philosophers as Wright did for its architects, although Russell was considerably more generous and forgiving than the irascible, dictatorial Wright. These Viennese, and especially Wittgenstein, overtook Russell in terms of philosophical innovation, but – except for Wittgenstein – they never lost their respect and admiration for the older Englishman. Karl Popper, in particular, revered Russell, as did many in the Vienna Circle.

The Principles of Mathematics was considered to be revolutionary because Russell argued that the entirety of mathematics could be derived from a few basic, logical principles, contrary to previous philosophers such as Kant who had argued that maths was quite distinct from logic. In the words of Ray Monk, Wittgenstein's biographer, 'For Russell, the importance of the issue lay in the difference between regarding mathematics as a body of certain, *objective* knowledge, and regarding it as a fundamentally *subjective* construction of the human mind.'[3] As we have seen, the German mathematician David Hilbert was also concerned with the same search for certain basic axioms of mathematics.

Russell was to spend the following years laying out these logical principles at inordinate length in *Principia Mathematica*, the first volume of which was published in 1910 and co-authored with another Cambridge philosopher and mathematician, A.N. Whitehead. The third and final volume was eventually published in 1913, leaving Russell intellectually drained. But he was fortunate (perhaps), in that having opened up an entirely new front in logic and mathematics, at this point the young Wittgenstein started to take up Russell's work, fresh and eager to continue his mentor's project by deploying logic and mathematics to probe language itself.

Wittgenstein, born in 1889, was similar to Russell in many ways, a scion of one of his own country's most eminent families. Unusually, he had not attended the University of Vienna, but moved to Berlin and thereafter Manchester to study aeronautics at the city's university. However, as soon as a friend introduced him to *The Principles of Mathematics* he quickly realised where his real interests lay. On 18 October 1911, the serious-minded and unusually nervous young Austrian presented himself at Russell's rooms at Trinity College, Cambridge, apparently without a prior introduction, wishing to place himself under Russell's guidance. At this point, Wittgenstein was concerned only to discover whether he too should become a philosopher. Such were the beginnings of a profoundly fruitful dialogue between Vienna, Britain and America in philosophy and mathematics.

The story of Wittgenstein's relationship with Russell and the influence of the younger man's *Tractatus Logico-Philosophicus* has often been recounted, and will not be repeated here.[4] As we saw in Chapter 4, the *Tractatus* was a starting-point for discussions about language and truth amongst the Vienna Circle, so the book played an important role in the evolution of the particular brand of philosophy, logical positivism, that came to be most closely associated with Vienna. Unsurprisingly, given these close links, Wittgenstein's work and logical positivism cast long shadows over university philosophy in Britain, particularly at Cambridge (where he died in 1951), and also, later, in America.

Almost uniquely for a philosopher, Wittgenstein's influence in Britain (and elsewhere) extended far beyond his chosen field of study. Even during his own lifetime, the Austrian had become a totemic cultural figure, lauded as much for his style of being as for anything he ever wrote, much of which is barely comprehensible. This is the Wittgenstein paradox, that a man who self-consciously dedicated himself to exactitude, rigour and a ruthless honesty in thought, language and life, is remembered as an enigmatic mystic as much as a logician. To the philosopher himself, the famous proposition 7 that ends the *Tractatus*, 'Whereof one cannot speak, thereof one must be silent', might have decluttered philosophy, and indeed language itself, thereby fulfilling his allotted task of putting philosophy on a sound basis. But these few words have also opened up his life and thought to the very opposite – intense imaginative speculation – on an industrial scale.

For as the literary critic Terry Eagleton has pointed out, it is Wittgenstein's commitment to *not knowing* that has excited and enthralled, rather than his commitment to truth and fact. It is this Wittgenstein, rather than the hyper-rationalist, that has so fascinated the artistic imagination in the century since the *Tractatus* appeared. 'Frege is a philosopher's philosopher, Bertrand Russell every shopkeeper's image of the sage, and Sartre the media's idea of an intellectual,' writes Eagleton, 'but Wittgenstein is the philosopher of poets and composers, playwrights and novelists, and snatches of the mighty *Tractatus* have even been set to music.'[5]

The cultural production that has been devoted to Wittgenstein is extensive, including Eagleton's own screenplay for British director Derek Jarman's film *Wittgenstein*. The writer and academic Marjorie Perloff, herself born in Vienna, chronicled the numerous plays, poems, installations and more that have been devoted to exploring every aspect of his life and work in her book *Wittgenstein's Ladder*, published in 1996, and since that date the list has only grown. If anything, the clubbing generation seems to be still more entranced by Wittgenstein than their elders. For a sampling of recent 'Ludwigmusik', check out, for instance, M.A. Numminen's subversion of the Wittgenstein cult in his song 'Wovon man nicht sprechen kann, darüber muss man schweigen' (Whereof one cannot speak, thereof one must be silent). Or see the *Tractatus* being taken rather too seriously and set to jazz/dance music in 2019 by Munich's Jazzrausch Bigband. The lyrics of 'Dancing Wittgenstein' really do begin with the famous opening proposition 'The world is all that is the case', but by way of compensation the Bigband's breezy rhythms are considerably more danceable than Numminen's ironic dirge.[6]

Perloff must be right in attributing so much of the world's obsession with Wittgenstein to his paradoxes; he was born one of the richest men in Europe, yet gave his fortune away and lived in spartan, rented rooms furnished with deck chairs; a war hero, he eschewed militarism; an intellectual giant, he worked as a humble schoolteacher for years in rural Austria. 'Wittgenstein comes to us,' Perloff writes, 'as the ultimate modernist outsider, the changeling who never stops reinventing himself, who never really "belongs", and whose presence is nevertheless so overwhelming that we can immediately identify it as Wittgenstein's.'[7]

In a sense, however, that 'overwhelming presence' has forever distorted the world's perceptions of the Viennese diaspora. It is ironic that of all their number it is the epigrammatic, mysterious Wittgenstein who has come to dominate popular perceptions of the Viennese intellectual, for in reality he was an outlier, an exception, rather than the rule. Most obviously, he was a loner who developed his philosophical strategies independently, whereas most of the intellectual production surveyed in this book was the result of collaboration, the organised, mediated clash of disciplines, theories and people. Wittgenstein remained studiously aloof from Vienna's intellectual life. Poor Moritz Schlick, for one, spent months trying to entice him to the Vienna Circle. 'What would Wittgenstein say here?' became a constant refrain of Schlick's at the Circle's meetings, to the increasing irritation of the other members. The truth is that Wittgenstein was rarely anywhere for very long, and his elusiveness only added to his elevated status. Yet this should never be mistaken for the Viennese intellectual method, even if the misconception remains, and, unfortunately, is unlikely ever to be rectified.

The methodological individualism of Ernst Gombrich

It is unlikely that Ernst Gombrich's work will ever get a jazz/ funk soundtrack, but he transformed his own discipline of art history as assuredly as Wittgenstein did philosophy. Like his fellow Viennese, Gombrich, born in 1909, came to Britain and prospered in a field where the Austrian capital had left Britain behind. Just as Russell tacitly acknowledged this lag in the work of the querulous Wittgenstein, so the equally patrician Kenneth Clark, England's leading young art historian of the day, recognized in Gombrich the skills and talent to modernise his own discipline.

In 1933 the library of the German exile Aby Warburg arrived in Britain and when, three years later, the youthful Gombrich came to carry out research there, art history in Britain was still mostly a matter of attribution. Gombrich, however, had started applying Popperian scientific concepts, as well as psychology, to art. Again, it was Viennese methodology that demanded the attention of the Anglo-Saxon world. Clark was shrewd enough to recognise that his own country had plenty to learn from the Vienna School of Art History, writing in the mid-1930s that the Viennese 'attempt to put the subject onto a broader and more humanistic basis comes at a moment when the dominant school of connoisseurship is practically exhausted in England'.[8] Clark helped the young immigrant climb up the greasy pole of his profession in his newly adopted country.

The Vienna School, of which Gombrich was an outstanding exemplar, had transformed the study of art during the second half of the nineteenth century. Inspired mainly by Rudolf von Eitelberger (appointed as associate professor at the University of Vienna in 1852), the Viennese sought to put the study of art onto an explicitly scientific basis, in the spirit of Ernst Mach, and to establish it therefore as a distinct discipline. Institutionally, this aim was achieved with the founding of the Institute of Art History in 1874.

Crucially, the Vienna School ruled out the idea that aesthetic judgements had any role to play in art-historical analysis. Instead, Eitelberger and his successors 'introduced the liberal paradigm of scientific research with agreed protocols of analysis, argumentation, and demonstration'.[9] The early Vienna School focused its energies on philology, translating and publishing textual sources relevant to understanding a painting or sculpture in its historical context. Added to this, the school developed a method of impartial, scientific visual analysis that stood apart from, and was in contrast to, the eye of the artist.

The new Viennese methodology began to gain wide recognition in the 1870s. Moreover, the Vienna School kept on evolving to adapt to the latest scientific advances as they unfolded. By the first decades of the new century, these included the novel disciplines of psychoanalysis and psychology, so it was only natural that a new generation of University of Vienna art historians should turn their attention to them. The most important of this rising generation were Ernst Kris, born in 1900, and Gombrich himself, born into a wealthy, very musical, assimilated Jewish family on the Ringstrasse. Gombrich was a decent cellist, his mother an excellent pianist and his elder sister a concert violinist (and music therapist). Gombrich's father had served a legal apprenticeship with Karl Popper's father, and the two offspring remained close friends and allies for the rest of their lives.

Kris was particularly keen to integrate psychoanalysis into the study of art. He was close to Freud's circle and was himself analysed by Helene Deutsch, head of training at the Ambulatorium, where Kris also briefly worked. Gombrich was less consumed by psychoanalysis, but fascinated by the new advances in cognitive psychology. In the 1930s Kris and Gombrich combined their skills and interests to explore the subject of caricature, approaching it, in the words of author Louis Rose, 'not as a low form of creativity or a debased mode of communication but as a distinctive psychological and cultural phenomenon with its own function and evolution'. As Rose points out, in the context of mid-1930s Vienna, the subject was also a simulacrum for political dissent, as the study was linked in part to a show in Vienna of the works of the French caricaturist Honoré Daumier, a democrat and anti-militarist.[10]

With rising anti-Semitism, however, both Kris and Gombrich were forced to move to London. The latter's first impressions of Britain's capital were not encouraging. 'London was grim, a dirty smelly city,' he recalled much later. 'It was freezing cold. My landlady lit a tiny fire which was so weak that it didn't warm the room at all. I had very little money . . . and usually ate in those Lyons or Express Dairy cafes which seemed very dirty and smelled of old fat.'[11] Nonetheless, whereas Kris swiftly moved on to New York in 1940, to teach at the New School for Social Research, Gombrich stayed in Britain, teaching mainly in London and Oxford before taking up a professorship at the Warburg Institute.

Although only in his mid-twenties, Gombrich was already equipped with most of the formidable intellectual apparatus that would mark his contribution to art history, substantially modernising the discipline in the process. Gombrich continued to use psychology to interpret shifts in artistic activity and creation, approaching images as mental constructs, the subject of his most influential book, *Art and Illusion*. In a very Viennese fashion, therefore, his most enduring contribution was the application of one discipline to another – psychology to the visual arts.

Equally, over the whole course of his productive life, Gombrich continued to wage Vienna's relentless war on German idealism and the metaphysical fog, flaying those who advocated 'absolute theories of human nature and society in defiance of the humane and liberal values that allow us to operate with open minds'.[12] He set out his arguments most eloquently in the essay 'In Search of Cultural History', published in 1969. Taking issue with the continuing (and then very fashionable) fixations with *Zeitgeist* and

Volksgeist in cultural history, Gombrich instead urged his readers to fix their attention 'firmly on the individual human being'. In another essay, he advised readers to consider 'living people in concrete situations'.

Like Popper, Gombrich nurtured a deep distrust of anything that smacked of historical inevitability and historicism, to use his friend's phrase. In his own discipline, Gombrich was constantly testing grand historical theories against the facts, only to find them wanting. One later commentator on Gombrich, Harry Mount, has summarised his approach as attending 'not to generalisations but to the specifics of individual cases assessed through a forensic analysis of factual evidence derived from primary sources'.[13] This remains as good a shorthand as any to describe the Viennese approach to social sciences, and it enabled Gombrich, together with Kenneth Clark himself, to become one of the most effective communicators about art, taste and culture of the modern era. Furthermore, Gombrich's success in this field was intimately bound up with his fellow émigrés' jolting transformation of Britain's fusty old trade of book publishing.

Bildung in books and on stage

Considering that the Viennese, in particular, were so steeped in books, it is perhaps not surprising that the émigrés should have had such an outsize impact on publishing, both in Britain and America. Indeed, their ambitions ranged beyond the mere physical production and communication of knowledge on paper, the brass tacks of the business. Many of the immigrants' thriving new publishing houses consciously set out to construct a fresh, transatlantic Anglo-American cosmopolitanism, a conscious substitute for the vanished central European culture they had left behind. These ambitions were conveyed very literally in the name of one of the most prestigious of the new imprints, founded in 1949 by the Viennese Walter Neurath and later his wife Eva. Thames & Hudson was a pointed tribute to the rivers running through London and New York, the two principal cities of refuge for many of those Europeans who fled Nazism.

The distinctive black livery of the Thames & Hudson art book remains an enticing symbol of the entrepreneurial skills that the Viennese, and other German-speaking immigrants, brought to a profession that was badly in need of shaking up by the 1930s. In the words of one historian of Anglo-American publishing, the émigrés:

> may be numbered among the wheel-horses who catapulted the book trades of Britain and the United States to that world-wide eminence that they still enjoy today. They brought an entirely new vision of and energetic pursuit of the cultural role of the book and journal in society, a vision which was quickly adopted and naturalised by an equally perspicacious band of native-born book people.[14]

What was this 'new vision'? Publishing in Britain, in particular, was an excessively tweedy affair in the 1930s, presided over by amateur generalists such as Sir Stanley Unwin. A few people had tried to jiggle the market a bit – notably Allen Lane, who founded Penguin Books in 1935, and Victor Gollancz, founder of the Left Book Club – but the Viennese diaspora brought some very particular new qualities to the business.

Most obviously, they were 'inveterate students of the subject matters in which they specialised their publishing lists'.[15] Walter Neurath was a prime example. Born in Vienna in 1903, he had studied art history at the city's university, like Gombrich, so was himself an expert in the main subject matter of Thames & Hudson. Before escaping to Britain in June 1938 he had run an art gallery in the city of his birth and published illustrated books. Men like Neurath were friends and intellectual partners of many of the authors they published, and thus themselves played important roles in the 'knowledge creation' of fields such as art history.

Neurath married erudition and integrity to a rich textual format, with good design and plentiful colour illustrations, essentially inventing the modern illustrated art book. They were pricey, but marketed firmly at a well-defined intelligentsia with disposable income. Herbert Read's brilliant *Concise History of Modern Painting* was first published by Thames & Hudson in 1959 and has remained in print ever since. The main competition to Thames & Hudson was offered by Phaidon Press, run by another exile, Béla Horovitz. Born in Budapest, after fighting for the empire in the First World War he had studied law at the University of Vienna. He started the Phaidon Press in the city in 1923, publishing art books but, again, escaped just after the *Anschluss*, helped by Unwin, managing to bring most of the files from the Vienna office over to London.

Phaidon established itself as the leader in large-format art books, landing several coups such as the catalogue to the drawings in the Royal Collection.[16] Like Neurath, Horovitz did much to shape the discipline of art history in the West, suggesting to Gombrich, for instance, whom he had known in Vienna, that he should write a new history of art incorporating his latest scholarship. This was the genesis of the phenomenally successful *The Story of Art*, first published by Phaidon in 1950. Now in its sixteenth edition, Gombrich's masterpiece has sold over 8 million copies in more than 30 languages, making it by some way the best-selling art book of all time.

Given Vienna's leadership role in the sciences during the interwar years, this was another field where specialisation could reap rich rewards. The German firm Springer Verlag had done most to develop scientific publishing in central Europe during the interwar years, and after 1945 a young immigrant to Britain from Czechoslovakia, Robert Maxwell, spotted the opportunity to import this tradition to the Anglo-Saxon publishing world. After a 'good war', the pushy, ebullient, entrepreneurial Maxwell was posted to the British occupation zone in Germany where he first came into contact with

Springer, which had barely survived the conflict. Seizing on the potential of the post-war science market, he proposed a tie-up between Springer and the British company Butterworths to publish and disseminate Springer's books and journals outside Germany. These were the origins of one of Europe's most successful post-war publishing ventures, later to become Pergamon Press. Maxwell, however, would have got nowhere without the skills of the remarkable Austrian-born Paul Rosbaud, born in 1896, the brains behind the Maxwell empire.

After gaining degrees in chemistry and metallurgy, Rosbaud started working with Springer in 1932, becoming a roving talent-scout for the German company and keeping abreast of all the latest scientific advances (such as nuclear fission). A keen Anglophile – the legacy of getting to know the British as a prisoner of war during the First World War – his ready access to scientists in the German-speaking world made him a valuable recruit to Britain's Secret Intelligence Service (SIS), to spy on the Nazis' progress towards developing an atom bomb. Together with Frank Foley, the SIS station chief in Berlin, he was also responsible for saving scores of Jewish families from the Holocaust.

Working in Britain after the war, he organised Butterworths' first commercial scientific publishing venture and became part-owner of Pergamon, founded by Maxwell in 1951. There he built the company's publishing list, founding the Maxwell fortune. Inevitably, as everyone did sooner or later, he fell out with Maxwell, and in 1956 moved to Interscience. Here he published the scientific equivalent of Gombrich's *Story of Art*, if less well known to the general reader: *Advanced Inorganic Chemistry*, by Geoffrey Wilkinson and F. Allen Cotton. It first appeared in 1962 and has also remained in print ever since.

Rosbaud, Neurath and Horovitz were very specialist publishers, as was Friedrich Praeger, who built his eponymous publishing company in New York specialising in anti-Communist literature. His most famous coup was to seize on Alexander Solzhenitsyn's

One Day in the Life of Ivan Denisovich, the great critique of Stalinism, have it translated and rush it into print. Other Viennese, however, were more catholic in their subject matter, none more so than the gregarious George Weidenfeld, probably Britain's most famous, and certainly best-connected, post-war publisher. Born in Vienna, he fled to Britain in 1938. After working for the BBC during the war, he founded Weidenfeld & Nicolson in 1949 together with Nigel Nicolson, the son of the novelist Vita Sackville-West and diplomat Harold Nicolson.

Weidenfeld was as promiscuous in friendship as in love, cultivating the great, the good and notorious in equal measure to put together one of the most glittering lists in the world. From his sumptuous second-floor apartment on the Chelsea embankment overlooking the Thames, a lavish Viennese-style eyrie decorated with Klimts and a Francis Bacon papal portrait, Weidenfeld spent decades schmoozing his way through the political and intellectual élites of the Western world, and beyond.

He made his initial fortune by taking a gamble on publishing Nabokov's sexboiler *Lolita*, but plodding political memoirs were usually more to his taste. Weidenfeld was particularly close to the Labour prime minister Harold Wilson. The politician's memoirs duly followed in the Weidenfeld imprint, as did those of Lyndon B. Johnson, Charles de Gaulle and many others. A notable Zionist since his Viennese days, Weidenfeld was also on good terms with the first generation of Israeli leaders and published the books of Golda Meir, Abba Eban and Chaim Herzog.

Weidenfeld, who died in January 2016 at the age of ninety-six, was much more than just a publisher; he was a cultural entrepreneur, involved with, or founding, an extraordinary range of institutions and organisations. Other Viennese immigrants to Britain, such as Stefan Zweig, who arrived in 1934 before moving on to New York, and Oskar Kokoschka, who spent the 1940s in London and Cornwall, worked on their own projects, but did not leave a noticeable legacy in the country that afforded them refuge. Viennese such as Weidenfeld were entirely different. So extensive were his political connections across Europe and beyond that he was known in Whitehall as 'Britain's other Foreign Office'. More so than most other Viennese, he also accepted honours from the city of his birth and promoted the cause of European unity, founded on the ideals of the Vienna of his youth. Mercifully, he never lived to see his adopted country leave the European Union.

Sir Rudolf Bing was another such cultural entrepreneur on both sides of the Atlantic. Born in Vienna in 1902 to a wealthy Jewish family, Bing studied art history at the University of Vienna before relocating to Berlin to work for a theatrical and artistic agency. Fleeing to Britain after 1934, one of his first jobs was as general manager to the newly founded Glyndebourne opera in the Sussex countryside. The first director of this quintessentially English event was the German émigré Fritz Busch, who hired Bing.

But it was only after the war that Bing developed his idea of 'an international festival in which the other nations of the world could join in paying tribute to Britain's courage and sacrifice in the struggle against Hitler'. The format, he considered, should be based on the Salzburg Festival, which started in 1920. Thus, in 1947, ably assisted by the British Council in Scotland, Bing inaugurated the first Edinburgh International Festival. Emerging from the devastation and divisions of war, the festival was to demonstrate 'the emergence of a truly international culture', starring musicians and singers from throughout Europe.[17] Appropriately, Bing invited the Vienna Philharmonic Orchestra, conducted by Bruno Walter, to open the first festival.

Bing remained in charge of his new festival until 1949 when he moved to America to take up the post of General Manager of New York's Metropolitan Opera, a post he held for a controversy-packed twenty-two years. This was the biggest job in world opera and Bing shaped the medium for decades thereafter. Nonetheless, his version of Salzburg/Glyndebourne in Scotland remains his most enduring legacy. It is now the world's largest arts festival, and in its intention to 'provide a platform for the flowering of the human spirit' also encapsulates much of the idealism and creativity of liberal Vienna, expressed through music and theatre in a Scottish castle.

Two cheers for Modernism

The Viennese in Britain such as Wittgenstein, Kris and Gombrich might have modernised important disciplines, just as the publishers reinvigorated the book trade, but continental Modernism as an artistic and aesthetic movement nonetheless struggled to gain a foothold, as has been well chronicled. The odd Woolf novel, penguin enclosure and lido apart, Modernism took a long time to make any inroads on conservative British taste, a source of stability in so many ways, but equally of resistance to change.

Two Viennese women, however, did manage to break the mould, after considerable struggle. They both emerged from the new fields of art and design in Vienna; together with the sciences it was the plastic arts that offered women the widest opportunities in the city. Many of these disciplines were relatively unformed, attracting a younger cohort of male teachers at freshly minted institutions who were keen to take women onto their courses. Of these institutions, the Kunstgewerbeschule, or School of Applied Arts, founded in 1867, was probably the most innovative and progressive; its original building still stands on the Ringstrasse. In 1900 a new course, in ceramics, was added to the syllabus. This attracted the interest of a young woman called Lucie Marie Gomperz, later known as Lucie Rie (see image p. 252).

She was born in 1902 into a wealthy, secular Jewish family. Her father, like many such in this book, was another graduate of Leopoldstadt. With his fortune secured, he enrolled the young Lucie at the first progressive girls' school founded in Vienna, by Dr Eugenie Schwarzwald, an educationalist and reformer. The line-up of teachers was certainly impressive, and adventurous: Kokoschka taught free drawing, Loos art history and Schoenberg music.[18] After this Rie entered the Kunstgewerbeschule, which was closely linked to the Wiener Werkstätte; Josef Hoffmann presided over both.

The training at the school was tough, combining academic rigour with an unusual degree of freedom to experiment individually, which suited Rie both emotionally and professionally. As her biographer writes, at this point she was already a New Woman of Red Vienna, in every sense, 'someone who wanted a professional education, the possibilities of a satisfying and fulfilling job and an independent existence'.[19] Artistically, she broke with the prevailing form of the Wiener Werkstätte, developing clean, minimal forms on the wheel in contrast to the more decorative style and ornamentation of the Werkstätte: 'Her approach was as revolutionary in its own way as that of Loos and Freud, who sought to unmask rather than obscure, seeking to remove layer after layer of illusion in quest of a kernel of truth and integrity.'[20]

In 1938 Rie, who had married in Vienna, escaped to London after the *Anschluss*. Almost completely unknown in Britain, she managed to bring over a few of her exquisite pots carefully wrapped in two suitcases. Helped by a couple of Viennese friends, Lotte Meitner-Graf, Lise Meitner's sister-in-law, who had set up a studio in Old Bond Street as a photographer, and the architect Ernst Freud (son of Sigmund, brother of Anna), she found a house and studio in Albion Mews, west London. This was her base for the rest of her life. Freud's young children helped her to settle in: Lucian, later the renowned artist, Clement, a politician, and Stephen, an iron-monger. She was henceforth a frequent visitor to the extended Freud clan in the Suffolk town of Walberswick, on the east coast of England, where Anna had a house. Many of Lucie's assistants were also Viennese refugees, but her closest aide was undoubtedly Hans Coper, a German, who graduated from Albion Mews to become a celebrated potter in his own right.

Rie's most important professional relationship, however, was with fellow ceramicist Bernard Leach. He drew his inspiration from the

East, especially Japan. Charismatic, if dogmatic, Leach was the archetypal artist-potter, rooted in the soil and craft of England's West Country. More than anyone, he had defined what 'craft work', whether in ceramics or anything else, should be. Leach was certainly not a Modernist, whereas Rie most emphatically was. Her pottery was determinedly metropolitan, his rural and local. In other words, he was as different from Rie intellectually, aesthetically and emotionally as it was possible to be. It is to their mutual credit, therefore, that Rie and Leach rubbed along as well as they did (he often stayed at Albion Mews on visits to London). Leach acknowledged her skill and importance, and thereby eased her path in her adopted country. Working in porcelain and stoneware, Rie gradually developed her own remarkable minimalist style, focusing on fine forms and surprising and sophisticated colour glazes. Flared vases and footed bowls became her signature pieces.

It took a long time for Rie's pots to be fully appreciated. By the 1960s, however, when she was given her own retrospective at the Arts Council, she had single-handedly dragged her branch of British art into the European mainstream. With a kind face and gentle manner, small, wiry and stooped, probably from bending over her wheel for decades, until a stroke in 1990 she remained as alert as ever, speaking 'an idiosyncratic English with a full Viennese accent'.[21] Today, her pieces are eagerly sought by international collectors. In 2020, Philips New York broke a then record for her work, auctioning a 14-centimetre-diameter footed bowl for $180,000. A year later Sotheby's sold a Lucie Rie bowl for $340,000. To the end, though, she refused to let her pots be exhibited in Austria.

Gaby Schreiber, born Wolff, was another Viennese Modernist who had a considerable impact on Britain. The upper-middle-class daughter of an industrialist, she also studied art and design in Vienna, and later Berlin, before fleeing to Britain in 1938. Design was then still heavily dominated by the indigenous *fin-de-siècle* Arts & Crafts movement. The country had yet to embrace the aesthetic of industrialism and machine-related design represented by the

Bauhaus, but as interest in this style grew after the war, so did demand for Schreiber's work. By the 1950s she was probably the most influential designer at work in Britain, despite the fact that her field was then, in the words of the historian Ulrike Walton-Jordan, a 'male bastion'.

There were few aspects of industry and retail to which Schreiber did not turn her hand, often producing work that was regarded, ironically, as quintessentially British. She was a star, for instance, of the 'Britain Can Make It' exhibition in 1946, to showcase the country's supposed industrial recovery from the Second World War. Schreiber designed the restaurants and shops for Marks & Spencer, but her most celebrated commissions were for the flag-carrying British Overseas Airways Corporation (BOAC). She was the first woman to design the interior of a passenger jet, the Comet IV, then the most advanced such plane in the world. The contemporary comforts of flying we owe partly to her; she abandoned the modest functionalism of early jet travel in favour of the luxuries and attention to detail that turned such planes into what one contemporary described as 'miniature hotel[s] in the shape of a large cigar'.[22]

The other side of the ledger

It is evident that an essential conduit of transmission from Vienna to Britain was usually a strong intellectual partnership (even if not always friendship), between, for instance, Russell and Wittgenstein in philosophy, Rie and Leach in ceramics, Gombrich and Clark in art history or the Welsh neurologist Ernest Jones and Freud in psychoanalysis. Jones became the first English-speaking psychoanalyst in the world, as well as Freud's biographer, paving the way for the older man's escape from Vienna to Britain in 1938. More than anyone, he prepared the intellectual ground abroad for the successful assimilation of Freudian psychoanalysis.

These Anglo-Viennese partnerships all contributed richly, and very directly, to British interwar and post-war culture, in the widest sense. However, other such partnerships – or more accurately conspiracies – sought to undermine that culture from within, and they were to prove just as significant, both for the history of Britain and the West more generally. The most momentous of these was struck up by a young Cambridge graduate, Kim Philby, and his Viennese lover, and later wife, Litzi Friedmann.

By the early 1930s, Vienna was brimming with young, enthusiastic communist activists, disillusioned, as we have seen, with what they regarded as the spinelessness of the city's Social Democrats. Just as central Europe at this point was a happy recruiting ground for the talent-scouts of the Rockefeller Foundation, so this was equally true of the foreign intelligence services of Soviet Russia and the Communist International, or Comintern, founded in 1919 to foment communist revolutions worldwide. Furthermore, by the time of the final confrontation between Red Vienna and the Heimwehr home guard in 1933–34 the city had also attracted young, idealistic foreigners to witness what they regarded as a climactic battle between the left and right in Europe. Among them were two Englishmen: Hugh Gaitskell, future leader of Britain's Labour Party, and, more significantly, Harold Adrian Russell Philby, better known as 'Kim', son of the establishment rebel and explorer Harry St John Philby. Philby's story is well documented, in as far as it is known at all, but Vienna's central contribution to the most productive spy ring in history is less well understood.

Both Gaitskell and Philby were scions of Britain's governing class, alumni of Winchester and Westminster, Oxford and Cambridge, respectively. Gaitskell, a social democrat, and Philby, already a convinced communist, both shed the last vestiges of their boyhood naïveté in the desperate, but exhilarating attempts to smuggle social democrats, *Schutzbund* paramilitary soldiers and communist fighters out of Vienna as the Heimwehr closed in. Gaitskell was aided in his efforts by the well-heeled socialist novelist Naomi Mitchison; they established an escape network that saved about 170 fighters.[23]

Some got out via Vienna's extensive sewer system and were dubbed the 'Kanalratten' – the sewer rats – by the Heimwehr. The sewers, at least, were memorialised in the post-war film noir *The Third Man*, directed by Carol Reed and scripted by the novelist Graham Greene. Certainly, Greene had been a colleague of Philby's in Britain's SIS during the war, so could have known of Philby's exploits first-hand – although the double agent himself later denied to his KGB handlers that the sewers had played any part in his specific operations. A scholastic mini-industry has flourished on the back of speculation about the exact provenance of the characters and scenes in the film. Was the mysterious, amoral Harry Lime, played by Orson Welles, based on Philby himself? Greene was certainly fascinated by the subterranean labyrinth of the rat-infested sewers; they form the backdrop for the climactic scenes of the film, leading to Lime's death.[24]

Whatever the truth, the events of Vienna 1934 changed Gaitskell, adding steel to the public schoolboy's youthful political commitment.[25] The ramifications for Philby were more dramatic still. Intellectually convinced by communism as an undergraduate at Cambridge, Philby had been sent to Vienna to help the cause by his Cambridge economics tutor Maurice Dobb, an avowed communist. Stopping off in Paris, the handsome, debonair young graduate was furnished with the address of some sympathisers with whom he could stay in Vienna. This was the family of Litzi Friedmann, still only twenty-three years old, yet already divorced. She was living with her parents, who took Philby in as a lodger. Friedmann was a passionate communist, a member of the Austrian party and already a member of the most secret arm of the Comintern, the International Liaison Department, or OMS. The bland moniker disguised the fact that it dealt mostly with international subversion and espionage, maintaining close links to OGPU (the intelligence and secret police service of the Soviet Union, afterwards the NKVD and eventually the KGB). Philby became the treasurer of Friedmann's communist cell. The hardened apparatchik and the enthusiastic Englishman looking for a cause became lovers.

Philby admired Friedmann's commitment and resourcefulness from the start. 'A frank and direct person,' he later recalled, 'Litzi came out and asked me how much money I had. I replied £100, which I hoped would last me about a year in Vienna. She made some calculations and announced, "That will leave you an excess of £25. You can give that to the International Organisation for Aid for Revolutionaries. We need it desperately." I liked her determination.'

Friedmann was equally struck: 'He was two years younger than me, and I was already divorced from my first husband and a member of the Party. He had come from Cambridge, where he had just completed his studies, was a very attractive man, behaved like a gentleman, and moreover, was a Marxist – a rare constellation. He stuttered, sometimes more and sometimes less, and like many people with a handicap he was very charming. We fell in love very quickly.'[26]

With the protection afforded him by a British passport, Philby fulfilled a vital role as a courier for the communist underground, both within Vienna itself and beyond. To save Friedmann herself from the vengeance of the Heimwehr as the left's resistance collapsed, he married her in a brief ceremony so she could escape. She rode pillion on his motorcycle back to London, where she was introduced to a rather surprised Philby mother. Shocked by the failure of socialism in Vienna and the general indifference of Britain and France to the bloody oppression of Austrian democracy, Philby returned more convinced than ever that communism was the only path. Infatuated with Friedmann, his cause seemed to be both right and romantic. But after the excitement of serving so directly in Vienna, how could he channel his energies back in humdrum London?

Only a few weeks after their return, Friedmann took her new husband to tea with an old friend and comrade from Vienna, born

Edith Suschitzky, now Edith Tudor-Hart. Like Friedmann, she too had married a sympathetic British communist, the surgeon Alexander Tudor-Hart, in order to escape from the clutches of the Austro-fascists. Born into the Jewish secular middle class, Edith and her brother Wolfgang came from a highly politicised family, deeply committed to Red Vienna. Like Friedmann, Tudor-Hart had joined the communists as a teenager, probably even before the apparent failure of the Social Democrats in the 1927 'July revolt'.

She came to London initially in 1925, aged just sixteen, to train as a Montessori teacher. She later studied photography at the Bauhaus in Germany in 1929, returning to London the following year. By now an open communist, she attracted the attention of MI5, Britain's domestic security agency, which deported her back to Austria in 1931. Her communist activities landed her in jail in Vienna for a month in the summer of 1933, but a year later, newly married to Alex Tudor-Hart, she returned to Britain for good. Thereafter she maintained her life as an open communist, regularly under surveillance by MI5; she was the 'accountant', as they recorded, for the Central Committee of the Austrian Communist Party in Britain, based at the Austrian Centre in west London. MI5 reported that she was of 'slim build, 5'6" tall, with blue-grey eyes', and blonde 'bobbed hair'. The fact that she was under official observation for much of her life in Britain – MI5 tapped her phone, steamed open her mail and broke into her flat – makes what she managed to achieve for the Soviets even more remarkable.[27]

By profession, Tudor-Hart could best be described as an activist-photographer. She was renowned for capturing the dismal living conditions of ordinary people during the depression, making a name for herself as a photographer of her adopted country's social divide. Her most memorable image was probably *Child Staring into Bakery Window*, in which an emaciated, ragged urchin gazes longingly at a bakery window stuffed with buns and cakes. It was her way of marking the occasion of King George V's silver jubilee in 1935. As Tudor-Hart's biographer writes, 'Both her life and art were guided by an ideal and her creativity was inseparable from her social commitment and revolutionary beliefs.'[28] Her brother, Wolfgang Suschitzky, was also a photographer, who escaped to Britain with his cousins in 1935.[29]

Tudor-Hart and her husband had already been working for the OMS for several years by 1934. She had also been recruited by the NKVD, particularly to look out for English sympathisers who might be useful to Moscow. Thus, when Friedmann arrived with her new husband for tea in May of that year, she was in a receptive frame of mind. Over the cakes, Philby regaled her with his tales of derring-do in Vienna. She quickly passed his details on to her own handler, the man who had himself recruited her to OGPU in Vienna, one Arnold Deutsch. He was intrigued, and asked Tudor-Hart to bring Philby along to a clandestine meeting.

OTTO and ERIC, EDITH and MARY

Deutsch was the top Soviet 'illegal' in Britain, running and recruiting agents from beyond the well-monitored confines of the Soviet embassy in Kensington. Knowing that she had been under surveillance by MI5, Tudor-Hart took Philby on a long, circuitous journey by taxi, tube and foot to his appointed meeting place with Deutsch, codename OTTO, on a bench by the boating lake in London's Regent's Park. Asked, after a lengthy interrogation, whether he would be willing to work under cover for communism, Philby barely hesitated, although at this point there was no mention of reporting directly to the Soviet intelligence service. The first thing that Deutsch asked Philby and Friedmann to do was to break off all their overt connections with Britain's official communist party, a necessary first step in building Philby's cover as a convincing member of Britain's establishment. Later, Philby had to give up Friedmann herself to make his new identity more credible; they divorced in 1946. This was probably the only emotional sacrifice that ever seriously mattered to the cold-hearted Philby. Later wives and children were discarded at will.

Deutsch was born in 1903 to Jewish parents, probably in Prague. His parents moved to Vienna when he was very young, and he later enrolled at the University of Vienna to study chemistry, philosophy and psychology. At the age of twenty-four he received a distinction in his PhD, in chemistry. He joined Austria's communist party and in about 1927 was also recruited by the Comintern. At about the same time he also started working for Wilhelm Reich's 'Sex-Pol' movement, running the Münster Verlag, a publishing house that issued Reich's articles advocating revolution through sexual liberation. Deutsch seems to have been devoted to Reich's politics, and moved with him to Berlin for a few years in about 1930.

Deutsch met Edith Suschitzky in Vienna in the mid-1920s, through the Sex-Pol movement, and they became lovers. Suschitzky was equally captivated by Reich's politics, and was sexually promiscuous by the standards of the day.[30] Deutsch now recruited the young Edith into OGPU, which valued her highly as an agent. It was Deutsch who gave her the curiously unimaginative codename of EDITH; perhaps it was intended as a double bluff. He wrote her psychological profile for his spymasters: 'She is modest, diligent and brave. She is prepared to do anything for us, but unfortunately she's not careful enough.'[31] Edith, in turn, introduced Litzi Friedmann to Deutsch; she was assigned the codename MARY.

In 1933, Deutsch, together with his equally committed Viennese wife Josefine, was summoned to Moscow for full training as an OGPU 'illegal' abroad. He was subsequently dispatched to London under cover of being an academic researcher at the University of London, living most of the time in Hampstead. The photo in his MI5 file reveals a handsome, confident man, well-groomed with fair, curly hair.[32] His modus operandi in Britain, which he probably designed himself, was to trawl through the country's leading universities for the best communist undergraduates and then cultivate them as long-term penetration agents in the corridors of powers. Deutsch, ably assisted by Tudor-Hart, proved to be the

perfect choice to befriend, recruit and run such well-born reneg-
ades from the British establishment. Indeed, it is perfectly possible
that no one *but* Deutsch could have recruited and successfully
exploited such unlikely material as the ramshackle, garrulous,
alcoholic and sexually indiscreet Guy Burgess, recommended to
Deutsch by the considerably more steely, self-controlled and
impressive Philby.

The key to Deutsch's success was his Viennese academic
background in psychology and philosophy, and particularly his
immersion in the Sex-Pol movement. This afforded him invaluable
insights into the motives of his most famous recruits, the 'Cambridge
Five' of Philby, Burgess, Donald Maclean, Anthony Blunt and John
Cairncross, all of whom were in revolt against their home country
across a broad front – politically, emotionally and sexually. More
plodding and narrow-minded spymasters might have baulked at
their unconventional and flamboyant sex lives, but not Deutsch. He
understood perfectly this blend of political and sexual resentfulness
as an opportunity. As Christopher Andrew, the pre-eminent
historian of modern intelligence, writes:

> Though four of the Five graduated from Cambridge with first-
> class honours, Deutsch's academic career was even more brilliant
> than theirs, his understanding of human nature more profound
> and his experience of life much broader. He combined a charis-
> matic personality and deep psychological insight with visionary
> faith in the future of a human race freed from all the exploit-
> ation and alienation of the capitalist system. His message of
> liberation had all the greater appeal to the Cambridge Five
> because it had a sexual as well as political dimension. Burgess
> and Blunt were homosexuals, Maclean a bisexual and Philby a
> heterosexual athlete.[33]

Philby remembered Deutsch fondly: 'He was a marvellous man,
simply marvellous. And the feeling never left me . . . The first thing

you noticed about him were his eyes. He looked at you as if there was nothing more important in life than talking to you existed at that moment ... And he had a marvellous sense of humour.'[34] Deutsch gave Philby the codename SYNOK ('son' in Russian) and encouraged his new recruit to identify other possible targets from his network of well-born Cambridge undergraduates. Maclean was thus the second recruit, Burgess the third, followed by Blunt and Cairncross.

Deutsch remains perhaps the most successful agent recruiter in the history of the Soviet intelligence services. During just five or six years, he probably recruited about twenty agents, all, most likely, in Britain. He was so revered by his bosses in Moscow that he was honoured with a portrait on the walls of the Memory Room of the First Chief Directorate, the inner sanctum of what was by then KGB headquarters.

Deutsch wrote the psychological evaluations of his recruits, revealed in their KGB files decades later. They are models of their kind. This is Deutsch's penetrating, Reichian analysis of Burgess, for example:

Many features of his character can be explained by the fact that he is a homosexual. He became one at Eton, where he grew up in an atmosphere of cynicism, opulence, hypocrisy and superficiality. As he is very clever and well educated, for him the Party was a saviour ... His personal degradation, drunkenness, irregular way of life and the feeling of being outside society was connected with this kind of life, but on the other hand his abhorrence of bourgeois morality came from this. This kind of life did not satisfy him.[35]

Deutsch identified a 'craving to be liked' as a weak spot, as he did with most of the Five; he consequently spent a lot of his time flattering and reassuring them.

The Cambridge Five recruited by the Viennese communists Deutsch, Tudor-Hart and Friedmann was not only the most successful spy ring on the Soviet side during the Cold War, it was probably the most accomplished in the entire history of espionage. Obeying their orders to penetrate the higher echelons of the British government, in quick succession Maclean joined the Foreign Office in 1935; Burgess MI6, in 1938; ditto Philby two years later. Blunt served with MI5 during the war and Cairncross in the Government Code and Cypher School at Bletchley Park and later in MI6. The urgent requirements of war meant that any vetting was perfunctory. Their impeccable establishment credentials did the rest.

Together, they must have handed over tens of thousands of secret documents to their Soviet controllers, covering everything from MI6's order of battle in post-war Europe to the inner workings of the Anglo-American alliance. Maclean smuggled out so many papers from the lackadaisical Foreign Office that his Soviet handlers struggled to keep up with photographing them. From the moment he entered the Foreign Office in London until his departure for a new assignment in France in 1938, Maclean handed over 45 boxes, each containing over 300 pages of stolen documents.[36]

Another Viennese on the barricades of Red Vienna with SYNOK and MARY in 1934 was a young chemistry student called Engelbert Broda. A convinced Marxist since his student days in the late 1920s, in 1930 he left the Social Democrats to join the communists. He became a leader of the underground communist cell in Vienna's first district, the very centre of the city. In 1935 he was imprisoned for a month for smuggling communist literature.[37]

Broda fled Vienna immediately after the *Anschluss* and came to Britain, where at some point the strikingly good-looking (and married) scientist became the next lover of Edith Tudor-Hart. Like her, he was an open communist, known to MI5 as serving on the same Central Committee of the Austrian Communist Party at the Austrian Centre in London. He was interned as an enemy alien in 1940, but released thereafter. In December 1941 he was given a job at the Cavendish Laboratory in Cambridge, part of a team working on Britain's secret programme to build an atomic bomb. MI5 advised against recruiting Broda because of his known communist connections, particularly to Tudor-Hart, but the spy agency was overruled, as one officer lamented: 'The Department of Scientific and Industrial Research ... considered that the exigencies of their department outweighed other objections in such employment.'[38]

MI5 was quite right to sound an alarm. Broda had already been recruited by the NKVD, possibly through EDITH herself. Assigned the codename ERIC, by 1942 Broda was supplying the Soviets with a stream of atomic secrets, a penetration that was only confirmed for certain with the opening of the NKVD files in 2009. In a memo from 22 December 1942, the NKVD was informed: 'Recently, "Edith" sent us a detailed report through Mary on the results and status of work on "Enormous", both in England and in the United States. "Eric" had given her this report on his own initiative to pass to the fraternal.' 'Enormous', appropriately, was the Soviet codename for the Allied atomic weapons programme. MI5 noted the continued contact between ERIC and EDITH in Britain, but never gathered any proof of espionage. It was a spectacular failure by the spooks.

Despite half-hearted efforts to compartmentalise the work of Britain's nuclear scientists, Broda seems to have enjoyed access to most Anglo-American developments in the field. The NKVD acknowledged that ERIC was their main source on the West's atomic research at this time. He was handing over documents to his Soviet handlers almost every fortnight; they described him as 'completely selfless in his work for us'.[39] Furthermore, Broda very probably recruited Alan Nunn May, a communist British scientist who handed over yet more nuclear secrets to Russia.

Broda was never caught, and returned to Vienna after the war to resume his academic career. May, however, was jailed for several years. MI5 remained puzzled, however, about several aspects of May's case, including his recruitment; he never broke under interrogation. But an intriguing clue was provided on May's release from jail – he quickly married Hilde Broda, Engelbert's first wife. ERIC, meanwhile, had remarried in Vienna. His new wife had fought with Tito's partisan forces in Yugoslavia.

So extensive was this Soviet penetration of the Anglo-American alliance that the full extent of the damage may not yet have been entirely discovered. In a preliminary calculus, it is safe to say that the network of deep-penetration agents recruited by Tudor-Hart and Deutsch severely damaged the West's prospects during the first half of the Cold War. Philby, in particular, betrayed hundreds of operatives working behind the Iron Curtain, condemning many of them to death. The atomic spies were even more harmful. At the very least, Broda and Nunn May, together with Klaus Fuchs, saved the Soviets billions of roubles and many years of arduous scientific research, enabling Russia to detonate a first bomb only four years after the Americans, much to the astonishment of the West. The revelation that so many of Britain's scientists, secret agents and mandarins were in fact working for the Soviets tarnished Anglo-American ties for years.

None of the atomic spies ever repented. Driven by ideology, they always claimed that they had been vindicated by events. Engelbert Broda's son Paul puts it this way: 'It is just as plausible that the activities of [these] scientists helped to prevent a Hot War as they were responsible for the Cold War. The balance of terror due to Russia gaining the Bomb has often been seen as having resulted in preventing war between the US and the USSR.'[40]

Of the Viennese spy ring, Deutsch was lucky to escape the Stalinist purges after his return to the Soviet Union from Britain in 1937. He is thought to have perished four years later aboard the *SS Donbass* when it was torpedoed by a German U-boat crossing the Atlantic. EDITH was interviewed by the authorities several times, especially after the defections of Maclean and Burgess in 1951 prompted MI5 to delve more deeply into the backgrounds of the Cambridge Five. She revealed nothing during interrogation. Nonetheless, divorced from her husband and harassed by MI5, she endured several nervous breakdowns before retiring to run a tiny antique shop in Brighton.[41]

She died in 1973, but her documentary photography has since been rediscovered and exhibited. If Deutsch can lay claim to being one of the most successful spymasters in history, Tudor-Hart was surely on a par with him as a talent-scout and recruiter. Blunt famously called her 'the grandmother of us all'.

Only MARY (Litzi Friedmann) survived to anything like a ripe old age. Obliged by the rules of espionage to distance herself from her husband to protect his cover, after leaving Philby she left Britain for East Germany. She remained silent about her second husband throughout. In 1984, then seventy-four years old, she returned to live quietly in Vienna. She died in 1991, three years after Philby. The last of the other Vienna Circle was gone.

Chapter 9

The World Reimagined:
War Work and the Open Society

J ust as the Viennese emigrants' technical skills had been enormously beneficial to America and Britain before the Second World War, so their direct experience of fascism and communism in central Europe made them even more valuable as the West confronted, first, Nazi Germany, and then the Soviet Union. In this context the Viennese exerted probably their most decisive long-term influence, encapsulated in a quartet of wartime books that remain political cornerstones, the subject of this chapter.

These were Hayek's *The Road to Serfdom*, published in 1944, the same year as Karl Polanyi's *The Great Transformation*; Karl Popper's *The Open Society and Its Enemies*, published the following year; and *Capitalism, Socialism and Democracy* by Joseph Schumpeter, from 1942. Collectively, they have defined the main contours of Western political discourse over the past seven or so decades. It is no coincidence that they were all published so close together, for the books continued debates that the authors had been having with each other

(opposite) An odd couple: Oskar Morgenstern and John von Neumann, authors of Theory of Games and Economic Behavior.

in Vienna for the previous twenty years. A fifth work, *Theory of Games and Economic Behavior*, by John von Neumann and Oskar Morgenstern, published in 1944, also emerged from these same Viennese wrangles. It was to have an equally important, if very different, bearing on the Cold War.

These writers were lionised by the West, but the flow of ideas and loyalties was not just one way, as Vienna's communist spies in Britain proved all too well. Just like Edith Tudor-Hart, many remained a deeper shade of red and made significant contributions to the Eastern bloc, unapologetic party members to the end. Take Margarete Schütte-Lihotzky, for instance, creator of the 'Frankfurt kitchen'. In 1930, together with a group of like-minded colleagues, she left Weimar Germany for the Soviet Union to help realise Stalin's first Five Year Plan. The task of Schütte-Lihotzky's 'May Brigade', as they were known, was to help construct the new industrial cities that were going to transform Russia from a peasant society into an industrial titan. Schütte-Lihotzky stayed until 1937. She spent the war in Turkey, returning to Vienna in 1947. She remained a committed communist, working on projects in Cuba, East Germany and China. She died in 2000, five days short of her 103rd birthday.

The composer Hanns Eisler followed a similar path. A disciple of Schoenberg in Vienna, Eisler was renowned for his collaborations with the communist playwright Bertolt Brecht. He also wrote several anthems for the left, including 'Solidarity Song', a staple of interwar anti-fascist street demonstrations. He joined Brecht in exile in California during the war, where he composed for Hollywood films, only to be deported in 1948 after his communist sympathies became an early focus of the McCarthyite enquiry into alleged subversion by the House Un-American Activities Committee.[1] He was eventually reunited with Brecht in East Germany, where he wrote the country's national anthem, one of the better examples of a usually lamentable genre. He died in East Berlin in 1962, and was buried close to Brecht in the city's Dorotheenstadt cemetery.

The hubris of reason

Nonetheless, the Viennese impact on Western thinking and culture in the 1940s and 1950s far outweighed these contributions to international communism. For if the critique of Red Vienna from the left drove people even further to the left, so it was on the right of politics. The Austrian School economists, in particular, having lived through the entirety of the great socialist experiment, developed a 'hostile intimacy' with collectivism of the left and right that was to sustain them for the rest of their lives.[2]

Ludwig von Mises was the most strident critic of planning in all its particulars, and his scorn only mounted as he witnessed Red Vienna in operation. The most enduring charge, as we have seen, was that Red Vienna was too interventionist and authoritarian, a 'nanny state'. Mises was joined in this critique by the younger Hayek. For both of them the villain of the piece was the ubiquitous Otto Neurath. Hayek's debates with John Maynard Keynes are well-known, but for Hayek himself Neurath was probably the more pernicious advocate of planning. As Hayek was to recall later, it was Neurath's 'extreme' belief in the scientific method, which Hayek labelled *positivism*, as well as Neurath's 'naïve' economics, and the perverse consequences of both, that forced him, reluctantly, to spend the later 1930s fundamentally revising his entire epistemology. This would emerge as *The Road to Serfdom*. At least Hayek would pay Neurath the honour of inspiring his most famous work: 'I owe it to Neurath's extreme position,' wrote Hayek, 'that I recognised [positivism] wouldn't do.'[3] Thus Neurath cemented his position as the intellectual punchbag of the Austrian School.

Hayek left Vienna for a professorship at the London School of Economics (LSE) in 1931. The timing was not coincidental. His principal backer at the LSE was Lionel Robbins, the youngest professor of economics in Britain and the newly-appointed head of the economics department. In the wake of the Wall Street crash of 1929 and the onset of the Great Depression, Robbins was leading a fightback on behalf of free-market economics against the increasingly popular notions of Keynes and his acolytes. Keynes's central contention was that free markets could evidently no longer provide full employment, and so it was now up to governments to boost 'aggregate demand', through ambitious schemes of public works and deficit spending. In particular, he argued for counter-cyclical fiscal policies to act *against* the natural functioning of the business cycle – one of the Austrian School's principal areas of interest.

Unusually, the youthful, amicable Robbins could read and speak German. He was therefore one of the few academics in the Anglo-Saxon world familiar with the Viennese economists, before translations of their work were readily available. He had visited Mises's circle in Vienna, and been impressed by Hayek's work at the Institute for Business Cycle Research. This, and four lectures that Hayek consequently gave at the LSE in early 1931, led to Robbins's offer of a chair. Mises's heir-apparent seemed just the right man to provide fresh intellectual ammunition in the war against Keynes. Hayek was to stay at the LSE until 1950. Robbins was his closest friend in Britain, and was to play a crucial role in spreading the ideas of the Austrian School more widely.

As required, Hayek joined battle with the Keynesians straight away. Robbins enlisted him to write a long review of Keynes's *A Treatise on Money* in the main journal of the British economics profession, *Economica*. Hayek's review was unusually critical, provoking Keynes, by now accustomed to almost universal acclaim, into a detailed reply. This led to an exchange of twelve letters between the two during the course of five months over the winter of 1931/32. It was the opening of hostilities between the Austrian School and the Keynesians. Hayek had established himself as the leading critic of Keynesianism in Britain, a position that was dimmed only slightly by his unexplained failure to review Keynes's theoretical magnum opus, *The General Theory of Employment, Interest and Money*, published in 1936.

By then, however, Hayek had embarked on a monumental project of his own, 'The Abuse and Decline of Reason', in which his critiques of Neurath and Keynes were synthesised into one overall attack on the fundamental basis of their thinking and political recommendations. Hayek never completed the work as a whole, but most of his writings from 1936 to 1944, the most important of his life, issued from this project.

In short, Hayek identified what he called 'scientism' as the fatal flaw in the grand designs of Neurath, Keynes and their ilk. He described this as the reflexive, unthinking application of the methods of the natural sciences to areas where they did not apply – such as economics and sociology, the territory of Red Vienna and Keynes's planned economy. Hayek's main point – the most influential he ever made – is that knowledge is too 'dispersed' and 'incomplete' in a modern society for even the self-appointed experts to plan. He called this the 'hubris of reason'. He argued that the 'scientific world view' of the logical positivists and the Machians had deluded people into believing that by applying their methodologies to the sphere of 'human action', they had severely overreached themselves, straining the scientific method beyond its capabilities. As a good Viennese rationalist himself, Hayek was at pains to point out that he was directing his complaints 'solely against a misuse of Science, not against the scientist in the special field where he is competent, but against the application of his mental habits in fields where he is not competent'.[4] The 'scientistic prejudice', as he called it, was, in fact, profoundly unscientific.

The obsession with scientism, in Hayek's opinion, had baleful consequences. Most importantly, its proponents failed to grasp 'how the independent action of many men can produce coherent wholes, persistent structures of relationships which serve important human purposes without having been designed for this end.'[5] Devotees of the scientistic fallacy – planners – assumed, wrongly, that if something served a human purpose, it must have been designed from scratch.

'From this idea,' writes the Hayek biographer Bruce Caldwell, 'it is but a small step to the even more dangerous view that we possess the ability to refashion social institutions at will. All such views overvalue the power of reason.'[6] Red Vienna, with its belief in creating *die neuen Menschen*, was a case in point. Necessarily, all planners and collectivists were infected with the disease of scientism, and also that of historicism, a belief in general theories of historical progression with predictive consequences – such as Marxism.

Hayek began to publish instalments of his grand critique in 1937, in *Economica*. The most important chunks were published as the two-part *Scientism and the Study of Society* in 1942 and 1943. However, erudite academic texts in specialist economics journals were never going to reach a wide audience. Yet for Hayek, who relocated to Cambridge with the LSE in 1940 once the Blitz started in London, the relevance of his new thesis only increased as the war progressed. The vogue for a Keynesian 'planned' economy and society had been real enough before the war, but now politicians of all hues clamoured for yet more planning, to win the war, and, more dangerously, to carry that planning into peacetime to deliver a more 'just' society. This is what drove Hayek to publish his new ideas in a more populist and provocative form. *The Road to Serfdom* was the result. As he wrote in the preface, by this juncture he felt that writing the book was a 'duty which I must not evade'. It was dedicated, famously, 'To the Socialists of all Parties'; it was also a heartfelt warning to the politicians of all countries.

Hayek never mentions Neurath and Red Vienna in the book, but they haunt the entire text. In the introduction, he asserts that *The Road to Serfdom* is 'the product of an experience as near as possible to twice living through the same period – or at least watching a very similar evolution of ideas'. The first experience he had in mind was Germany 'during and after' the First World War, the period when Neurath's idea of a war economy, in Hayek's view, inevitably developed into (National) Socialism. It had been the same story in Austria itself; the Austrian School beheld little difference between

Neurath's 'socialist' economy and the corporate state of the Austro-fascists. Both entailed a similar diminution of individual freedom and private enterprise in favour of a commensurate rise in the power and extent of state intervention and bureaucracy.

As Britain's politicians celebrated the publication of the Beveridge Report in 1942, the country's own blueprint for a Tandler-style 'cradle to the grave' welfare state, Hayek warned:

> Few are ready to recognise that the rise of Fascism and Nazism was not a reaction against the socialist trends of the preceding period, but a necessary outcome of those tendencies . . . Many who think themselves infinitely superior to the aberrations of Nazism and sincerely hate all its manifestations, work at the same time for ideals whose realisation would lead straight to the abhorred tyranny.[7]

As it turned out, a few Nazis, at least, would not have disagreed with this analysis. The RAF dropped thousands of copies of an abridged version of Beveridge's report over Germany to persuade the suffering populace that Britain's vision of the future was better than Hitler's. Hayek would doubtless have been gratified to learn that a couple of these propaganda pamphlets were found in Hitler's bunker after the end of the war, heavily annotated. The Nazis apparently concluded that Beveridge's scheme was very similar to, and indeed somewhat in advance of, what National Socialism was trying to achieve.[8]

A Viennese front: Popper joins Hayek

The Road to Serfdom was shocking stuff for a war-weary British readership. Five years into the conflict, with no discernible end in sight, especially in the Far East, most Britons were clinging on with the promise of a New Jerusalem, a better post-war world in which a beneficent state would guarantee jobs, health and education. There would be no going back to the dole queues of the 1930s. The Labour Party's election manifesto of 1945, 'Let Us Face the Future', successfully captured this optimism. Yet Hayek's slim text poured a large bucket of icy cold water on this vision. It was an overnight sensation. With paper severely rationed, the publishers struggled to keep up with an expanded print run.

One person who was not shocked, however, was Popper. Quite separately, he had been thinking along very similar lines to Hayek, but from a different perspective. Whereas Hayek, under the influence of Mises, had been an early critic of Red Vienna, Popper had been an integral part of it, a committed Social Democrat and a student of the Bühlers, whom he revered.

As a student of the scientific worldview, inevitably Popper was drawn to the Vienna Circle. He was never a formal member, but attended several meetings. More significantly, he offered the most convincing critique of their project, and particularly of their hero Wittgenstein; rather than focusing on language (what can and cannot be said), Popper argued that it was more vital to demarcate true science from pseudo-science (in which category he placed Wittgenstein *and* Freud).

His critique centred on what he termed the 'falsification principle', Popper's philosophical formula for distinguishing 'science' from 'non-science'. For a theory to be considered truly scientific, it must be able to be tested and falsified. To take a famous example, the statement 'All swans are white' can be disproved by the sighting of just one black swan. Psychoanalytic claims were thus inherently untestable; if the analyst suggested that a dream had shown that a patient harboured suppressed feelings of anger against his mother, there was no way to prove the theory wrong. Most of the Circle were intrigued by Popper's reasoning, if not entirely convinced.[9]

Coincidentally, Hayek and Popper had thus been worrying away at the same problem – the overreach of the scientific method. Popper further developed his ideas in *The Poverty of Historicism*, a long paper that he completed in 1936 and read out at seminars in his home country and Britain. It was updated and published as a book only in 1957. One of those seminars was Hayek's own at the LSE, and the older Viennese was immediately struck with the similarities to his own 'Abuse and Decline of Reason' project.

Popper proposed that only 'piecemeal social engineering' was rationally possible, or desirable, as distinct from the large-scale utopian, societal engineering advocated by Neurath, the communists and fascists. In particular, Popper blamed the Marxist theorising of his youth for central Europe's collapse. As his biographer, Malachi Haim Hacohen paraphrases his subject's thinking at this point: 'Instead of making history, historicists searched for inexorable historical laws, hoping to ride them. Instead of planning institutions, they prophesied the collapse of capitalism. This was a prescription for inaction. After each failure, socialists revised their interpretations. Meanwhile the Fascists acted.'[10]

Popper, an assimilated Jew and Social Democrat, was himself a victim of such inaction; from the mid-1930s it was clear that he would have to leave his home city. Like many Viennese Jews he began an increasingly frantic search for a job overseas, which eventually led him to an unlikely post at Canterbury College in Christchurch, New Zealand, where he stayed for the duration of the war. Despite having met each other just once, Hayek and Popper corresponded regularly and at length throughout the hostilities, shaping and informing each other's work.[11] Essentially, from the late 1930s to the end of the war they were working as an intellectual tag team. Just as *The Poverty of Historicism* reflected many of Hayek's misgivings about the abuse of science and reason, so Popper's *The Open Society and Its Enemies*, published in 1945, mirrored much of what Hayek was writing in *The Road to Serfdom*. As Popper wrote to his fellow warrior, after each had seen drafts of the other's work in 1943, they were clearly 'fighting the same battle on different fronts'.[12] Both authors regarded these books as war work, their own contributions to the Allies' causes of democracy and freedom.

The intellectual link between Hayek, Popper's philosophical work at the Vienna Circle and the very different *Open Society*, essentially a work of political theory, is provided by the 'falsification principle'. In the end, only free societies could test policies in government until they were proved *wrong* – Liz Truss's disastrous six-week spell in Downing Street in 2022 being an excellent case in point. The open society was *only* open if it was open to being proved wrong. Hayek shared the same insight, but used different language. For him, free competition (of political ideas as much as products or businesses) was the essential 'discovery process' that would determine what worked, and what did not. Such competition was only available in an open society.[13]

Despite their confluence of interests, Popper and Hayek were very different characters, and these differences extended to their politics as well. Popper was short, fiery and forceful. In debate he set out to dominate and unsettle his opponents. His student seminars at the LSE, where he taught after the war, were notoriously intimidating – wags dubbed them 'The Open Society by one of its enemies'. Many, including Moritz Schlick, thought him boorish, intolerant and bullying. His confrontation with Wittgenstein – whom he despised as an overprivileged, half-mystical poseur – at a meeting of the Moral Sciences Club in Cambridge in 1946 is legendary. Riled by Popper's aggressive attack on an aspect of his philosophy, the elder Viennese started brandishing a poker before storming out of the room.[14] Never a particularly sociable man, Popper buried himself away with his wife 'Hennie' in the countryside at Penn, in Buckinghamshire, for most of his time in Britain, as far away from his colleagues at the LSE as was contractually possible. Devoted solely to his work, the Poppers had vowed not to have any children due to circumstances during the war. Karl was lionised by statesmen and students alike; one of the latter was the financier George Soros, who founded the Open Society Foundations in his teacher's honour, financing it with \$32 billion of his personal fortune.

Hayek, by contrast, was relatively urbane, mild-mannered and sociable, able, apparently, to get along with almost anyone, whatever their intellectual and temperamental differences. Photographs accurately convey the image of an endlessly patient but steely interlocutor, a professor who would always argue his point but was infrequently provoked to anger. Very rarely did Hayek fall out with anyone, although he did so badly with his British mentor Robbins over the break-up of his first marriage. Robbins was appalled by Hayek's treatment of his first wife, whom he divorced to marry an old girlfriend, his cousin Helene Bitterlich. Robbins and Hayek were only reconciled years later.

Just as Hayek enjoyed cordial relations with his great adversary Keynes, with whom he spent time in Cambridge during the war, so he formed a lifelong friendship with Popper. He was also, at this stage of Popper's career, infinitely helpful to the younger man. He published *The Poverty of Historicism* in the journal *Economica*. Together with Ernst Gombrich he found a publisher for *The Open Society* and, crucially, he brought Popper back from New Zealand, securing him a professorship at the LSE in 1945. Popper was forever in his debt, and Hayek remained about the only person to whom Popper was unfailingly courteous.

Perhaps this personal relationship, a story of two compatriots helping each other to find new moorings in exile, helped to obscure their political differences. These were, nonetheless, substantial. To a degree, Popper remained true to his Red Vienna roots to the end. His advocacy of 'piecemeal social engineering' suggested that some level of planned social change was possible, whereas Hayek increasingly believed that a full-blooded free-market system was the only way forward, and that any compromises between economic liberalism and collectivism, of the right or left, were impossible.

Popper's biographer argues that, in fact, Hayek persuaded Popper of this view, but it is noticeable that Popper never joined the post-war Hayekian crusade for the restoration of free-market economics, or what came to be called 'neoliberalism'. Out of deference to a friend, perhaps, Popper attended the first edition of Hayek's post-war international thought-collective, the Mont Pelerin Society, of which more later, but never again. Indeed, the two men seemed to swap roles. Before the war, Popper was the political activist in Red Vienna, Hayek the aloof academic; after the war, Hayek threw himself into international political activism whereas Popper retreated into political quietude in Buckinghamshire, devoting his energies solely to the study of scientific methodology. Was this Popper's only possible answer, perhaps, to what Hayek had persuaded him was the political cul-de-sac of Red Vienna?

Churchill's calamity

The content of *The Road to Serfdom* as much as *The Open Society* was shaped by the historical contingencies of war. Although Hayek was clearly attacking the totalitarian tendencies of both left and right, due to the fact that he was writing at a time when Britain's brave Soviet ally, Uncle Joe, was at the height of his popularity, the Viennese thought better of assaulting the Soviet Union directly. It was probably a wise decision in the circumstances. Simultaneously, George Orwell, much better known than Hayek, was struggling to find a publisher for his own dissection of Soviet totalitarianism, *Animal Farm*.

The case of *The Open Society* was rather different. The totalitarianism that was the target of Popper's book, traced through the works of Plato, Hegel and Marx, was clearly fascism. But, written in New Zealand during the first half of the war, given the time it took to find a publisher for the manuscript and get it onto the bookshelves, the war was over and fascism, apparently, vanquished. Minds had already turned to the problem of containing the Soviet Union's ambition to control at least half the continent of Europe. *The Open Society* was thus largely read in the context of the onset of the Cold War, and was widely interpreted as a defence of open,

Western liberal democracies against the seductive promises of socialism and communism.

Readers accordingly invested *The Open Society* with their own contemporary preoccupations. The book was an extremely good example of what the French sociologist Pierre Bourdieu has dubbed the 'prism effect', where texts circulate internationally out of their immediate context 'and don't bring with them the field of production of which they are a product'. This can give rise to 'formidable misunderstandings', writes Bourdieu, but with 'good or bad consequences'.[15] Regardless of Popper's original intent, *The Open Society*, even more so than *The Road to Serfdom*, was taken as a definitive exposition of the West's political outlook, or at least what the NATO alliance aspired to, for the following four decades and more. Popper himself never disowned this narrative. For defenders of Western values the misreading, or perhaps it would be better to call it the invested reading, of *The Open Society* only had good consequences.

In sum, in those vital post-war years Popper and Hayek provided the best intellectual ammunition for those who were concerned that the Anglo-American alliance might be making the fundamental error of mistaking communism for what it *claimed to be* rather than what it actually was – another totalitarian system akin to National Socialism. Voters had got used to seeing politics on a left–right axis for decades. The Viennese argued that it was now more realistic to look at politics on an individualist–collectivist axis, or liberal capitalism versus fascism/communism.

This insight prefigured a fundamental shift in political thinking. There is no doubt that both *The Road to Serfdom* and *The Open Society* were ahead of their time, as any such paradigm-shifting works should be. Unsurprisingly, one reader who was outraged by *The Road to Serfdom* was Otto Neurath. Hayek's punchbag gave the book a relatively generous public review, but his annotations in his own copy reveal a much more scathing, if not inaccurate, assessment: 'His technique: overstate a case, create a caricature of it, then fight it and then kill it. . . .'[16] At this late moment, Neurath wanted to engage in an open debate with Hayek about the methodology of scientism and totalitarianism. Hayek, however, refused to be drawn.

To some, the boldness and clarity of Hayek's message served as a clarion call. As the author had intended, it was quickly seized on by the right-of-centre in both Britain and America. In Britain, Conservative politicians, anxious about the apparent drift of their own party to the left during the war, quickly dispatched copies to their party leader Winston Churchill, then preparing for a general election campaign in the summer of 1945. Hayek, the hitherto obscure Austrian professor, now became a central focus of the celebrated general election of July 1945.

An exhausted Churchill, bereft of any message of his own for the electorate, picked up Hayek's thesis with gusto, if clumsily. As I have argued elsewhere, there is no evidence that the extremely busy prime minister read *The Road to Serfdom* in full, or even in part, but he would undoubtedly have gathered the gist of it from his advisers, in particular from Ralph Assheton, the Conservative Party chairman.[17]

Churchill's first broadcast of the election campaign reiterated Hayek's thesis of well-meaning interventionism inevitably leading to a totalitarian future. But it was the way that Churchill framed Hayek's argument that did lasting damage: 'No Socialist Government conducting the entire life and industry of the country could afford to allow free, sharp, or violently-worded expressions of public discontent,' growled the great war leader into the microphone. 'They would have to fall back on some form of Gestapo, no doubt very humanely directed in the first instance.'

The vision of his labour opponent, the impeccably mild-mannered Clement Attlee, as a jack-booted gauleiter was so preposterous, and so insulting to a man who had been Churchill's immediate deputy for the previous five years, that the prime minister's campaign imploded from the start. Churchill also managed to discredit Hayek at the same time; Attlee cleverly blamed the Viennese professor for

Churchill's bizarre assault in his own broadcast reply the following night.[18] From now on, in Britain, if people thought about Hayek at all, it was as some eccentric, half-crazed continental professor. The image would endure for years.

However maladroit the wording of his broadcast, Churchill never regretted the general argument. A few conservatives grasped what their leader was trying to say, following up with their own similarly crafted attacks on the Labour Party during the campaign. But to no avail. Churchill's blundering certainly contributed to the Tories' losing the election by a landslide, bested by Attlee's vision of a New Jerusalem. But the seeds of Hayek's message in Britain had been sown. Another early reader of *The Road to Serfdom* was a perky young Oxford chemistry student, Margaret Roberts. Another reader, probably of the *Reader's Digest* version, was a Hollywood film actor and aspiring politician, Ronald Reagan.[19]

The Austrian School goes to America, and Switzerland

The Road to Serfdom not only attracted a lot of attention, and vitriol, in Britain but also in the United States. Even more so than in Hayek's adopted country, the book made him an overnight celebrity. Helped on its way by a laudatory review from the free-marketeer Henry Hazlitt in the *New York Times*, the book became an unlikely commercial success, making the best-seller list. Hazlitt described it as 'one of the most important books of our generation', noting the irony that 'the great British liberal tradition . . . of Adam Smith and Hume, of Macaulay and Mill . . . should find in England its ablest contemporary defender – not in a native Englishman, but in an Austrian exile'.[20] While Hayek was slowly crossing the Atlantic for a book promotion tour in March 1945, a condensed copy of *The Road to Serfdom* was published in the April edition of *Reader's Digest*, selling millions of copies.

As Hayek put it himself, the success of this edition 'completely altered the position'.[21] Arriving in New York, he was virtually mobbed. The original plan for the visiting professor to go on a relatively low-key book tour around some of America's more obscure colleges and campuses was ripped up; instead, Hayek embarked on a travelling circus 'as far as the mountains and back', speaking to scores of large audiences.

For those American businessmen who had been fighting a rearguard action against Roosevelt's New Deal policies, *The Road to Serfdom* was a gift. Hayek became their anointed warrior for capitalism. The prominent journalist Walter Lippmann was an early and powerful backer, as was the businessman Leonard Read, an admirer of Mises. Indeed, to a degree, Hayek's tumultuous reception in America had been prepared for him not only by Mises, who had emigrated to America in 1940 with a grant from the Rockefeller Foundation, but also by his fellow Viennese Joseph Schumpeter, whose own seminal exposition of free-market systems, *Capitalism, Socialism and Democracy*, had been published in 1942.

Schumpeter, born in 1883, was two years younger than Mises but considerably older than Hayek. Despite being taught by several members of the first generation of the Austrian School, and sharing their views, the rather grand and politically conservative Schumpeter was never a paid-up member, working beyond the confines of Mises's *Privatseminar* and the other loci of the interwar Austrian School. He had moved to America permanently in 1932 to take up a teaching post at Harvard. Increasingly, during the 1930s, he found his intellectual authority at Harvard waning as his students devoured the new Keynesianism. What Schumpeter himself regarded as his own magnum opus, *Business Cycles: A Theoretical, Historical, and Statistical Analysis of the Capitalist Process*, appeared in 1939, but at over 1,000 pages it was barely read and had little impact. It was at this point, depressed by the war and unhappy at Harvard, that Schumpeter conceived of his most enduring work.

As Hayek had done in *The Road to Serfdom*, Schumpeter embarked on a more accessible account of his ideas in *Capitalism, Socialism and Democracy*. He had some novel points to make about the last two, but it was his analysis of capitalism that remains the best ever penned. In particular, he placed the entrepreneur firmly at the centre of events. The entrepreneur was the innovator responsible for wealth and prosperity, the driver of 'creative destruction', the central process driving the capitalist system onwards. 'Economic progress in capitalist society,' he wrote memorably, 'means turmoil.' Here, Schumpeter consciously echoed Marx's own introduction to *The Communist Manifesto*: 'All that is solid melts into air.' Schumpeter's academic texts before the First World War had first developed this concept of the entrepreneur, his most important contribution to economics.

By the same token, however, Schumpeter warned that 'creative destruction' also made capitalism vulnerable to its ideological opponents, such as socialism. By contrast, he argued, the main virtue of capitalism, wealth creation was a long-haul process and often too subtle to readily appreciate. Its downsides – inequality, a monopolising tendency, occasional recessions, dislocations and resulting unemployment (all inevitable consequences of 'creative destruction') – were more conspicuous. In short, capitalism could be the victim of its very success.

Schumpeter's was thus a more pessimistic work than Hayek's or Popper's. Whereas the latter two offered spirited defences of a classical liberal order, Schumpeter seemed to be suggesting that the game was up. He was assailed by some capitalists and economic liberals for his defeatist tone.[22] Neither was his as directly provocative a book as Hayek's, so its message took longer to percolate through America's political and academic eco-systems. Only when the second edition was published in 1947 did *Capitalism* start reaching a wide readership. By the time that the third edition appeared a few years later, Schumpeter was famous.[23] In the long run, *Capitalism* was probably more influential than *The Road to Serfdom*, not for its defeatism but for its ringing advocacy of the entrepreneur. Certainly, American free-marketeers such as Hazlitt, Lippmann and Read took notice. Inspired also by Hayek, and the objectivist writer Ayn

Rand, Hazlitt and Read set up the Foundation for Economic Education (FEE), the first distinctly libertarian think-tank, with which Read was associated until his death in 1983.[24]

In the beginning the FEE was largely supported by the William Volker Fund, founded by the eponymous home-furnishings mogul in Kansas City in 1932. After his death in 1947, the fund was administered by his nephew Harold Luhnow. He wasn't much of an intellectual, but he did believe instinctively in free enterprise and was consequently 'captivated' by a speech he heard Hayek give to the Economic Club of Detroit on his book tour.[25] Prompted to read *The Road to Serfdom*, Luhnow decided to focus much of the Volker Fund's money and energies on promoting the Austrian School, publishing their works as well as paying for professorships for the Viennese in America. The fund was responsible for financing Hayek's chair at the University of Chicago, to where he moved in 1950. With about $15 million at his disposal, a huge sum in 1947, Luhnow had the resources to make a considerable impact, and he did. For decades, the FEE and the Volker Fund were in large part responsible for the percolation of Austrian School ideas throughout north America and beyond.

One of the first and most far-reaching decisions of the FEE and Volker Fund (together with the Bank of England) was to support Hayek's idea of establishing an international think-tank to revive interest in the ideas of economic liberalism and the Austrian School. Originally, Read had urged Hayek to write an American version of *Road to Serfdom* specifically for a local audience, but after much dithering this plan came to nothing. Instead, Read provided funds for Hayek to corral the leading economic liberals of his day for a meeting in Switzerland in 1947. Here, Hayek gathered together the threads of the Austrian School's story to date, to discuss how to roll back the incoming tides of statism and Keynesianism. This first meeting included Popper, Mises, Robbins and a young economist from Chicago, Milton Friedman. Lippmann and Read also attended, as well as several German economists.[26] Robbins drafted their initial statement of aims, which included, among other imperatives, a commitment to 'the redefinition of the functions of the state so as to distinguish more clearly between the totalitarian and liberal order'.

The quarrelsome participants were unable to agree on which great liberal precursor they should name their think-tank after, so as a compromise they settled for the name of the mountain on which their hotel was located, Mont Pelerin. From the start the think-tank was a very Viennese creation, modelled on Mises's *Privatseminar*. Participants were drawn from a wide range of disciplines – history, law as well as economics – and there was always a rich mix of academics and others, including, sometimes, politicians. This dissolved some of the boundaries between theorists and practitioners.

The job of thinkers like Mises and Hayek was to sway the 'second-hand dealers' in ideas, those journalists, broadcasters, writers and more who wielded the decisive influence over the general public, thus shaping the intellectual (and electoral) environment in which democratic politicians had to operate. As one American backer put it, 'What the highbrows upstairs talk about today has such a decisive influence on the public opinion of tomorrow.'[27] Furthermore, at the meeting in 1947 Hayek explicitly accepted that theirs could only be a 'long-run effort', and that Mont Pelerin members had to be 'concerned not so much with what would be immediately practicable, but with the beliefs which must regain ascendance if the dangers are to be averted which at the moment threaten individual freedom'.

Asked by admirers how they could help the cause, Hayek's advice was often to found a think-tank, to shape public and political opinion. One British supporter who took Hayek at his word was a Battle of Britain fighter pilot called Antony Fisher, who founded the Institute of Economic Affairs in 1955 on the proceeds of his successful chicken-farming business. This became the most influential institution in the revival of economic liberal ideas in post-war Britain and, together with the Fabian Society, the most important think-tank in the country's history.[28]

An unlikely duo: Polanyi and Drucker

Completely overshadowed by the oeuvre of Schumpeter, Hayek and Popper at the time, the fourth of the Viennese quartet of wartime texts was the only one to mount any sort of defence of Red Vienna. *Origins of Our Time: The Great Transformation*, better known just as *The Great Transformation*, by Karl Polanyi, was a slow burn. Virtually ignored by the mainstream press and media when it was published in 1944 (save for one unflattering review in the *New York Times*), *The Great Transformation* sold only about 1,700 copies at first.

In the long run, however, Polanyi's book proved to be just as persuasive as anything written by his Austrian peers. *The Great Transformation* would only come into its own in the 1990s, long after Polanyi himself had died, when its concepts and arguments began to be deployed as an effective rejoinder to the advance of 'neoliberalism', then sweeping all before it. Appropriately, Polanyi's productive afterlife continued the arguments he had enjoined with Mises and Neurath during the 'socialist calculation debate' of the early 1920s.

Like Popper, Polanyi had embraced Red Vienna. Unlike the younger philosopher, however, Polanyi was steeped in the traditions and theory of European socialism, particularly the British 'guild socialism' and Fabianism of writers like G.D.H. Cole and R.H. Tawney. As was evident in his contributions to the socialist calculation debate, Polanyi was trying to find a 'third way' between the communist-style collectivism of a Neurath and the free-market ideology of a Mises, and believed that he had found it in Red Vienna. He revelled in the apparent union of the radical intelligentsia – people like himself – with a mass working-class movement. His biographer describes how he 'experienced an epiphany' as he looked on admiringly at one of the massive May Day demonstrations in Vienna, when thousands of workers marched proudly round the Ringstrasse, bands playing and banners aloft.[29]

Just as Popper contemplated the cataclysm that had overtaken Europe from an enforced exile, so too Polanyi. He lived in Britain first, from 1933, eking out a living as a lecturer for the Workers' Educational Association. In the early war years, however, he was able to escape to a liberal arts college at Bennington, in Vermont, where he lived on a Rockefeller Fellowship from 1940 to 1943. He had been recommended to the position by a friend and admirer from Vienna, also on the faculty at Bennington, one Peter Drucker, who had also been marching around the Ringstrasse in the 1920s, remembering a particular workers' procession as 'the happiest day of my life'.[30]

In retrospect, the founders of alternative economics and management studies would seem to have been unlikely bedfellows, even more so than the fierce Red Vienna activist Popper and the mild-mannered Hayek. But for a few years, at least, Polanyi and Drucker, twenty-three years his junior, shaped and enriched each other's thinking, with long-lasting consequences for both their disciplines. As Drucker wrote to Polanyi on his seventy-fifth birthday, 'I doubt whether anyone has been more deeply formed by your influence and friendship.'[31]

Drucker was born in Vienna in 1909 into a Protestant house-hold. Unlike the entrepreneurial Polanyi *père*, Drucker's father was a senior civil servant, and Peter grew up surrounded by the leading lights of liberal Vienna, including Schumpeter and Mises. After finishing *Gymnasium*, Drucker moved first to Germany and then to London, working as an economist and journalist. He then emigrated permanently to America in 1937, working at Bennington College from 1942 to 1949. By contrast with the frugal, intensely intellectual Polanyi, Drucker was rather grand and worldly, a man of expansive gestures. As he gradually acquired the moniker of 'the guru's guru', bestowed on him by students of business and finance, so the official photographs tended to mimic Rodin's 'Thinker', the great domed head propped up by a pensive hand and surrounded by books.

Drucker's first personal encounter with Polanyi in 1927 tells its own story. Having sought Polanyi out to congratulate him on his journalism, the younger man was invited to share a Christmas meal with Karl, his wife Ilona and their very young daughter in their tiny Viennese flat. Decades later, recounting the event, Drucker was still clearly traumatised by what he called 'the worst meal' of his life: barely peeled, half-raw potatoes – with 'not even margarine. This was Christmas dinner!!'[32]

However, what Polanyi and Drucker did have in common was a shared intellectual concern with finding an alternative economic system both to unbridled capitalism, which they viewed as having brought about the interwar crisis in Europe, and its antithesis, unbridled collectivism – be it fascism or communism. In late 1939, Drucker published his first book, *The End of Economic Man*, which was closely followed by a second, *The Future of Industrial Man*. The first, particularly, was what we would now call a sociological interpretation of the rise of totalitarianism, in which he eerily predicted many of the awful events that would soon come to pass during the war itself. In common with several other writers of the day, he declared the death of *homo economicus*, anticipating some of the themes of *The Great Transformation*.

One enthusiastic reviewer of *The End of Economic Man* was Winston Churchill, who began: 'Mr. Drucker is one of those writers to whom almost anything can be forgiven because he not only has a mind of his own, but has the gift of starting other minds along a stimulating line of thought.' Drucker later claimed that Churchill was so impressed by his analysis that when he became prime minister fifteen months later he 'ordered that every British officer candidate be issued a copy of the book', although I have found no independent evidence to verify this.[33]

Regardless of the impression he left on Churchill, writing these two books certainly made Drucker the perfect sounding-board for Polanyi as the latter worked at the drafts of his own magnum opus at Bennington. The Drucker and Polanyi families bonded closely in Vermont. Ilona worked as a lecturer in the sciences at Bennington, while Doris Drucker took courses in physics and mathematics. By all accounts they would spend long, stimulating nights round the fire putting the world to rights.[34]

For Polanyi, even more so than Drucker, the interwar rupture in European history – the 'great transformation' of the title – had been caused by the atomisation of societies produced by free-market capitalism. He boldly set out his stall on the first page of his tract, arguing that, if left to itself, the 'self-adjusting market' would have 'annihilated the human and natural substance of society'.[35] Inevitably, in Polanyi's account, society had therefore 'taken measures to protect itself' – through social legislation, protectionist policies, corporatism and eventually fascism and communism – which had 'endangered society' even more. Polanyi famously called this dialectical cycle of capitalism and reaction the 'double movement'.

His thesis bore more than a passing resemblance to Schumpeter's concept of capitalism as 'creative destruction'. The very big difference between the two Viennese, however, was that whereas Schumpeter teased out the virtues and benefits of such creativity amidst the destruction (as Drucker also did), in Polanyi's account such a process was merely destructive. He maintained that market capitalism had rent society asunder by 'disembedding' the economic from the societal sphere – thus making people slaves to a ruthless, alienating economic system.

In particular, the fundamental delusion of nineteenth-century capitalism was to have treated human beings and nature ('land' in Polanyi's language) merely as commodities, to be bought and sold like cars or clothes. In fact, Polanyi argued, 'according to the empirical definition of a commodity' they were obviously nothing of the kind; people and nature are specifically not produced for sale.[36] Yet the market economy had subjected them to the same laws of supply and demand as everything else, leading, unsurprisingly, to a severe reaction. Socialist pioneers such as Robert Owen – Polanyi's hero – had managed to combine industrial production with a duty of care for both his workers and nature, and for Polanyi this was the ambition that had fired Red Vienna.

Polanyi's concept of fictitious commodities was his most important contribution to political theory. The vital difference with Drucker was that whereas the younger man believed the market had a vital role to play if it could be tamed and controlled, Polanyi believed that the market as it had developed apart from society was fundamentally flawed. Equally, in the end Drucker distrusted the state more than the market. Even before the end of the war, by which time he had been contracted to carry out a scientific investigation of the inner workings of General Motors, Drucker thought that he had in fact alighted on the one entity that could advance society beyond the binary cul-de-sac of the free market/collectivism. As the academic Daniel Immerwahr writes:

> Drucker pinned his hopes on the institution that he believed played the largest role in subordinating market to society: the corporation. His experience in the business world had taught him that corporations were anything but slaves to the imperatives of supply and demand and he hoped that, as social actors, they could act as responsible leaders in the new industrial age.[37]

The result of Drucker's two-year sojourn at General Motors was his most famous book, *The Concept of the Corporation*, which launched his career as a management guru. The hallmarks of his thinking thereafter, particularly his embedding of management in social and political theory, owed much to those years at Bennington and his dialogue with Polanyi. For Drucker, the management of organisations (not just businesses) now had to be studied rigorously in order for societies to function better; in so doing, he essentially founded the field of management studies. One of his most celebrated recommendations, that bosses should regard their employees as 'resources' rather than merely staff, recognising that they would per se have valuable knowledge to contribute to an organisation, was an example of Drucker's distinctive approach that owed much to Polanyi.

Unlike Popper, Hayek, Schumpeter and Drucker, Polanyi attracted few disciples during his lifetime and led a sometimes precarious existence as a lecturer in New York. (His brother Michael was better known, and was ideologically closer to the Austrian School in exile. Michael attended the first meeting of the Mont Pelerin Society.)[38] Nonetheless, *The Great Transformation* had laid the foundations for later movements of economic democracy and 'green' economic thinking.

Game theory and the Cold War

Not all Viennese, however, rushed to take up more didactic political positions as a response to the European crisis of the 1930s and 1940s. Some believed that too much politics was precisely the problem, not an answer. Among this group were several mathematicians, all sometime members of Vienna's Mathematics Colloquium, including Oskar Morgenstern, John von Neumann and Abraham Wald. The last had been born in Kolozsvár, Transylvania, which was then in Hungary, but was educated at the University of Vienna and took a PhD under the mathematician Karl Menger.

Morgenstern, born in 1902 in Germany, gained a PhD in political science from the University of Vienna where he became a professor of economics. A grand, haughty figure, his mother was the illegitimate daughter of German Emperor Frederick III. One colleague described him as 'Napoleonic': in later life he was prone to ride around Princeton University on horseback in a business suit. He was a member of Mises's *Privatseminar*, and also close to the Vienna Circle. From his variety of perches, Morgenstern could keep a weather-eye on the progress of these particular strands of Viennese thinking, and by the mid-1930s he was becoming increasingly worried.

In particular, he felt that Mises, certainly, and latterly Hayek, had abandoned the highest standards of the Austrian School by introducing 'value judgements' into their work. This was the central charge of his 1934 book, translated into English as *The Limits of Economics*. Here, Morgenstern broke definitively with his former colleagues. His diary increasingly filled up with random criticisms of Hayek – 'He is totally crazy', reads one entry.[39] Not that this mattered much to Morgenstern personally, as most of those economists had already abandoned Vienna by the time he himself got out on a fellowship from the Carnegie Endowment for International Peace. Hayek, for his part, wrote a spiky letter to Morgenstern on receiving *The Limits of Economics*, complaining particularly about the latter's 'rude' attacks on Mises.[40]

Morgenstern did not reserve his ire just for his fellow-Viennese. He was equally scornful of Keynes, another man who, in his opinion, had sullied economics with politics. In response to a letter from the Viennese economist Gottfried Haberler, Morgenstern confided to his diary in 1943 that the Cambridge guru was 'one of the biggest charlatans who ever appeared on the economic scene. And everybody is on their belly before him. Someone should really match up to him one of these days, he is brilliant, very intelligent and his opponents are no match for him.'[41] Perhaps that someone could be Morgenstern himself?

Increasingly, Morgenstern travelled in the opposite direction to his more activist peers in the Vienna Circle and the Austrian School. Morgenstern looked instead to mathematics as a purer, objective language to describe social action. This drew him closer to Neumann, who in 1933 had been offered a lifetime professorship at the newly founded and enviably well-endowed Institute for Advanced Study in Princeton. The brilliant Hungarian had written a paper in 1926, published two years later, on the application of mathematics to games, and human behaviour. Partly his interest had been piqued by the old central European tradition of playing chess.[42] This paper introduced the concept of 'zerosum games', in which one person's gain can only be at another's expense. He used a particular decision rule, called the Minimax theorem, to prove his case. The paper was called *On the Theory of Parlour Games*.

It stirred little interest at the time, however, and after 1928 Neumann left the subject alone – until Morgenstern prompted him to revisit it in the early 1940s. By this time Morgenstern himself had left Vienna for Princeton University and had also started to explore similar ideas, specifically related to economics. He had started a paper introducing economists to game theory, at which point Neumann suggested that they cooperate and write together. This paper grew longer and longer, and eventually ended up as a seminal book, *Theory of Games and Economic Behavior*, published in 1944.

Like Drucker and Polanyi, Morgenstern and Neumann were an odd couple (see image p. 284). Beside the towering Morgenstern, Neumann appeared small, impish and, by the 1940s, rather plump. But his eyes – 'brown, large, vivacious, and full of expression', remarked a close friend – betrayed his quicksilver mind and boundless curiosity.[43] Completely absorbed in his mental life, he barely noticed the emotional needs of those around him, leading to the break-up of his first marriage in 1937. The gregarious Morgenstern, on the other hand, scandalised Princeton on first arrival by dating a beautiful redheaded bank teller called Dorothy Young, with whom he had two children.

Theory of Games was their only collaboration, but was quickly acknowledged to be the foundational text for a new discipline, game theory, and particularly its application to economics. One historian, Robert Leonard, has described the book as a 'manifesto for the use of set theory and discrete mathematics in the social realm'.[44] Morgenstern himself wrote the most widely read part of the book, the introduction, which reflected his critique of contemporary economics. He argued that economists had not framed their analysis of social problems accurately enough, particularly regarding the behaviour of individuals at a micro level – a clear swipe at Keynes, amongst others. Game theory, he proposed, would allow them to do so with mathematical precision. Broadly, Morgenstern proposed that all social situations can be described in terms of coalitional games, and that all the range of possible outcomes in a game could be identified. These are 'solutions' – 'a set of rules for each participant which tell him how to behave in every situation which may conceivably arise'. Morgenstern's ringing introduction was backed up by hundreds of pages' worth of Neumann's dense equations and calculations.

The book was received respectfully in the academic press, but also merited a review in the *New York Times*, which turned *Theory of Games and Economic Behavior* into an unlikely hit. Just as importantly, game theory was quickly put to work for the war effort, for which Neumann, in particular, worked in a bewildering variety of capacities, including weapons testing. From 1943 the Hungarian started working part-time on the Manhattan Project.

Wald was also gainfully employed on war work, although in a very different capacity. He was a star mind at the now legendary, but then very secret, Statistical Research Group (SRG), part of the Applied Mathematics Group set up by the government at Columbia University. Here, America's best statisticians were put to work on behalf of the armed forces. Wald, as a recent immigrant from Vienna, had not even got formal security clearance, but was let loose on all the top-secret projects regardless. Milton Friedman also worked there.

Wald's most telling contribution at the SRG, which may have saved thousands of lives, was to develop the concept of 'survivorship bias', originally in relation to the endurance of American bombers over Europe. The air force came to the SRG with a specific question – where should they better armour their planes in order to reduce losses from enemy fighters and flak? The airmen handed Wald copious statistical data demonstrating where the most damage was on their B-17s when they returned to base. The air force expected Wald to suggest that some of these heavily-hit areas, the fuselage for instance, should be better protected. But Wald pointed out that these statistics related to planes that had survived an attack well enough to limp home, whereas what they really had to consider were the planes that had *not* returned. Arguing that hits by German shells would, statistically, be distributed randomly, he argued that the numbers of damaged engines observed in planes that returned to base were far fewer than randomness should predict. This indicated that the engines were the weak point. So these received more armour, to great effect. While at the SRG, Wald also invented the sequential analysis of statistics, allowing for better quality control on industrial production lines.

In the short term, game theory reached its apotheosis at the RAND Corporation, set up by the Douglas Aircraft Company and the Air Force at Santa Monica, California, in 1948 to analyse the new defence environment in the atomic age. The acronym came from 'research and development'. From the start, RAND drew heavily on the techniques of game theory; Neumann and Morgenstern themselves were both closely involved in developing the new institution's capacity through to the 1950s.[45]

This is where the Cold War was gamed, the consequences of nuclear war calibrated. The Strategic War Planning Game, or SWAP, was a common operational model. A small initial team was quickly expanded with the addition of scores of social scientists, economists and anthropologists. Gradually, Neumann stepped back from RAND but, as Robert Leonard writes:

There, now outgrowing its founder, game theory was sustained, initially as a technique promising precision and control in military engagement, and then as a machinery of thought, so to speak, helping the qualitative analysis of strategic problems. Throughout, the new analytics of bargaining and coalition-formation helped constitute a new culture of laboratory experimentation and game-play.[46]

RAND, together with the output of Hayek, Popper, Schumpeter and Drucker, put Viennese thinking at the heart of the Cold War.

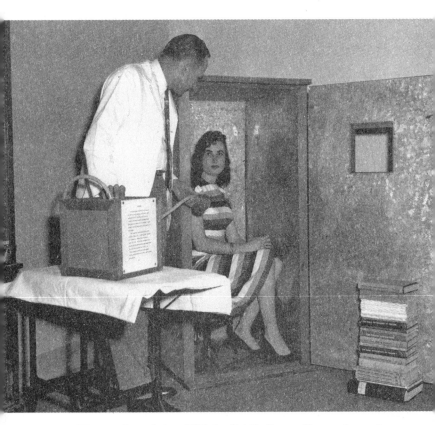

The sexual revolution: Wilhelm Reich's Orgone Energy Accumulator.

Chapter 10

Sex, Shopping and the Sovereign Consumer

O n 29 August 1909, a Viennese gentleman and his Swiss acolyte disembarked from the *George Washington* liner at Hoboken, New Jersey, to begin their first visit to America. Sigmund Freud and Carl Jung had spent the eight-day passage from Bremen analysing each other's dreams. They had been invited to speak at an international scientific conference at Clark University, Massachusetts, convened by the university president G. Stanley Hall. He also wanted to award Freud the degree of Doctor of Law, a rare accolade for the Viennese visitor at a time when, for those who had heard of him at all, his ideas were regarded as deeply flawed, if not downright scandalous. Hall, a psychologist himself, was one of Freud's few American admirers.

But even if psychoanalysis took time to permeate the mainstream of American life, it is hard to quibble with the historian John Burnham's assertion that 'the impact of Freud's ideas in the United States, for good or for ill, was indeed a major historical event of the twentieth century'. The pioneer of psychoanalysis had a much greater impact on America than anywhere else, and since this came at a time when the country was beginning to assert its global economic and cultural hegemony his influence was further amplified.[1]

Indeed, from the 1940s to the 1970s, Freudian ideas not only exerted a stranglehold over the discipline of psychoanalysis (and psychiatry more generally), they were also omnipresent in American (and Western) culture. This would probably have shocked Freud himself had he lived to see it. The Viennese father of psychoanalysis had always regarded America as singularly unpromising ground for his theories due to the nation's supposed 'prudery' and 'materialism'. As he wrote dismissively to Jung in 1908, weighing up the merits of bothering with the invitation to Clark University at all: 'Once they discover the sexual core of our psychological theories they will drop us.'[2]

Nonetheless, Freud was gratified by the attention. He regarded his five Clark lectures as the first official recognition of his achievements. All the same, his American sortie in 1909 was not only his first, it was also to be his last. His violent prejudices against all things American, as we have seen, must have played a part in that.

Fortunately for psychoanalysis there were other, less intolerant, Europeans who were prepared to swallow their snobbery and campaign for 'Freudianism' on his behalf. The most important was Abraham Brill. Born in Galicia in 1874, he had fled an oppressive family aged just fifteen for New York, arriving almost penniless. After graduating with his MD from Columbia University, he studied under the psychiatrist Eugen Bleuler in Switzerland and steeped himself in Freudianism. Fully converted, on returning to America he appointed himself as Freud's spokesman and principal advocate there. Brill was Freud's first translator into English (*Some Papers on Hysteria*), and was duly on hand to show him around New York City in the days before Freud delivered his Clark University lectures.

Freud's other tour guide that week was the young Welshman Ernest Jones, then on a fellowship at the University of Toronto. Just as Jones had done most to propagate Freudianism in Britain, so Brill founded the New York Psychoanalytic Society in 1911, the principal staging post for Freudianism in America. This was very much a satellite station of Vienna's Psychoanalytic Society. From his perch in New York, Brill effectively oversaw the growth of psychoanalysis as an accepted discipline in his adopted country, aided and abetted by the trickle of Viennese Freudians who moved to New York in the interwar years. This trickle turned to a flood after 1938.

One of those post-*Anschluss* arrivals, for example, was the Vienna-born Bruno Bettelheim, who managed to get a job quickly at the University of Chicago. Having been held for ten months by the Nazis at Dachau and Buchenwald, one of his first published works in America, *Individual and Mass Behavior in Extreme Situations*, was based on his experiences at the concentration camps. For the Allies, this became one of the standard early reference works for any systematic analysis of the murderous brutality of the Nazi regime. During the 1960s and 1970s Bettelheim went on to become one of the best-known faces of psychoanalysis in America, writing and lecturing particularly about autism and emotionally disturbed children. His analysis of how fairy tales could help childhood development, *The Uses of Enchantment*, published in 1976, was a best-seller. Only after his suicide in 1990 was Bettelheim's reputation severely tarnished with accusations of plagiarism, of falsifying his academic credentials and even of cruel and abusive behaviour towards his students and colleagues.[3]

So great was the influx of Viennese-trained central European psychoanalysts that they rapidly swamped any home-grown American attempts to develop psychoanalysis, and the study of mental health more generally, in any way other than what Freud himself had ordained. This set the stage for what became known as the 'Freud wars'. The Viennese immigrants, such as Fritz Wittels and particularly Heinz Hartmann (born in Vienna in 1894 and considered to be one of the founders of 'ego psychology'), insisted on Freudian orthodoxy, linking all mental problems to libido and penis envy. They ruthlessly policed the discipline through their leadership of the New York Society and later the American

Psychoanalytic Association, co-founded by Brill. Dissenters, who included German immigrants, Americans and many women, were kept out of the New York group; more often than not they founded their own rival institutes and associations.[4]

Freud's great adversary from Vienna, Alfred Adler, also established his own tradition in America, and beyond. In 1932, facing the closure of his clinics in Europe due to anti-Semitism, Adler gained a permanent position at Long Island University. Joined in America by his daughter, Alexandra, they set up the Alfred Adler Mental Hygiene Clinic in New York. After Adler's death in 1937, another Viennese psychoanalyst, Rudolf Dreikurs, took up the leadership of the Adlerians, helping to found the North American Society of Adlerian Psychology in 1952. Dreikurs was to Adler what Brill was to Freud. The society remains the centre for propagating Adler's ideas, including the notion of the inferiority complex, ensuring that the two great Viennese schools of mainstream psychoanalysis continue to divide opinion to this day.

Capitalism meets the id

These clashes within the rancorous, closed world of professional psychoanalysis were significant, especially for the future course of mental health more generally, but they also reverberated beyond the confines of the couch. For of considerably more importance to wider American and Western culture, and the subject mainly of this chapter, was the explosive impact of psychoanalysis and the broader study of unconscious motivation on the trajectory of post-war capitalism – what became known as consumer culture.

It was not only orthodox Freudians who played an important role here, but also those Viennese dissenters who broke with Freudianism, such as Wilhelm Reich. Indeed, the Viennese who worked within the American capitalist system were able to draw on an almost inexhaustible reservoir of skills and disciplines that had been developed in Red Vienna, originally to further the cause of socialism, but now applied equally well to capitalism. This enabled them to become extraordinarily innovative at the operational level of capitalism, applying new techniques and modes of thinking to almost every aspect of commerce and business, from public relations (PR) to design, from marketing to venture capital, from advertising to entrepreneurship, from shop design to consumer behaviour.

In this context, the close intertwining of Viennese methodologies with American capitalism pre-dated the more formal dominance of Austrian School economics as a theoretical framework for modern capitalism – to be examined in the next chapter – by several decades. From the 1920s onwards, Viennese émigrés were already reshaping and reinvigorating American business practices. As Jan Logemann, an economic historian, writes: 'Imbued with "outsider knowledge" as Europeans with backgrounds in arts and academia, the émigré consumer engineers provided a crucial innovative impulse to American consumer capitalism.'[5]

Of all this 'outsider knowledge', the most critical was psychoanalysis (and psychology more widely). Freudians offered the crucial insight for business that people – consumers – could be driven by unconscious feelings and desires as much as by more rational and deliberative decision-making processes. It was another example of the Viennese skill at applying one idea – psychoanalysis – to a completely new field. Furthermore, especially after the financial crash of 1929 and the consequent Great Depression, American industry, desperate to stimulate demand, was surprisingly open to innovation – even if that meant some executives spending more time than they might have wished exploring the finer points of human libido.

Torches of freedom

It was thus no coincidence that the first Viennese émigré to have a significant impact on American capitalism was Freud's own nephew, the dapper, convivial and irrepressible Edward Bernays.

A good-looking man with close-cropped hair and a fashionable moustache, Eddy, as he was widely known, was the son of Ely Bernays and Freud's elder sister Anna. Freud had himself married Ely's sister Martha. Ely and Anna moved to the United States in the 1890s, possibly to avoid scandal in Vienna as the philandering Ely had fathered several illegitimate children. This strained relations between Ely and his brother-in-law, who was understandably furious on his sister's behalf. Freud did not even attend their wedding.

Nonetheless, Eddy Bernays's intricate but rarely tranquil relationship with the Freuds served him extremely well. He fashioned a career by applying his (rather garbled) understandings of psychoanalysis and psychiatry to sales and marketing; he is usually hailed as the founder of the public relations industry. Bernays consulted with his uncle and, in New York, also with Brill, who furnished him with some of his most valuable insights into human – and thus consumer – behaviour. As Freud's reputation prospered in America after the First World War, so did Bernays's. The connection to his increasingly famous uncle became his calling card. Bernays repaid the favour, helping his uncle financially and acting effectively as his literary agent in America.

Previously, companies had taken a utilitarian approach to selling products, appealing strictly to the practical merits of their wares. Swayed by Freudianism, however, Bernays showed firms how to start investing their products with emotional meaning and psychological significance. His most famous campaign set out to persuade women to smoke Lucky Strike cigarettes. In the 1920s it was still taboo for women to smoke in public, but Bernays, after consulting Brill, hit on the ingenious idea of playing on this very prohibition. He marketed the cigarettes as 'Torches of Freedom', appealing to younger women who felt constrained by patriarchal limits on their personal behaviour. Bernays arranged for women to smoke Lucky Strikes in public on prominent occasions, such as the 1929 Easter Day parade in New York, and the habit quickly caught on. One

Harvard historian of science and medicine, Allan Brandt, has called this 'a publicity stunt of genuine historical significance', reluctantly acknowledging the American Tobacco Company's success in shaping and promoting 'the cigarette's status as the symbol of the independent feminist and the bold, glamorous flapper'.[6]

Bernays was also the first to enlist 'experts' to endorse products. He persuaded a former president of Britain's Society of Medical Officers of Health, for instance, to recommend that 'the correct way' to end a meal was not with a dessert, which would cause tooth decay, but rather 'with fruit, coffee and a cigarette . . . the cigarette disinfects the mouth and soothes the nerves'. Bernays would go much further down this dark road, inventing entire bogus organisations – 'fronts' – to disguise corporate involvement in publishing positive information about their own products. Such 'information', of course, could be wholly misleading; his biographer has called him 'the father of spin', but he might equally be remembered as the father of fake news.

Bernays peddled his techniques for most of America's biggest companies, including General Electric and the United Fruit Company, through to the 1960s. He was also the first PR executive to work effectively in that grey area between politics and big business, mingling confidently with the political class of Washington DC. It was Bernays, for example, who led the massive disinformation campaign on behalf of the United Fruit Company to persuade Americans that Guatemala was on the verge of turning communist, thus prompting the Eisenhower administration to engineer a coup in 1954 against the mildly socialist president Jacobo Árbenz. Behind this was the fear held by United Fruit that Árbenz might remove some of its privileges in the country or even move against its massive landholdings. He was replaced by a CIA-friendly dictator, precipitating decades of bloody civil war in the Central American republic.

With hindsight, it is easy to condemn Bernays for such activities, but the indefatigable PR man, like his Viennese peers, always saw his work in the context of the Cold War. Studying and exploiting the dramatic influence of the media was too important, he argued, to be left to the fascists who had destroyed his own city, or the communists. Democratic propaganda, retorted Bernays, should be – needed to be – just as robust and sophisticated. His book *Crystallizing Public Opinion*, published in 1923, was the founding text of the discipline. For better and for worse, he was certainly responsible for creating many of the techniques employed in corporate public relations to this day.

Alien invasion, and the study of mass media

If Bernays, for all his significance, can be accused of peddling Freudianism as snake oil, other Viennese émigrés provided much more rigour, and integrity, to the nascent fields of marketing, advertising and the like. They were to add numbers to Bernays's emotions. Of the more academically trained products of Red Vienna to arrive in 1930s America, the most important in this respect was Paul Lazarsfeld, who was to help found the disciplines of modern sociology and media studies. Not only was the young sociologist a catch in his own right, but he also brought with him a cluster of mostly Bühler-trained associates who were to transform many aspects of American academia and business over the following decades. He was, as he described himself, 'a connecting cog'.[7]

Like so many other Viennese, the sociologist's links to America began with a Rockefeller Foundation fellowship in 1933. Lazarsfeld impressed his American hosts with the range of new techniques for measuring, quantifying and analysing public opinion that he had developed in Vienna. Consequently, from 1936 onwards he was encouraged to found, or co-found, a succession of organisations and institutions in America closely modelled on his Research Centre for Economic Psychology, all following his Viennese funding model. Lazarsfeld himself saw the opportunities early on, writing home in 1934 to reflect on the lack of expertise in psychology and market research in America, meaning that European experts might be welcomed with 'great enthusiasm'.[8] Lazarsfeld dismissively described the market research that he found in America at the time as 'simple nose-counting'.[9]

His very first such organisation in America, in Newark, New Jersey, combined academic and consumer research, relying for its money on a blend of government commissions, particularly from a New Deal agency, the National Youth Administration, and commercial contracts. Lazarsfeld carried out a survey on milk consumption for the state-funded Milk Research Council of New York, for instance, but also completed a study of the home movie market for Eastman Kodak.

Lazarsfeld continued the communications research that his Viennese centre had pioneered, and in 1937 two leading American academics, the Princeton psychiatrist Hadley Cantril and Frank Stanton, later the president of CBS, created a niche for him to remain in America permanently as head of the newly created Office of Radio Research (ORR). In 1938, Lazarsfeld explicitly set out the new research aims of the ORR, in the process overhauling the entire study of mass media in the West. Hitherto, such research had mainly focused on technical engineering issues – frequency allocations and the like. Now, Lazarsfeld argued, it was time to go further: 'Who should broadcast, what and why, has been the main concern in the past. *To whom one should broadcast, what, and why, has now come to the foreground of general interest.*'[10] Of those who joined him from Vienna, his outstanding hire was, fortuitously, his second wife, Herta Herzog. Being a specialist in audience research, she was particularly suited to the media work at the ORR, also known among social scientists as the Princeton Radio Project. Ernest Dichter was also drawn to this group, as well as other alumni of the Vienna Research Centre, including Hans Zeisel.

In 1939 Lazarsfeld moved to Columbia University in New York, where shortly afterwards he set up what would eventually be called the Bureau of Applied Social Research. During this time, Lazarsfeld and his group perfected many of the most important techniques, often derived from their earlier work back home, that are still used today by social scientists, polling organisations, marketing and advertising agencies. Lazarsfeld himself had written what amounted to his group's manifesto in 1935, *The Art of Asking WHY in Marketing Research: Three Principles Underlying the Formulation of Questionnaires.* Here he critiqued the shortcomings of standard questionnaires and surveys, arguing, from his Vienna experience, for a much broader and more sophisticated approach. He demonstrated that it was now possible to apply scientific methods to revealing people's motivations, and to quantify these accurately.

Of all these new scientific market research methods, the most enduring and celebrated was the focus group, largely the creation of Herzog. This technique was refined at Columbia with two other American sociologists, Robert Merton and Patricia Kendall, who then codified the work in an academic article in 1946, citing Herzog's contribution only in passing. Her subsequent admirers have been rightly outraged by what one has called 'the symbolic annihilation of Herzog from this history of the focused interview'.[11] Unfortunately, only at the age of ninety-nine did she finally claim the focus group for herself. 'That is my invention,' she declared. 'I did not invent very much, but the focus group for sure.'[12]

Her husband fared better with the Lazarsfeld-Stanton Program Analyzer, developed in 1938. This was, essentially, a chart recorder, hitched up to listeners to capture their reactions to radio shows. In its crudest form, it consisted of a button in either hand of a listener seated in a studio. He or she was invited to press the green button if they liked something, and red if they did not – and to continue pressing as long as these reactions continued. Each button then sent an electronic impulse to separate red and black pens marking lines on a roll of paper running continuously through a machine. The impulses caused the pens to deviate from the norm, thus recording the listener's continuous reactions as a series of zig-zags. Simple, but the forerunner of all subsequent reaction tests. Corporations, as well as government agencies, quickly saw the usefulness of the Viennese group's work.

The most memorable single piece of work produced by the Lazarsfeld cluster, however, was the study of listeners' reactions to Orson Welles's notorious radio adaptation of H.G. Wells's science fiction novel *The War of the Worlds*. Broadcast on 30 October 1938, the radio version took the form of a highly convincing newscast, apparently chronicling the Martian invasion in real time. There were breathless reports from the 'battlefield', where the Martians were being engaged with heavy artillery. 'Officials' warned that New Jersey had been seized, and appealed for everyone to leave their homes. The result was, supposedly, widespread panic – many people believed that the Martians had actually arrived.

The very next day, Herzog, prompted by Lazarsfeld, set out from the ORR to conduct in-depth interviews in New York City and New Jersey with many of those who had panicked, as well as those who had not. The ORR followed this up with long questionnaire surveys conducted weeks afterwards, as well as analysing 12,500 newspaper reports of the event. This mix of qualitative and quant-itative research was eventually published in 1940 as *The Invasion from Mars: A Study in the Psychology of Panic*, and became nearly as well known as the broadcast itself. Many listeners had been so alarmed by the programme that, paralysed by fear, they abandoned all hope of survival. The study showed very vividly how much trust listeners now invested in the radio.[13] The study remains one of the most famous in the history of communications research.

The Bureau of Applied Social Research endured until 1977. During the Second World War, a scaled-down outfit carried on its work, mainly for the war effort. One of the Bureau's monographs, *Mass Persuasion*, for instance, assessed the role that radio had played in convincing so many Americans to invest in war bonds. After 1945, Lazarsfeld and his colleagues continued to innovate in the field of communications research, developing the 'two-step flow' model of communications theory. Rather than people forming their opinions directly from reading or listening to the mass media, two-step flow described how information flowed first from the mass media to opinion-formers (such as journalists) and from them to the public. The model was first formulated in Lazarsfeld's book *The People's Choice*, of 1948, co-authored with two colleagues. This was based on research gathered during the 1940 and 1944 presidential elections, and the insights were subsequently used in many American political campaigns.

From the 1950s onwards, Lazarsfeld concentrated much more on pure sociology, publishing one of the most important textbooks on the subject, *The Language of Social Research*. He is usually hailed as a founder of modern empirical, or mathematical, sociology, and institutes were opened throughout the West based on the model of the Bureau. But if Lazarsfeld inhabited a space between academia and business, his protégé Ernest Dichter pushed Viennese methodologies much further in the direction purely of business.

Know your customers

The Austrian School economists had theorised that the true value of a product was decided by how much a customer wanted to buy it, rather than by how much it had cost to produce. But if companies were to profit from this concept, first they had to find out what drove people to buy one make of saloon car, or soda pop, over its rival. What motivated customers to differentiate between very similar products in a crowded market? The answers to this question would give corporations a weighty competitive advantage, and it was Dichter who made it his life's work to help them find out.

Dichter was born, literally, into the sales business in 1907. His family were assimilated Jews, and his grandfather, Leopold, had founded one of Vienna's great department stores, the Warenhaus Dichter. Much of the Dichter family lived above the shop, and were also expected to work there. Young Ernest was in charge of the window displays, and, by one account, was the first to notice that customers were more likely to part with their cash with music playing in the background. At the University of Vienna he was drawn to the gaggle of clever students around the Bühlers, including Lazarsfeld. Dichter's Viennese background determined his later career; steeped in retailing, he also drew on the city's rich medley of intellectual disciplines to shape an entirely new field – motivation research – that would influence profoundly the modern advertising and retail industries.[14]

From the Bühlers, Dichter learned about psychology, psycholinguistics and self-realisation. When he was forced to flee Vienna in 1938, Dichter naturally teamed up with Lazarsfeld at Columbia University. But on top of imbibing Lazarsfeld's quantitative research, Dichter also drew deeply on Freud for a wider and more psychoanalytically-inclined interpretation of his interviewees' responses during the 'in-depth' interview sessions. Thus, as Stefan Schwarzkopf, one of Dichter's biographers, argues, he used a 'more colourful melange' of research methods than Lazarsfeld. Dichter took lessons in psychoanalysis from a colleague of Freud's and at one point was considering whether to become a psychoanalyst himself. Dichter even lived on the same Viennese street as the man himself, although there is no evidence that the two ever met. Nonetheless, he was obviously sufficiently well versed in the discipline to conceptualise the consumer as 'a hidden realm of desires, full of taboos, repression and secrets'.[15] If psychoanalysis had been developed to help extremely distressed people in a therapeutic context, Dichter's lifework was to show that it offered equally profound insights into everyday behaviour – like shopping.

In what was to be a common theme for many of the Viennese émigrés, as we saw with the architects and filmmakers in Chapter 7, Dichter regarded it as his job to persuade Americans to overcome their own inhibitions (mostly sexual, the 'prudery' that had concerned Freud), that they might consume, prosper and prevail. This was Dichter's version of Cold War politics, and his intent was every bit as serious as Popper's or Hayek's. More than any other Viennese exile, Dichter was determined to be more American than the Americans, or more accurately, a certain type of American. On arrival he immediately got elocution lessons, ridding himself of the thick Teutonic accent that Lazarsfeld and others retained. The 'Ernst' was quickly dropped in favour of Ernest. Unlike Lazarsfeld, who remained a notional socialist all his life, Dichter eagerly embraced American capitalism, picking up a roster of corporate clients soon after he branched out to set up his own consultancy. As the sociologist Daniel Horowitz writes, 'Compared with all the others who fled Europe as Nazism spread across the continent, Dichter celebrated commercial culture, salesmanship and the good life, as defined by the increasing spread of materialism.'[16]

Dichter had witnessed the misery of famine and destitution at first hand in Vienna in the early 1920s, which clearly had a lasting effect on him. As his disgruntled children testified, tired of his parsimonious ways around the house, their father retained a lifelong dread of poverty. His own, previously middle-class family had been immiserated by Vienna's spiralling inflation. Consequently, perhaps, Dichter became one of the most purposeful and straightforward advocates of the virtues of prosperity. In a famous phrase, he described himself as a 'general on the battlefield of free enterprise'. Even his detractors warmed to Dichter's sunny personality. With his horn-rimmed glasses, bow ties, thinning red hair and a ready quote for journalists on almost any subject, the jaunty Dichter, pipe in hand, became the archetype of the mid-century American adman.[17]

Before Dichter's arrival, America already had a growing market research industry. The 'profession' was being formalised, and in 1937 the American Marketing Association was established. Companies were accustomed to using the perceptions of interview-led research to analyse markets and explore their customers.[18] Some had already toyed with Freud, but the whole business was still relatively slapdash and unsystematic. Those picked to answer the marketing men's questions were too often members of their own families, or friends. The questions were usually cursory and superficial.

Dichter offered an infinitely more meticulous approach to market research. With a new methodological exactitude, he delineated the emotional and psychological appeal of brands. Today, we are so saturated by companies selling us 'feelings' and 'lifestyles' that it is hard to imagine a time when they merely tried to sell anything by virtue of its practical usefulness. Back in the 1940s, however, Dichter's methods were electrifying. For strait-laced, Republican-leaning, mid-century American executives his approach was novel to the point of shocking, even titillating. And when they consulted their bottom lines, it proved to be massively profitable.

Sex sells

Take Dichter's earliest assignment, in 1939, for Compton Advertising, the agency for Ivory Soap. In what was to be the very first instance of motivation research in America, Dichter subjected 100 carefully selected people to interviews lasting several hours, to discover how they really viewed soap. Much to the executives' surprise, Dichter told them that their innocent-looking bars of fats and oils were about something much more intimate than just getting clean. Dichter revealed that bathing with soap was in fact a sensual experience: 'One of the few occasions when the puritanical American was allowed to caress himself or herself.' A special time for women was the Saturday night bath before going out on a date, anticipating romance. 'Bathing,' as he explained, 'in its old, ritualistic, anthro-pological sense, is getting rid of all your bad feelings, your sins, your immorality, and cleansing yourself, baptism, etc.'

Based on these judgements, Dichter recommended a new slogan for the brand: 'For a fresh start . . . take an Ivory bath.' As his wife Hedy later said, her husband had hit on the golden truth that 'soap was more than soap, and a bath was more than a bath'.[19]

Companies flocked to hear about what Dichter called the 'hidden desires' of consumers. 'He was able,' writes Ronald Fullerton, 'to demonstrate operationally that "sex sells".'[20] If his work on soap got his foot through America's corporate door, it was his research for Chrysler that made his reputation. The struggling car giant hired Dichter to sell its Plymouth models. Dichter famously classified the car market in terms of sex appeal for men – an enduring trope. The dashing convertible was a mistress, while the sedan was the wife (gender stereotypes were the order of the day). Anticipating post-Modernist literary theory, he explained how a new car was in fact a 'semiotic system, a sign system', allowing a man to buy energy, success and strength off a garage forecourt.[21] He encouraged advertisers to sex up their car advertising: 'It fits me like a glove' was one suggestion. The companies obliged, bringing in the ubiquitous models who draped themselves over bonnets at testosterone-charged motor shows for the rest of the century.

Dichter was equally frank about the appeal of hot dogs. What *really* motivated people to buy food, he surmised, might be as much to do with sex as nutrition. Asked how to market hot dogs by Swift & Co., Dichter, drawing on focus group research, advised that the steamed sausage in a bun was deceptively complex. It was easy to eat, and thus popular with youngsters, even 'democratic'. But 'on a deeper psychological level', he declared, the hot dog provided 'an oral satisfaction comparable to cigarettes'. Dichter therefore proposed that different marketing strategies should be aimed specifically at the 'sensuous hot dog eater' and the 'delicate hot dog eater' (the latter probably a woman); the erotic parallels were 'unavoidable and probably desirable as long as they are done in good taste'.

Swift & Co., Ivory Soap, Chrysler and many more paid handsomely for these insights and designed vast adverting campaigns around them. Throughout, Dichter maintained his Viennese intellectual and organisational modus operandi. For a start, he was keen to advertise the theoretical underpinnings of his work as well as profit from its practical application. He wrote often at the intersection between academia and business – for the *Harvard Business Review*, for instance. In a groundbreaking 1947 article he laid out his new approach in full, arguing that marketeers had to address consumers' emotions, irrational behaviour and unconscious drives if they were really to understand them.

Dichter expanded further on this theme in his first book, *The Psychology of Everyday Living*.

In 1946, he set up the Institute for Research in Mass Motivations in a large, rambling mansion just outside New York. It survived on the fees that Dichter and his colleagues charged corporations for motivation research, yet maintained strong links to academia. There was considerable overlap with Lazarsfeld's Bureau at Columbia; sometimes they were working for the same clients. Dichter borrowed liberally from the latest developments in psychoanalysis, using 'free association' techniques, role-playing and Thematic Apperception Tests, originally designed to diagnose emotional disorders. Dichter also borrowed from anthropology and Lorenz's animal behaviourism.

Scores of people were eventually employed at Dichter's institute. By 1952, Dichter was widely acknowledged as the leader in his field, the star of that year's American Marketing Association annual convention in Chicago. Throughout that decade and the next, Dichter and his methods were the gold standard for the marketing and advertising industries in America. His work consequently affected almost every other branch of contemporary retail. If products embodied certain emotional qualities, for instance, then this had to be conveyed in the packaging. Walter Landor, the foremost packaging designer of the era (an immigrant from Munich via London), collaborated closely with Dichter's institute on several motivation research projects. Dichter, for instance, suggested that exactly as a bath was more than just a bath, so coffee was 'more than just coffee . . . [it is] a symbol of warmth and comfort and a way of life'. Landor consequently redesigned coffee cans for his client, S&W Fine Foods. Landor described this integration of motivation research into packaging as 'consumer response design'. Thus, 'packaging itself became primarily a marketing device'.[22]

Dichter's only serious rival in America was a German émigré called Alfred Politz, who championed the more traditional quantitative methods. Politz maintained, quaintly, that customers' reactions to more obvious retailing signals such as price were at least as important as their unfulfilled desires.[23] The jousts between Politz and Dichter at marketing conferences during the 1950s were the nearest the profession got to a blood sport.

Herzog on Madison Avenue

Motivation research was widely known as 'The Viennese School' of advertising. Hans Zeisel, the lawyer and sociologist who worked with Lazarsfeld and Dichter on market research after also fleeing Austria in 1938, later defined this distinctive approach as the blend of qualitative methods, emphasising the role of the unconscious, with empirical methods. But the fact that this methodology could be thought of as a 'school' in its own right owed almost as much to the redoubtable Herzog, 'the most powerful woman in the American advertising community', as it did to Dichter.[24] Overshadowed by such a relentless self-publicist, however, she remains much less well-known.[25]

As we saw, Herzog had followed Lazarsfeld over from Vienna in 1935. She worked principally on the Radio Project at Princeton and Columbia. Like her then husband (they divorced in 1945), Herzog was as much a theorist of communications, an academic, as a practitioner, but in 1943 she was invited to join the advertising behemoth McCann-Erickson, specifically to import all the methods that she and Lazarsfeld had developed in Vienna and New York. This was the first time that a mainstream agency started using all the new insights of psychology, psychoanalysis and communications research. Herzog further developed the focus group at McCann's, but also introduced personality tests and the 'eye camera', to record pupil dilations in response to visual materials. Herzog also ensured that McCann acquired exclusive rights to the Lazarsfeld-Stanton content analyser.[26]

By 1948 Herzog was deputy head of McCann. She led a separate, in-house research unit in the agency, called Marplan, to experiment with new methodologies, making it into a boutique version of Dichter's institute, employing psychologists as well as more formal market researchers. Herzog and Dichter both developed the idea of a brand 'image', derived from *imago* (the Latin word for 'image') that Freud had used. Brand images, for Herzog, were 'the sum total of impressions the consumer receives from many sources . . . [to create] a sort of brand personality which is similar for the consuming public at large, although different consumer groups may have different attitudes towards it'.[27]

In 1964 Herzog was made director of the first-ever dedicated think-tank in advertising: 'Jack Tinker and Partners', set up by McCann. Having emerged from academia originally, she eventually returned to it, in Germany and Austria, dying in her home country in 2010 at the age of ninety-nine. Towards the end of her life she wrote one of the best viewers' analyses of the two American soap operas that mesmerised large audiences in the 1980s, *Dallas* and *Dynasty*.

From the 1950s onwards, the 'Vienna School' was reaching a worldwide audience. Dichter was opening offices throughout the West, reimporting to Europe the ideas that had originated in Vienna. Herzog travelled to most of McCann's outposts worldwide in the late 1950s, training her younger colleagues. McCann was the first multinational agency to establish satellite offices in those countries where its biggest clients operated, and Herzog was its main draw. Dichter's methods were particularly popular in Germany, where his offices carried out 488 studies for companies between 1950 and 1972, as against about 3,000 in the United States. In Britain Dichter opened a large office in Whitfield Street, London, employing no fewer than eight psychologists. But he was probably most influential in France. Marcel Bleustein-Blanchet, the young founder of the agency Publicis in 1926, spoke admiringly of Dichter as 'the magician', and incorporated many of his techniques into his own practices. He regularly invited Dichter to talk to his executives; Publicis is now the third-largest agency in the world by revenue.

Architects of prosperity

In order for Dichter's cherished consumer society to prosper, retailers had to improve not only the way that they advertised, but also how to tempt customers into their shops. Before internet shopping, the physical environment of the retailer was all-important, particularly the window display. Up to the First World War, however, little thought had been given to this critical subject. Stores, and their windows, were often just crammed with products stacked up in no particular order, presenting merely a forbidding and confusing wall of merchandise to any casual shopper. But from the 1920s onwards, Viennese designers and architects were at the forefront of modernising the shopping experience, eventually leading to the greatest pre-internet retail innovation of them all.

Viennese designers were particularly well suited to retail for, as we have seen, they regarded their ideas as applicable to all structures and buildings, regardless of their use. This gave them enormous freedom and flexibility. One of the most eccentric, and sadly neglected, of Vienna's designers, Friedrich Kiesler, came up with his basic creative concept while in his early twenties at the city's *Technische Hochschule*. Space, he considered, should be 'endlessly fluid . . . freed of walls and other boundaries . . .'. He dedicated the rest of his professional life to implementing this doctrine. He was known simply as Doktor Raum (Doctor Space) among journalists and critics.[28]

Born in the 1890s, on the farthest peripheries of the empire in Chernivtsi, the state capital of Bukovina, now in western Ukraine, Kiesler, from an assimilated Jewish family, flourished in Vienna. Like most Viennese designers, he dissolved the boundaries in his own profession, working on everything from theatrical set designs, through gallery installations to biomorphic homes, where the shape of the walls and roofs evoked living forms. For photographers, he liked to pose embracing a model of one of these futuristic dwellings, often sporting a beret. It was his preoccupation with space that prompted the newly opened and very prestigious luxury department store Saks on Fifth Avenue to invite Kiesler to design their shop windows in 1927.

True to form, the aggressively original Kiesler quickly junked the clutter:

[He] removed all the partitions between the hitherto segmented shop windows to create a continuous stage upon which the individual garments entered into dialogue with one another . . . the juxtaposition of a generous expanse of space and an isolated and detail-rich exhibition piece drew attention [and], most of all, the generous emptiness came to be the expression of exclusive elegance.[29]

Kiesler thus helped to convey the impression that a fur coat purchased at Saks (as Dichter was also to argue) was imbued with qualities above and beyond its immediate function of giving warmth. The consumer had bought into an élite, luxury lifestyle.

Kiesler's design was the template for all upmarket retail stores to this day. He laid out his thoughts on the subject in *Contemporary Art Applied to the Store and its Display*, published in 1930. Here, he described the lessons of his Saks Fifth Avenue experience. Kiesler wanted to fuse Modernism with retail, to make the shopper a genuine participant in the drama of consumption. In so doing, however, he was also perfectly clear about the ultimate aim of the exercise. 'CREATE DEMAND', he enjoined. 'You must stimulate desire. That is why shop windows, institutional propaganda, and advertising were created and why their importance is continually increasing.'

Kiesler's work for Saks, and his life on the fringes of the Surrealist movement, attracted other commissions. In 1929 he built the Film Guild Cinema in New York's Greenwich Village, the first to have a flexible 'Screen-o-scope' that could expand the projection to the ceiling or the side walls. But his most important contribution to American, and Western, history was perhaps a commission he received from the art collector Peggy Guggenheim to design her new gallery of contemporary art. Kiesler's name was suggested to her by a friend, as she wrote in her memoirs:

Kiesler was the most advanced architect of the century, so I thought this was a good suggestion . . . He was a little man about five feet tall with a Napoleon complex. He was an unrecognized genius and I gave him a chance, to create something really sensational. He told me that I would not be known to posterity for my collection of paintings, but for the way he presented them to the world in his revolutionary setting.[30]

Kiesler was not wrong. Eschewing anything so boring as hanging Guggenheim's canvases on the wall, in one gallery he suspended them, unframed, protruding from the walls mounted on baseball bats. The walls were curved, made of gum wood, and the lights flickered on and off every three seconds, to general dismay. The opening night of her show Art Of This Century, on 20 October 1942, created the 'terrific stir' that she had been hoping for, mostly thanks to Kiesler.[31] With the benefit of hindsight, this exhibition is usually taken as a significant moment in introducing American taste to European Modernism, and later the more indigenous Abstract Expressionism. American artists on display at the Guggenheim show included Jackson Pollock and Clyfford Still.

From here on, the curatorial environment for art would be at least as important as the objects on display, much like Kiesler's shops. Despite these triumphs, however, Doctor Space struggled after the war, increasingly shunned by his peers. A rare vindication came with his extraordinary design for the Israel Museum's Shrine of the Book, completed in Jerusalem just before his death in 1965. He exited in style, at least; at his funeral the painter Robert Rauschenberg rolled a car tyre through the church nave up to the coffin where he painted it blue, yellow, green, white and red as a symbolic wreath.

Giving Vienna a roof: the invention of the mall

The most important Viennese of all in respect to the architecture of retailing was, however, Victor Gruen, born Viktor Grünbaum to an assimilated Jewish family in 1903. His father, Adolf, was a wealthy lawyer, mainly for clients in the theatre business, and the young Victor was educated at the *Realgymnasium* in central Vienna. At the Vienna Academy of Fine Arts, like many others, he fell under the spell of Adolf Loos, who provided inspiration for his work for the rest of his career.

Coming of age in Red Vienna, Gruen, as we have seen, was a staunch socialist. By night he was a regular on the irreverent and intensely anti-bourgeois cabaret circuit. By day, he worked as an apprentice in an architectural firm, helping supervise the building of one of the city council's municipal housing projects. This was the unlikely background for the future inventor of the shopping mall.

In the later 1930s, a change of tack was forced on Gruen by the rapidly changing political situation in Vienna. For a start, the collapse of the Social Democrats spelled the end of lucrative commissions on the municipal housing projects. Gruen had to turn to commercial contracts to survive. From 1936, he began to design stores for some of Vienna's retailers in the First District, such as the Bristol Parfumerie. Like those other devotees of Loos, Kiesler and Frankl, he decluttered the shop front and the interior, and, drawing on his theatrical and cabaret experience, employed the clever use of mirrors to artificially exaggerate the interior space. Then, on 28 May 1938, after the *Anschluss*, he fled Vienna, bound for New York.

Broke and eager for work, Gruen was quickly snapped up by New York retailers, eager to apply the skills he had demonstrated in Vienna to their own shops. At this point, retail design was still beneath most homegrown architects, so the more flexible and adaptable Viennese had the nascent field to themselves. After all, in the best traditions of the Wiener Werkstätte, Gruen was merely applying smart design to all the paraphernalia of commerce and retail, from signage to window displays, from calligraphy to letterheads. Teaming up with a New York partner, Morris Ketchum, Gruen was soon working on two upmarket boutiques on Fifth Avenue, Lederer de Paris, and Ciro's jewellery store. Here the two men designed the first arcade entrance to a store, a motif borrowed from Vienna and other central European cities, making Ciro more accessible to the casual street-shopper.

Retailers, stirred by how Gruen could stimulate 'impulse sales' with these new designs, were impressed and commissions poured in. In 1941, a fellow store designer, Morris Lapidus, praised Gruen's achievements in a weighty article in *Architectural Record*, recommending them as the best of contemporary design. The *New York Times*, meanwhile, sourly complained that the likes of Gruen were using trickery to create a 'frightening hypnotism of the public'. One critic complained his shops were so beguiling they were like 'mousetraps'.[32] That, as Gruen might have pointed out, was exactly the point.

Thereafter Gruen was seldom out of work. In 1941 he moved to Los Angeles, setting up home in the Hollywood Hills with his second wife Elsie Krummeck, a successful interior designer in her own right. He quickly attracted the attention of the Grayson-Robinson chain of mid-market department stores; the rapid expansion of the stores formed the vast bulk of Gruen's flourishing business into the early 1950s. As the Grayson stores grew in size and moved beyond the old downtown locations, so Gruen turned his mind to what he increasingly saw as the ills of contemporary American living – the social fragmentation of the 'distant sprawling suburbs', vast, featureless terrains dominated by the car and the tyranny of the freeway, leading to 'communities without hearts'.

He set out his critique at length in his magnum opus *The Urban Crisis: Diagnosis and Cure*. He contrasted American suburban sprawl with the organic, more democratic and intimate virtues of his birthplace, filtered, no doubt, through the lens of his youthful socialism:

The city is the countless cafes and sidewalk cafes of Vienna, from the ornate ones for the well-to-do to the little ones called *Tchochs*, where a person with little money may spend hours over a cup of coffee and a newspaper . . . the city is the community of soul and spirit rising from an audience in a theatre or at the opera, or from those attending services in a church.[33]

Gruen therefore set himself the task of overcoming the alienation of the suburbs by creating a new environment in which to shop, socialise and be entertained. Sporting a bow tie and braces, photos usually depict an expressive Gruen poring over his latest maquette, enthusing about his idea for transforming America.

This, then, was the advent of the shopping mall. To Gruen, the mall represented a utopian vision of American society, and indeed humanity, yet it was in fact a peculiarly Viennese mix of the socialist values of fraternity and solidarity with commerce and business. Gruen's prime concern was always to pull customers into shops. But the mall was also a space where hitherto alienated Americans could sip espressos, watch movies, wander and chat, as the idealised Viennese of Gruen's youth had done. The mall, as Gruen's biographer writes, was 'a new outlet for that primary human instinct, to mingle with other humans'.

Gruen arrived at this solution only step by step, but by 1954 he was ready to build his first recognisable mall, called 'Northland', in Detroit, then one of the fastest growing cities in America. Here, for the first time, about 100 outlets were grouped together around one central anchor store, with 'courts', 'terraces', 'malls' or 'lanes' connecting them, interspersed with grassy areas, colonnaded walks, sculptures and fountains. It was a new city. Restaurants and cafés abounded; there were also banks, a post office and an infirmary. Crucially, cars were left aside in huge outdoor parking lots. People could now mingle indoors, in an air-conditioned environment (another innovation), free of petrol fumes. The more perceptive critics appreciated the mall's clear

Vienna for Americans: Southdale mall, designed by Victor Gruen.

European influences. In *Ladies' Home Journal*, the journalist Dorothy Thompson praised Gruen's creation as 'extremely practical' and 'perfectly beautiful . . . a model of enlightened planning and social cooperation'. As she sensed: 'Something of the Vienna waltz pervades Northland'.[34]

The mall was an instant hit – up to 50,000 people crowded in every day. Some came to shop, others just to gawk. Northland's success allowed Gruen to plan on a much larger scale for his next extravaganza, in Edina, Minnesota. Southdale Mall opened in October 1956, with seventy-two stores, and for the first time they were *all* enclosed under the same roof, completing the full evolution to today's malls. As well as the retailers spread out over two floors, Southdale boasted a goldfish pond, sculptures, mosaics and tropical plants. The 'garden court', in the middle of the mall, was a wonder of the age, with a towering eucalyptus tree and an aviary. It was, as *Life* magazine trilled, the 'splashiest center in the U.S.'.

An instant American classic was born. Soon every developer was scrambling to build one. By 1960, just four years after

Southdale opened, an astounding 4,500 such shopping centres had been built in America alone, and by 1975 that figure had increased to 16,400. It seems safe to say that Gruen remains one of the most influential architects, if not *the* most, in post-war American history, and maybe even the world. Gruen not only reinvented shopping, he also permanently changed urban geography around the globe.

True to his Loosian routes, Gruen was particularly proud of Southdale's blank facades, his own antidote to the scruffy, confusing, neon-lit ugliness of traditional downtown. In his own mind, Gruen conceived of Southdale as a community hub for a vast new 'blight-proof neighbourhood', with the mall as the 'city centre'. Thus Gruen reconciled his Viennese socialism with American capitalism. In a broad perspective, like most of the other emigrants from Red Vienna, he viewed his work as strengthening democracy and capitalism against totalitarianism and communism. Yet at the same time he envisaged the mall as a powerful instrument to create entirely new living spaces in order to bring America's different classes and ethnicities closer together, thereby helping to meet the challenges of poverty and discrimination that had plagued interwar Vienna.

This was not quite how it turned out, of course, at least in his own lifetime. Gruen himself designed scores of malls, but cheap imitations also mushroomed across the country, and beyond, cannibalising each other. He regretted the developers' lack of interest in what he considered to be the social and economic potential of the mall to unite communities. By the 1970s, in America, malls had too often become victims of demographic trends that Gruen deplored, as crime-infested inner cities emptied into the suburbs. A shiny new mall could easily become the magnet for 'white flight', thereby turning them into racially defined ghettoes, hubs of fearful white exclusiveness – exactly the reverse of what Gruen had intended.

Yet in a longer perspective, the story does not look so bad. Demography has shifted again in the mall's favour. To an extent, the white flight to the suburbs has been reversed. Malls in America, in particular, now host a greater variety of peoples than before, although allegations about the racial profiling of Hispanics and Afro-Americans while shopping have led to protests and boycotts. Also, the mall has evolved, as Gruen would have wished. Now they could be better described as centres of 'retailtainment'. As the internet has eaten into the market for bricks-and-mortar shopping, so mall-owners have turned ever more to events and 'experiences' to make up the difference. The *ne plus ultra* of contemporary malls is the $5 billion American Dream in New Jersey. Besides the shops, this boasts the 'largest indoor water park in North America', a 'real snow' ski resort, and the Western hemisphere's 'largest indoor theme park'. Malls of course spread far beyond America. Europe's biggest mall is Westfield, in west London, just slightly ahead of various glitzy behemoths in Russia and Croatia. Such destinations are a world away from Southdale but, more so than ever, they encapsulate the spirit of Gruen's vision. Westfield, for one, is probably London's most multiethnic and multi-faith retailtainment space.

Into the Orgasmatron: Reich and the counter-culture

The Viennese engineers of America's consumer culture such as Dichter and Gruen never used Red Vienna's concept of *die neuen Menschen* in their discourse about building America's post-war society. But it is not hard to see the parallels in the way that they enthused about post-war American women and men as liberated, post-political, democratic consumers choosing and expressing new lifestyles amidst an abundance of material prosperity. More than any of his contemporaries, Dichter venerated these 'world customers' united together in the peaceful pursuit of self-fulfilment. The economist William Hutt, a member of the Mont Pelerin Society, had coined the expression 'sovereign consumer' to describe Dichter's vision. As Stefan Schwarzkopf explains:

Dichter predicted that national cultural differences between consumers worldwide were in terminal decline as the world's people came closer to each other and more consumer products moved across borders . . . motivation analysis offered to lift all human beings out of their regressive embedding in cultural, religious, national, racial and political ties and declared them – as consumers – to be the rulers of a new world in which traditional boundaries and separations no longer mattered.[35]

Another Viennese who offered a similarly ambitious vision of personal liberation in America was Wilhelm Reich, the author of *The Sexual Revolution*. He sought to bring people to full consciousness not through shopping, but sex. In so doing he shaped the emotional and intellectual environments in which Vienna's consumer engineers worked. Some claim that he ushered in America's sexual revolution (if the country had one). He was certainly a prophet of the 1960s counter-culture.

As we saw in Chapter 4, Reich had helped to run Freud's outpatients' clinic, the Ambulatorium, in Vienna from 1922 to the end of the decade, but by the mid-1930s the orgasm-obsessed Reich had been ostracised from the mainstream psychoanalytic profession. By the time he crossed the Atlantic, Reich was a man cast adrift, in all senses. In America, however, he was to find a surprisingly devoted audience. For Reich arrived in New York with a new concept, or to be more specific, a new device. Towards the end of his European exile, he had been feverishly working on what he dubbed the Orgone Energy Accumulator (see image p. 314). This was a box, about the size of a telephone booth, fabricated of alternating layers of wood, glass, steel wire and several organic materials. One sat inside this contraption, he maintained, to attract and to amplify 'orgone', a previously undetected energy composed of vital atoms of the life-force. He called the interaction between the orgone in the atmosphere and in the body 'orgonic lamination'.

Reich attributed many benefits to using the box on a regular basis, preferably daily. He promoted it as a means of alleviating cancer but, above all, the Accumulator was supposed to raise the user's 'orgastic' potency, or sex drive. As perhaps no one could have predicted, for a swathe of young Americans coming of age after the Second World War, the Accumulator took on a kind of shamanic significance well beyond the physical reality. It became the prop of a new counter-culture, the symbol of a yearning for new freedoms amidst the mainstream, buttoned-up America of the Eisenhower years.

As Christopher Turner, a Reich biographer, argues, the Austrian 'offered bohemians and intellectuals who had lost faith in Marxism, but who did not want to resign themselves to Freudian pessimism, a language of opposition ... In celebrating the anarchy of the orgasm, in trying to explode their sense of alienation with pleasure, the left were able to justify their retreat from traditional politics.'[36] In *The Mass Psychology of Fascism* Reich had already pointed the way, arguing that there were no 'class distinctions when it comes to character'; everyone was either 'reactionary' or, more encouragingly, 'revolutionary' and 'free minded'.[37] In short, anyone could join the Reichian revolution, as long as they weren't 'square', to use a period term.

Amongst those American 'bohemians and intellectuals', the first to call on Reich, shortly after the dropping of the atom bombs in the summer of 1945, was the bisexual, self-proclaimed anarchist and provocateur Paul Goodman, later author of a best-selling account of youth culture called *Growing Up Absurd*. Reich, Goodman proclaimed, was exactly the guru for a new generation anxious to escape the binary politics of the Cold War. For Goodman, Reich promised to restore a repressed populace to 'sexual health and animal spirits', a condition of such bliss that they would no longer 'tolerate the mechanical and routine jobs they have been working at, but turn (at whatever general inconvenience) to work that is spontaneous and directly meaningful'.[38]

Largely through Goodman's propaganda work, Reich's supposed manifesto for personal and sexual fulfilment quickly caught on with the Beat Generation. The novelist Norman Mailer was an early devotee. He attributed his own sexual and political awakening to reading Reich's *The Function of the Orgasm* after it was finally published in English in 1942. This was a cult book for aspiring hipsters, and widely quoted. All the other early precursors of the counter-culture read and absorbed Reich, including William S. Burroughs, Allen Ginsberg and Jack Kerouac.

The pugnacious Mailer was especially partisan, publicising Reich's ideas in *Village Voice*, the bible of New York's alternative arts scene. In *The White Negro* of 1957, a pen-portrait of his generation, Mailer described how the hipster 'seeks love . . . love as the search for an orgasm more apocalyptic than the one that preceded it'. God, he wrote, was 'energy, life, sex, force . . . the Reichian's orgone'. All these hipsters used the orgone box. Reich himself constructed them to buy or rent at his orgone research headquarters in Maine. Burroughs kept one in his garden; Mailer went to the lengths of making his own. Even the James Bond actor Sean Connery was a fan. The box became a well-worn trope of the counter-culture, until Woody Allen mercilessly parodied it as the 'Orgasmatron' in his 1973 film *Sleeper*. The spoof effectively ended the orgone box's useful life.

Naturally, the antics of Goodman and Mailer scandalised mainstream America. That was the point. They brought Reich and his ideas national reach, but also made him a hate-figure for conservatives and the East Coast establishment. Particularly damaging was an article in *Harper's Magazine* in April 1947 by the journalist Mildred Brady, entitled 'The New Cult of Sex and Anarchy'. This cast Reich (and his box) as the dangerous leader of a wild new youth movement centred on San Francisco, intent on corrupting the nation. Abridged versions of Brady's work were republished under equally lurid headlines – 'Is the World Sexually Sick?', asked one.

The notoriety unleashed a scramble for Reich's books and boxes. One beneficiary was Richard Neutra. Those bohemian Californians who were reared on Reich (and before him, Lovell) were, as the writer Sylvia Lavin argues, exactly the same people who turned to Neutra's architecture, which seemed to offer the same dreams of 'climate control, better sex, improved health and happiness' as did the Orgone Accumulator.[39] One couple, Josephine and Robert Chuey, a poetess and painter, commissioned a dream-house by Neutra in 1954 that became a gathering place for orgone box users and followers of Timothy Leary, the poet and advocate of LSD.

Ironically, however, Reich himself largely disavowed his role in these first stirrings of America's counter-cultural revolution. The beatniks appropriated his sexology, but severely distorted his views in the process. Although Reich did advocate the perfect orgasm, one that 'completely absorbed the participants in tender and all-consuming pleasure', this could only be achieved *within the union of a loving couple*. Reich, as his biographer Christopher Turner points out, was very definitely not an advocate of 'free-love. He was for love, not senseless promiscuity . . . he was against homosexuality and dirty jokes.' He was, in the end, a bourgeois Viennese.

It is difficult, therefore, even at this distance, to separate out the real Wilhelm Reich from the largely mythical hero of his supporters and the subversive ogre of his detractors. So certain was the federal government that he was a dangerous leader of a pernicious sex cult that he was hounded for years by the Federal Drug Administration (FDA), determined to prove that he was a fraud. At one point the FDA was unbelievably spending a quarter of its entire national budget trying to prove its case. Equally, the FBI worried about his radical politics and his membership of the old German communist party, but found nothing against him. He was eventually sentenced to two years in prison for contempt of court after the FDA charged him. He would not survive this blow. He died in his cell in 1957 awaiting a parole hearing. Astonishingly, in an unsettling echo of the Nazi bonfires of Jewish literature in the 1930s, the FDA ordered all his books and papers to be burned, although his orgone laboratory in Maine survives as a museum.

The manner of his death, of course, gave America's 1960s rebels a martyr, further muddying the waters. In 1964, as the swinging sixties and the 'sexual revolution' were gathering pace, even the sober *Time* magazine was elevating Reich to the status of a 'prophet', much for the worse. Bemoaning the 'cult of pop hedonism' and 'phony sexual sophistication', the arbiter of middle America duly laid most of these horrors at the feet of Dr Reich. This was how the magazine opened its long, alarmist report on the 'second' sexual revolution:

> The Orgone Box is a half-forgotten invention of the late Dr Wilhelm Reich, one of Sigmund Freud's more brilliant disciples, who in his middle years turned into an almost classic specimen of the mad scientist ... Hundreds of people hopefully bought it before the U.S. Government declared the device a fraud in 1954 and jailed its inventor. *And yet, in a special sense, Dr. Reich may have been a prophet. For now it sometimes seems that all America is one big Orgone Box* ... [today] the big machine works on its subjects continuously, day and night. From innumerable screens and stages, posters and pages, it flashes the larger-than-life-sized images of sex ... And constantly, over the intellectual Muzak, comes the message that sex will save you and libido make you free.[40]

By this time, Reich's reputation was so tethered to the Orgone Box that nobody bothered to read his original works. *Time* ended its piece with a stern rejoinder to what it saw as the cesspool of Reichian licence and indecency. 'When sex is pursued only for pleasure, or only for gain, or even only to fill a void in society or in the soul, it becomes elusive, impersonal, ultimately disappointing.' In truth, Reich himself would probably have agreed with most of that.

Welcome to the counter-revolution: the economist F.A. Hayek at the height of his influence, in London, 1983.

Chapter 11

A Viennese Apotheosis:
The Ascent of the Austrian School

In 1957 the hitherto obscure American journalist Vance Packard published his first book, *The Hidden Persuaders*. Written in a breezy and accessible style, it quickly became a best-seller, and has never been out of print since. For the first time, Packard took readers behind the scenes of all the latest techniques in advertising and marketing, exposing, principally, the mysteries of motivation research. Packard's main charge, sensational for the time, was that the 'depth boys', as he called Dichter and his acolytes, were manipulating people into buying consumer goods that they might not otherwise choose to purchase, or even need. As Packard wrote:

> All this probing and manipulation has its constructive and its amusing aspects; but also, I think it is fair to say, it has seriously antihumanistic implications. Much of it seems to represent regress rather than progress for man in the long struggle to become a rational and self-guiding being. Something new, in fact, seems to be entering the pattern of American life with the growing power of our persuaders.[1]

Packard's book was attacked for its flimsy footnotes and lack of hard evidence, but that didn't matter. Against the background of the Cold

War and the general hysteria over brain-washing at the time (*The Manchurian Candidate*, about American prisoners of war hypnotised by the North Koreans, starring Frank Sinatra, was released a few years later, in 1962), Packard's book struck a chord. It is regarded as a founding text of the modern critique of consumerism and capitalism, shaping public opinion on the malevolent influence of advertising and prompting the subsequent regulation of the industry. This chapter examines how much of this came to be blamed on the Viennese emigrants and exiles, even if this setback was closely followed by the apotheosis of Viennese influence – the ascent of the Austrian School of economists.

A cultural backlash

The Hidden Persuaders turned Dichter into a punchbag for all the early critics of consumer capitalism, such as the consumer-rights activist Ralph Nader. Dichter's case histories and methods were referenced frequently by Packard, who returned to the attack in several subsequent books such as *The Waste Makers* and *The Status Seekers*. Not that Packard's assault seemed to make much of a dent in Dichter's own business. The apparent 'persuasiveness' of Dichter's techniques recounted by Packard seemed to be so impressive that his list of clients just grew longer.

Furthermore, perhaps things were not as bad as they appeared, for as Packard himself conceded in *The Hidden Persuaders*: 'We still have a strong defence available against such persuaders; we can choose not to be persuaded. In virtually all situations we still have the choice, and we cannot be too seriously manipulated if we know what is going on.'[2] Indeed, for succeeding generations of consumers, thoroughly *au fait* with the language, symbolism and visual vocabulary of advertising and marketing, purchasing branded goods held no such fears of being tricked and exploited. And amongst those who contributed most to decoding modern capitalism for them was Dichter himself. He had nothing to hide. A relentless self-publicist, he ended up writing seventeen books about his craft, as well as numerous articles. In 1960, Dichter set out his own long riposte to Packard in *The Strategy of Desire*, his most famous work, defending himself against any charges of covert manipulation and brainwashing. By 1965, the advertising business in America was doing as well as ever, posting record-breaking revenues of $14.7 billion, over 2 per cent of the national GDP.[3]

Nonetheless, Packard's book marked the beginning of a clear backlash against not only motivation research but also the pervasive influence of Viennese empirical methodologies more generally. Complementary to Packard, the writer Betty Friedan kick-started the second wave of American feminism in 1963 with the publication of her celebrated book *The Feminine Mystique*. She took aim at those such as Dichter and Bernays who appeared to be seducing women into becoming passive stay-at-home housewives, whose biggest decision of the day was whether to serve up a hearty or light breakfast for the family (Bernays advised hearty, to help America's bacon producers). Friedan was very focused on middle-class women in the new, affluent suburbs. Herself Jewish, with a talent for exaggeration, Friedan compared the sprawling, all-mod-cons homes of these trapped women as 'comfortable concentration camps'.[4]

Friedan assailed Dichter for showing how corporations could use 'marketing strategies to transform the suburban housewife into a person who sought fulfilment as she baked a cake or polished a floor'. Dichter and his ilk stood 'guilty of persuading housewives to stay at home, mesmerized in front of a television set, their nonsexual human needs unnamed, unsatisfied, drained by the sexual sell into the buying of things . . .'.[5] Consumer culture had duped women, trapped by the feminine mystique. Friedan was herself trapped in a disintegrating marriage in the suburbs at the time, but argued positively that women should develop a healthy identity through leading more purposeful lives than being slaves to housework.

Others took aim at the vogue for the sort of systematic and integrated strategic thinking that characterised the culture of the

RAND Corporation, which by 1960s and 1970s permeated all corners of the military-industrial complex. Most notoriously, the concept of Mutually Assured Destruction emerged from Herman Kahn's work at the RAND. The application of such thinking to the prosecution of increasingly unpopular wars did not help. Take General Systems Theory (GST), for example, pioneered by the Viennese theoretical biologist Ludwig von Bertalanffy. As we saw in Chapter 1, GST was, in short, a theoretical model for applying the underlying principles of an 'open system' – one (as in human beings) which interacts continuously and dynamically with the environment around it – to all systems, and then modelling those principles mathematically. GST was enormously influential in post-war America, especially among inventors, architects and futurists (such as Buckminster Fuller), as well as the more formal scientific community. Bertalanffy himself was lionised by an army of devoted followers who put him up for a Nobel Prize. But, almost inevitably, GST was also deployed by the American military to examine its effectiveness in the war in Vietnam. Although, as Bertalanffy himself pointed out, if the army had used GST correctly it would have anticipated 'the ultimate failure of the U.S. military involvement by focusing on such non-military factors as Vietnamese history, culture, and nationalism, along with the morale of our fighting men in a war of such political and ethical ambiguity'.[6]

Regardless, such dubious applications of systems thinking left GST and the RAND wide open to criticism, parody and even mockery. The RAND worldview was brilliantly satirised by the director Stanley Kubrick in his 1964 film *Dr. Strangelove or: How I Learned to Stop Worrying and Love the Bomb*. Peter Sellers's sinister Dr Strangelove was an amalgam of Von Neumann, Kahn, the former Nazi rocket scientist Wernher von Braun and maybe also Neumann's Hungarian compatriot Edward Teller, the 'father of the H-Bomb'. The comic magpie Sellers also used the trope of the mad, German-speaking scientist Rotwang in Fritz Lang's *Metropolis* to flesh out the character of Strangelove, complete with an artificial arm involuntarily convulsing into a Nazi salute. Like all the best satire, *Dr. Strangelove* was uncomfortably close to the truth. Neumann, a fierce opponent of both Nazism and communism, was constantly urging the American military to use the bomb on the Soviet Union before it had acquired a sufficient deterrence of its own. It was only too easy to imagine the boffins at RAND calculating the film's 'mineshaft gap' with the same deadly earnestness as they really did calculate the 'missile gap'.

Culture wars and the Great Refusal

Thus an entirely new critique of Western society and capitalism had started to develop in the late 1950s, and it took very careful aim at exactly those Viennese consumer engineers and the broader range of thinkers and ideologues behind America's Cold War society – a critique that would develop into what became known as the politics of the 'New Left'. Broadly, the New Left accepted (unlike pre-war socialists) that capitalism was unmatched in stimulating economic growth and lifting people out of poverty. Instead, New Left intellectuals focused on the allegedly perverse, negative and disruptive psychological and emotional consequences of consumer capitalism, and the whole idea that 'society and democracy could be strengthened through the intelligent application of rational analysis to social problems'.[7]

The New Left borrowed heavily from the Frankfurt School of neo-Marxist critical theory, as developed by a generation of German intellectuals such as Walter Benjamin, Theodor Adorno, Max Horkheimer and Herbert Marcuse. They were mainly responsible for founding the Institute for Social Research in Frankfurt in 1924. Many of these theorists were Jewish, and were forced to escape to America where they spent the war (except Benjamin, who died by his own hand on the run in Spain in 1940). Adorno and Horkheimer picked up the pieces in Frankfurt after the war ended, but Marcuse stayed on teaching at the universities of Harvard, Brandeis and finally the University of California San Diego. It was Marcuse who now published the most trenchant and wide-ranging attack on not only the Dichterian universe, but the whole Viennese mode of thinking, characterised by Marcuse as the 'radical empiricist onslaught'.[8] Or, in another phrase, hyper-rationalism. His book *One-Dimensional Man*, published in the same year as *Dr. Strangelove* was released, cemented the sixty-six-year-old Marcuse's reputation as the 'father of the New Left'.

Unknown to most of the readers, however, in an important sense *One-Dimensional Man* marked not the beginning but rather the climax of a long battle between the critical theorists and the Viennese, which had begun in the 1930s. The divisions between the two schools of thought were profound, and delineated one of the principal cleavages in European philosophy that continues to this day, with significant political consequences. Whereas the Viennese, broadly, argued for a Machian universe in which men and women dealt in objectively constructing arguments and perspectives built on neutral facts, numbers and data, 'critical theory' argued that this was a dangerous illusion. In fact, so the argument went, it was impossible to have an objective stance before a world of facts because such men and women failed to realise, as one modern interpreter of the Frankfurt School writes, that 'he or she is not a free-floating intellectual but a lackey of capitalism, complicit, albeit often unwittingly, in the suffering caused by its exploitative nature'. Against the Viennese tradition, therefore, Horkheimer pitted critical theory, whereby social and political reality determined the outcomes of scientific work, not the other way round.[9] The Viennese themselves, on the other hand, detected the old foe of metaphysics in critical theory, often dismissing its conclusions as 'speculative' – a favourite form of abuse.

The skirmishing between these two very different worldviews had begun in the early 1930s with the logical positivists' attack on German idealism, Heidegger and metaphysics. Critical theory emerged precisely from this tradition; Marcuse himself had spent the 1920s studying with Heidegger and was heavily influenced by the older philosopher. Horkheimer penned the Frankfurt School's most comprehensive riposte to logical positivism in his 1937 essay 'The Latest Attack on Metaphysics', arguing that the Viennese philosophers held 'only to what is, to the guarantee of facts', thus divorcing their discipline from the wider context of political and social domination.[10]

Likewise, Lazarsfeld tussled with Adorno during the early years of the war when the Viennese hired the latter to work on his Radio Research Project in Newark. Lazarsfeld was particularly keen to work with Adorno, an established music critic, in order to test out some early theories on how audiences reacted to music on the radio – before the war, music occupied a good half of all broadcast time. However, very different approaches to the work quickly emerged. Whereas Lazarsfeld wanted to refine techniques of audience research to reveal *why* and *how* people listened to the radio, Adorno insisted on the primacy of his theory-based approach to the work – for *theory*, apparently, rendered such empirical work and all Lazarsfeld's 'clumsy research apparatus' superfluous.[11]

Rather than concentrating on the audience, Adorno argued, they should instead be questioning the social bases that supported the production and dissemination of mass culture through the media. Music, according to Adorno, had become commodified, like all goods under capitalism, and the further society proceeded down this track, the more individual choice and taste would be eroded. Beethoven, for instance, had become a victim of this society – by constant repetition on the radio, his music had degenerated from a vital force to a museum piece. All mass 'culture' was the same under monopoly capitalism, Adorno claimed.[12] Adorno produced no evidence to support his views – Lazarsfeld dismissed them, of course, as merely 'speculative'.

One-Dimensional Man was, therefore, a distillation of thirty or so years of intellectual warfare against what Marcuse considered to be the sins of Vienna. Rather than emancipating people through extending personal choice, as Dichter argued, Marcuse charged that post-war capitalism had merely generated compliance and submission to a highly restrictive and regimented way of life. By reducing people to mindless shoppers hankering after commodified pleasure and instant gratification, Dichterian capitalism had removed their ability to think critically and, by implication, subversively. These were the 'one-dimensional' people of the title – so many mall-rats. There was no free choice in such a society. Men, and women, were in fact slaves to 'false needs', 'superimposed on the individual by particular social interests ... the needs which perpetuate toil, aggressiveness, misery and injustice'.[13]

The responsibility for this dystopia lay, apparently, with the 'rational universe', foremost among them the radical empiricists. Ludwig Wittgenstein is mentioned several times in this context, as are the heirs to Vienna's logical positivists such as the British linguistic philosopher J.L. Austin and Willard Van Orman Quine, a visitor to the Vienna Circle's discussions in the 1930s. More broadly, Marcuse was taking aim at the application of such thinking to all aspects of life, creating a 'totalitarian universe of technological rationality', the RAND world, blocking 'all escape'.[14]

Michel Foucault, France's foremost post-modern philosopher, launched a very similar critique in a celebrated series of lectures on the then new phenomenon of neoliberalism at the Collège de France in early 1979. He, too, picked on the baleful influence of the 'logical positivism of the Vienna School', equating the philosophical tendency to filter 'every statement whatsoever in terms of contradiction, lack of consistency, nonsense' with the market's debilitating attacks on public administration and government, not on moral or ethical grounds, but in 'strictly economic and market terms'.[15] The high priest of Britain's New Left, Perry Anderson, similarly lamented the pernicious consequences of the Viennese migration to Britain in a famous essay, 'Components of the National Culture', published in the *New Left Review*.

But what to do about this rationalist assault? This was the weak point of the armchair philosophers of the Frankfurt School. Unlike the Viennese, who were very good at changing the world, the critical theorists could only interpret it. Unlike Packard, Marcuse asserted that there was nowhere left to hide from the pervasive indoctrination. Even sex, 'libido', had been mobilised and 'integrated into work and public relations, and is thus made more susceptible to (controlled) satisfaction'.[16] Marcuse feebly urged on his readers a 'Great Refusal' to conform, without offering the slightest hint of what this was to be.

In the end, Marcuse bequeathed this puzzle to the student generation of the 1960s, for whom he became a prophet of cultural revolution, his books brandished on the barricades. The opaque and provocative slogans of the 1968 rebels, 'Beneath the paving stones – the beach!', or 'Boredom is counterrevolutionary', were designed precisely to advertise the great refusal of the hyper-rational universe: 'Be realistic, demand the impossible' was another well-worn slogan. A rejection of corporate culture and the hidden persuaders became essential components of the alternative lifestyle, akin to rejecting the 'oppression' of the Johnson and Nixon administrations. 'Turn on, tune in and drop out' was as good a definition as any of Marcuse's Great Refusal.

It is easy to see, in this context, how Reich also became a hero to the counter-culture. Reich's apparent message of sexual liberation, of a better orgasm, was itself elevated into a Great Refusal of 'square' culture, claimed by a new generation (of men) who channelled his ideas into a proto-hippie lifestyle.[17] In the end, Reichianism ended up as a mainly therapeutic culture on the West Coast, dedicated to self-discovery and self-realisation – or self-absorption and selfishness, take your pick. The Esalen Institute, located on a dramatic outcrop by Big Sur, on the Californian coast, became the main outpost of Reich's ideas during the 1960s and beyond; the main teacher there during its hippy heyday was the German-born Fritz Perls, himself a student of Reich's in Vienna in the late 1920s, and later in Berlin.

Mises and American libertarianism

The outcome of the great intellectual joust between the radical empiricists and those advocating a Great Refusal was never clear-cut. Drugs, and the hedonism of rock music, were the surest path to a Great Refusal in the 1960s; amongst this generation the culture war was definitely won by the New Left, helpfully united with other strands of leftist politics in opposition to the Vietnam War.

At the same time, however, the extent to which much of the counter-culture was itself essentially capitalist cannot be underestimated. Schumpeterian entrepreneurs still built successful enterprises to meet new demands and lifestyles, only in radically new commercial spaces; such hippie capitalists and their brands included Richard Branson of Virgin, Anita Roddick of the Body Shop, Ben Cohen and Jerry Greenfields of the ice cream brand and even Steve Jobs of Apple, imbued with a vision of the liberating power of cyberspace, available to all through the personal computer.[18] As early as the mid-1970s, this maturing counter-cultural generation had reconciled itself to the idea that the best way to express one's individuality was not to *withdraw* from the supposedly controlling eye of mainstream society, but to create fresh brands to allow for alternative lifestyles *within* society. Whether choosing to fly, buy records, open a bank account or go to the gym, Virgin came to offer a distinct alternative to mainstream competitors – but it was still a Dichterian brand offering a service to be bought.

Eventually, the differences between companies like Virgin and others were to erode almost entirely, especially with the general acceptance of 'corporate social responsibility' even within the citadels of square capitalism. The hippy brands thus created a new mainstream, just as the shift in sexual and social mores from the 1950s rendered the cultural critique of the New Left almost redundant. In this sense, the emancipatory political economy of the New Left dovetailed neatly with an upcoming generation of libertarians, later to be grouped as the New Right. So much so, indeed, that one of their number, an eclectic New York intellectual called Murray Rothbard, started a short-lived journal to explore the areas of crossover between the two supposedly contradictory traditions, revealingly entitled *Left and Right: A Journal of Libertarian Thought*. And Rothbard's hero and mentor was Ludwig von Mises, certainly no counter-cultural hedonist but nonetheless an apostle of the economic and personal freedoms espoused by younger generations.

Mises had hurriedly left an academic perch in Geneva in 1940 for New York where, after several years of struggling to find regular work, the Volker Fund paid for a visiting professorship at New York University (NYU); Mises was there from 1945 until his retirement in 1969. Here, the Austrian attempted to recreate something of his old Viennese *Privatseminar* in NYU's Graduate School of Business. This second iteration of the Mises seminar started in 1948, when he was already sixty-seven, and lasted for the next twenty-one years. Attendance was not as coveted as it had been in Vienna; and the location, a dingy, impersonal classroom in the bowels of the university, not a patch on his old office in Vienna. Even the post-seminar chow, at a Childs Restaurant, never matched that of Vienna's Zum Grünen Anker. Nonetheless, the impact of this second Mises seminar, especially on the American libertarian movement and Tea Party Republicanism, was profound.

Mises remained as intransigent in his hostility to the prevailing New Deal/Keynesian political consensus as ever, so for those likeminded souls who found their way to his seminar the old man's voice was welcome and refreshing. Particularly after the publication of his major post-Vienna book, *On Human Action*, in 1949, for the nascent libertarian right of American politics Mises quickly became something of a cult figure. Only Ayn Rand, of *Atlas Shrugged*, could be said to have matched his status in these circles; she reportedly attended the Mises seminar on occasion, as, more regularly, did other Austrian School groupies such as Leonard Read and Henry Hazlitt. But the most important figure in disseminating

Mises's ultra-liberalism was Rothbard himself, the moving spirit of the modern libertarian movement and an advocate of anarcho-capitalism.

His most important book *Man, Economy and State*, published in 1962, was written with the explicit aim of making the ideas of Mises's dense and meandering *On Human Action* accessible to a wider public. Another influential devotee of the Mises seminar was the economist Israel Kirzner, who became a professor of economics at NYU. Through Mises, Kirzner and others, NYU thus became a rival centre to Chicago for the reception and study of Austrian School economics.[19] The billionaire businessman Charles Koch also took up Austrian School ideas to help found the Center for the Study of Market Processes (later the Mercatus Center), first at Rutgers and later at George Mason University, now the principal centre for research in the tradition of Mises and Hayek. Koch also co-founded the Cato Institute think-tank in 1977, an important point of influence in the Reagan administrations.

Mises died in New York in 1973, aged ninety-two. Almost exactly a year later, to the surprise of many, Hayek shared the Nobel Prize in Economic Science, the first non-Keynesian to be so honoured. Two years later, in 1976, Milton Friedman was similarly recognised. Unlike Hayek, therefore, Mises never lived to see the intellectual pendulum swing back in favour of Austrian-style economics. But he might have been cheered to know that acolytes such as Rothbard and Kirzner, and politicians such as congressman and three-times presidential candidate Ronald Paul, played their roles in shifting American politics away from collectivism during the Reagan revolution of the 1980s. The younger Paul, Rand Paul, carried the tradition into the Trump era.

Strikingly, all these Misites valued the paterfamilias of the Austrian School precisely *because* he had become so inflexible and immoderate in his views. There was considerably less give-and-take at the Mises seminar 2.0 than there had been in Vienna; in New York it was more about listening respectfully to the guru's very firm opinions. Such dogmatism might have been a valuable quality in an intellectual entombed in a classroom at NYU, but as practised in the real world it would fuel extremist politics. As Ronald Paul wrote of his mentor:

Mises never yielded to any temptation to soften his stand to be more acceptable to the conventional economic community, which proved him to be a man of strong will and character ... His determination and consistency were buoyed by the confidence that he was right, and that rectitude was all that mattered ... I have tried to emulate him.[20]

The location of the Mises Institute, founded in his honour by Rothbard, Paul and others in 1982, is telling. The city of Auburn, Alabama is well removed from the ideological muddles and messy compromises required of politics in Washington DC. It is the perfect place to cultivate ideological purity.[21]

Furthermore, anarcho-capitalists such as Rothbard moved far beyond Mises in advocating the complete abolition of the state in favour of free markets; in this world individuals would even be free to choose their own judicial agencies and 'police forces' to fit their own preferences. Mises and other Viennese, such as Hayek, always believed in a minimal state, to provide shared public goods such as the courts, police and army.[22] Indeed, as we will see below, the rule of law and the necessity for a strong state became an increasing intellectual concern for the internationalist-minded Viennese émigrés, even as some of their erstwhile admirers were drifting off to the wilder shores of right-wing economic nationalism, Tea Party or even alt-right politics.[23]

To the mountaintop: the revival of the Austrian School

If Mises gained his own discreet, influential following in America, his erstwhile protégé Hayek was all the time cultivating a wider audience on a bigger stage (see image p. 348). Throughout the apparent ascendancy of the New Left and the long reign of Keynesian economics, the most organised, coherent and combative of all the Viennese 'schools' or 'circles', the 'Austrian School' of economists, now led by Hayek, was quietly gaining ground. The original members of the Austrian School, like Vienna's philosophers, scientists and others, had been scattered by the war, mainly to Britain and America, and occasionally to Switzerland. Yet this hardly mattered as they met and communed constantly through Hayek's Mont Pelerin Society (MPS), founded, as we have seen, in 1947 to roll back the tide of collectivist, Keynesian-style planning.[24] It was, essentially, the first Mises seminar on a global scale. By the 1950s the MPS had about 500 members and hosted annual meetings, and sub-meetings, around the world. It remained, however, relatively obscure (as its participants would have wished), especially when compared to the other international liberal capitalist gatherings of the post-war world. The MPS has been compared to the World Economic Forum, for instance, founded in 1971 by the German Klaus Schwab, but in truth the MPS was always more academic and tightly focused.

This was Hayek's doing. As the founder, he chose the participants initially, a mix of academics, businesspeople and journalists. But if Hayek was relatively ecumenical as to the professional background of those he invited, he also insisted on a fairly rigid commitment to the politics and economics of free-market liberalism – against the wishes of colleagues such as Popper, who wanted to cast the net more widely so as to form a broader humanitarian camp. Certainly, Hayek's camp turned out to be very male and white, even if, gradually, more economists from the developing world started to join the MPS from the 1960s onwards. To date, there have only been two women presidents (out of thirty-three), the libertarian campaigner Linda Whetstone and the economist Victoria Curzon-Price.

Hayek's ideological diktat might have excluded Social Democrats and others useful to the more general cause of anti-communism, but in return it gave the MPS an intellectual coherence that members valued. It was the Chicago economist, Milton Friedman, a faithful MPS member from the very beginning, who employed the moniker 'Neoliberalism', in a pamphlet published in 1951 on 'Neoliberalism and its Prospects'. The term 'neoliberalism' was already in circulation before Friedman picked it up, but as members of the MPS began to use the phrase themselves, so it gradually came to be used as a shorthand to describe the general orientation of their collective thinking.[25]

More than anything, the MPS functioned as a support network at a time when these views were deeply unfashionable, especially in university faculties where most MPS members worked. Often, a member would be the sole economic liberal in his or her department, so Hayek's organisation offered almost unique opportunities for intellectual exchange, encouragement and networking. From the mid-1950s onwards, those British politicians who were central to the Thatcherite revolution in the 1980s began, sporadically, to attend meetings. First came Enoch Powell, and later Geoffrey Howe, Thatcher's future Chancellor of the Exchequer, John Biffen and Sir Keith Joseph, her political mentor. Not the least of Hayek's achievements was that he always seemed able to secure ample funding from sympathetic American backers and foundations for his meetings, the more so after the MPS began to meet in America itself rather than just in Europe; the first such gathering was at Princeton in 1958. Meetings were often held in plush hotels, preferably with a mountain backdrop and views over a lake. All very Austrian, as the participants observed.

The MPS was never, in fact, as one-dimensional as it might have seemed. There were four identifiable sub-groups at the early meetings, which allowed for plenty of vigorous arguments in subsequent decades. The Viennese-in-exile, at first, were certainly the most important, intellectually: Hayek, Popper, Mises, Machlup and later Haberler. Popper attended only the first meeting. But just as influential, in the short term at least, were the German economists who developed the school of 'Ordoliberalism', named after their journal

Ordo (Order), founded in 1948. By the early 1950s all the leading lights of Ordoliberalism had joined the MPS: Wilhelm Röpke (present in 1947), Walter Eucken, Ludwig Erhard, Franz Böhm and Friedrich Maier.

During this period they were the main architects of the Social Market Economy, which allowed for a greater role of the state in the economy than Mises, especially, but also Hayek, could accept.[26] In this respect the Ordoliberals took their cue from Schumpeter, acknowledging that the state had to provide a social and political framework for markets in order that they might benefit the maximum number of people. Regardless of the Austrians' objections, in practice the Social Market Economy was incontrovertibly successful, laying the foundations for Germany's 'economic miracle' of the 1950s and 1960s and the country's subsequent prosperity. Erhard, finance minister from 1949 to 1963 and thereafter Chancellor, was particularly lauded by succeeding generations of economists and politicians intent on emulating Germany's spectacular success.[27]

In the longer term, the Anglo-American contingent of the MPS was even more influential. Milton Friedman was a founding member, as were Frank Knight, Aaron Director and George Stigler; Friedman and Stigler were both formative influences in the Chicago School of free-market economics. Hayek himself crossed the Atlantic in 1950 to take up a professorship at the University of Chicago, a post financed by the Volker Fund, the early paymasters of the MPS. Before long, almost every member of the Chicago School was Pelerinesque; of the seventy-six economic advisers on Ronald Reagan's 1980 presidential election team, twenty-two were MPS members.

From Britain, Lionel Robbins attended, as did Stanley Dennison and John Jewkes, both of whom played key roles in maintaining some intellectual interest in economic liberalism even as Keynes triumphed in the land of Smith and Locke. Lastly, the MPS encompassed a small but important continental European contingent, which would include the Frenchmen Raymond Aron and Maurice Allais as well as the great Luigi Einaudi. As, successively, governor of the Bank of Italy, finance minister and president, Einaudi did as much as anyone to restore Italy's post-war finances and entrench democracy, thus saving the country from communism.

Almost inevitably there were splits in the ranks, making a nonsense of the notion that the MPS was a rigidly controlled 'thought collective'. There were vocal disagreements over the formation of the European Economic Community in 1957, for instance. Was this a laudable stab at a rules-based free-trade zone, or a protectionist bloc right at the heart of the world trade system? Or both? The question of intellectual property rights was equally divisive. Were they barriers to the free circulation of ideas and knowledge, or legal protections necessary *to ensure* the circulation of ideas and knowledge? The Swiss-German Röpke advocated an explicitly white, Christian capitalism at odds with the liberalism of his MPS colleagues. He was a vocal defender of apartheid South Africa, writing in 1964 that if the white population were to grant full political equality to the black population, this would invite 'national suicide'. As he drifted further away from his European neoliberal colleagues, so Röpke was enthusiastically embraced by the American neo-Conservatives around William Buckley. One of Röpke's Swiss backers wrote to him despairingly from South Africa after a conversation with Hayek that the Austrian 'now advocates one man one vote and race mixing'. He concluded contemptuously: 'Nothing surprises me about Hayek anymore.'[28]

Increasingly, the Viennese operated a hub-and-spoke system of intellectual influence. The MPS acted as the fulcrum and inspiration for hundreds of other such free-market orientated think-tanks founded around the world from the 1950s onwards. Again, this was Hayek's particular contribution to the battle of ideas; for him, like-minded academics and thinkers first had to recapture the intellectual high ground from Keynesians and collectivists before they could reasonably start translating their abstract notions of 'freedom' and 'liberty' into policy.[29] Britain's Institute of Economic Affairs, founded in 1955, was an early prototype of such outfits. In the United States the American Enterprise Institute (as the original American Enterprise Association had been renamed in 1962) and Heritage Foundation, founded in 1973, were both very influential on the right, especially during the Reagan era, and served as models for such think-tanks elsewhere. The first resident scholar at the American Enterprise Institute was Gottfried Haberler; the long-time head of the Heritage Foundation, Edwin Feulner, was a graduate student of Karl Popper's at the LSE. Celebrating his ascent to the presidency in 1980 at a dinner hosted by the Conservative Political Action Conference, Reagan paid tribute to his political precursors – such as Barry Goldwater – but also expressed his gratitude to Hayek, Mises and Friedman 'for their intellectual acuity in dark times'.[30]

The founder of the Institute of Economic Affairs, Antony Fisher, went on to set up the Manhattan Institute and later the Atlas Network, an international umbrella organisation for free-market think-tanks which, by one count, could boast of over 500 partner organisations in almost 100 countries around the world. These networks were particularly influential in backing local initiatives to set up economic liberal think-tanks in Latin America from the 1980s onwards (such as Hernando de Soto's Institute for Liberty and Democracy in Peru) and later in Asia.[31] The MPS may have been the organising brain of this campaign, but its hundreds of offshoots throughout the world purposefully created a ready-made toolkit for politicians of many hues – conservatives and notional socialists – to respond in similar ways to the same geo-political events. Together, they prepared a deep intellectual reservoir of neoliberal thought into which politicians could dip, or plunge, as they wanted.

The Thatcher government of 1979 to 1990 and the Reagan presidency of 1980 to 1988, in particular, certainly plunged, as has been well documented. But from the mid-1980s countries such as Mexico,

China and then Russia also began their own turns to more free-enterprise economies.[32] But it is worth emphasising here that the turn to Austrian School economic liberalism in the world from the mid-1970s onwards, the creation of the Washington Consensus, was not inevitable. Events – such as the oil price shock of 1973, the high inflation of the 1970s – certainly worked in favour of the Austrian economists, but it was the way in which politicians responded to these events, largely with economic policies forged by members of the MPS, that mattered.

This was the result of decades of relentless campaigning by the likes of Hayek, Machlup and Friedman, those 'academic scribblers' and 'defunct economists' (to quote Keynes), who usually turn out to have had such a bearing on the 'madmen in authority'. Fisher was knighted for his endeavours by Mrs Thatcher a month before he died. Hayek was appointed a Companion of Honour by Queen Elizabeth II in 1984 for 'his services to the study of economics', a day that he later described as the happiest in his life. In 1991, the year before his death, Hayek was also awarded the Presidential Medal of Freedom by President George H.W. Bush.

The 'double order': recreating Austro-Hungary at a global level

From the 1950s onwards, Hayek travelled widely, acting principally as chief diplomat for the Austrian School. Affable and well-connected, he was ideally suited to the role. But his major contributions to economics were behind him. Instead, he turned increasingly to consider how the free market could be sustained, and protected, by the rule of law, producing what he regarded as his masterpiece on politics and economics, *The Constitution of Liberty*, in 1960. Mrs Thatcher was prone to bang it on the desk in front of recalcitrant colleagues. 'This is what we believe in now!' she would bark. The three volumes of *Law, Legislation and Liberty* duly followed in the 1970s.

As well as providing the high theory and economic analysis for the turn to market liberalism in the 1970s, the Viennese were also very active at an institutional level – working within existing institutions to promote a global free-trade order, or inventing them from scratch if need be. The Austrian School contributed very little to the creation of those institutions that came into being at the end of the Second World War to found the new, American-dominated Western economic system: the International Monetary Fund, the World Bank and the General Agreement on Tariffs and Trade (GATT), collectively known as the Bretton Woods system. But members of the Austrian School, notably Machlup and Haberler, did subsequently influence these institutions to match their own vision of a global free-trade system guaranteed by internationally agreed laws and regulations. In all, the relatively unknown Machlup was probably the most influential in this respect. Indeed, he was probably the most successful Viennese émigré economist in America, enjoying a string of academic appointments at the Universities of Buffalo, Johns Hopkins and Princeton. He was also head of the International Economic Association, one of the discipline's leading, and most ecumenical, professional bodies, from 1971 to 1974. In retirement he joined the faculty of New York University.

The historian Quinn Slobodian has traced the Austrian vision of a global free-trade order, or what might be called 'economic federalism', back to the original discussions between members of the Mises Circle and Ordoliberals such as Röpke and William Rappard in the 1930s. These economists were confronted with the rush to protectionism and economic nationalism in the wake of the Wall Street crash of 1929 and the subsequent Great Depression. For these early neoliberals, the abandonment by the British Empire of free trade with the rest of the world in 1932, with the imposition of a system of 'imperial preference' at the Ottawa Conference, sounded the death knell of the long round of globalisation that had endured since the mid-nineteenth century (albeit with the interruption of the First World War).

The economic federalism proposed by those who would later go on to form the core of the MPS owed much to the search for new forms of global governance clustered around the Geneva-based League of Nations. But their model of global economic federalism also owed a great deal to a nostalgia for the old Austro-Hungarian empire, which they regarded as a model liberal regime. The term 'empire' confuses matters here, because unlike the contemporaneous British, French and Belgian empires (to name a few), the Austro-Hungarian version was not built on conquest, territorial aggression and slavery but rather on treaties and dynastic marriages. Vitally, also, it had no overseas territories. To a significant degree, therefore, it was not founded on coercion. The large internal market allowed for the free movement of people (labour), capital, goods and knowledge, yet, as we saw in the first chapter, a strong central authority (the monarchy) guaranteed and protected the cultural and linguistic identities of the many different peoples within the entity. This was what some Austrians dubbed a 'double order', or as Hayek described it, thinking specifically of Austro-Hungary, 'a double government, a cultural and an economic government'.[33]

This was the Viennese economist's vision of the world economy, the essence of contemporary 'globalisation', a term popularised by the Harvard professor Theodore Levitt in 1981. The Viennese accepted the proliferation of nation states that followed the break-up of the Austro-Hungarian empire – there was no going back on that. So the task for the neoliberals now was, in the phrase of Slobodian, 'to keep the nation but defang it', so as to allow the global market to function as one unit. Hence the turn to law for Hayek and others, as they sought ways to strengthen the regulatory powers of global institutions in order to override national obstructions to global flows of trade, capital and information.[34]

The main body that they alighted on to do this was the secretariat of the GATT; as early as 1958 Haberler was commissioned to write a comprehensive report on the organisation, in which he argued that although it was useful, trade liberalisation had not gone nearly far enough. It was a major turning-point in the history of the GATT (which evolved into the World Trade Organization in 1995). Thereafter, from the late 1970s onwards, three lawyers and academics, Jan Tumlir, Frieder Roessler and Ernst-Ulrich Petersmann, set the GATT on a sound and sustainable legal basis, to realise more closely the vision of a double order. Roessler and Petersmann were both German, inspired directly by their country's Ordoliberals, and the Austrian School more widely. Tumlir, a Czech émigré to America, was the head of the GATT's Economic Research and Analysis Division for eighteen years. All three pushed to give the world trading system a 'constitutional backbone'.[35]

When Roessler, who had grown up amidst the ruins of Dresden at the end of the war, arrived at the GATT in 1973, he was surprised to find that the organisation did not even have a legal affairs division; trade deals were done apparently on an ad hoc basis between contracting parties, known as the 'management' approach. Petersmann was advised by his second boss after joining the GATT to work like a 'U-boat . . . with low visibility and without provoking disputes over legal advice'.[36] Only in 1983 was an Office of Legal Affairs set up, accommodating both Roessler and Petersmann, and the procedures to follow for trade disputes were thereafter given a more formal legal basis. As Roessler later recalled, 'the presence of lawyers was gradually accepted, first as unavoidable, then as useful, and finally, as indispensable'.[37] The culmination of their work was the so-called 'Uruguay Round' of trade negotiations, the most complex in history, which in 1995 brought 123 countries into a new era of free trade, complete with a robust new Dispute Settlement Body. It was the nearest the world ever got to 'economic federalism' in practice.

Those countries which signed up to this system benefited immensely from the efficiencies and wealth that trade would bring (see China, for example), but they had to abide by the complex rules (covering no less than 22,000 pages) against tariffs, hidden subsidies and other barriers to trade that, ideally, created a level playing field. The highest court of the WTO, the Appellate Body, set up in 1995, has become the ultimate arbiter in trade disputes, operating like a Habsburg monarch in the federal trading system. All the while, countries could retain their unique values, politics and institutions (such as the Communist Party of China).

If Haberler had set the ball rolling on trade liberalisation, Machlup was instrumental in paving the way for the new world of floating exchange rates, the other essential grease of the modern trading system. An era of fixed exchange rates, with the dollar essentially pegged to the gold standard, prevailed after the end of the Second World War. It was supported by some of the older Viennese, mainly Mises and Hayek, but increasingly the younger Viennese – Haberler and Machlup – acknowledged its main defect; to maintain the values of these fixed currencies, countries were often obliged to enforce strict capital controls (or exchange controls), thereby severely limiting the circulation of money, and thus goods, in the global economy. Extraordinary as it may seem today, in 1966, more than two decades after the end of the economic emergency of the Second World War, British citizens going abroad, for instance, were limited to a travel allowance of just £50 a year outside the sterling area, for fear of straining the government's ability to maintain the value of sterling against other currencies, causing a run on the pound. This constraint was only removed in 1979.

Machlup was principally responsible for reforming this creaky system with the founding of the little-known, but vitally important, Bellagio Group in 1963. Machlup was the first chairman, assisted by two other prominent critics of the Bretton Woods system, the Belgian-born Robert Triffin and the Hungarian-born William Fellner (both held academic posts in America). The group consisted of academics, treasury and central bank officials, and came to be tasked by the G-10, an enlarged version of the G-7 group of rich countries, with the specific task of framing proposals to move to a new regime of floating exchange rates. Like the MPS, the group derived its name from the location of its early meetings at the Rockefeller Foundation Center at the sumptuous Villa Serbelloni overlooking the town of Bellagio in Italy. The group also had a strongly Austrian School flavour, as eight of the thirty-two participants were members of the MPS. Machlup and Haberler were ever present at the frequent Bellagio conferences, driving the group on to convert the politicians, in particular, to the virtues of ending fixed exchange rates. At a Bellagio meeting in 1965, Machlup decreed impatiently that if the politicians were 'unwilling to discuss, let alone adopt' flexible exchange rates, the experts had to 'get busy teaching the politicians because they lag behind in their intellectual development'.[38]

Eventually, of course, the politicians did see the wisdom of Machlup's arguments. Under the dual economic pressures of the Vietnam war and funding the Great Society of his predecessor, President Richard Nixon ended the gold convertibility of the dollar in 1971. Most countries followed suit, moving to floating exchange rates, or at least controlled floats as in the various iterations of the European Monetary System, the precursor of the euro. Its job apparently done, the Bellagio Group wound up in 1974, although it was subsequently revived in 1996. Machlup died in 1983, twelve years before the older Haberler. They were the hidden hands of the Austrian School's revolution, providing the persistent, long-term economic diplomacy on official committees and government bodies that Mises, for one, could never have endured, and would probably have scorned.

The knowledge economy

Machlup, together with Peter Drucker, also did most to advance the theoretical analysis of modern capitalism from the 1960s onwards, responsible for spotting and elucidating the fundamental shift from an economic system based on manual labour to one based on knowledge – the 'knowledge economy', as Drucker popularised the term. From now on, at least in advanced societies, knowledge workers, those whose value lies in what they have in their head rather than what they can do with their hands, would command a premium. It was no coincidence that two Viennese should come up with this concept. As I argued in Chapter 4, the Viennese method of intellectual production going right back to the 1920s created, in its own way, the first recognisable knowledge economy.

There are stirrings of this thesis in Drucker's famous study of General Motors (GM), *Concept of the Corporation*. With echoes of Red Vienna, as we have seen, and his collaboration with Polanyi, he admonished GM for its 'assembly-line mentality'. He recommended, effectively, team-working throughout, whereby each worker, however humble, could contribute his or her knowledge of the assembly line into a large pool of expertise that would help to improve constantly the production process, thereby empowering them along the way. Urging managers to regard workers as an intellectual resource, rather than merely as a unit of production, was radical stuff for the time, and ignored by most Western companies.

The Japanese, however, were much more receptive. Rebuilding a devastated economy after the war, Japanese managers incorporated Drucker's principles into their own industries, with stunning success. If Drucker was merely admired in America, he was revered in Japan: his classic *The Practice of Management* sold 1 million copies there, out of 5 million worldwide.[39] The Japanese eventually re-exported Drucker's ideas back to America and Europe as they built their own car factories there, leaving Detroit and Britain's strike-prone British Leyland assembly lines high and dry.

It was only in 1962, however, that Machlup, rather than Drucker, wrote the first path-breaking, extended analysis of the knowledge economy, *The Production and Distribution of Knowledge in the United States*, published by Princeton University Press. For the first time, Machlup used an economist's toolkit in an attempt to measure the full extent of the knowledge economy, beyond the usual suspects such as higher education and companies' research and development departments. His was a daringly synoptic, but realistic, view of knowledge, embracing not only scientific but 'ordinary' knowledge as well: 'We may designate as knowledge anything that is known by somebody.' He also included in his definition the production and distribution of knowledge. This wider definition of the knowledge economy is now commonplace, and Machlup's original terms are still largely in use to quantify knowledge economies today.[40] His work was amplified by Gary Becker's theories on human capital formation. Becker, a Chicago School economist, was also a member, and one-time president, of the MPS, winning a Nobel Prize for his concept of human capital in 1992.

Machlup's conclusions on the state of America's knowledge economy, after reviewing the available data over hundreds of pages, were alarming – that America faced a 'great scarcity of brainpower in our labour force'.[41] He therefore advocated a complete overhaul of the public school system, to 'turn out not only a much larger élite of top-rate knowledge producers and knowledge users but also broad masses of people whose intellectual attainment is well above the national average'.[42] Like all the Viennese exiles, Machlup framed this in existential terms; without such reforms, and an efficient knowledge economy, he argued, America's 'national security, or even survival', would be under threat.

Drucker took up a lot of Machlup's thinking years later in *The Age of Discontinuity*, published in 1968. In so doing, and in emphasising the personal responsibility of managers and their crucial roles in the survival of business organisations, Drucker became, in the words of one recent historian of management theory, perhaps 'the most widely read management thinker of all time'. He inspired unlikely levels of devotion, which, to give him his due, he often tried to deflect. One South Korean businessman was so impressed that he changed his own name to Peter Drucker.[43]

But how to turn the fruits of 'knowledge work' into tangible, monetised outcomes – products? This was the role of Schumpeter's entrepreneur, as Machlup and Drucker acknowledged. In contrast to the Keynesian, corporatist states of the 1950s, the Austrian School, in its widest sense, including even Drucker, who never attended a

Mont Pelerin meeting, advocated a capitalism that put the entrepreneur at the heart of the economic system, as the principal creative spur to wealth creation. This was Schumpeter's profound contribution to political economy, to push the entrepreneur, as he put it, to centre-stage, to describe and promote the role of the essential risk-taker who pushes capitalism forwards. Today, business executives and journalists talk incessantly of 'disruptors', usually digital, such as Elon Musk or Jeff Bezos. In truth, these are merely the long-standing Schumpeterian actors who harness capital to new technology in order to meet consumer demands in more efficient and effective ways. Schumpeter made their role immanent.

Drucker was the first intellectual to take management seriously as a discrete professional activity, in and of itself. In the Viennese tradition, he drew on many other disciplines – psychology, history, philosophy and economics – to create the 'effective' manager. Drucker worked to restructure the corporation as a flexible, market-sensitive entity, with the ability to innovate even at scale. He worked through case histories and concrete examples to make his arguments, a technique that was to dominate management literature. But again and again, he always came back to the essential role of the modern entrepreneur. This is his own description from *Management*, published in 1974: 'The want a business satisfies may have been felt by customers ... but it remained a potential want until business people converted it into effective action. Only then are there customers and a market.'

Together, Drucker and Schumpeter can take much of the credit for elevating the role of the entrepreneur to the prominent position that she or he now occupies in Western societies. It was only in the 1960s that the first 'entrepreneurship' courses were offered in America, at Stanford and New York Universities (where Mises held his seminars), followed shortly by the first entrepreneurship MBA at the University of Southern California. A decade later several hundred schools and universities were offering entrepreneurship courses and programmes.[44] The supply-side economics of the

Thatcher and Reagan era were but a series of policies to allow the entrepreneur to flourish once again. The 'entrepreneurial society' has now become a fashionable cliché, but it took many decades of incessant argument and persuasion to reach this point.

In a wider context, the Austrian School argued that only the entrepreneurial economy, or at the very least Germany's post-war social market economy, guaranteed the Open Society and the sort of diversity of peoples and views that had prevailed in pre-war Vienna. As well as free markets, the entire philosophical systems of critical rationalism and scientific methodology were equally important determinants of a liberal polity based on the rule of law.

Overall, it is difficult to think of any intellectual movement since the Marxist-Leninists of the late nineteenth and early twentieth centuries that has reorientated political and economic thinking so profoundly, and been so assiduously and coherently organised. By the 1970s, the Austrian School offered an all-embracing vision of a new political economy that claimed to lift people out of poverty and produce economic growth. This vision had been worked out in detail, from trade to monetary to taxation policies, all available in handy, readable pamphlets published by the innumerable offshoots of the MPS.

Furthermore, the Viennese worked very much at an operational level, just as much as at a grand theoretical level. The Austrian School swept through Wall Street as well as the financial bureaucracies on both sides of the Atlantic. Successive chairs of the Federal Reserve, the legendary Paul Volcker (1979–87) and Alan Greenspan (1987–2006) had both imbibed their Hayek at university and beyond. Volcker, in particular, looked to Hayek in his struggles to bring soaring inflation down in the early 1980s. His draconian interest-rate policy proved unpopular but ultimately successful; in 1979, when Volcker began his experiment with monetary targets, inflation was running at over 12 per cent, but three years later it had been reduced to just under 6 per cent.[45]

Greenspan, a disciple of the eccentric Russian-born writer and philosopher Ayn Rand as much as the Austrian School, aimed to run an equally tight ship.

The vision frays: enter Polanyi

In the competitive global marketplace of ideas, to put it in Austrian School terms, the ascendancy of the Viennese brand of neoliberalism lasted from the mid-1970s through to about 2010. I write 'ascendancy' advisedly, rather than 'dominance' or 'hegemony', for the politicians and international financial bureaucrats who operationalised neoliberalism never achieved as much as is often ascribed to them. Take world trade, a key marker for economic federalism. The Uruguay Round of 1994 was a triumph, but it also proved to be the last ever such multilateral trade agreement under the reformed WTO. The Thatcherites and Reaganites made some modest inroads into the size of government budgets and bureaucracies, but these should not be overestimated. In Britain, at least, public spending (pandemics aside) as a share of GDP still fluctuates around 40 per cent, slightly more than it was by the time Thatcher had left office.

Nonetheless, neoliberalism also made significant gains. In both Britain and America, and subsequently elsewhere, important sectors of the economy, such as financial services and utilities, were deregulated. More so in Britain, industries were privatised, and trade-union power curtailed. Furthermore, as the political scientist Gary Gerstle points out, one symptom of an ideology's political success is when the 'opposition party has to acquiesce in accepting ideas that they were previously opposed to'.[46] In Britain, Tony Blair's New Labour accepted most of Mrs Thatcher's economic reforms after it won power in 1997, whilst in America Bill Clinton's triangulating Democrats accepted most of Reagan's reforms and embraced free trade, ratifying the North American Free Trade Agreement, for instance, which came into force in 1994.

With hindsight, it is clear that the high-water mark of the modern free-trade global trading system came in 2008, when total international trade peaked on the eve of the financial crash and subsequent recession of 2008–09.[47] These events, more than anything, shook people's faith in the fundamentals of the free-trade system, much as the crash in 1929 had done in Hayek's and Mises's own time. On the right, similar to the interwar years, the near-total collapse of the international banking system provoked another round of economic nationalism, led by a fresh wave of populists such as Donald Trump in the US, Boris Johnson in Britain, Jair Bolsonaro in Brazil and Viktor Orbán in Hungary. Russia's Vladimir Putin was certainly emboldened by the crisis.

Trump, in particular, repudiated the neoliberal order, blaming it for America's relative economic decline vis-à-vis countries like China. A general decoupling of economic and trading links has ensued, illustrated by the renegotiation of the North American Free Trade Agreement and Trump's trade war against China. Brexit was another revolt against neoliberalism. Globalisation is not categorically over, but it is certainly under severe strain.

On the left, the crises of our time have led to a remarkable rehabilitation of Karl Polanyi, the old sparring partner of Mises and Otto Neurath in Vienna. *The Great Transformation* had fallen into almost total obscurity after it was first published, but after being translated into German in 1977 it gathered a new and receptive readership in Europe and beyond. As people read it in the 1980s, so it seemed to offer the alternative economics that the left had been lacking since the demise of the command economy. Andreas Novy, a contemporary writer on Polanyi, argues that he was above all a 'moral economist', harbouring a profound dislike of mass consumption and materialism. He therefore disdained in equal measure the sort of Keynesian welfare capitalism that prevailed in the 1950s (during his own lifetime) just as much as he would have been appalled by the free-market capitalist revival of the 1980s and 1990s, distinguished, according to its critics, by the triumph of greed and self-interest.

Polanyi offered a clear alternative, an 'ethical horizon of a post-market society', as Novy argues. With each successive stock market crash and financial crisis from Black Monday of 1987, through the dot-com bubble of 2000 and finally and most devastatingly to the great subprime mortgage crisis of 2007–09, so Polanyi's central contention as to the disembeddedness of free-market capitalism became more persuasive. Each shock came about due to an irrational exuberance in the capitalist financial system, consequently throwing millions out of work in the real economy of corner-shops and car-makers. Those people seemed to be inno-cent victims of poor decisions made by others trying to maximise their self-interest; the self-regulating market, as Polanyi had predicted, seemed to be anything but.

Furthermore, as concerns about environmental degradation and global warming moved up political agendas from the early 2000s, so Polanyi's original analysis of the commodification of land became more pressing. His early insistence that land – nature – was not a tradeable asset, just as labour – men and women – wasn't either, took on a fresh relevance. In the Polanyian system, an embedded economy would protect these assets from any kind of trade or exploitation. It is easy to see, therefore, why he has been anointed as a founder of environmental economics, or indeed 'heterodox economics', disciplines that are now infused with his concepts and terminology.

Many contemporary economists and thinkers view environmental issues through a strictly Polanyian framework. Take this recent account of his relevance to the climate-change debate by three academics in the journal *New Political Economy*:

The increasing commodification of nature has accelerated climate change. Increasing quantities and types of fossil fuels have been extracted, priced, sold in markets and subsequently burned. Fossil fuels, as natural conditions of production, represent an example of what Polanyi . . . calls a 'fictitious commodity'. Fossil fuels were not created for the purpose of being bought or sold in a market but existed for thousands of years below ground, part of the land or nature . . . By incorporating fictitious commodities into market systems without protective measures, Polanyi argues we run the risk of destroying the social and natural dimensions of our world.[48]

It was Polanyi's own double movement, against the market and in defence of the environment, that has made him so relevant today. Polanyi was integral to the 'Greening of the Reds', a dramatic political shift in Europe over the past two decades, particularly in Germany. Many, however, have thus erroneously fingered capitalism and markets as the sole sources of environmental damage, ignoring the horrifying ecological consequences of the pell-mell industrialisation driven by Eastern bloc command economies from the 1950s to 1980s, unconstrained by any countervailing democratic or consumer pressures.[49]

Regardless, Polanyi societies, meetings and institutes have proliferated, often organised by his daughter Kari Polanyi Levitt, herself a development economist. In a pale imitation of Hayek's intellectual movement on the right, so Polanyi's movement of the left has filtered out into the public discourse on challenging neoliberalism; the economist Joseph Stiglitz has looked forward to 'The coming great transformation', an explicit nod to Polanyi.[50] Even the World Economic Forum entitled their gathering at Davos in 2012 'The Great Transformation: New models to address old challenges', a clear sign that Polanyi has now joined the mainstream.

Polanyi's heirs, advocates and cheerleaders also managed to influence political thinking both in the United States and Britain. In the former, Bernie Sanders has been a vehicle for much of that thinking, as was Jeremy Corbyn in Britain, leader of the Labour Party from 2015 to 2020, although it is not clear whether either man would have read much Polanyi themselves.[51] What is clear, however, is that both succeeded in enthusing and motivating a fresh generation of activists with Polanyi's radical politics. Corbyn came surprisingly close to winning a general election in 2017, while Sanders came second only to Joe Biden in the 2020 Democratic Party presidential primary, winning almost 10 million votes, or 26 per cent of the total, well ahead of his nearest rivals. These were remarkable results for very progressive, leftist candidates.

That they didn't do even better, however, owed a great deal to Polanyi's old Viennese opponents. Thus, the debates over the optimum way to organise economic life that began in an obscure academic journal in 1920 continue to reverberate down the subsequent century and more, even if most people have long forgotten how it all started in the first place.

Conclusion: The Politics of Genius versus the Empire of Critical Rationalism

Otto Neurath was one of the very last people to escape continental Europe as the Wehrmacht advanced rapidly across the Low Countries in May 1940. The moving spirit of Red Vienna endured a perilous journey across the North Sea from the Netherlands to Britain with Marie Reidemeister, later his wife. Grabbing just a couple of suitcases, they jumped into a rickety, overcrowded motorised lifeboat, from which they watched the port of Rotterdam burning as they headed out into open waters. Fortunately, they were eventually picked up by a British warship which deposited them at Dover.

After internment on the Isle of Man, Neurath and Reidemeister were released in February 1941 and subsequently moved to Oxford. Like many other Viennese in these pages, Neurath now had plenty of time to reflect on the bloody calamity that had overtaken his homeland, and the whole of Europe. Unlike Hayek, Popper and others he never produced a systematic, fully rounded treatise on the crisis of his times – perhaps by now the great polymath was just exhausted – but he nonetheless worried away at the central questions in letters, articles and essays. Why had National Socialism taken root in the Germanic countries, and not elsewhere? What was special about the 'German climate', or the 'German atmosphere', as he called it, which had produced the terrors of Nazism, an ideology that had eviscerated not only a whole people but also his home city and its intellectual culture, leaving him a wandering exile for the last decade or so of his life.

One part of the answer, it seemed to Neurath, lay in the specific role of the 'genius' as perceived in German literature and philosophy – the over-exalted personality directed solely by his, and occasionally her, own visions and intuitions. As Günther Sandner, a Neurath biographer, writes, such a genius 'was felt to be exempt from rules and restrictions and allowed to act above the law because he is not to be judged in the same way as ordinary people. In this sense, a genius could even resort to criminal actions, while the masses needed to obey.'[1] This described Hitler, of course, but it might also serve as a shorthand for all populist leaders, to a greater or lesser extent, down to our own time. Hitler and the National Socialists claimed to be anti-élitist and were also anti-pluralist, another hallmark of the populist. The irony was not lost on Neurath that, for all his lifelong opposition to what he identified as this particular strand in ethnic German culture, the high priest of the cult of (male) genius was himself Viennese – the misogynistic, anti-Semitic Otto Weininger, fêted and fated in equal measure. Weininger, above all, had insisted on the *duty* of genius, that the fulfilment of the genius's vision – for a country, for a 'race' even – had to rank above all else, including the individual's conscience.

Neurath was quite right to identify this strand of messianic politics, and to locate its origins, in part, in his own hometown. Thankfully, however, Vienna was also responsible for reinvigorating, and in many respects pioneering, the school of thought that was the antithesis to the politics of genius, namely critical rationalism. This was the hallmark of Red Vienna, the interwar culture of so many Viennese intellectuals who, like Neurath, fled abroad: the architects, economists, sociologists, historians, physicists, photographers and ceramicists of these pages. All these women and men were, of course, extremely clever in a formal, academic sense, but they were not *geniuses* in the

Weiningerian sense of the word, nor did they aspire to be. Indeed, they consciously endeavoured to be the exact opposite. Rather than intuiting, or resorting to, the self-intoxicating power of rhetoric, these Viennese were evidence-led, and rigorous (to the point of self-lacerating) in the manner in which they weighed and used that evidence. Neurath and Hayek might have wrangled about the extent to which it was legitimate to apply the theoretical apparatus of social science to the study of economics, but they were both fully within Vienna's pale of critical rationalism, as distinct from the National Socialists' explicit campaign of 'de-rationalisation'. This gave them much more in common with each other than either cared to acknowledge.

Heterodoxy united by methodology

Furthermore, the liberal Viennese usually started with the lives and concerns of ordinary people as their primary 'evidence' – Kant's 'crooked timber [of] humankind'. Eschewing the vast impersonal forces of class and nation that bewitched so many of their contemporaries, Viennese architects, craftsmen, social scientists, economists and more, always tried to start their work with real people, whether it be Richard Neutra interrogating his clients as to their architectural needs; Herta Herzog's focus groups; Lazarsfeld's and Jahoda's investigation of the unemployed at Marienthal; Hayek's concern with the free interplay of market forces in economics; or Josef Frank's opposition to what he regarded as the lifeless square blocks that passed for modern architecture, imposed on people by authoritarian designers in the name of abstract principle.

For Frank, the purpose of a building 'was not to determine human actions but to allow the inhabitants to live as they wanted, freely and without fixed rules'.[2] Furthermore, as the Austrian historian of the social sciences, Christian Fleck, writes of Marie Jahoda, they generally all insisted 'that research should serve people instead of perpetuating the unworldliness of the ivory tower'.[3] This was the real hallmark of the generation of intellectuals who grew up in the shadow of Red Vienna; they were Druckerian knowledge workers, in the modern sense of applying the latest academically developed ideas to the full praxis of societies, from applying philosophy to everyday language to applying modern psychology to the appreciation of art, from applying Taylorism to the kitchen and the theory of atomic fission to nuclear weapons.

The Viennese earned a reputation for being integrators and synthesisers themselves – think of General Systems Theory, Lorenz's animal behaviourism or psychoanalysis. Thus, they have often been lumped together as 'Modernists', in the philosophical and aesthetic sense. Yet, as I hope I have shown, their output was far too heterodox to be easily classified. The architect Robert Venturi, in his famous blast against Modernism in *Complexity and Contradiction in Architecture* (1966), called for 'messy vitality over obvious unity'. The phrase could have served as a leitmotif for so much of what the Viennese were trying to demonstrate in their various fields, just as it is also a pretty good description of the virtues of the old Habsburg empire. Belatedly, Venturi and his partner and wife Denise Scott Brown only discovered Josef Frank's writings and oeuvre after he had died in 1967 – but the two Americans immediately recognised him as an unacknowledged precursor of their own work.

For more often than not the Viennese prefigured a post-modernist disposition in their concern for diversity and eclecticism. Surely Hayek was essentially correct to argue that the hallmark of contemporary society is the decentralisation, or dispersal, of knowledge, implying that the best decision-making is made by those with local knowledge, rather than central planners, however many degrees they might possess. It is no coincidence that Wikipedia, the online encyclopaedia, was directly inspired by Hayek's work. Co-founder Jimmy Wales read Hayek's essential essay on the subject, 'The Use of Knowledge in Society', published in 1945, as an undergraduate, which persuaded him to create a platform to enable the decentralised dissemination of knowledge, curated by local volunteers, freely available to all. Wikipedia is now the world's largest reference website, used by millions, of whom nearly 130,000 regularly contribute and edit articles.

The Viennese usually returned to the marketplace of constantly evolving individual needs and taste to inform and guide their work. They were united more by intellectual temperament than anything else, a willingness to take on and use the full diversity of knowledge allied to a relentless pursuit of truth through methodological rigour. Consequently, they did more than their fair share to extend the boundaries of humanity in a civilised society, working for the rights of children, for instance, the legalisation of homosexuality and the extension of counselling and other therapies. Change came incrementally, perhaps too slowly for anyone to register the true magnitude of some of the shifts in attitude and behaviours for which they were responsible. Equally, the Viennese abroad were usually the first to push at the boundaries of free speech and expression, in literature, in art and design and particularly, as we have seen, in the films of prudish Hollywood.

This, essentially, is what made the Viennese diaspora instinctively anti-totalitarian, and why they flourished in, and indeed led, the West intellectually after 1945. Ernst Gombrich, for all his eminence and accomplishments, was desperately concerned not to leave a 'school' of thought behind, for that would have negated an entire life's work dedicated to methodological individualism. Their temperament is one reason why the Viennese never received the acclaim that they deserved, precisely because they themselves consciously avoided attaching their names to all the new disciplines and fields of study that they founded. Humility was a personal characteristic shared by many, often to the frustration of biographers and historians.[4]

By its very nature, Vienna's empire of critical rationalism was pluralist and inclusive, in that they privileged their intellectual disposition over the cruel and sectarian identity politics of ethno-nationalism that gradually closed minds and hardened hearts throughout Europe after the First World War, as it continues to do today. Vienna flourished precisely because it was a refreshingly Open Society, to people previously excluded from cultural and intellectual production, such as women, Jews and indeed the vast variety of ethnicities from throughout the sprawling Austro-Hungarian empire. Perhaps this very diversity of peoples also made the young radicals of Red Vienna unusually good collaborators, give or take a Popper or Wittgenstein. For all their directness of speech, they had to learn how to listen, and to collaborate. This could maybe explain why so many of Vienna's cultural, economic and political ideas were successfully incubated in the city's numerous circles and think-tanks, specifically designed spaces and forums for collective intellectual endeavour. Institutionalising ideas in this way, through the Vienna Circle or the Mont Pelerin Society, helped with their reception in spreading those ideas throughout the West.

Such collaborative intellectual production also helped to continually break down the mind-forged manacles of professional and academic self-interest that characterised their peers elsewhere. These extraordinary Viennese moved easily and fluidly between business and academia, the arts and sciences, philosophy and the design of door handles. That these artificial categories were merely for other people was a conviction that seized the Viennese during their youthful days at the university, or even earlier, while tending to the terrariums in their Ringstrasse apartments. From this liberating embrace of intellectual heterodoxy and political pluralism flowed the ideas that have shaped the world right up to our present day. We are all in their debt.

Endnotes

Acknowledgements

1. Richard Cockett, *Thinking the Unthinkable: Think-Tanks and the Economic Counter-Revolution, 1931–1983* (HarperCollins, 1994).

Introduction

1. For a recent discussion of these 'Atlantic Crossings', see Jan Logemann and Mary Nolan (eds), 'More Atlantic Crossings? European Voices and the Postwar Atlantic Community', *Bulletin of the German Historical Institute*, supplement 10 (2014).
2. For an earlier revisionist view of Schorske's work by several authors, see Steven Beller (ed.), *Rethinking Vienna 1900*, Vol. 3, *Austrian and Habsburg Studies* (Berghahn Books, 2001).
3. Edward Timms, 'School for Socialism: Karl Seitz and the Cultural Politics of Vienna', in Judith Beniston and Robert Vilain (eds), *Culture and Politics in Red Vienna*, *Austrian Studies*, vol. 14 (2006), p. 46.

Chapter 1 Growing Up Viennese: An Education in Liberalism

1. Joseph Roth, *The Emperor's Tomb* (Granta, 2013), pp. 11–12.
2. Pieter Judson, *The Habsburg Empire: A New History* (Harvard University Press, 2016), p. 341.
3. Carl Schorske, *Fin-de-Siècle Vienna : Politics and Culture* (Vintage Books, 1981), p. 31.
4. Adolf Hitler, *Mein Kampf*, trans. James Murphy (Hurst & Blackett, 1939), p. 24.
5. Patrick McGilligan, *Fritz Lang: The Nature of the Beast* (University of Minnesota Press, 1997), pp. 6–7.
6. Maureen Healy, *Vienna and the Fall of the Habsburg Empire* (Cambridge University Press, 2004), p. 4.
7. Johannes Feichtinger and Gary Cohen, 'The Habsburg Central European Experience', *Austrian and Habsburg Studies*, vol. 17 (2014), p. 5.

8. Victor Gruen, *The Heart of Our Cities: The Urban Crisis: Diagnosis and Cure* (Thames & Hudson, 1965), p. 153.

9. William M. Johnston, *Vienna: The Golden Age, 1815–1914* (Clarkson M. Potter, 1981), p. 234.

10. McGilligan, *Fritz Lang*, p. 23.

11. Quoted by Roman Horak in his essay 'Metropolitan Culture/Popular Pleasures: Modernism, Football and Politics in Interwar Vienna', in Siegfried Gehrmann (ed.), *Football and Regional Identity in Europe* (LIT Verlag, 1997), p. 107.

12. Jonathan Wilson, *Inverting the Pyramid: The History of Football Tactics* (Weidenfeld & Nicolson, 2018), p. 75.

13. Lisa Silverman, *Becoming Austrians: Jews and Culture Between the World Wars* (Oxford University Press, 2015), p. 23.

14. See Steven Beller, *Vienna and the Jews, 1867–1938: A Cultural History* (Cambridge University Press, 1995). See also George E. Berkley, *Vienna and Its Jews: The Tragedy of Success, 1880s–1980s* (Madison Books, 1988), and Silverman, *Becoming Austrians*, for scholarly and convincing interpretations of Vienna's Jewish history. Also Lisa Silverman and Wolfgang Maderthaner, '"Wiener Kriese": Jewishness, Politics, and Culture in Interwar Vienna', in Deborah Holmes and Lisa Silverman (eds), *Interwar Vienna: Culture Between Tradition and Modernity* (Camden House, 2009).

15. David Luft, *Eros and Inwardness in Vienna: Weininger, Musil, Doderer* (University of Chicago Press, 2003), p. 15.

16. Quoted in Matthew Rampley, *The Vienna School of Art History: Empire and the Politics of Scholarship, 1847–1918* (Pennsylvania State University Press, 2013), p. 15.

17. Ibid., pp. 16–17.

18. Gary Cohen, *Education and Middle-Class Society in Imperial Austria, 1848–1918* (Purdue University Press, Indiana, 1996) p. 37.

19. The authorities were much more cautious when it came to universities, and no new ones were founded in the Austrian half of the empire during the same period.

20 Cohen, *Education*, p. 96.

21. Ibid., pp. 58–60.

22. Richard Neutra, *Life and Shape* (Atara Press, 2009), p. 46.

23. Beller, *Vienna and the Jews*, p. 93.

24. Cohen, *Education*, p. 153.

25. Ibid., p. 177.

26. The complexities of Jewish attitudes towards 'German' high culture are captured brilliantly by the music critic Alex Ross in *Wagnerism: Art and Politics in the Shadow of Music* (4th Estate, 2020). Despite Wagner's well-publicised anti-Semitic essays, for many Viennese and German Jews an appreciation of Wagner's music nonetheless remained an important symbol of assimilation. As Ross writes, 'An attachment to Wagner served as a kind of shield, minimizing their otherness and advertising their nationalist bona fides' (p. 255).

27. Beller, *Vienna and the Jews*, p. 163.

28. Hayek's letter is reprinted in full on pp. 305–11 of *The Collected Works of F.A. Hayek*, Vol. 13, *Studies on the Abuse and Decline of Reason*, ed. Bruce Caldwell (Routledge, 2010).

29. Stefan Zweig, *The World of Yesterday* (University of Nebraska Press, 2013), pp. 52–3.

30. Peter Drucker, *Adventures of a Bystander* (Transaction Publishers, 1994), ebook 202/923.

31. Cohen, *Education*, p. 219.

32. Wolfgang Reiter, 'Karl Przibram: Radioactivity, Crystals, and Colors', *Physics in Perspective*, vol. 21 (August 2019), https://doi.org/10.1007/s00016-019-00242-z.

33. The story of the tiger in Lorenz's study was told to the author by his grandson, the present owner of the Lorenz house at Altenberg.

34. These details of Kammerer's life scientific are from Klaus Taschwer, *The Case of Paul Kammerer: The Most Controversial Biologist of His Time* (Bunim & Bannigan, 2016).

35. Bruce Caldwell and Hansjoerg Klausinger, *Hayek: A Life, 1899–1950* (University of Chicago Press, 2022), p. 41.

36. These details about Hayek's early life are from Alan Ebenstein, *Friedrich Hayek: A Biography* (Palgrave, 2001), pp. 11–13.

37. Stephen Kresge and Leif Wenar (eds), *Hayek on Hayek: An Autobiographical Dialogue* (Routledge, 1994), pp. 51–2.

38. William M. Johnston, 'Von Bertalanffy's Place in Austrian Thought', in William Gray and Nicholas Rizzo (eds), *Unity Through Diversity: A Festschrift for Ludwig von Bertalanffy* (Gordon and Breach Science Publishers, 1973), p. 27.

39. Stephen Beniansky, *Journey to the Edge of Reason: The Life of Kurt Gödel* (W.W. Norton, 2021), p. 138.

40. Zweig, *World of Yesterday*, p. 62.

41. For a contemporary appreciation of Kraus and a commentary on his relevance, see Jonathan Franzen, *The Kraus Project: Essays by Karl Kraus* (Farrar, Straus and Giroux, 2013). For much more on Kraus and his Viennese context, see Edward Timms, *Karl Kraus, Apocalyptic Satirist: The Post-War Crisis and the Rise of the Swastika* (Yale University Press, 2005).

42. Erwin Dekker has written persuasively of this unique Viennese culture in his book *The Viennese Students of Civilization: The Meaning and Context of Austrian Economics Reconsidered* (Cambridge University Press, 2016). For instance: 'While in many other European countries modern universities were coming to dominate the intellectual atmosphere, Viennese intellectual life took place within the social sphere. While knowledge production became organised along disciplinary lines in many other European countries (and the United States), intellectual life in Vienna remained both broad and relatively informal' (p. 30).

43. For a very good example of this mix of private 'informal' and formal public contributions to a Viennese education, see Deborah Coen's group biography of the Exner family: *Vienna in the Age of Uncertainty: Science, Liberalism, and Private Life* (University of Chicago Press, 2007). Over three generations, between 1802 and 1886, the Exner dynasty produced no fewer than ten professors at Austrian universities, mainly scientists. Karl Frisch, who married into the Exner family, won the Nobel Prize in biology.

44. Wolfgang Reiter charts this scientific background very well in his article 'Karl Przibram: Radioactivity, Crystals, and Colors'. See also Mitchell Ash (ed.), *Science in the Metropolis: Vienna in Transnational Context, 1848–1918* (Routledge, 2020).

45. For more on these connections, see Mitchell Ash, 'Multiple Modernisms in Context: The Sciences, Technology and Culture in Vienna around 1900', in Robert Bud, Paul Greenhalgh, Frank James and Morag Shiach (eds), *Being Modern: The Cultural Impact of Science in the Early Twentieth Century* (UCL Press, 2018), pp. 23–39.

46. For the influence of Mach on Viennese empiricism, see for example Karl Sigmund, *Exact Thinking in Demented Times: The Vienna Circle and the Epic Quest for the Foundations of Science* (Basic Books, 2017).

47. Ibid., p. 78.

48. Ludwig von Mises, *Memoirs* (Ludwig von Mises Institute, 2012).
49. Luft, *Eros and Inwardness*, pp. 94–5.
50. Ash, 'Multiple Modernisms in Context'.
51. John Blackmore, *Ernst Mach: His Work, Life, and Influence* (University of California Press, 1972), p. 187.
52. See Judith Beniston's essay on 'Body Politics in Arthur Schnitzler's Professor Bernhardi', in Carolin Duttlinger, Kevin Hilliard and Charlie Louth (eds), *From Enlightenment to Modernism: Three Centuries of German Literature* (Legenda, 2021).
53. Theodor Alexander, 'From the Scientific to the Supernatural in Schnitzler', *The South Central Bulletin: Studies by Members of the SCLA*, vol. 31, no. 4 (1971), p. 164.
54. As well as *La Ronde*, Schnitzler's novella *Traumnovelle* (Dream Story) was made into a film by Stanley Kubrick, *Eyes Wide Shut*, starring Tom Cruise and Nicole Kidman. Some critics dubbed it an erotic thriller.
55. Quoted in Schorske, *Fin-de-Siècle Vienna*, p. 11.
56. For more on the influence of Mach on James and other contemporary philosophers see Gerald Holton, 'From the Vienna Circle to Harvard Square', in Friedrich Stadler (ed.), *Scientific Philosophy: Origins and Developments, Vienna Circle Institute Yearbook*, vol. 1 (1993).
57. Quoted in Schorske, *Fin-de-Siècle Vienna*, p. 233.
58. For an excellent account of how Darwinism permeated German political debate and thought in the late nineteenth century, see Paul Weindling, *Health, Race and German Politics Between National Unification and Nazism, 1870–1945* (Cambridge University Press, 1989), pp. 25–48.
59. See Klaus Taschwer, *The Case of Paul Kammerer*, pp. 46–60, for a fuller account of Vienna's neo-Lamarckism.
60. Neutra, *Life and Shape*, p. 49.
61. George Newman, *Finding Harmony: A Family's Journey Across Europe and Beyond* (self-published, 2013), p. 79.
62. Karl Menger, *Reminiscences of the Vienna Circle and the Mathematical Colloquium* (Kluwer Academic Publishers, 1994), p. 9.
63. Karl Popper, *Unended Quest: An Intellectual Biography* (Routledge, 1992), p. 53.
64. Quoted by David Edmonds, *The Murder of Professor Schlick: The Rise and Fall of the Vienna Circle* (Princeton University Press, 2020), p. 201.
65. Ludwig Wittgenstein, *Notebooks, 1914–1916* (Basil Blackwell, 1961), p. 40.
66. Maurice O'Connor Drury, 'Some Notes on Conversations with Wittgenstein', in *The Selected Writings of Maurice O'Connor Drury: On Wittgenstein, Philosophy, Religion and Psychiatry* (Bloomsbury Academic, 2018), p. 828.
67. Ray Monk, *Ludwig Wittgenstein: The Duty of Genius* (Jonathan Cape, 1990), p. 7.
68. Elana Shapira, *Style and Seduction: Jewish Patrons, Architecture, and Design in Fin de Siècle Vienna* (Brandeis University Press, 2016), p. 58.
69. Ibid., pp. 8–9.
70. Several Jewish artists were very conscious of this dilemma, of the apparent Jewishness of what was supposed to be a universal aesthetic. The writer Hugo von Hofmannsthal was one such, and this concern partly prompted his involvement in founding the Salzburg Festival in 1920. See Silverman, *Becoming Austrians*, pp. 164–7, for a useful discussion of this point.
71. Rampley, *The Vienna School of Art History*, p. 153.
72. For more on Waerndorfer's patronage of the Wiener Werkstätte and the arts more generally, see Shapira, *Style and Seduction*, pp. 122–42.
73. Quote by Schorske, *Fin-de-Siècle Vienna*, p. 326.

74. Ernst Gombrich, *The Visual Arts in Vienna circa 1900: Reflections on the Jewish Catastrophe* (Austrian Cultural Institute, 1997), p. 11.
75. The quote is from a former partner of Gruen's, Cesar Pelli, quoted by Jeffrey Hardwick, *Mall Maker: Victor Gruen, Architect of an American Dream* (University of Pennsylvania Press, 2004), p. 132.
76. Neutra, *Life and Shape*, p. 103.
77. Judson, *The Habsburg Empire*, pp. 363–70.
78. Quoted by Taschwer, *The Case of Paul Kammerer*, p. 139.
79. My guide, Stefan Zweig, was a rare exception.
80. McGilligan, *Fritz Lang*, p. 37.
81. Ibid., p. 38.
82. Zweig's suicide was prompted mainly by his depression, and his despair at the course of the Second World War. He made his final decision to end his life after the fall of Singapore to the Japanese. It is reasonable to read *The World of Yesterday* as a literary last testament, an adieu to the cosmopolitan world in which he had grown up. For more details on Zweig and his masterpiece, see Oliver Matuschek, *Three Lives: A Biography of Stefan Zweig* (Pushkin Press, 2011).
83. Richard Swedberg, *Joseph A. Schumpeter: His Life and Work* (Polity Press, 1991), p. 146.
84. Quoted in Marjorie Perloff, *Edge of Irony: Modernism in the Shadow of the Habsburg Empire* (University of Chicago Press, 2016).

Chapter 2 Black Vienna and the Birth of Populist Politics

1. Schorske, *Fin-de-Siècle Vienna*, p. 119.
2. Quoted in Wolfgang Maderthaner and Lutz Musner, *Unruly Masses: The Other Side of Fin-de-Siècle Vienna* (Berghahn Books, 2008), p. 53.
3. Allan Janik and Stephen Toulmin, *Wittgenstein's Vienna* (Ivan R. Dee, 1996), p. 51.
4. Ibid., p. 7.
5. Quoted in Brigitte Hamann, *Hitler's Vienna: A Portrait of the Tyrant as a Young Man* (Taurus Parke Paperbacks, 2010), p. 237.
6. Schorske, *Fin-de-Siècle Vienna*, pp. 120–6.
7. Hamann, *Hitler's Vienna*, p. 240.
8. See Silverman, *Becoming Austrians*, for an excellent account of *The City Without Jews* and also of the murder of Bettauer soon after the release of the film version of the book.
9. Hitler, *Mein Kampf*, pp. 88–90.
10. Quoted by Maderthaner and Musner, *Unruly Masses*, p. 132.
11. John Boyer, *Culture and Political Crisis in Vienna: Christian Socialism in Power, 1897–1918* (University of Chicago Press, 1995), p. 1. Boyer's book discusses Lueger's mayoralty in detail: 'With modest financial and intellectual resources Karl Lueger and his colleagues had broken thirty years of Liberal rule in the capital, representing perhaps the most extraordinary shift in voter loyalties ever experienced in a major Central European city before the First World War.'
12. See also Janik and Toulmin, *Wittgenstein's Vienna*, pp. 53–7.
13. Hamann, *Hitler's Vienna*, p. 298.
14. Ibid., p. 282.
15. Boyer, *Culture and Political Crisis*, p. 55.

16. Quoted in Rob McFarland, Georg Spitaler and Ingo Zechner, *The Red Vienna Sourcebook* (Camden House, 2020), p. 612.
17. Schorske, *Fin-de-Siècle Vienna*, pp. 163–8.
18. Bruce Pauley, *From Prejudice to Persecution: A History of Austrian Anti-Semitism* (University of North Carolina Press, 1992), p. 223.
19. See Janek Wasserman, *The Marginal Revolutionaries: How Austrian Economists Fought the War of Ideas* (Yale University Press, 2019), pp. 17–18.
20. Ibid., p. 105.
21. Taschwer, *The Case of Paul Kammerer*, pp. 176–7.
22. Zweig, *The World of Yesterday*, p. 85.
23. Pauley, *From Prejudice to Persecution*, p. 124.
24. Ibid., p. 129.
25. Friedrich Stadler, *The Vienna Circle: Studies in the Origins, Development, and Influence of Logical Empiricism* (Springer, 2001), p. 291.
26. Benno Weiser Varon, *Confessions of a Lucky Jew* (Associated University Presses, 1999).
27. Quoted by Taschwer, *The Case of Paul Kammerer*, p. 7.
28. Wasserman, *The Marginal Revolutionaries*.

Chapter 3 The New Human

1. Tony Judt, *Ill Fares the Land* (Penguin, 2010), p. 98.
2. Quoted by Helmut Gruber, *Red Vienna: Experiments in Working Class Culture, 1919–34* (Oxford University Press, 1991), p. 6.
3. These numbers are quoted by Healy, *Vienna and the Fall of the Habsburg Empire*, pp. 41–4.
4. Judson, *The Habsburg Empire*, pp. 399–403, for this quote and more on the food crisis.
5. For more on Austria's treatment at the Versailles peace conference, see Margaret MacMillan, *Paris 1919: Six Months That Changed the World* (Random House, 2002), Chapter 19.
6. Zweig, *The World of Yesterday*, p. 305.
7. Pauley, *From Prejudice to Persecution*, p. 211.
8. Healy, *Vienna and the Fall of the Habsburg Empire*, p. 255.
9. These figures are quoted by Éve Blau in *The Architecture of Red Vienna 1919–1934* (MIT Press, 1999), p. 28.
10. Esther Menaker, *Appointment in Vienna: The American Psychoanalyst Recalls Her Student Days in Pre-War Austria* (St Martin's Press, 1989), p. 157.
11. Zweig, *The World of Yesterday*, p. 316.
12. Ibid., pp. 316–17. For an entertaining discussion of Zweig's claims about the English unemployed in Salzburg, see Rhys Griffiths, 'Strange Guests at the Hotel de l'Europe', *History Today*, 20 November 2014.
13. Richard Sterba, *Reminiscences of a Viennese Psychoanalyst* (Wayne State University Press, 1982), pp. 21–2.
14. See Christian Fleck, *A Transatlantic History of the Social Sciences: Robber Barons, the Third Reich and the Invention of Empirical Social Research* (Bloomsbury Academic, 2011), for the Rockefeller Foundation's money.
15. See the symposium on post-war American aid to Austria at: https://www.aaf-online.org/index.php/news-details/items/symposium-post-wwi-relief-aid-in-austria-and-central-europe-september-26-27-2019-vienna.html (accessed 2021).
16. Silverman, *Becoming Austrians*, p. 12.
17. Pauley, *From Prejudice to Persecution*, p. 139.

18. In this sense the Social Democrats were devoted Gramscians before Gramsci, attempting to shatter the 'cultural hegemony' that the bourgeoisie exerted in order to maintain their economic power.
19. Quoted in Thomas Uebel, Nancy Cartwright, Jordi Cat and Lola Fleck (eds), *Otto Neurath: Philosophy Between Science and Politics* (Cambridge University Press, 2008), p. 24.
20. See the work of Dr Tatjana Buklijas, 'Cultures of Death and Politics of Corpse Supply: Anatomy in Vienna, 1849–1914', *Bulletin of the History of Medicine*, vol. 82, no. 3 (2008), pp. 578–607.
21. See Birgit Nemec, 'Anatomical Modernity in Red Vienna: Textbook for Systematic Anatomy and the Politics of Visual Milieus', *Sudhoffs Archiv*, vol. 99, no. 1 (2015), pp. 44–72.
22. Gruber, *Red Vienna*, p. 7.
23. Otto Neurath, *From Hieroglyphics to Isotype: A Visual Autobiography*, ed. Matthew Eve (Hyphen Press, 2010), p. 23.
24. See, for instance, Neurath's essays 'A System of Socialisation' and 'Total Socialisation' in *Otto Neurath: Economic Writings, Selections 1904–1945*, ed. Thomas Uebel and Robert Cohen (Kluwer Academic Publishers, 2004).
25. Ibid., p. 3.
26. A plaque on the former Palais Epstein now commemorates the Vienna School Authority on the Ringstrasse.
27. Friedrich Hayek, 'Remembering My Cousin Ludwig Wittgenstein', in *The Collected Works of F.A. Hayek*, Vol. 4, *Remembering My Cousin Ludwig Wittgenstein* (University of Chicago Press, 1992).
28. Healy, *Vienna and the Fall of the Habsburg Empire*, p. 307.
29. See Blau, *Architecture of Red Vienna*, pp. 86–9, for a fuller account of these settlements.
30. Quotes from Otto Neurath in McFarland et al., *The Red Vienna Sourcebook*, pp. 392 and 397.
31. Blau, *Architecture of Red Vienna*, pp. 253–60.
32. Another prominent advocate of neo-Lamarckian social reform was Rudolf Goldscheid, who proposed that what he termed 'human economy' should take precedence over the profit motive. For a good discussion of his work in this context, see Paul Weindling, 'A City Regenerated: Eugenics, Race and Welfare', in Holmes and Silverman, *Interwar Vienna*.
33. Quoted by Mitchell Ash in his chapter 'Psychology and Politics in Interwar Vienna: The Vienna Psychological Institute, 1922–1942', in *Psychology in Twentieth-Century Thought and Society*, ed. Mitchell Ash and W.R. Woodward (Cambridge University Press, 1987).
34. Quoted in McFarland et al., *Red Vienna Sourcebook*, p. 143.
35. Clemens von Pirquet, *An Outline of the Pirquet System of Nutrition* (W.B. Saunders Company, 1922).
36. See Blau, *Architecture of Red Vienna*, p. 39.
37. The circumstances of Sindelar's life and death have been the subject of several books, blogs and documentaries. See, for instance, Wilson, *Inverting the Pyramid*, p. 100, or the BBC documentary *Fascism and Football* (2003).
38. Quoted in McFarland et al., *Red Vienna Sourcebook*, p. 358, from an article by Deutsch first published in 1928.
39. The permanent exhibition on Red Vienna in the Washhouse No. 2 of the Karl-Marx-Hof gives an excellent overview of the organised activities on offer in the city at the time.
40. *Spectator*, 5 October 1929.

45. Budiansky, *Journey to the Edge of Reason*, p. 280.
46. Ananyo Bhattacharya, *The Man from the Future: The Visionary Life of John von Neumann* (Allen Lane, 2021), pp. 139–43.
47. Alan Turing, 'On Computable Numbers, with an Application to the *Entscheidungsproblem*', published in two parts, 1936–7, *Proceedings of the London Mathematical Society*, pp. 42, 230–65.
48. See Alan Ebenstein, *Hayek's Journey: The Mind of Friedrich Hayek* (Palgrave, 2003), pp. 20–35, for a good account of the development of the Austrian School in Vienna.
49. His younger brother, Richard, was a renowned mathematician and physicist, later a professor at Harvard University. An aviator, he gave the first ever university course on powered flight.
50. Mises, *Memoirs*, p. 61.
51. Quinn Slobodian, *Globalists: The End of Empire and the Birth of Neoliberalism* (Harvard University Press, 2018), pp. 31–2.
52. Ibid., pp. 70–1.
53. Mises, *Memoirs*, p. 81.
54. Dekker, *Viennese Students of Civilization*.
55. Although not until 1936 was it published in English for the first time.
56. Ludwig von Mises, *Socialism: An Economic and Sociological Analysis* (Jonathan Cape, 2nd edn, 1951), p. 25.
57. Mises, *Memoirs*, p. 32.
58. See Neurath's essays 'A System of Socialisation' and 'Total Socialisation' in *Otto Neurath: Economic Writings*, eds Uebel and Cohen.
59. Mises, *Socialism*, p. 1.
60. Ibid., p. 122.
61. See Bruce Caldwell, *Hayek's Challenge* (University of Chicago Press, 2004,) pp. 110–20, for the Neurath vs Mises debate.
62. Caldwell and Klausinger, *Hayek: A Life*, p. 146.
63. Neurath, *Otto Neurath: Economic Writings*, eds Uebel and Cohen, p. 11.
64. For a short but informative account of the firebrand Ilona Polanyi's life, see Veronika Helfert, 'Born a Rebel, Always a Rebel', in Andreas Novy (ed.), *Karl Polanyi: The Life and Works of an Epochal Thinker* (Falter Verlag, 2020), pp. 61–5.
65. See Gareth Dale, *Karl Polanyi: The Limits of the Market* (Polity Press, 2010), pp. 20–32, for a longer discussion of Polanyi's contribution to the socialist calculation debate.

Chapter 5 The Muse Has Had Enough: Feminism and Socialism

1. The letter can be found at: http://outofthequestion.org/Additional-Resources/Documents.aspx (accessed 2021).
2. Leora Auslander, 'The Boundaries of Jewishness, Or When Is a Cultural Practice Jewish?', *Modern Jewish Studies*, vol. 8, no. 1 (2009).
3. Harriet Anderson, *Utopian Feminism: Women's Movements in Fin-de-Siècle Vienna* (Yale University Press, 1992), p. 3.
4. Luft, *Eros and Inwardness*, p. 45. The author gives a more charitable interpretation of Weininger, arguing that his book 'is a critique of the women's movement, but in a rather peculiar way that argues for what Weininger regarded as true women's liberation' (p. 81).
5. Ibid., p. 69.
6. David Stern and Béla Szabados, *Wittgenstein Reads Weininger* (Cambridge University Press, 2004), p. 8.

7. Anderson, *Utopian Feminism*, p. 4.
8. Hamann, *Hitler's Vienna*, p. 228.
9. Schorske, *Fin-de-Siècle Vienna*, Chapter 5.
10. Zweig, *The World of Yesterday*, p. 78.
11. Menger, *Reminiscences of the Vienna Circle*, p. 60.
12. These figures are from Maria Rentetzi, *Trafficking Materials and Gendered Experimental Practices: Radium Research in Early 20th-Century Vienna* (Columbia University Press, 2009), pp. 81–2.
13. Quoted by Andersen, *Utopian Feminism*, p. 10.
14. Hamann, *Hitler's Vienna*, p. 366.
15. Zweig, *The World of Yesterday*, p. 109.
16. There is an excellent, if dispiriting, account of just such a wretched marriage in Karina Urbach's biography of her grandmother growing up in Vienna in the first decades of the century. See Karina Urbach, *Alice's Book: How the Nazis Stole My Grandmother's Cookbook* (MacLehose Press, 2022).
17. McEwen, *Sexual Knowledge*, ebook p. 545/769.
18. Silverman, *Becoming Austrians*, pp. 52–4.
19. Blau, *Architecture of Red Vienna*, p. 204.
20. Marianne Pollak, 'From Crinoline Dress to Bobbed Hair: Revolution and Fashion', in McFarland et al., *Red Vienna Sourcebook*, pp. 240–2.
21. For more on Leichter in the context of Red Vienna, see Gruber, *Red Vienna*, pp. 148–50.
22. Francisca de Haan, Krassimira Daskalova and Anna Loutfi (eds), *Biographical Dictionary of Women's Movements and Feminisms: Central, Southern and South Eastern Europe* (Central European University Press, 2006), entry on Leichter by Gabriella Hauch.
23. Blau, *Architecture of Red Vienna*, pp. 184–5.
24. Ruth Oldenziel and Karin Zachmann (eds), *Cold War Kitchen: Americanization, Technology, and European Users* (MIT Press, 2009), p. 12.
25. Helmut Gruber, 'Sexuality in "Red Vienna": Socialist Party Conceptions and Programs and Working-Class Life, 1920–34', *International Labour and Working-Class History*, no. 31 (Spring 1987), pp. 37–68.
26. Herta Herzog sketched details of her life in a letter to a putative biographer; it is available online at: http://outofthequestion.org/userfiles/file/Herta%20Herzog%20 (Sept%2012%201994%20to%20Elisabeth%20Perse).pdf (accessed 2021).
27. Christian Fleck has a fascinating article on the relations between Herzog, Jahoda and Lazarsfeld: 'Lazarsfeld's Wives, or: What Happened to Women Sociologists in the Twentieth Century', *International Review of Sociology*, vol. 31, no. 1 (2021).
28. Herta Herzog, http://outofthequestion.org/ (accessed 2021).
29. For a discussion on their relative contributions to the book, see Lisa Held, 'Profile of Else Frenkel-Brunswik', at: https://feministvoices.com/profiles/else-frenkel-brunswik (accessed 2021).
30. Rentetzi, *Trafficking Materials*, pp. 81–3.
31. Information provided by Wolfgang Reiter, a historian (and veteran) of the Radium Institute.
32. The proportion of women working at the Radium Institute and the Vivarium still surpasses the proportions of women in similar roles in Britain today, for instance. At the time of writing, 26 per cent of those graduating in STEM subjects (dated back to 2019) are women, whilst women hold 24 per cent of jobs in the science sector. For a full breakdown see: https://www.stemwomen.co.uk/blog/2021/01/women-in-stem-percentages-of-women-in-stem-statistics (accessed 2021).

33. Rentetzi, *Trafficking Materials*, p. 121.
34. See Ruth Lewin Sime, *Lise Meitner: A Life in Physics* (University of California Press, 1996).
35. Richard Rhodes, *Hedy's Folly: The Life and Breakthrough Inventions of Hedy Lamarr, the Most Beautiful Woman in the World* (Doubleday, 2011).
36. I am grateful to Andrea Winklbauer for suggesting these quotes, mainly from Hedy Lamarr's disputed autobiography *Ecstasy and Me: My Life as a Woman* (Ishi Press, 2014). Ms Winklbauer curated the exhibition on Hedy Lamarr's life at Vienna's Jewish Museum, entitled *Lady Bluetooth*.
37. The patent can still be viewed online at: https://patents.google.com/patent/US2292387 (accessed 2021).
38. Rhodes, *Hedy's Folly*, p. 102.
39. Timms and Hughes (eds), *Intellectual Migration*, p. 235.
40. Nick Midgley, 'Anna Freud: The Hampstead War Nurseries and the Role of Direct Observation of Children for Psychoanalysis', *International Journal of Psychoanalysis*, vol. 88, no. 4 (2007), pp. 939–59.
41. For a further discussion of the work of the Hampstead Nursery and its pedagogy, see Michal Shapira, 'Anna Freud Shaping Child Education and Providing "Democratic Citizenship" in Britain', in Elana Shapira and Daniel Finzi (eds), *Freud and the Émigrés: Austrian Émigrés, Exiles and the Legacy of Psychoanalysis in Britain, 1930–1970* (Palgrave Macmillan, 2020).
42. Ilse Hellman, *From War Babies to Grandmothers* (Karnac Books, 1990), pp. 79–102.
43. These facts and other details about the film *A Two-Year-Old Goes to Hospital* are from Justyna Wierzchowska, '"Nurse! I Want My Mummy!" Empathy as Methodology in the Documentary Film *A Two-Year-Old Goes to Hospital* (1952)', *Theories and Practices of Visual Culture*, no. 26 (2019–20).
44. Bowlby and Robertson were probably the most important campaigners on this issue, but other doctors, parents' pressure groups and some sympathetic hospitals also contributed to bringing about reform. See Frank van der Horst and René van der Veer, 'Changing Attitudes Towards the Care of Children in Hospital: A New Assessment of the Influence of the Work of Bowlby and Robertson in the UK, 1940–1970', *Attachment and Human Development*, vol. 11, no. 2 (March 2009), pp. 119–42.
45. Quoted in Nick Midgley, *Reading Anna Freud* (Routledge, 2013), p. 185.
46. Ibid., pp. 186–90.
47. Timms and Hughes (eds), *Intellectual Migration*, p. 226.
48. Riccardo Steiner, *Transition, Change, Creativity: Repercussion of the New Diaspora on Aspects of British Psychoanalysis* (Routledge, 2000).
49. Quoted by Schorske, *Fin-de-Siècle Vienna*, p. 328.
50. Some of her story is told by Megan Brandow-Faller in her essay on Emmy Zweybrück-Prochaska in *Erasures and Eradications in Modern Viennese Art, Architecture and Design*, ed. Megan Brandow-Faller and Laura Morowitz (Routledge, 2022).
51. For more on Cizek, the *Jugendstil* and the birth of art therapy see Joseph Weber, 'The Jugendstil and Its Relationship to the Development of Child-Centered Art' (PhD thesis, St Louis University, 1988), available at: https://www.proquest.com/openview/e0d123436d9b93489576663d4cd3f363/1.pdf?pq-origsite=gscholar&cbl=18750&diss=y (accessed 2021).
52. For the best academic account of the Theresienstadt drawings, see Nick Stargardt, 'Children's Art of the Holocaust', *Past & Present*, no. 161 (November 1998), pp. 191–235.

53. Susan Goldman Rubin, *Fireflies in the Dark: The Story of Friedl Dicker-Brandeis and the Children of Terezín* (Holiday House, 2000), p. 15.
54. Quoted by a survivor of the Maagal in Linney Wix, *Through a Narrow Window: Friedl Dicker-Brandeis and Her Terezín Students* (University of New Mexico Press, 2010), p. xi.
55. Ibid., p. 4.
56. Rubin, *Fireflies in the Dark*, p. 21.
57. Lani Gerity and Susan Ainlay Anand, *The Legacy of Edith Kramer: A Multifaceted View* (Routledge, 2018), p. xvii.
58. See ibid. for the best account of Kramer's life and work.

Chapter 6 The War on Science and the End of Vienna

1. J.E. Smyth, *Fred Zinnemann and the Cinema of Resistance* (University Press of Mississippi, 2014), p. 96.
2. Fred Zinnemann, *A Life in the Movies: An Autobiography* (Bloomsbury, 1992), pp. 96–7.
3. Ibid., p. 11.
4. Karl Popper uses the phrase, for instance, in his autobiography *Unended Quest*.
5. There is a debate as to whether Hitler himself actually read this book.
6. Erwin Baur, Eugen Fischer and Fritz Lenz, *Foundations of Human Heredity and Racial Hygiene* (George Allen, 1931), p. 699.
7. Ibid., p. 607.
8. Kammerer was not the only Viennese opposed to racial hygiene theories with whom Lenz took issue. The German also waged a running intellectual battle against other Viennese biologists such as Friedrich Hertz and Ignaz Zollschan. Hertz was an early critic of Nazi-style race theories and in particular the attempts to use these theories to justify anti-Semitism. Zollschan was an early critic of Houston Stewart Chamberlain's race theories. See Paul Weindling, 'Central Europe Confronts German Racial Hygiene: Friedrich Hertz, Hugo Iltis and Ignaz Zollschan as Critics of Racial Hygiene', in Marius Turda and Paul Weindling (eds), *Blood and Homeland: Eugenics and Racial Nationalism in Central and Southeast Europe, 1900–1940* (Central European University Press, 2007).
9. Gerd Müller (ed.), *Vivarium: Experimental, Quantitative, and Theoretical Biology at Vienna's Biologische Versuchsanstalt* (MIT Press, 2017), pp. 4–10.
10. Weindling, 'A City Regenerated', in Holmes and Silverman (eds), *Interwar Vienna*, p. 82.
11. Cheryl Logan, *Hormones, Heredity, and Race: Spectacular Failure in Interwar Vienna* (Rutgers University Press, 2013), p. 99.
12. Paul Weindling argues this point well in 'A City Regenerated'. For a more detailed discussion of Tandler's attitudes towards eugenics, see McEwen, *Sexual Knowledge*, Chapter 1.
13. Stefan Kühl, *For the Betterment of the Race: The Rise and Fall of the International Movement for Eugenics and National Hygiene* (Palgrave Macmillan, 2013), p. 67.
14. Footnote on p. 675 of Baur, Fischer and Lenz, *Foundations of Human Heredity*.
15. Taschwer, *The Case of Paul Kammerer*.
16. Logan, *Hormones, Heredity, and Race*, p. 27.
17. Ibid., p. 38.
18. Chandak Sengoopta, *The Most Secret Quintessence of Life: Sex, Glands, and Hormones, 1850–1950* (University of Chicago Press, 2006), p. 78.

19. McEwen, *Sexual Knowledge*, Chapter 6.
20. Sengoopta, *The Most Secret Quintessence*, p. 83.
21. See, for instance, Noël Coward's *Private Lives*, or *Black Oxen*, a novel by Gertrude Atherton.
22. See Chandak Sengoopta, 'Dr Steinach Coming to Make Old Young!: Sex Glands, Vasectomy and the Quest for Rejuvenation in the Roaring Twenties', *Endeavour*, vol. 27, no. 3 (September 2003).
23. See Stefan Kühl's two books on the subject, from which the following paragraphs are largely drawn: *Eugenics, American Racism, and German National Socialism* (Oxford University Press, 1994), and *For the Betterment of the Race* (Palgrave Macmillan, 2013).
24. See Chapter 2 of James Whitman's *Hitler's American Model: The United States and the Making of Nazi Race Law* (Princeton University Press, 2018) for an extended discussion of how American legislation and Jim Crow laws informed the drafting of the Nuremberg Laws.
25. Weindling, 'A City Regenerated', in Holmes and Silverman (eds), *Interwar Vienna*.
26. Ibid., p. 101.
27. Pauley, *From Prejudice to Persecution*, pp. 270–2.
28. Edith Sheffer, *Asperger's Children: The Origins of Autism in Nazi Vienna* (W.W. Norton, 2018), ebook p. 149/769.
29. Klaus Taschwer, 'Expelled, Burnt, Sold, Forgotten and Suppressed: The Permanent Destruction of the Institute for Experimental Biology and its Academic Staff', in Johannes Feichtinger, Herbert Matis, Stefan Sienhell and Heidemarie Uhl (eds), *The Academy of Sciences in Vienna 1938 to 1945* (Austrian Academy of Sciences Press, 2014), p. 109.
30. Logan, *Hormones, Heredity, and Race*, Chapter 8.
31. Estimate by Robert Hubenstorf, quoted by Herwig Czech, 'From Welfare to Selection: Vienna's Public Health Office and the Implementation of Racial Hygiene Policies under the Nazi Regime', in Turda and Weindling (eds), *Blood and Homeland*, p. 320.
32. Sheffer, *Asperger's Children*, ebook p. 154/768.
33. For a fuller account of the Vienna Circle in America, see Feigl's memoir in Fleming and Bailyn (eds), *The Intellectual Migration*, pp. 659–73.
34. See Edmonds, *The Murder of Professor Schlick*, Chapter 15. There is now a memorial plaque on the flight of stairs where Schlick was killed.
35. A point made by Lisa Silverman in *Becoming Austrians*, p. 60.
36. Quoted by Logan, *Hormones, Heredity, and Race*, p. 116.
37. Pauley, *From Prejudice to Persecution*, p. 280.
38. Quoted by Philippe Sands in *The Ratline: Love, Lies and Justice on the Trail of a Nazi Fugitive* (Weidenfeld & Nicolson, 2020), pp. 59–60.
39. Evan Burr Bukey, *Hitler's Austria: Popular Sentiment in the Nazi Era, 1938–1945* (University of North Carolina Press, 2000), p. 26.
40. Edmonds, *The Murder of Professor Schlick*, p. 188.
41. For more on the Nazi occupation of Vienna, see Thomas Weyr, *The Setting of the Pearl: Vienna under Hitler* (Oxford University Press, 2005).
42. This figure, and those of Kristallnacht, from Bukey, *Hitler's Austria*, pp. 142–5.
43. Pauley, *From Prejudice to Persecution*, pp. 284–5.
44. Famously, Hitler and Wittgenstein overlapped by one year at the school, but there is no firm evidence that they either knew each other or were classmates. This has not forestalled a blizzard of speculation as to their *real* relationship at this time. See,

for example, the highly imaginative book by Kimberley Cornish, *The Jew of Linz: Wittgenstein, Hitler, and Their Secret Battle for the Mind* (Century Books, 1998).

45. These figures are from Gerhard Sonnert and Gerald Holton, *What Happened to the Children Who Fled Nazi Persecution* (Palgrave Macmillan, 2006), p. 16.
46. Quoted by Pauley, *From Prejudice to Persecution*, p. xix.
47. Bertrand Perz, 'The Austrian Connection: SS and Police Leader Odilo Globocnik and His Staff in the Lublin District', *Holocaust and Genocide Studies*, vol. 29, no. 3 (Winter 2015), pp. 400–30.
48. Philippe Sands writes at length about the enduring convictions and loyalties of Otto and Charlotte Wächter in *The Ratline*.
49. Richard Burkhardt, *Konrad Lorenz: Patterns of Behavior* (University of Chicago Press, 2005), p. 238.
50. Ibid., p. 244.
51. Ibid., p. 278.
52. Sheffer, *Asperger's Children*, ebook p. 282/768.
53. Ibid., ebook p. 523/786.
54. For excellent, short accounts of the exclusion of neo-Lamarckian biology from the 'central dogma', and its consequences, see the essays 'The Exclusion of Soft ("Lamarckian") Inheritance from the Modern Synthesis' by Snait Gissis and Eva Jablonka, and 'Why Did the Modern Synthesis Give Short Shrift to "Soft Inheritance"' by Adam Wilkins, both in *Transformations of Lamarckism: From Subtle Fluids to Molecular Biology*, ed. Snait B. Gissis and Eva Jablonka (MIT Press, 2011).
55. Eva Jablonka and Marion Lamb, *Inheritance Systems and the Extended Evolutionary Synthesis* (Cambridge University Press, 2020).
56. Pauley, *From Prejudice to Persecution*, p. 303.
57. Sheldon Rubenfeld and Susan Benedict (eds), *Human Subjects Research after the Holocaust* (Springer, 2014), p. 118.
58. Feichtinger, Matis, Sienell and Uhl (eds), *The Academy of Sciences*, p. 7.

Chapter 7 Awake, Slumbering Giant! The Viennese Discover America

1. The article is reproduced in McFarland et al., *Red Vienna Sourcebook*, pp. 573–7.
2. Gay, *Freud*, pp. 563, 567.
3. Quoted in Long, *The Looshaus*, p. 21.
4. Neutra, *Life and Shape*, p. 182.
5. See Ehrhard Bahr, *Weimar on the Pacific: German Exile Culture in Los Angeles and the Crisis of Modernism* (University of California Press, 2007), pp. 149–50.
6. Christopher Long, *Paul T. Frankl and Modern American Design* (Yale University Press, 2007), p. 25.
7. Ibid., p. 69.
8. For a full appreciation of Urban as a set designer, see the long essay by Arnold Aronson at: http://www.columbia.edu/cu/lweb/eresources/archives/rbml/urban/architectOfDreams/text.html (accessed 2021).
9. See the essay by Janis Staggs, 'Joseph Urban and Cosmopolitan Productions', in Christian Witt-Dörring and Janis Staggs (eds), *Wiener Werkstätte 1903–1932: The Luxury of Beauty* (Prestel, 2017), p. 506.
10. For an account of the American failure of the Wiener Werkstätte, ibid., pp. 468–505.
11. Famously, *Casablanca*, the best-known Hollywood film of its time, featured only two American-born actors: Humphrey Bogart himself, and Dooley Wilson, the African-American who plays Sam, the pianist.

12. Brendan Carroll, *The Last Prodigy: A Biography of Erich Wolfgang Korngold* (Amadeus Press, 1997), p. 21.
13. Dorothy Lamb Crawford, *A Windfall of Musicians: Hitler's Émigrés and Exiles in Southern California* (Yale University Press, 2009), p. 178.
14. Ross, *The Rest is Noise*, p. 292.
15. McGilligan, *Fritz Lang*, p. 104.
16. Zinnemann, *A Life in the Movies*.
17. Chris Fujiwara, *The World and Its Double: The Life and Work of Otto Preminger* (Faber & Faber, 2008), p. 74.
18. Both examples from ibid., pp. 73 and 79.
19. Neutra, *Life and Shape*, p. 209.
20. For a good description of the Schindler House, and some lavish colour plates, see Judith Sheine, *R.M. Schindler* (Phaidon, 2001), pp. 106–14.
21. Quoted by Judith Sheine and Robert Sweeney, *Schindler, Kings Road, and Southern California Modernism* (University of California Press, 2012).
22. Ibid., p. 92.
23. Sylvia Lavin, *Form Follows Libido: Architecture and Richard Neutra in a Psychoanalytic Culture* (MIT Press, 2007), p. 47.
24. Sylvia Lavin, 'Open the Box: Richard Neutra and the Psychology of the Domestic Environment', *Assemblage*, no. 40 (December 1999), p. 18.
25. For a good summary of Biorealism, see Rupert Spade, *Richard Neutra* (Thames & Hudson, 1971), pp. 16–17.
26. Thomas Hines, *Architecture of the Sun: Los Angeles Modernism, 1900–1970* (Rizzoli, 2010), p. 315.
27. For an excellent account of Neutra's working style and character, see Alex Ross, 'Vanishing Act', *New Yorker*, 27 September 2021.
28. Lavin, 'Open the Box', pp. 12–13.
29. Bahr, *Weimar on the Pacific*, p. 169.

Chapter 8 The Balm of Muddle: The Viennese in Britain

1. Quotes from Günther Sandner, 'The German Climate and Its Opposite: Otto Neurath in England, 1940–45', in A. Grenville and A. Reiter (eds), *Political Exile and Exile Politics in Britain after 1933*, Yearbook of the Research Centre for German and Austrian Exile Studies, vol. 12 (2011), pp. 67–85.
2. Perry Anderson, *English Questions* (Verso, 1992), p. 65.
3. Monk, *Ludwig Wittgenstein*, p. 31.
4. See for instance Ray Monk's biographies of Wittgenstein and of Bertrand Russell, *The Spirit of Solitude* (Free Press, 2016), and the works of the Wittgenstein scholar Brian McGuinness.
5. Derek Jarman, *Wittgenstein: The Terry Eagleton Script, the Derek Jarman Film* (British Film Institute, 1993), p. 5.
6. See: https://axel-duerkop.de/en/post/wittgenstein-in-music/ and https://www.youtube.com/watch?v=57PWqFowq-4 (both accessed 2021).
7. Marjorie Perloff, *Wittgenstein's Ladder: Poetic Language and the Strangeness of the Ordinary* (University of Chicago Press, 1996), pp. 7–8.
8. Timms and Hughes (eds), *Intellectual Migration*, pp. 55–6.
9. Rampley, *The Vienna School of Art History*, p. 30.
10. Louis Rose, *Psychology, Art, and Antifascism: Ernst Kris, E.H. Gombrich, and the Politics of Caricature* (Yale University Press, 2016), pp. 2–4.

11. Quoted in Daniel Snowman, *The Hitler Émigrés: The Cultural Impact on Britain of Refugees from Nazism* (Pimlico, 2003), p. 96.

12. Martin Kemp, 'Gombrich and Leonardo', in Paul Taylor (ed.), *Meditations on a Heritage: Papers on the Work and Legacy of Sir Ernst Gombrich* (Paul Holberton Publishing in association with the Warburg Institute, 2014), p. 163.

13. Ibid., p. 25.

14. Richard Abel and Gordon Graham, *Immigrant Publishers: The Impact of Expatriate Publishers in Britain and America in the 20th Century* (Transaction Publishers, 2009), pp. 4–5.

15. Ibid., p. 5.

16. Snowman, *The Hitler Émigrés*, pp. 241–2.

17. Ibid., p. 217.

18. Emmanuel Cooper, *Lucie Rie: Modernist Potter* (Yale University Press, 2012), p. 25.

19. Ibid., p. 39.

20. Ibid., p. 49.

21. Ibid., p. 252.

22. See the essay by Ulrike Walton-Jordan, 'Designs for the Future: Gaby Schreiber as an Exponent of Bauhaus Principles in Britain', in Timms and Hughes (eds), *Intellectual Migration*.

23. See Mitchison's account of her experiences in Vienna in her *Vienna Diary* (Harrison Smith and Robert Hass, 1934).

24. For a good summary of *The Third Man*'s possible relationship to real life, see, for example, Thomas Riegler, 'The Spy Story Behind *The Third Man*', *Journal of Austrian-American History*, vol. 4 (2020), pp. 1–37.

25. Brian Brivati, *Hugh Gaitskell* (Richard Cohen Books, 1996), p. 38.

26. Quoted by Riegler, 'The Spy Story', p. 13.

27. For a short, reliable account of Edith Tudor-Hart's early life, see Charmain Brinson and Richard Dove, *A Matter of Intelligence: MI5 and the Surveillance of Anti-Nazi Refugees, 1933–1950* (Manchester University Press, 2014), pp. 81–4.

28. Daria Santini, *The Exiles: Actors, Artists and Writers Who Fled the Nazis for London* (Bloomsbury, 2019), p. 55.

29. Ibid. pp. 50–6 for their family background. Wolfgang made films for the Ministry of Information during the war. He was also the cinematographer on *Get Carter*, the best British gangster film ever made, starring Michael Caine. Perhaps only an outsider could have managed to make the terraces and slag heaps of a sodden Newcastle look quite so exotic.

30. Another of Edith Tudor-Hart's lovers, in the early 1950s, was the psychoanalyst and paediatrician Donald Winnicott.

31. Quoted by John Costello and Oleg Tsarev, *Deadly Illusions* (Century, 1993), p. 448.

32. His MI5 file, KV 2/4428, can be examined online at: https://discovery.nation-alarchives.gov.uk/details/r/C17023797 (accessed 2021).

33. Christopher Andrew and Vasili Mitrokhin, *The Mitrokhin Archive: The KGB in Europe and the West* (Allen Lane, 1999).

34. Genrikh Borovik, *The Philby Files: The Secret Life of the Master Spy – KGB Archives Revealed* (Little Brown, 1994), p. 29.

35. Costello and Tsarev, *Deadly Illusions*, p. 227.

36. Ibid., p. 219.

37. See Paul Broda, *Scientist Spies: A Memoir of My Three Parents and the Atom Bomb* (Matador Books, 2011), Part One.

38. From Engelbert Broda's MI5 file at KV 2/2350 in the National Archives.
39. John Earl Haynes, Harvey Klehr and Alexander Vassiliev, *Spies: The Rise and Fall of the KGB in America* (Yale University Press, 2009), p. 67.
40. Broda, *Scientist Spies*, p. xv.
41. Her life story has been told by her family and friends in a documentary, *Tracking Edith*, released in 2016 and produced by Lillian Birnbaum.

Chapter 9 The World Reimagined: War Work and the Open Society

1. See Bahr, *Weimar on the Pacific*, for a lively account of Brecht and Eisler's unlikely sojourn among the palm trees on the Pacific coast.
2. The phrase 'hostile intimacy' is from Anderson, *English Questions*, p. 274.
3. Kresge and Wenar (eds), *Hayek on Hayek*, p. 50.
4. *The Collected Works of F.A. Hayek*, ed. Caldwell, Vol. 13, p. 166.
5. Ibid., p. 142.
6. Ibid., p. 13.
7. F.A. Hayek, *The Road to Serfdom* (Routledge, 1986), p. 3.
8. John Bew, *Citizen Clem: A Biography of Attlee* (Riverrun, 2017), pp. 339–40.
9. See Edmonds, *The Murder of Professor Schlick*, pp. 163–9, for a succinct account of Popper's differences with the Circle. In this particular case, Neurath's criticism of Popper was to hold up over time.
10. Malachi H. Hacohen, *Karl Popper: The Formative Years, 1902–1945* (Cambridge University Press, 2001), p. 378.
11. For instance, see pp. 36–7 of Bruce Caldwell's introduction to *The Collected Works of F.A. Hayek*, Vol. 13, for an account of Popper's discussion of Hayek's concept of 'scientism' which led to Hayek amending his own definition of the term in later editions of the essay.
12. Caldwell and Klausinger, *Hayek: A Life*, p. 555.
13. I am grateful to David Edmonds, the writer on the Vienna Circle, for a discussion on this point.
14. This one incident has become the subject of books, films and more. See, for instance, the recent text by David Edmonds and John Eidinow, *Wittgenstein's Poker: The Story of a Ten-Minute Argument Between Two Great Philosophers* (Faber & Faber, 2005).
15. See Pierre Bourdieu's essay 'The Social Conditions for the International Circulation of Ideas', in Richard Shusterman (ed.), *Bourdieu: A Critical Reader* (Blackwell, 1999).
16. Quoted by Friedrich Stadler in Timms and Hughes (eds), *Intellectual Migration*, p. 170.
17. Cockett, *Thinking the Unthinkable*, pp. 92–3.
18. For Churchill's broadcast and Hayek's role in the 1945 campaign, ibid., pp. 93–9, and Richard Toye, 'Winston Churchill's "Crazy Broadcast": Party, Nation, and the 1945 Gestapo Speech', *Journal of British Studies*, vol. 49, no. 3 (July 2010), pp. 655–80.
19. See Edward Yager, *Ronald Reagan's Journey: Democrat to Republican* (Rowman and Littlefield, 2006), pp. 102–3, for a discussion of exactly when Reagan read *The Road to Serfdom*.
20. The irony was not lost on Hayek either. He later wrote that when he arrived in London he shared the nineteenth-century moral and political tradition of 'liberalism', 'which was essentially British', and in which he felt 'very much at home'. But he soon became aware that 'the most powerful current intellectual influence, the Bertrand Russell, H.G. Wells, G.B. Shaw, J.M. Keynes, and practically the

whole literary world were against it. I felt a radical British liberal but was soon regarded by most intellectual colleagues and students as a reactionary, yet feeling more British than they. . . .' Quoted in Caldwell and Klausinger, *Hayek: A Life*, p. 334.

21. Kresge and Wenar (eds), *Hayek on Hayek*, p. 103.

22. See Chapter 4 of Dekker's *Viennese Students of Civilization* for more on the contrasts between, on the one hand, Schumpeter and, on the other, Hayek and Popper.

23. Swedberg, *Joseph A. Schumpeter*, p. 151.

24. Wasserman, *The Marginal Revolutionaries*, Chapter 5.

25. Kim Phillips-Fein, *Invisible Hands: The Making of the Conservative Movement from the New Deal to Reagan* (W.W. Norton, 2009), p. 42.

26. The Mont Pelerin Society was in part inspired by a gathering in Paris in 1938 in honour of Lippmann, the *Colloque Walter Lippmann*. Organised by the French philosopher Louis Rougier, this meeting featured several of those who participated in the first Mont Pelerin meeting, including Hayek himself.

27. Phillips-Fein, *Invisible Hands*, p. 45.

28. Cockett, *Thinking the Unthinkable*, pp. 122–99.

29. Dale, *Karl Polanyi*, p. 100.

30. Drucker, *Adventures of a Bystander*, ebook p. 27/923.

31. Quoted by Daniel Immerwahr, 'Polanyi in the United States: Peter Drucker, Karl Polanyi and the Midcentury Critique of Economic Society', *Journal of the History of Ideas*, vol. 70, no. 3 (July 2009), pp. 445–66.

32. Drucker, *Adventures of a Bystander*, ebook p. 338/923. The Polanyi family have hotly disputed Drucker's account of the meal, arguing that Ilona was always a good cook and would never have served just potatoes on such an important occasion, however young and undistinguished the guest.

33. Drucker's account can be found in Peter F. Drucker, *A Functioning Society: Community, Society, and Polity in the Twentieth Century* (Routledge, 2011), p. 27. I am grateful to Richard Straub for pointing out this reference.

34. See Aaron Barcant, 'Coexistence: Karl Polanyi and Peter Drucker Navigating Mid-Century Crises', paper for the Peter Drucker Society (August 2019).

35. Karl Polanyi, *Origins of Our Time: The Great Transformation* (Victor Gollancz, 1945), p. 13.

36. Ibid., p 78; and see Dale, *Karl Polanyi*, p. 50, for a useful commentary.

37. Immerwahr, 'Polanyi in the United States', pp. 445–66.

38. See, for instance, Martin Beddeleem, 'Michael Polanyi: Pivotal Figure of Early Neoliberalism', paper given at the Polanyi Society Annual Meeting (Boston, 17–18 November 2017), available at: http://polanyisociety.org/2017pprs/Beddeleem_Polanyi-Pivotal-Figure-early-neoliberalism10-19-17.pdf (accessed 2021).

39. Robert Leonard, *Von Neumann, Morgenstern, and the Creation of Game Theory: From Chess to Social Science, 1900–1960* (Cambridge University Press, 2010), p. 168.

40. Ibid.

41. Quoted in ibid., pp. 258–9.

42. See Bhattacharya, *The Man from the Future*, pp. 141–5, for an excellent account of the evolution of Von Neumann's thinking on chess and game theory.

43. Ibid., p. 71.

44. Leonard, *Von Neumann*, p. 243.

45. See Bhattacharya, *The Man from the Future*, p. 189.

46. Leonard, *Von Neumann*, p. 344.

Chapter 10 Sex, Shopping and the Sovereign Consumer

1. See John Burnham (ed.), *After Freud Left: A Century of Psychoanalysis in America* (University of Chicago Press, 2012).
2. See Gay, *Freud*, pp. 206–13, for the visit to Clark University.
3. See, for instance, Richard Pollak's relentless dismantling of Bettelheim's life and work in *The Creation of Dr. B: A Biography of Bruno Bettelheim* (Touchstone Books, 1998). By this account, Bettelheim was nothing but a malevolent charlatan.
4. See, for instance, the German immigrant psychoanalyst Karen Horney, who clashed with orthodox Freudians on their application to women of the master's reductionist sexual theories. The first key text of modern feminism, Simone de Beauvoir's *The Second Sex*, published in 1949, also took aim at Freud. For a good, short essay on the early feminist critique of Freud, see Naomi Segal, 'Freud and the Question of Women', in Naomi Segal and Edward Timms (eds), *Freud in Exile: Psychoanalysis and Its Vicissitudes* (Yale University Press, 1988).
5. Logemann, *Engineered to Sell*, p. 6.
6. Quoted in Larry Tye, *The Father of Spin: Edward Bernays and the Birth of Public Relations* (Holt Paperbacks, 1988), p. 34.
7. See Lazarsfeld's own memoir in Fleming and Bailyn (eds), *The Intellectual Migration*, p. 271.
8. Quoted in Tye, *Father of Spin*, p. 57.
9. See Lazarsfeld's memoir in Fleming and Bailyn (eds), *The Intellectual Migration*, p. 295.
10. Fleck, *Transatlantic History of the Social Sciences*, p. 171, author's emphasis.
11. Elisabeth Klaus and Josef Seethaler (eds), *What Do We Really Know about Herta Herzog?* (Peter Lang Academic Press, 2016), p. 72.
12. Ibid., p. 133.
13. See Jerabek, *Paul Lazarsfeld*, pp. 82–9, for a good account of the Mars study.
14. I am grateful to Michael Haas for referring me to Ernest Dichter's family background in retail. Ernest's cousin was the composer and music critic Walter Arlen who as a young man also worked in the family store. Arlen told Haas the story about Dichter noticing that customers responded well to piped music. See also a blog post here from Haas commemorating Arlen's 100th birthday: https://forbiddenmusic.org/2020/07/17/on-july-31-2020-the-composer-walter-arlen-turns-100
15. Stefan Schwarzkopf and Rainer Gries (eds), *Ernest Dichter and Motivation Research: New Perspectives on the Making of Post-War Consumer Culture* (Palgrave Macmillan, 2010), p. 6.
16. Daniel Horowitz, 'From Vienna to the United States and Back: Ernest Dichter and American Consumer Culture', in ibid., p. 55.
17. Vance Packard, *The Hidden Persuaders* (IG Publishing, 2007), p. 57.
18. Lawrence R. Samuel, *Freud on Madison Avenue: Motivation Research and Subliminal Advertising in America* (University of Pennsylvania Press, 2010), pp. 5–6.
19. Ibid., p. 34. See also Rena Bartos, 'Ernest Dichter: Motive Interpreter', *Journal of Advertising Research* (February–March 1986), p. 15.
20. Ronald Fullerton, 'Ernest Dichter: The Motivational Researcher', in Schwarzkopf and Gries (eds), *Ernest Dichter*, p. 59.
21. Ibid., pp. 112–15.
22. Logemann, *Engineered to Sell*, pp. 205–12.
23. For more on the rivalry between Dichter and Politz, a former physicist, see Samuel, *Freud on Madison Avenue*, pp. 63–73.
24. Quote from Fullerton, 'Ernest Dichter', in Schwarzkopf and Gries (eds), *Ernest Dichter*, p. 59.

25. For a discussion of Herzog's role as a woman at Columbia and at McCann, see the excellent short volume edited by Klaus and Seethaler (eds), *What Do We Really Know about Herta Herzog?*, particularly the chapter by Peter Simonson, 'Herta Herzog and the Founding Mothers of Mass Communication Research'.

26. See her own account of her career at McCann at: http://outofthequestion.org/userfiles/file/Herta%20Herzog%20(Sept%2012%201994%20to%20Elisabeth%20Perse).pdf (accessed 2021).

27. Quoted by Simonson, 'Herta Herzog', in Klaus and Seethaler (eds), *What Do We Really Know about Herta Herzog?*, p. 75.

28. Christoph Thun-Hohenstein, Dieter Bogner, Maria Lind and Barbel Vischer (eds), *Friedrich Kiesler: Life Visions* (MAK, 2016), p. 9.

29. Ibid., p. 109.

30. Peggy Guggenheim, *Out of This Century: Confessions of an Art Addict* (Andre Deutsch, 1980), p. 270.

31. Ibid., p. 274.

32. Quoted in 'Birth, Death, and Shopping: The Rise and Fall of the Shopping Mall', *The Economist*, 22 December 2007.

33. Gruen, *The Heart of Our Cities*, pp. 24–7.

34. Quoted by Jeffrey Hardwick, *Mall Maker: Victor Gruen, Architect of an American Dream* (University of Pennsylvania Press, 2004), p. 131.

35. Schwarzkopf and Gries (eds), *Ernest Dichter*, p. 288.

36. Turner, *Adventures in the Orgasmatron*, p. 249.

37. Reich, *The Mass Psychology of Fascism*, p. xxiv.

38. Turner, *Adventures in the Orgasmatron*, p. 246.

39. Lavin, *Form Follows Libido*, p. 13.

40. 'Morals: The Second Sexual Revolution', *Time*, 24 January 1964, available at: http://content.time.com/time/subscriber/article/0,33009,875692-11,00.html (accessed 2021).

Chapter 11 A Viennese Apotheosis: The Ascent of the Austrian School

1. Packard, *The Hidden Persuaders*, p. 34.

2. Ibid., p. 239.

3. From Molly Niesen, 'Crisis of Consumerism: Advertising, Activism, and the Battle over the U.S. Federal Trade Commission, 1969–1980' (PhD thesis, University of Illinois at Urbana-Champaign, 2013), p. 38, available at: https://www.ideals.illinois.edu/items/46622 (accessed 2021).

4. Daniel Horowitz, *Betty Friedan and the Making of The Feminine Mystique: The American Left, the Cold War, and Modern Feminism* (University of Massachusetts Press, 1998), p. 205.

5. Ibid., p. 214.

6. Mark Davidson, *Uncommon Sense: The Life and Thought of Ludwig von Bertalanffy, Father of General Systems Theory* (J.P. Tarcher, 1983), p. 33.

7. Mie Augier and James March, quoted by Morgen Witzel, *A History of Management Thought* (Routledge, 2016).

8. Herbert Marcuse, *One-Dimensional Man* (Beacon Press, 1964), p. 13.

9. Stuart Jeffries, *Grand Hotel Abyss: The Lives of the Frankfurt School* (Verso, 2017), p. 146.

10. Max Horkheimer, 'The Latest Attack on Metaphysics', in Ruth Groff (ed.), *Subject and Object: Frankfurt School Writings on Epistemology, Ontology and Method* (Bloomsbury Academic, 2014).

11. See Lorenz Jäger, *Adorno: A Political Biography* (Yale University Press, 2004), p. 104.

12. Adorno's critique, developed at the Radio Research Project, was to form the basis of one of the most enduring chapters, on the evils of mass culture, in the most celebrated text of the Frankfurt School, *Dialectic of Enlightenment*, by Adorno and Horkheimer, published in 1944.

13. Marcuse, *One-Dimensional Man*, p. 5.

14. Ibid., p. 123.

15. Michel Foucault, *The Birth of Biopolitics: Lectures at the Collège de France* (Palgrave Macmillan, 2008), p. 247.

16. Marcuse, *One-Dimensional Man*, p. 75.

17. These points are all well made by Reich's long-suffering wife Ilse in her memoir, *Wilhelm Reich: A Personal Biography* (St Martin's Press, 1969).

18. For more on the connection between early Silicon Valley, the counter-culture and the New Left see Gary Gerstle's book *The Rise and Fall of the Neoliberal Order: America and the World in the Free Market Era* (Oxford University Press, 2022).

19. For more details on Mises's NYU seminar, see Sebastian Caré, 'Ludwig von Mises's New York University Seminar (1948–1969): The Covert Migration of Austrian Liberalism to the United States', *Raisons politiques*, vol. 71, no. 3 (2018), pp. 17–41.

20. Quoted by Caré, ibid., p. 1.

21. For more on the Mises Institute and its influence, even in Jair Bolsonaro's Brazil, see Niklas Olsen and Quinn Slobodian, 'Locating Ludwig von Mises: Introduction', *Journal of the History of Ideas*, vol. 82, no. 2 (April 2022), pp. 257–67.

22. For more on the profound differences between Mises and the likes of Rothbard, see Jacob Jensen, 'Repurposing Mises: Murray Rothbard and the Birth of Anarchocapitalism', *Journal of the History of Ideas*, vol. 82, no. 2 (April 2022), pp. 315–32.

23. For a further study of the appropriation of Austrian School liberalism by the 'Alternative Right' in America and the points of contact with the MPS, see Quinn Slobodian, 'Anti-'68ers and the Racist-Libertarian Alliance: How a Schism Among Austrian Neoliberals Helped Spawn the Alt Right', *Cultural Politics*, vol. 15, no. 3 (November 2019), pp. 372–86.

24. For a deeper look at how Hayek came to found the MPS, see Jeremy Shearmur, 'The Other Path to Mont Pelerin', in Robert Leeson (ed.), *Hayek: A Collaborative Biography*, Part IV (Palgrave Macmillan, 2015).

25. See *The Collected Works of Milton Friedman*, compiled and edited by Robert Leeson and Charles Palm (Hoover Institution Press, 2017).

26. For more on the frosty relations between Mises, in particular, and the Ordoliberals see Joshua Rahtz, 'Two Types of Separation: Ludwig von Mises and German Neoliberalism', *Journal of the History of Ideas*, vol. 82, no. 2 (April 2022), pp. 293–313.

27. For a longer discussion of the Ordoliberals and their relationship with the MPS see Daniel Stedman Jones, *Masters of the Universe: Hayek, Friedman, and the Birth of Neoliberal Politics* (Princeton University Press, 2012), Chapter 3.

28. Quoted by Quinn Slobodian in his essay 'The World Economy and the Colour Line: Wilhelm Röpke, Apartheid and the White Atlantic', in Logemann and Nolan (eds), 'More Atlantic Crossings?', p. 64.

29. Dieter Plehwe has mapped the influence of the MPS and its members on this neoliberal network in the introduction to Philip Mirowski and Dieter Plehwe (eds), *The Road from Mont Pelerin: The Making of the Neoliberal Thought Collective* (Harvard University Press, 2009).

30. Quoted in Phillips-Fein, *Invisible Hands*, p. 261.

31. For more on de Soto and the Institute for Liberty and Democracy see Timothy Mitchell, 'How Neoliberalism Makes Its World: The Urban Property Rights Project

in Peru', in Mirowski and Plehwe (eds), *The Road from Mont Pelerin*. More controversially, Friedman and Hayek advised the dictator General Augusto Pinochet in Chile during the late 1970s. For a good short account of the Chilean 'experiment', see Karin Fischer, 'The Influence of Neoliberals in Chile Before, During, and After Pinochet', also in Mirowski and Plehwe (eds), *The Road from Mont Pelerin*.

32. For a thorough account, for instance, of Hayek's impact on China, see Malcolm Warner (ed.), *The Diffusion of F.A. Hayek's Thoughts in Mainland China and Taiwan* (Routledge, 2017).

33. Slobodian, 'The World Economy and the Colour Line', p. 50.

34. The supreme importance that the rule of law played in the worldview of members of the Mont Pelerin Society was captured very well by one of their number, Michael Polanyi, the brother of Karl. In *The Logic of Liberty: Reflections and Rejoinders* (University of Chicago Press, 1951), p. 34, he wrote: 'The main function of a system of jurisdiction is to govern the spontaneous order of economic life. The system of law must develop and reinforce the rules according to which the competitive mechanism of production and distribution operate.'

35. Pascal Lamy, 'The New World of Trade: The Third Jan Tumlir Lecture', in *Jan Tumlir Policy Essays*, no. 01/2015, European Centre for International Political Economy (ÉCIPE).

36. Ernst-Ulrich Petersmann, 'The Establishment of a GATT Office of Legal Affairs and the Limits of "Public Reason" in the GATT/WTO Dispute Settlement System', in Gabrielle Marceau (ed.), *A History of Law and Lawyers in the GATT and WTO: The Development of the Rule of Law in the Multilateral Trading System* (Cambridge University Press, 2015), p. 187.

37. Frieder Roessler, 'The Role of Law in International Trade Relations and the Establishment of the Legal Affairs Division of the GATT', in Marceau (ed.), *A History of Law and Lawyers*, pp. 167–8.

38. Quoted by Matthias Schmeltzer, 'What Comes After Bretton Woods? Neoliberals Debate and Fight for a Future Monetary Order', in Dieter Plehwe, Quinn Slobodian and Philip Mirowski (eds), *Nine Lives of Neoliberalism* (Verso, 2020).

39. Chuck Ueno, 'Peter Drucker's Influence in Japan', *People and Strategy*, vol. 32, no. 4 (2009).

40. See Benoit Godin, 'The Knowledge Economy: Fritz Machlup's Construction of a Synthetic Concept', *Project on the History and Sociology of STI Statistics*, Working Paper no. 37 (2008), for a useful recent discussion of Machlup's book.

41. Fritz Machlup, *The Production and Distribution of Knowledge in the United States* (Princeton University Press, 1962), p. 133.

42. Ibid., p. 135.

43. Witzel, *A History of Management Thought*, p. 92.

44. The details on entrepreneurship courses are from Dieter Plehwe, 'Schumpeter Revival? How Neoliberals Revised the Image of the Entrepreneur', in Plehwe, Slobodian and Mirowski (eds), *Nine Lives of Neoliberalism*.

45. See Sebastian Mallaby, *The Man Who Knew: The Life and Times of Alan Greenspan* (Bloomsbury, 2016), pp. 232–3.

46. Conversation with Gary Gerstle.

47. Gerstle, *The Rise and Fall of the Neoliberal Order*, p. 273.

48. Diana Stuart, Ryan Gunderson and Brian Petersen, 'Climate Change and the Polanyian Countermovement: Carbon Markets or Degrowth?', *New Political Economy*, vol. 24, no. 1 (2017), available at: https://www.cssn.org/wp-content/uploads/2020/12/Climate-Change-and-the-Polanyian-Counter-movement-Carbon-Markets-or-Degrowth-Ryan-Gunderson.pdf (accessed 2021). There

are many more examples of the same, such as Giulia Iannuzzi, 'The Significance of Polanyi's Contribution: An Interpretation of the Neoliberalization and Commodification of Nature', *Janus Net*, vol. 9 (2018), available at: https://www.researchgate.net/publication/324849571_The_significance_of_Polanyi's_contribution_an_interpretation_of_the_neoliberalization_and_commodifica-tion_of_nature (accessed 2021).

49. The article 'Clean Up or Clear Out', *The Economist*, 9 December 1999 (https://www.economist.com/europe/1999/12/09/clean-up-or-clear-out, accessed 2021) details the horrors of air pollution in the north of what is now the Czech Republic from the 1950s on. One sizeable part of the former communist territory, largely overlapping the old Austro-Hungarian empire comprised of northern Bohemia, south-east East Germany and south-west Poland, became known as 'the triangle of death'. Here acid rain created an apocalyptic wasteland. Trees were reduced to charred twigs, visibility to a few yards, and residents only emerged from their homes in gasmasks (as I well remember observing as I drove through). Life expectancy was shortened, and children were evacuated to the mountains for months at a time. The Czech authorities resorted to offering a bonus to people to live in the area for more than ten years. Locally, this was known as 'burial money'.

50. See Joseph E. Stiglitz, 'The Coming Great Transformation', *Journal of Policy Modeling*, vol. 39 (2017), pp. 625–38, available at: https://www8.gsb.columbia.edu/faculty/jstiglitz/sites/jstiglitz/files/The%20Coming%20Great%20Transformation%20Final.pdf (accessed 2021). And also Robert Kuttner, 'The Man from Red Vienna', *New York Review of Books*, 2 December 2017.

51. For discussions of the influence of Polanyi on Sanders and Corbyn, see Patrick Iber, 'Karl Polanyi for President', *Dissent*, 23 May 2016 (https://www.dissentmagazine.org/online_articles/karl-polanyi-explainer-great-transformation-bernie-sanders, accessed 2021), and Mike Konczal, 'Corbynomics Would Change Britain – But Not in the Way Most People Think', *The Economist*, 17 May 2018.

Conclusion The Politics of Genius and the Empire of Critical Rationalism

1. Sandner, Günther, 'The German Climate and Its Opposite: Otto Neurath in England, 1940–45', in A. Grenville and A. Reiter (eds), *Political Exile and Exile Politics in Britain after 1933* (Yearbook of the Research Centre for German and Austrian Exile Studies, vol. 12, 2011), p. 76.

2. Long, *Josef Frank*, pp. 260–1.

3. Fleck, *Transatlantic History of the Social Sciences*, p. 8.

4. This did not, of course, stop the later devotees and acolytes of the Viennese in these pages from founding hundreds of eponymous think-tanks, institutes and foundations in their honour. Indeed, this is one measure of the influence that they exerted worldwide. To give but a few examples, consider the Peter Drucker Forum, the Mises Institute, the Karl Polanyi Institute of Political Economy, the Anna Freud Centre, the Melanie Klein Trust, the North American Society for Adlerian Psychology, the Neutra Institute for Survival Through Design, the British Wittgenstein Society, the Konrad Lorenz Institute for Evolution and Cognition Research, the Kurt Gödel Research Institute and the Bertalanffy Center for the Study of Systems Science. There are many more. Hayek alone, through the Mont Pelerin Society, inspired the foundation of several hundred think-tanks and research organisations throughout the world, all of which curate his memory and valorise his ideas. Similarly, the International Psychoanalytic Foundation, founded by Freud in 1910, now has hundreds of branches and over 10,000 members.

Bibliography

This is intended as a guide to the texts that I found most useful for writing this book rather than an exhaustive bibliography on the history of Vienna. All editions refer to those that I used, rather than the original year of publication.

By the Viennese writers and intellectuals themselves, and their contemporaries

Adler, Alfred, *The Practice and Theory of Individual Psychology* (Kegan Paul, Trench, Trubner & Co., 1924)
Adorno, Theodor and Max Horkheimer, *Dialectic of Enlightenment* (Verso, 1992)
Aichhorn, August, *Wayward Youth* (Putnam, 1936)
Baur, Erwin, Eugen Fischer and Fritz Lenz, *Foundations of Human Heredity and Racial Hygiene* (George Allen, 1931)
Bernays, Edward, *Propaganda*, intro. Mark Crispin Miller (IG Publishing, 2005)
Bertalanffy, Ludwig von, *Problems of Life* (Watts & Co., 1952)
Canetti, Elias, *The Memoirs of Elias Canetti: The Tongue Set Free; The Torch in My Ear; The Play of the Eyes* (Farrar, Straus and Giroux, 2000)
Dichter, Ernest, *The Psychology of Everyday Living* (Kessinger Publishing, 2010)
___, *The Strategy of Desire* (Martino Fine Books, 2012)
Drucker, Peter, *Adventures of a Bystander* (Transaction Publishers, 1994)
___, *The Age of Discontinuity: Guidelines to Our Changing Society* (Transaction Publishers, 1992)
___, *Concept of the Corporation* (John Day, 1972)
___, *The Essential Drucker* (Routledge, 2007)
___, *The Future of Industrial Man; A Conservative Approach* (John Day, 1942)
Frankl, Viktor, *Man's Search for Meaning* (Rider, 2014)
___, *Yes to Life, In Spite of Everything* (Rider, 2020)
Freud, Anna, *Before the Best Interests of the Child* (Free Press, 1986)
___, *Beyond the Best Interests of the Child* (Free Press, 1984)
___, *The Ego and the Mechanisms of Defence* (Routledge, 1992)
___, *In the Best Interests of the Child* (Macmillan, 1986)
Freud, Sigmund, *Civilization and Its Discontents* (Penguin Classics, 2005)
___, *Three Essays on the Theory of Sexuality* (Verso, 2017)

Friedman, Milton, *The Collected Works of Milton Friedman*, ed. Robert Leeson and Charles Palm (Hoover Institution Press, 2017)

Gombrich, Ernst, *Art and Illusion: A Study in the Psychology of Pictorial Representation* (Phaidon, 2002)

___, *The Story of Art* (Phaidon, 2006)

___, *The Visual Arts in Vienna circa 1900: Reflections on the Jewish Catastrophe* (Austrian Cultural Institute, 1997)

Gruen, Victor, *The Heart of Our Cities: The Urban Crisis: Diagnosis and Cure* (Thames & Hudson, 1965)

Guggenheim, Peggy, *Out of This Century: Confessions of an Art Addict* (Andre Deutsch, 1980)

Hahn, Hans, *Empiricism, Logic and Mathematics* (Kluwer, 1980)

Hayek, F.A., *The Collected Works of F.A. Hayek*, Vol. 1, *The Fatal Conceit: The Errors of Socialism*, ed. W.W. Bartley III (Routledge, 2001)

___, *The Collected Works of F.A. Hayek*, Vol. 4, *Remembering My Cousin Ludwig Wittgenstein* (University of Chicago Press, 1992)

___, *The Collected Works of F.A. Hayek*, Vol. 13, *Studies on the Abuse and Decline of Reason*, ed. Bruce Caldwell (Routledge, 2010)

___, *Hayek on Hayek: An Autobiographical Dialogue*, ed. Stephen Kresge and Leif Wenar (Routledge, 1994)

___, *New Studies in Philosophy, Politics, Economics and the History of Ideas* (Routledge, 1977)

___, *The Road to Serfdom* (Routledge, 1991)

Hellman, Ilse, *From War Babies to Grandmothers* (Karnac Books, 1990)

Hitler, Adolf, *Mein Kampf*, trans. James Murphy (Hurst & Blackett, 1939)

Jahoda, Marie, Paul Lazarsfeld and Hans Zeisel, *Marienthal: The Sociography of an Unemployed Community* (Transaction Publishers, 2002)

Leach, Bernard, *Beyond East and West: Memoirs, Portraits and Essays* (Faber & Faber, 1978)

Lorenz, Konrad, *The Foundations of Ethology* (Springer, 1981)

___, *King Solomon's Ring* (Methuen & Co. Ltd, 1952)

___, *On Aggression* (Routledge, 2002)

Machlup, Fritz, *The Production and Distribution of Knowledge in the United States* (Princeton University Press, 1962)

Marcuse, Herbert, *One-Dimensional Man* (Beacon Press, 1964)

Menaker, Esther, *Appointment in Vienna: The American Psychoanalyst Recalls Her Student Days in Pre-War Austria* (St Martin's Press, 1989)

Menger, Karl, *Reminiscences of the Vienna Circle and the Mathematical Colloquium* (Kluwer Academic Publishers, 1994)

Mises, Ludwig von, *Memoirs* (Ludwig von Mises Institute, 2012)

___, *Socialism: An Economic and Sociological Analysis* (Jonathan Cape, 1951)

Mitchison, Naomi, *Vienna Diary* (Harrison Smith and Robert Hass, 1934)

Musil, Robert, *The Man Without Qualities* (Picador, 1997)

Neurath, Otto, *From Hieroglyphics to Isotype: A Visual Autobiography*, ed. Matthew Eve (Hyphen Press, 2010)

___, *Otto Neurath: Economic Writings, Selections 1904–1945*, ed. Thomas Uebel and Robert Cohen (Kluwer Academic Publishers, 2004)

Neutra, Richard, *Life and Shape* (Atara Press, 2009)

___, *Survival Through Design* (Oxford University Press, 1954)

Newman, George, *Finding Harmony: A Family's Journey Across Europe and Beyond* (George Newman, 2013)

Philby, Kim, *My Silent War* (Arrow, 2018)
Pirquet, Clemens von, *An Outline of the Pirquet System of Nutrition* (W.B. Saunders Company, 1922)
Polanyi, Karl, *The Great Transformation: The Political and Economic Origins of our Time* (Victor Gollancz, 1945)
Polanyi, Michael, *The Logic of Liberty: Reflections and Rejoinders* (University of Chicago Press, 1951)
Popper, Karl, *The Open Society and Its Enemies* (Routledge, 1969)
___, *The Poverty of Historicism* (Routledge, 1991)
___, *Unended Quest: An Intellectual Autobiography* (Routledge, 1992)
Reich, Ilse, *Wilhelm Reich: A Personal Biography* (St Martin's Press, 1969)
Reich, Wilhelm, *The Function of the Orgasm* (Panther, 1970)
___, *The Mass Psychology of Fascism* (Farrar, Straus and Giroux, 1970)
___, *The Sexual Revolution: Towards a Self-regulating Character Structure* (Farrar, Straus and Giroux, 1974)
Roth, Joseph, *The Emperor's Tomb* (Granta, 2013)
___, *A Life in Letters*, ed. Michael Hofmann (Granta, 2012)
___, *The Radetzky March* (Penguin, 2000)
Schnitzler, Arthur, *A Dream Story* (Penguin, 1999)
___, *La Ronde* (Timeless Classics, 2014)
Schumpeter, Joseph, *Capitalism, Socialism and Democracy* (Routledge, 1994)
Sterba, Richard, *Reminiscences of a Viennese Psychoanalyst* (Wayne State University Press, 1982)
Varon, Benno Weiser, *Confessions of a Lucky Jew* (Associated University Presses, 1999)
Von Neumann, John and Oskar Morgenstern, *Theory of Games and Economic Behavior* (Princeton University Press, 2007)
Weininger, Otto, *Sex and Character: An Investigation of Fundamental Principles*, ed. Daniel Steuer and Laura Marcus, trans. Ladislaus Löb (Indiana University Press, 2005)
Wittgenstein, Ludwig, *Notebooks, 1914–1916* (Basil Blackwell, 1961)
___, *Philosophical Investigations* (Blackwell, 1978)
___, *Tractatus Logico-Philosophicus* (Routledge, 1974)
Zinnemann, Fred, *A Life in the Movies: An Autobiography* (Bloomsbury, 1992)
Zweig, Stefan, *Messages from a Lost World: Europe on the Brink* (Pushkin Press, 2017)
___, *The World of Yesterday* (University of Nebraska Press, 2013)

Secondary sources

Abel, Richard and Gordon Graham, *Immigrant Publishers: The Impact of Expatriate Publishers in Britain and America in the 20th Century* (Transaction Publishers, 2009)
Alexander, Theodor, 'From the Scientific to the Supernatural in Schnitzler', *The South Central Bulletin: Studies by Members of the SCLA*, vol. 31, no. 4 (1971), pp. 164–7
Andersen, Esben Sloth, *Joseph Schumpeter* (Palgrave Macmillan, 2011)
Anderson, Harriet, *Utopian Feminism: Women's Movements in Fin-de-Siècle Vienna* (Yale University Press, 1992)
Anderson, Perry, *English Questions* (Verso, 1992)
___, *A Zone of Engagement* (Verso, 1992)
Andrew, Christopher and Oleg Gordievsky, *KGB: The Inside Story* (Hodder and Stoughton, 1990)

Andrew, Christopher and Vasili Mitrokhin, *The Mitrokhin Archive: The KGB in Europe and the West* (Allen Lane, 1999)

Ash, Mitchell, 'Multiple Modernisms in Context: The Sciences, Technology and Culture in Vienna around 1900', in Robert Bud, Paul Greenhalgh, Frank James and Morag Shiach (eds), *Being Modern: The Cultural Impact of Science in the Early Twentieth Century* (UCL Press, 2018)

___, 'Psychology and Politics in Interwar Vienna: The Vienna Psychological Institute, 1922–1942', in Mitchell Ash and W.R. Woodward (eds), *Psychology in Twentieth-Century Thought and Society* (Cambridge University Press, 1987)

___, (ed.), *Science in the Metropolis: Vienna in Transnational Context, 1848–1918* (Routledge, 2020)

Aulenbacher, Brigitte, Markus Marterbauer, Andreas Novy, Kari Polanyi Levitt and Armin Thurnher (eds), *Karl Polanyi: The Life and Works of an Epochal Thinker* (Falter Verlag, 2020)

Auslander, Leora, 'The Boundaries of Jewishness, Or When Is a Cultural Practice Jewish?', *Modern Jewish Studies*, vol. 8, no. 1 (2009)

Bahr, Ehrhard, *Weimar on the Pacific: German Exile Culture in Los Angeles and the Crisis of Modernism* (University of California Press, 2007)

Barcant, Aaron, 'Coexistence: Karl Polanyi and Peter Drucker Navigating Mid-Century Crises', paper for the Peter Drucker Society (August 2019)

Bartos, Rena, 'Ernest Dichter: Motive Interpreter', *Journal of Advertising Research* (February–March 1986)

Beller, Steven, *Vienna and the Jews, 1867–1938: A Cultural History* (Cambridge University Press, 1995)

Beller, Steven (ed.), *Rethinking Vienna 1900*, Vol. 3, *Austrian and Habsburg Studies* (Berghahn Books, 2001)

Beniston, Judith, 'Body Politics in Arthur Schnitzler's Professor Bernhardi', in Carolin Duttlinger, Kevin Hilliard and Charlie Louth (eds), *From the Enlightenment to Modernism: Three Centuries of German Literature* (Legenda, 2021)

___, 'Schnitzler and the Place of Tendentious Drama', *Austrian Studies*, vol. 27 (2019)

Beniston, Judith and Robert Vilain (eds), *Culture and Politics in Red Vienna*, *Austrian Studies*, vol. 14 (2006)

Berkley, George E., *Vienna and Its Jews: The Tragedy of Success, 1880s–1980s* (Madison Books, 1988)

Berry, Mark, *Critical Lives: Arnold Schoenberg* (Reaktion Books, 2019)

Bew, John, *Citizen Clem: A Biography of Attlee* (Riverrun, 2017)

Bhattacharya, Ananyo, *The Man from the Future: The Visionary Life of John von Neumann* (Allen Lane, 2021)

Blackmore, John, *Ernst Mach: His Work, Life, and Influence* (University of California Press, 1972)

Blau, Eve, *The Architecture of Red Vienna 1919–1934* (MIT Press, 1999)

Borovik, Genrikh, *The Philby Files: The Secret Life of the Master Spy – KGB Archives Revealed* (Little Brown, 1994)

Borsi, Franco and Ezio Godoli, *Vienna 1900: Architecture and Design* (Lund Humphries, 1986)

Bourdieu, Pierre, 'The Social Conditions for the International Circulation of Ideas', in Richard Shusterman (ed.), *Bourdieu: A Critical Reader* (Blackwell, 1999)

Boyer, John, *Culture and Political Crisis in Vienna: Christian Socialism in Power, 1897–1918* (University of Chicago Press, 1995)

Brandow-Faller, Megan and Laura Morowitz (eds), *Erasures and Eradications in Modern Viennese Art, Architecture and Design* (Routledge, 2022)

Brinson, Charmain and Richard Dove, *A Matter of Intelligence: MI5 and the Surveillance of Anti-Nazi Refugees, 1933–1950* (Manchester University Press, 2014)

Brivati, Brian, *Hugh Gaitskell* (Richard Cohen Books, 1996)

Broda, Paul, *Scientist Spies: A Memoir of My Three Parents and the Atom Bomb* (Matador Books, 2011)

Brown, Andrew, 'The Viennese Connection: Engelbert Broda, Alan Nunn May and Atomic Espionage', *Intelligence and National Security*, vol. 24 (2009)

Budiansky, Stephen, *Journey to the Edge of Reason: The Life of Kurt Gödel* (W.W. Norton, 2021)

Bukey, Evan Burr, *Hitler's Austria: Popular Sentiment in the Nazi Era, 1938–1945* (University of North Carolina Press, 2000)

Buklijas, Tatjana, 'Cultures of Death and Politics of Corpse Supply: Anatomy in Vienna, 1848–1914', *Bulletin of the History of Medicine*, vol. 82, no. 3 (2008)

Burke, Christopher, Eric Kindel and Sue Walker (eds), *Isotype: Design and Contexts, 1925–1971* (Hyphen Press, 2013)

Burkhardt, Richard, *Konrad Lorenz: Patterns of Behavior* (University of Chicago Press, 2005)

Burnham, John (ed.), *After Freud Left: A Century of Psychoanalysis in America* (University of Chicago Press, 2012)

Caldwell, Bruce, *Hayek's Challenge* (University of Chicago Press, 2004)

Caldwell, Bruce and Hansjoerg Klausinger, *Hayek: A Life, 1899–1950* (University of Chicago Press, 2022)

Caré, Sebastian, 'Ludwig von Mises's New York University Seminar (1948–1969): The Covert Migration of Austrian Liberalism to the United States', *Raisons Politiques*, vol. 71, no. 3 (2018)

Carroll, Brendan, *The Last Prodigy: A Biography of Erich Wolfgang Korngold* (Amadeus Press, 1997)

Cockett, Richard, *Thinking the Unthinkable: Think-Tanks and the Economic Counter-Revolution, 1931–1983* (HarperCollins, 1994)

Coen, Deborah, *Vienna in the Age of Uncertainty: Science, Liberalism, and Private Life* (University of Chicago Press, 2007)

Cohen, Gary, *Education and Middle-Class Society in Imperial Austria, 1848–1918* (Purdue University Press, 1996)

Cooper, Emmanuel, *Lucie Rie: Modernist Potter* (Yale University Press, 2012)

Cornish, Kimberley, *The Jew of Linz: Wittgenstein, Hitler and Their Secret Battle for the Mind* (Century Books, 1998)

Costello, John and Oleg Tsarev, *Deadly Illusions* (Century, 1993)

Crawford, Dorothy Lamb, *A Windfall of Musicians: Hitler's Émigrés and Exiles in Southern California* (Yale University Press, 2009)

Czech, Herwig, 'From Welfare to Selection: Vienna's Public Health Office and the Implementation of Racial Hygiene Policies under the Nazi Regime', in Marius Turda and Paul Weindling (eds), *Blood and Homeland: Eugenics and Racial Nationalism in Central and Southeast Europe, 1900–1940* (Central European University Press, 2007)

Dale, Gareth, *Karl Polanyi: A Life on the Left* (Polity Press, 2010)

___, *Karl Polanyi: A Life on the Left* (Columbia University Press, 2016)

Danto, Elizabeth Ann, *Freud's Free Clinics: Psychoanalysis and Social Justice, 1918–1938* (Columbia University Press, 2005)

Davidson, Mark, *Uncommon Sense: The Life and Thought of Ludwig von Bertalanffy, Father of General Systems Theory* (J.P. Tarcher, 1983)

Dawson, John, *Logical Dilemmas: The Life and Work of Kurt Gödel* (AK Peters, 1997)

De Haan, Francisca, Krassimira Daskalova and Anna Loutfi (eds), *Biographical Dictionary of Women's Movements and Feminisms: Central, Southern and South Eastern Europe* (Central European University Press, 2006)

De Waal, Edmund, *The Hare with Amber Eyes: A Hidden Inheritance* (Vintage, 2011)

Dekker, Erwin, *The Viennese Students of Civilization: The Meaning and Context of Austrian Economics Reconsidered* (Cambridge University Press, 2016)

Drury, Maurice O'Connor, 'Some Notes on Conversations with Wittgenstein', in *The Selected Writings of Maurice O'Connor Drury: On Wittgenstein, Philosophy, Religion and Psychiatry* (Bloomsbury Academic, 2018)

Dyson, George, *Turing's Cathedral: The Origins of the Digital Universe* (Penguin, 2012)

Ebenstein, Alan, *Friedrich Hayek: A Biography* (Palgrave, 2001)

___, *Hayek's Journey: The Mind of Friedrich Hayek* (Palgrave, 2003)

Edmonds, David, *The Murder of Professor Schlick: The Rise and Fall of the Vienna Circle* (Princeton University Press, 2020)

Edmonds, David and John Eidinow, *Wittgenstein's Poker: The Story of a Ten-Minute Argument Between Two Great Philosophers* (Faber & Faber, 2005)

Erbacher, Christian (ed.), *Friedrich August von Hayek's Draft Biography of Ludwig Wittgenstein: The Text and Its History* (Mentis, 2019)

Erker, Linda, Wolfgang Schütz, Harald Sitte and Oliver Rathkolb (eds), 'Anschluss 1938: Aftermath on Medicine and Society', *Central European Journal of Medicine*, supplement 5 (January 2018)

Feichtinger, Johannes, Anil Bhatti and Cornelia Hülmbauer (eds), *How to Write the Global History of Knowledge-Making: Interaction, Circulation and the Transgression of Cultural Differences* (Springer, 2020)

Feichtinger, Johannes and Gary Cohen, *Understanding Multiculturalism: The Habsburg Central European Experience* (Berghahn Books, 2014)

Feichtinger, Johannes, Herbert Matis, Stefan Sienell and Heidemarie Uhl (eds), *The Academy of Sciences in Vienna, 1938 to 1945* (Austrian Academy of Sciences Press, 2014)

Fischer, Karin, 'The Influence of Neoliberals in Chile Before, During, and After Pinochet', in Philip Mirowski and Dieter Plehwe (eds), *The Road from Mont Pelerin: The Making of the Neoliberal Thought Collective* (Harvard University Press, 2009)

Fleck, Christian, 'Lazarsfeld's Wives, or: What Happened to Women Sociologists in the Twentieth Century', *International Review of Sociology*, vol. 31, no. 1 (2021)

___, *A Transatlantic History of the Social Sciences: Robber Barons, the Third Reich and the Invention of Empirical Social Research* (Bloomsbury Academic, 2011)

Fleming, Donald and Bernard Bailyn (eds), *The Intellectual Migration: Europe and America, 1930–1960* (Harvard University Press, 1969)

Foucault, Michel, *The Birth of Biopolitics: Lectures at the Collège de France* (Palgrave Macmillan, 2008)

Franzen, Jonathan, *The Kraus Project: Essays by Karl Kraus* (Farrar, Straus and Giroux, 2013)

Freis, David, *Psycho-Politics between the World Wars: Psychiatry and Society in Germany, Austria and Switzerland* (Palgrave Macmillan, 2019)

Fujiwara, Chris, *The World and Its Double: The Life and Work of Otto Preminger* (Faber & Faber, 2008)

Gay, Peter, *Freud: A Life for Our Time* (J.M. Dent & Sons Ltd, 1988)

George, Alys, *The Naked Truth: Vienna, Modernity and the Body* (University of Chicago Press, 2020)

Gerity, Lani and Susan Ainlay Anand, *The Legacy of Edith Kramer: A Multifaceted View* (Routledge, 2018)

Gerstle, Gary, *The Rise and Fall of the Neoliberal Order: America and the World in the Free Market Era* (Oxford University Press, 2022)

Gill, Brendan, *Many Masks: A Life of Frank Lloyd Wright* (Heinemann, 1988)

Gissis, Snait B. and Eva Jablonka (eds), *Transformations of Lamarckism: From Subtle Fluids to Molecular Biology* (MIT Press, 2011)

Godin, Benoît, 'The Knowledge Economy: Fritz Machlup's Construction of a Synthetic Concept', *Project on the History and Sociology of STI Statistics*, Working Paper no. 37 (2008)

Griffiths, Rhys, 'Strange Guests at the Hotel de l'Europe', *History Today*, 20 November 2014

Grosskurth, Phyliss, *Melanie Klein: Her World and Her Work* (Alfred Knopf, 1986)

Gruber, Helmut, *Red Vienna: Experiments in Working-Class Culture, 1919–1934* (Oxford University Press, 1991)

___, 'Sexuality in "Red Vienna": Socialist Party Conceptions and Programs and Working-Class Life, 1920–34', *International Labour and Working-Class History*, no. 31 (Spring 1987)

Gunning, Tom, *The Films of Fritz Lang: Allegories of Vision and Modernity* (British Film Institute, 2000)

Hacohen, Malachi H., *Karl Popper: The Formative Years, 1902–1945* (Cambridge University Press, 2001)

Hamann, Brigitte, *Hitler's Vienna: A Portrait of the Tyrant as a Young Man* (Taurus Parke Paperbacks, 2010)

Hartwell, Max, *A History of the Mont Pelerin Society* (Liberty Fund, 1995)

Haynes, John Earl, Harvey Klehr and Alexander Vassiliev, *Spies: The Rise and Fall of the KGB in America* (Yale University Press, 2009)

Healy, Maureen, *Vienna and the Fall of the Habsburg Empire* (Cambridge University Press, 2004)

Heertje, Arnold, *Schumpeter's Vision: Capitalism, Socialism and Democracy after 40 Years* (Praeger Publishers, 1981)

Helfert, Veronika, 'Born a Rebel, Always a Rebel', in Andreas Novy (ed.), *Karl Polanyi: The Life and Works of an Epochal Thinker* (Falter Verlag, 2020)

Herzog, Dagmar, *Cold War Freud: Psychoanalysis in an Age of Catastrophe* (Cambridge University Press, 2009)

Hines, Thomas, *Architecture of the Sun: Los Angeles Modernism, 1900–1970* (Rizzoli, 2010)

___, *Richard Neutra and the Search for Modern Architecture* (Oxford University Press, 1982)

Hirsch, Foster, *Otto Preminger: The Man Who Would Be King* (Alfred Knopf, 2007)

Hoffman, Edward, *The Drive for Self: Alfred Adler and the Founding of Individual Psychology* (Addison-Wesley Publishing, 1994)

Holmes, Deborah and Lisa Silverman (eds), *Interwar Vienna: Culture Between Tradition and Modernity* (Camden House, 2009)

Holton, Gerald, 'From the Vienna Circle to Harvard Square', in Friedrich Stadler (ed.), *Scientific Philosophy: Origins and Developments*, *Vienna Circle Institute Yearbook*, vol. 1 (1993)

Horak, Roman, 'Metropolitan Culture/Popular Pleasures: Modernism, Football and Politics in Interwar Vienna', in Siegfried Gehrmann (ed.), *Football and Regional Identity in Europe* (LIT Verlag, 1997)

Horowitz, Daniel, *Betty Friedan and the Making of* The Feminine Mystique*: The American Left, the Cold War, and Modern Feminism* (University of Massachusetts Press, 1998)

Immerwahr, Daniel, 'Polanyi in the United States: Peter Drucker, Karl Polanyi and the Midcentury Critique of Economic Society', *Journal of the History of Ideas*, vol. 70, no. 3 (July 2009)

Jablonka, Eva and Marion Lamb, *Inheritance Systems and the Extended Evolutionary Synthesis* (Cambridge University Press, 2020)

Jäger, Lorenz, *Adorno: A Political Biography* (Yale University Press, 2004)

Janik, Allan and Stephen Toulmin, *Wittgenstein's Vienna* (Ivan R. Dee, 1996)

Jarman, Derek, *Wittgenstein: The Terry Eagleton Script, the Derek Jarman Film* (British Film Institute, 1993)

Jay, Martin, *The Dialectical Imagination: A History of the Frankfurt School and the Institute of Social Research, 1923–1950* (University of California Press, 1996)

Jeffries, Stuart, *Grand Hotel Abyss: The Lives of the Frankfurt School* (Verso, 2017)

Jensen, Jacob, 'Repurposing Mises: Murray Rothbard and the Birth of Anarchocapitalism', *Journal of the History of Ideas*, vol. 82, no. 2 (April 2022)

Jerabek, Hynek, *Paul Lazarsfeld and the Origins of Communications Research* (Routledge, 2017)

Johnson, Julian, 'Anton Webern, the Social Democratic Kunststelle and Musical Modernism', in Judith Beniston and Robert Vilain (eds), *Culture and Politics in Red Vienna, Austrian Studies*, vol. 14 (2006)

Johnston, William M., *The Austrian Mind: An Intellectual and Social History 1848–1938* (University of California Press, 1983)

___, *Vienna: The Golden Age, 1815–1914* (Clarkson M. Potter, 1981)

___, 'Von Bertalanffy's Place in Austrian Thought' in William Gray and Nicholas Rizzo (eds), *Unity Through Diversity: A Festschrift for Ludwig von Bertalanffy* (Gordon and Breach Science Publishers, 1973)

Judson, Pieter, *The Habsburg Empire: A New History* (Harvard University Press, 2016)

Judt, Tony, *Ill Fares the Land* (Penguin, 2010)

Kershaw, Ian, *Hitler 1889–1936: Hubris* (Penguin, 1999)

Klaus, Elisabeth and Josef Seethaler (eds), *What Do We Really Know about Herta Herzog?* (Peter Lang Academic Research, 2016)

Kühl, Stefan, *Eugenics, American Racism and German National Socialism* (Oxford University Press, 1994)

___, *For the Betterment of the Race: The Rise and Fall of the International Movement for Eugenics and National Hygiene* (Palgrave Macmillan, 2013)

Kuttner, Robert, 'The Man from Red Vienna', *New York Review of Books*, 21 December 2017

Lamy, Pascal, 'The New World of Trade: The Third Jan Tumlir Lecture', in *Jan Tumlir Policy Essays*, no. 01/2015, European Centre for International Political Economy (ÉCIPE)

Lavin, Sylvia, *Form Follows Libido: Architecture and Richard Neutra in a Psychoanalytic Culture* (MIT Press, 2007)

Leonard, Robert, *Von Neumann, Morgenstern, and the Creation of Game Theory: From Chess to Social Science, 1900–1960* (Cambridge University Press, 2010)

Logan, Cheryl, *Hormones, Heredity, and Race: Spectacular Failure in Interwar Vienna* (Rutgers University Press, 2013)

Logemann, Jan *Engineered to Sell: European Émigrés and the Making of Consumer Capitalism* (University of Chicago Press, 2019)

419

Logemann, Jan and Mary Nolan (eds), 'More Atlantic Crossings? European Voices and the Postwar Atlantic Community', *Bulletin of the German Historical Institute*, supplement 10 (2014)

Long, Christopher, *Adolf Loos on Trial* (Kant, 2017)

___, *Josef Frank: Life and Work* (University of Chicago Press, 2002)

___, *The Looshaus* (Yale University Press, 2011)

___, 'The Origins and Context of Adolf Loos's "Ornament and Crime"', *Journal of the Society of Architectural Historians*, vol. 68, no. 2 (June 2009)

___, *Paul T. Frankl and Modern American Design* (Yale University Press, 2007)

Luft, David, *Eros and Inwardness in Vienna: Weininger, Musil, Doderer* (University of Chicago Press, 2003)

McCraw, Thomas, *Prophet of Innovation: Joseph Schumpeter and Creative Destruction* (Harvard University Press, 2007)

McEwen, Britta, *Sexual Knowledge: Feeling, Fact, and Social Reform in Vienna, 1900–1934* (Berghahn Books, 2016)

McFarland, Rob, Georg Spitaler and Ingo Zechner, *The Red Vienna Sourcebook* (Camden House, 2020)

McGilligan, Patrick, *Fritz Lang: The Nature of the Beast* (University of Minnesota Press, 1997)

MacMillan, Margaret, *Paris 1919: Six Months that Changed the World* (Random House, 2002)

Maderthaner, Wolfgang and Lutz Musner, *Unruly Masses: The Other Side of Fin-de-Siècle Vienna* (Berghahn Books, 2008)

Makarova, Elena, *Friedl Dicker-Brandeis: Ein Leben für Kunst und Lehre* (Verlag Christian Brandstätter, 1999)

Mallaby, Sebastian, *The Man Who Knew: The Life and Times of Alan Greenspan* (Bloomsbury, 2016)

Marceau, Gabrielle (ed.), *A History of Law and Lawyers in the GATT and WTO: The Development of the Rule of Law in the Multilateral Trading System* (Cambridge University Press, 2015)

Mayer-Hirzberger, Anita, 'The Takeover of Social Democratic Musical Institutions by the Austrian "Corporate State"', in Judith Beniston and Robert Vilain (eds), *Culture and Politics in Red Vienna, Austrian Studies*, vol. 14 (2006)

Menger, Karl, *Reminiscences of the Vienna Circle and the Mathematical Colloquium* (Kluwer Academic Publishers, 1994)

Midgley, Nick, 'Anna Freud: The Hampstead War Nurseries and the Role of Direct Observation of Children for Psychoanalysis', *International Journal of Psychoanalysis*, vol. 88, no. 4 (2007)

___, *Reading Anna Freud* (Routledge, 2013)

Mirowski, Philip and Dieter Plehwe (eds), *The Road from Mont Pelerin: The Making of the Neoliberal Thought Collective* (Harvard University Press, 2009)

Mitchell, Timothy, 'How Neoliberalism Makes its World: The Urban Property Rights Project in Peru', in Philip Mirowski and Dieter Plehwe (eds), *The Road from Mont Pelerin: The Making of the Neoliberal Thought Collective* (Harvard University Press, 2009)

Monk, Ray, *Ludwig Wittgenstein: The Duty of Genius* (Jonathan Cape, 1990)

Mosse, Werner (ed.), *Second Chance: Two Centuries of German-Speaking Jews in the United Kingdom* (J.C.B. Mohr, 1991)

Müller, Gerd (ed.), *Vivarium: Experimental, Quantitative, and Theoretical Biology at Vienna's Biologische Versuchsanstalt* (MIT Press, 2017)

Muxeneder, Therese, 'The Hegemony of German Music: Schoenberg's Vienna as the Musical Center of the German-Speaking World', in Deborah Holmes and Lisa

Silverman (eds), *Interwar Vienna: Culture Between Tradition and Modernity* (Camden House, 2009)

Nemec, Birgit, 'Anatomical Modernity in Red Vienna: Textbook for Systematic Anatomy and the Politics of Visual Milieus', *Sudhoffs Archiv*, vol. 99, no. 1 (2015)

Niesen, Molly, 'Crisis of Consumerism: Advertising, Activism, and the Battle over the U.S. Federal Trade Commission, 1969–1980' (PhD thesis, University of Illinois at Urbana-Champaign, 2013), available at: https://www.ideals.illinois.edu/items/46622 (accessed 2021)

Oechslin, Werner, *Otto Wagner, Adolf Loos, and the Road to Modern Architecture* (Cambridge University Press, 2002)

Oldenziel, Ruth and Karin Zachmann (eds), *Cold War Kitchen: Americanization, Technology, and European Users* (MIT Press, 2009)

Olsen, Niklas and Quinn Slobodian, 'Locating Ludwig von Mises: Introduction', *Journal of the History of Ideas*, vol. 82, no. 2 (April 2022)

Ott, Hugo, *Martin Heidegger: A Political Life* (HarperCollins, 1953)

Packard, Vance, *The Hidden Persuaders* (IG Publishing, 2007)

Pauley, Bruce, *From Prejudice to Persecution: A History of Austrian Anti-Semitism* (University of North Carolina Press, 1992)

Pearlman, Jill, 'The Spies Who Came into the Modernist Fold: The Covert Life in Hampstead's Lawn Road Flats', *Journal of the Society of Architectural Historians*, vol. 72, no. 3 (September 2013)

Perloff, Marjorie, *Edge of Irony: Modernism in the Shadow of the Habsburg Empire* (University of Chicago Press, 2016)

___, *The Vienna Paradox: A Memoir* (New Directions Publishing, 2004)

___, *Wittgenstein's Ladder: Poetic Language and the Strangeness of the Ordinary* (University of Chicago Press, 1996)

Perz, Bertrand, 'The Austrian Connection: SS and Police Leader Odilo Globocnik and His Staff in the Lublin District', *Holocaust and Genocide Studies*, vol. 29, no. 3 (Winter 2015)

Petersmann, Ernst-Ulrich, 'The Establishment of a GATT Office of Legal Affairs and the Limits of "Public Reason" in the GATT/WTO Dispute Settlement System', in Gabrielle Marceau (ed.), *A History of Law and Lawyers in the GATT and WTO: The Development of the Rule of Law in the Multilateral Trading System* (Cambridge University Press, 2015)

Phillips-Fein, Kim, *Invisible Hands: The Making of the Conservative Movement from the New Deal to Reagan* (W.W. Norton, 2009)

Plehwe, Dieter, Quinn Slobodian and Philip Mirowski (eds), *Nine Lives of Neoliberalism* (Verso, 2020)

Pollak, Richard, *The Creation of Dr. B: A Biography of Bruno Bettelheim* (Touchstone Books, 1998)

Prochnik, George, *The Impossible Exile: Stefan Zweig at the End of the World* (Granta, 2014)

Pytell, Timothy, *Viktor Frankl's Search for Meaning: An Emblematic 20th-Century Life* (Berghahn Books, 2020)

Rahtz, Joshua, 'Two Types of Separation: Ludwig von Mises and German Neoliberalism', *Journal of the History of Ideas*, vol. 82, no. 2 (April 2022)

Rampley, Matthew, *The Vienna School of Art History: Empire and the Politics of Scholarship, 1847–1918* (Pennsylvania State University Press, 2013)

Reisman, George, 'Ayn Rand and Ludwig von Mises', *Journal of Ayn Rand Studies*, vol. 6, no. 2 (Spring 2005)

Reiter, Wolfgang, 'Karl Przibram: Radioactivity, Crystals, and Colors', *Physics in Perspective*, vol. 21 (August 2019), https://doi.org/10.1007/s00016-019-00242-z (accessed 2021)

Reiter, Wolfgang and Herbert Matis (eds), *Darwin in Zentraleuropa* (LIT Verlag, 2018)

Rentetzi, Maria, *Trafficking Materials and Gendered Experimental Practices: Radium Research in Early 20th-Century Vienna* (Columbia University Press, 2009)

Rhodes, Richard, *Hedy's Folly: The Life and Breakthrough Inventions of Hedy Lamarr, the Most Beautiful Woman in the World* (Doubleday, 2011)

Riegler, Thomas, 'The Spy Story Behind *The Third Man*', *Journal of Austrian-American History*, vol. 4 (2020)

Roessler, Frieder, 'The Role of Law in International Trade Relations and the Establishment of the Legal Affairs Division of the GATT', in Gabrielle Marceau (ed.), *A History of Law and Lawyers in the GATT and WTO: The Development of the Rule of Law in the Multilateral Trading System* (Cambridge University Press, 2015)

Rose, Louis, *Psychology, Art, and Antifascism: Ernst Kris, E.H. Gombrich, and the Politics of Caricature* (Yale University Press, 2016)

Ross, Alex, *The Rest is Noise: Listening to the Twentieth Century* (Farrar, Straus and Giroux, 2007)

___, 'Vanishing Act', *New Yorker*, 27 September 2021

___, *Wagnerism: Art and Politics in the Shadow of Music* (4th Estate, 2020)

Rowland, Alison and Peter Simonson, 'The Founding Mothers of Communication Research: Toward a History of a Gendered Assemblage', *Critical Studies in Media Communication*, vol. 31, no. 1 (March 2014)

Rubenfeld, Sheldon and Susan Benedict (eds), *Human Subjects Research after the Holocaust* (Springer, 2014)

Rubin, Susan Goldman, *Fireflies in the Dark: The Story of Friedl Dicker-Brandeis and the Children of Terezín* (Holiday House, 2000)

Samuel, Lawrence R., *Freud on Madison Avenue: Motivation Research and Subliminal Advertising in America* (University of Pennsylvania Press, 2010)

Sandner, Günther, 'The German Climate and Its Opposite: Otto Neurath in England, 1940–45', in A. Grenville and A. Reiter (eds), *Political Exile and Exile Politics in Britain after 1933, Yearbook of the Research Centre for German and Austrian Exile Studies*, vol. 12 (2011)

Sands, Philippe, *The Ratline: Love, Lies and Justice on the Trail of a Nazi Fugitive* (Weidenfeld & Nicolson, 2020)

Santini, Daria, *The Exiles: Actors, Artists and Writers Who Fled the Nazis for London* (Bloomsbury, 2019)

Schmelzer, Matthias, 'What Comes After Bretton Woods? Neoliberals Debate and Fight for a Future Monetary Order', in Dieter Plehwe, Quinn Slobodian and Philip Mirowski (eds), *Nine Lives of Neoliberalism* (Verso, 2020)

Schorske, Carl, *Fin-de-Siècle Vienna: Politics and Culture* (Vintage Books, 1981)

Schwarzkopf, Stefan and Rainer Gries (eds), *Ernest Dichter and Motivation Research: New Perspectives on the Making of Post-War Consumer Culture* (Palgrave Macmillan, 2010)

Segal, Naomi, 'Freud and the Question of Women', in Naomi Segal and Edward Timms (eds), *Freud in Exile: Psychoanalysis and Its Vicissitudes* (Yale University Press, 1988)

Sengoopta, Chandak, *The Most Secret Quintessence of Life: Sex, Glands, and Hormones, 1850–1950* (University of Chicago Press, 2006)

Shapira, Elana, *Style and Seduction: Jewish Patrons, Architecture, and Design in Fin de Siècle Vienna* (Brandeis University Press, 2016)

Shapira, Elana and Daniel Finzi (eds), *Freud and the Émigrés: Austrian Émigrés, Exiles and the Legacy of Psychoanalysis in Britain, 1930–1970* (Palgrave Macmillan, 2020)

Shapira, Michal, 'Anna Freud Shaping Child Education and Providing "Democratic Citizenship" in Britain', in Elana Shapira and Daniel Finzi (eds), *Freud and the Émigrés: Austrian Émigrés, Exiles and the Legacy of Psychoanalysis in Britain, 1930–1970* (Palgrave Macmillan, 2020)

Shearmur, Jeremy, 'The Other Path to Mont Pelerin', in Robert Leeson (ed.), *Hayek: A Collaborative Biography*, Part IV (Palgrave Macmillan, 2015)

Sheffer, Edith, *Asperger's Children: The Origins of Autism in Nazi Vienna* (W.W. Norton, 2018)

Sheine, Judith, *R.M. Schindler* (Phaidon, 2001)

Sheine, Judith and Robert Sweeney, *Schindler, Kings Road, and Southern California Modernism* (University of California Press, 2012)

Sigmund, Karl, *Exact Thinking in Demented Times: The Vienna Circle and the Epic Quest for the Foundations of Science* (Basic Books, 2017)

Sikov, Ed, *On Sunset Boulevard: The Life and Times of Billy Wilder* (Hyperion, 1998)

Silverman, Lisa, *Becoming Austrians: Jews and Culture Between the World Wars* (Oxford University Press, 2015)

Sime, Ruth Lewin, *Lise Meitner: A Life in Physics* (University of California Press, 1996)

Slobodian, Quinn, *Globalists: The End of Empire and the Birth of Neoliberalism* (Harvard University Press, 2018)

Slobodian, Quinn, 'Anti-'68ers and the Racist-Libertarian Alliance: How a Schism Among Austrian Neoliberals Helped Spawn the Alt Right', *Cultural Politics*, vol. 15, no. 3 (November 2019)

___, *Globalists: The End of Empire and the Birth of Neoliberalism* (Harvard University Press, 2018)

Smyth, J.E., *Fred Zinnemann and the Cinema of Resistance* (University Press of Mississippi, 2014)

Snowman, Daniel, *The Hitler Émigrés: The Cultural Impact on Britain of Refugees from Nazism* (Pimlico, 2003)

Sonnert, Gerhard and Gerald Holton, *What Happened to the Children Who Fled Nazi Persecution* (Palgrave Macmillan, 2006)

Spade, Rupert, *Richard Neutra* (Thames & Hudson, 1971)

Spaulding, E. Wilder, *The Quiet Invaders: The Story of the Austrian Impact upon America* (Österreichischer Bundesverlag für Unterricht, Wissenschaft und Kunst, 1968)

Spiel, Hilde, *Vienna's Golden Autumn, 1866–1938* (Weidenfeld & Nicolson, 1987)

Stadler, Friedrich, *The Vienna Circle: Studies in the Origins, Development, and Influence of Logical Empiricism* (Springer, 2001)

Stadler, Friedrich and Christoph Limbeck-Lilienau, *Der Wiener Kreis: Texte und Bilder zum Logischen Empirismus* (LIT Verlag, 2015)

Staggs, Janis, 'Joseph Urban and Cosmopolitan Productions', in Christian Witt-Dörring and Janis Staggs (eds), *Wiener Werkstätte 1903–1932: The Luxury of Beauty* (Prestel, 2017)

Stedman Jones, Daniel, *Masters of the Universe: Hayek, Friedman, and the Birth of Neoliberal Politics* (Princeton University Press, 2012)

Stern, Alexandra Minna, *Eugenic Nation: Faults and Frontiers of Better Breeding in Modern America* (University of California Press, 2015)

Stern, David and Béla Szabados, *Wittgenstein Reads Weininger* (Cambridge University Press, 2009)

Swales, Martin, *Arthur Schnitzler: A Critical Study* (Oxford University Press, 1971)

Swedberg, Richard, *Joseph A. Schumpeter: His Life and Work* (Polity Press, 1991)

Taschwer, Klaus, *The Case of Paul Kammerer: The Most Controversial Biologist of His Time* (Bunim & Bannigan, 2016)

___, 'Destroyed Research in Nazi Vienna: The Tragic Fate of the Institute for Experimental Biology in Austria', *Mètode Science Studies Journal*, vol. 10 (2020)

___, *Hochburg des Antisemitismus: Der Niedergang der Universität Wien im 20. Jahrhundert* (Czernin, 2015)

Taschwer, Klaus, Andreas Huber and Linda Erker, *Der Deutsche Klub: Austro-Nazis in der Hofburg* (Czernin, 2020)

Taylor, Paul (ed.), *Meditations on a Heritage: Papers on the Work and Legacy of Sir Ernst Gombrich* (Paul Holberton Publishing in association with the Warburg Institute, 2014)

Thun-Hohenstein, Christoph, Dieter Bogner, Maria Lind and Barbel Vischer (eds), *Friedrich Kiesler: Life Visions* (MAK, 2016)

Timms, Edward, *Karl Kraus, Apocalyptic Satirist: The Post-War Crisis and the Rise of the Swastika* (Yale University Press, 2005)

___, 'School for Socialism: Karl Seitz and the Cultural Politics of Vienna', in Judith Beniston and Robert Vilain (eds), *Culture and Politics in Red Vienna, Austrian Studies*, vol. 14 (2006)

Timms, Edward and Jon Hughes (eds), *Intellectual Migration and Cultural Transformation: Refugees from National Socialism in the English-Speaking World* (Springer Wien, 2003)

Toye, Richard, 'Winston Churchill's "Crazy Broadcast": Party, Nation, and the 1945 Gestapo Speech', *Journal of British Studies*, vol. 49, no. 3 (July 2010)

Turner, Christopher, *Adventures in the Orgasmatron: Wilhelm Reich and the Invention of Sex* (4th Estate, 2011)

Uebel, Thomas, Nancy Cartwright, Jordi Cat and Lola Fleck (eds), *Otto Neurath: Philosophy Between Science and Politics* (Cambridge University Press, 2008)

Ueno, Chuck, 'Peter Drucker's Influence in Japan', *People and Strategy*, vol. 32, no. 4 (2009)

Van der Horst, Frank and René van der Veer, 'Changing Attitudes Towards the Care of Children in Hospital: A New Assessment of the Influence of the Work of Bowlby and Robertson in the UK, 1940–1970', *Attachment and Human Development*, vol. 11, no. 2 (March 2009)

Walton-Jordan, Ulrike, 'Designs for the Future: Gaby Schreiber as an Exponent of Bauhaus Principles in Britain', in Edward Timms and Jon Hughes (eds), *Intellectual Migration and Cultural Transformation: Refugees from National Socialism in the English-Speaking World* (Springer Wien, 2003)

Warner, Malcolm (ed.), *The Diffusion of F.A. Hayek's Thoughts in Mainland China and Taiwan* (Routledge, 2017)

Warren, John, 'David Josef Bach and the "Musik- und Theaterfest of 1924"', in Judith Beniston and Robert Vilain (eds), *Culture and Politics in Red Vienna, Austrian Studies*, vol. 14 (2006)

Wasserman, Janek, *Black Vienna: The Radical Right in the Red City* (Cornell University Press, 2017)

___, *The Marginal Revolutionaries: How Austrian Economists Fought the War of Ideas* (Yale University Press, 2019)

Weber, Joseph, 'The Jugendstil and Its Relationship to the Development of Child-Centered Art Education' (PhD thesis, St Louis University, 1983), available at:

https://www.proquest.com/openview/e0d123436d9b93489576663d4cd3f363/1.
pdf?pq-origsite=gscholar&cbl=18750&diss=y (accessed 2022)

Weindling, Paul, 'Central Europe Confronts German Racial Hygiene: Friedrich Hertz, Hugo Iltis and Ignaz Zollschan as Critics of Racial Hygiene', in Marius Turda and Paul Weindling (eds), *Blood and Homeland: Eugenics and Racial Nationalism in Central and Southeast Europe, 1900–1940* (Central European University Press, 2007)

___, 'A City Regenerated: Eugenics, Race and Welfare', in Deborah Holmes and Lisa Silverman (eds), *Interwar Vienna: Culture Between Tradition and Modernity* (Camden House, 2009)

___, *Health, Race and German Politics Between National Unification and Nazism, 1870–1945* (Cambridge University Press, 1989)

Weyr, Thomas, *The Setting of the Pearl: Vienna under Hitler* (Oxford University Press, 2005)

Whitman, James, *Hitler's American Model: The United States and the Making of Nazi Race Law* (Princeton University Press, 2018)

Wierzchowska, Justyna, '"Nurse! I Want My Mummy!" Empathy as Methodology in the Documentary Film *A Two-Year-Old Goes to Hospital* (1952)', *Theories and Practices of Visual Culture*, no. 26 (2019–20)

Wilson, Jonathan, *Inverting the Pyramid: The History of Football Tactics* (Weidenfeld & Nicolson, 2018)

Wistrich, Robert, *Socialism and the Jews: The Dilemmas of Assimilation in Germany and Austria-Hungary* (Associated University Presses, 1982)

Witt-Dörring, Christian and Janis Staggs (eds), *Wiener Werkstätte 1903–1932: The Luxury of Beauty* (Prestel, 2017)

Witzel, Morgen, *A History of Management Thought* (Routledge, 2016)

Wix, Linney, *Through a Narrow Window: Friedl Dicker-Brandeis and Her Terezín Students* (University of New Mexico Press, 2010)

Yager, Edward, *Ronald Reagan's Journey: Democrat to Republican* (Rowman and Littlefield, 2006)

Young-Bruehl, Elisabeth, *Anna Freud* (Macmillan, 1989)

Index

Page references in italics refer to illustrations.

Also by the author:

Twilight of Truth: Chamberlain, Appeasement and the Manipulation of the Press (1989)
My Dear Max: The Letters of Brendan Bracken to Lord Beaverbrook (ed.) (1990)
David Astor and the Observer (1991)
Thinking the Unthinkable: The Economic Counter-Revolution, 1931–1983 (1994)
Anatomy of Decline: The Political Journalism of Peter Jenkins (ed., with Brian Brivati) (1995)
New Left, New Right and Beyond: Taking the Sixties Seriously (ed., with Alan Hooper, Geoff Andrews and Michael Williams) (1999)
Sudan: Darfur and the Failure of an African State (2010)
Blood, Dreams and Gold: The Changing Face of Burma (2015)